CORPORATE GOVERNANCE: DOES ANY SIZE FIT?

ADVANCES IN PUBLIC INTEREST ACCOUNTING

Series Editor: Cheryl R. Lehman

ADVANCES IN PUBLIC INTEREST ACCOUNTING   VOLUME 11

CORPORATE GOVERNANCE: DOES ANY SIZE FIT?

EDITED BY

CHERYL R. LEHMAN

Hofstra University, New York, USA

ASSOCIATE EDITORS

TONY TINKER

Baruch College, The City University of New York, USA

BARBARA MERINO

University of North Texas, USA

MARILYN NEIMARK

Baruch College, The City University of New York, USA

2005

ELSEVIER
JAI

Amsterdam – Boston – Heidelberg – London – New York – Oxford
Paris – San Diego – San Francisco – Singapore – Sydney – Tokyo

𝓁-27905056

ELSEVIER B.V.
Radarweg 29
P.O. Box 211
1000 AE Amsterdam
The Netherlands

ELSEVIER Inc.
525 B Street, Suite 1900
San Diego
CA 92101-4495
USA

ELSEVIER Ltd
The Boulevard, Langford
Lane, Kidlington
Oxford OX5 1GB
UK

ELSEVIER Ltd
84 Theobalds Road
London
WC1X 8RR
UK

First edition 2005

British Library Cataloguing in Publication Data
A catalogue record is available from the British Library.

ISBN: 0-7623-1205-X
ISSN: 1041-7060 (Series)

♾ The paper used in this publication meets the requirements of ANSI/NISO Z39.48-1992 (Permanence of Paper).
Printed in The Netherlands.

CONTENTS

LIST OF CONTRIBUTORS

Maureen Bickley	Graduate School of Business, Curtin University of Technology, Western Australia
Rebecca Boden	Bristol Business School, University of the West of England, Bristol, UK
Frank Clarke	School of Business, University of Sydney, Sydney, Australia
Graeme Dean	School of Business, University of Sydney, Sydney, Australia
Jack Flanagan	School of Business and Informatics, Australian Catholic University, North Sydney, Australia
Cameron Graham	Haskayne School of Business, University of Calgary, Alberta, Canada
Duncan Green	Haskayne School of Business, University of Calgary, Alberta, Canada
David A. Holloway	Murdoch Business School, Murdoch University, Murdoch, Australia
Stewart Lawrence	Department of Accounting, University of Waikato, New Zealand
John Little	CREDO, Australian Catholic University, Australia
James C. Lockhart	College of Business, Massey University, New Zealand
Anna Maria E. Mendoza	School of Management, University of Asia and the Pacific, Philippines

Margaret Nowak	Graduate School of Business, Curtin University of Technology, Western Australia
Dianne van Rhyn	Murdoch Business School, Murdoch University, Murdoch, Australia
John Roberts	The Judge Institute of Management Studies, University of Cambridge, UK
Grant Samkin	Department of Accounting, University of Waikato, New Zealand
Kala Saravanamuthu	New England Business School, University of New England, Australia
Vivien T. Supangco	College of Business Administration, University of the Philippines, Philippines
Mike Taitoko	College of Business, Massey University, New Zealand
Maria Teresa B. Tolosa	Center for Organization Research and Development, Ateneo de Manila University, Philippines
Ted Watts	School of Accounting and Finance, University of Wollongong, Australia
Loong Wong	Central Coast School of Business, University of Newcastle, Australia
Guanghua Yu	Faculty of Law, University of Hong Kong, Hong Kong

LIST OF AD HOC REVIEWERS

Tyrone Carlin
Macquarie Graduate School of
Management

Philip Yim Kwong Cheng
Australian National University

Jean Jacques Du Plessis
Deakin University

Duncan Green
University of Calgary

Jack Flanagan
Australian Catholic University

David Holloway
Murdoch University

John Horsley
Manukau Institute of Technology

Ernest Jordan
Macquarie Graduate School of
Management

James Lockhart
Massey University

Alan Lowe
University of Waikato

Sue McGowan
University of South Australia

Juliet McKee
New Zealand

Mary Ellen Oliverio
New York

Geeta Singh
University of Wollongong

EDITORIAL BOARD

CORPORATE GOVERNANCE: DOES ANY SIZE FIT?

Kala Saravanamuthu

The papers compiled in this special issue have been presented at the conference on "Corporate Governance and Ethics: Beyond Contemporary Perspectives" that has been held in June 2004 in Sydney, Australia.[1] The conference has brought together the three disciplines that impact on governance issues: accounting, management, and law. This issue reflects this interdisciplinary approach to the subject matter.

The conference theme captures the possibility that the rationale underpinning of the construction of contemporary governance may be inappropriate for the challenges of the 21st century. It raises the obvious question: What is corporate governance? Tricker (1994) associates it with managing the organization in the interest of its shareholders. It implies a concern with agency in the context of the separation of ownership and control functions in public corporations (Berle & Means, 1967; Fama & Jensen, 1983). However, even as far back as 1932, Berle and Means have gone further in expressing unease over the implied prioritization of equity interests over broader social ones. Their third recommendation encourages shareholders to eventually "yield before the larger interests of society":

> the owners of passive property, by surrendering control and responsibility over active property, have surrendered the right that the corporation should be operated in their sole interest... At the same time, the controlling groups...have in their own interest broken the bars of tradition which require that the corporation be operated solely for the benefit of the owners of passive property. This...alternative offers a wholly new concept of

Corporate Governance: Does Any Size Fit?
Advances in Public Interest Accounting, Volume 11, 1–11
Copyright © 2005 by Elsevier Ltd.
ISSN: 1041-7060/doi:10.1016/S1041-7060(05)11001-3

1

corporate activity. Neither the claims of ownership nor those of control can stand against the paramount interest of the community... Rigid enforcement of property rights as a temporary protection against plundering by control would not stand in the way of the modification of these rights in the interest of other groups. When a convincing system of community obligations is worked out and is generally accepted, in that moment the passive property right of today must yield before the larger interests of society... It is conceivable – indeed it seems almost essential if the corporate system is to survive, – that the "control" of the great corporations should develop into a purely neutral technocracy, balancing a variety of claims by various groups in the community and assigning to each a portion of the income stream on the basis public policy rather than private cupidity.

                                                                    (Berle & Means, 1967, p. 312)

Two questions immediately come to mind in the context of 21st century governance principles: firstly, the extent to which governance should embrace inclusiveness of the other, and secondly the process of ascertaining the rights of the other in a just and equitable manner. The second question will be addressed later. In the case of the former, the OECD (1999) has extended the boundary of accountability to include stakeholders such as employees. However, judging by Mr. Greenwood's (a U.S. Congressman) exasperated response at the conclusion of the Hearing on The Financial Collapse of Enron (Part 4),[2] contemporary governance mechanisms are unable to protect investors themselves:

My only comment in closing would be that once again the commentary from the witnesses is that the company failed because of loss of confidence of the investors, which sounds an awful lot to me like blaming the victims, the people who lost money failed because they failed to have confidence in the company itself (Subcommittee on Oversight and Investigations of Committee on Energy and Commerce, House of Representatives, 2002, p. 91).

Therefore, what is the likelihood that corporate (and agency) responsibility will be extended beyond the interests of shareholders in this century? There is little doubt that the corporation cannot appear to shirk from its responsibility to non-financial stakeholders even though conventional governance mechanisms do not seem to have the capacity to rein in management excesses. Any attempt to understand (and perhaps resolve) this dilemma requires starting at the beginning by problematising the very meaning of the term, governance: Does governance merely refer to rules and systems, or does it encompass a means of shaping organizational behavior and its social consequences? This special issue is divided into three sections. The first section problematises the appropriateness of popular rule-based governance approaches. Section 2 considers governance issues that are unique to various national contexts before drawing conclusions about governance as a universal concept. Section 3 goes beyond critique in suggesting ways of developing governance approaches that are better suited to engendering ethical outcomes.

In section 1, Clarke and Dean (this issue) provocatively swim against the worldwide tide of prescribing more rules to fix the Enron-type financial disasters. They call for the "less, rather than more" regulatory measures. The authors examine the consequences of relying on the "invisible hand of self interest" which separates ownership and control of property before asserting that (perhaps) "one size doesn't fit any". Effective stewardship (ideally) rests on the probity of the stewards but it is probably unattainable: it comes as no surprise that the 1844 Companies Act requires annual accounts to be audited by a shareholder. The dilemma may be surmised as follows: corporate governance has to become a means of curbing managerial opportunism and self-interest, but does it have the capacity to do so? The authors extend Berle and Means' reservations about the underlying divergence of management-shareholder interests to warn that the modern corporation could become ungovernable because contemporary governance prescriptions fail to address the structural origins of the agency impasse.

Yu (this issue) also begins with the Berle and Means concern with the separation of ownership and control of corporate equity. He adopts a functionalist approach in examining whether common governance principles may be applied across the board regardless of different historical, social, legal and political contexts. Yu scrutinizes the circumstances under which English takeover law has been transplanted into China (and subsequently modified) before concluding that one size does not fit all (even under a functional analysis of governance).

The final paper in this section (Boden, this issue) provides a larger socioeconomic context for interrogating the appropriateness of contemporary governance approaches. Her Foucauldian interrogation of the ethical implications of the concept of governance reveals how the corporate regime (of practice) has shaped contemporary notions of governmentality along the lines of economic morality. It means that unacceptable moral outcomes are not regarded as governance failures. However, such corporate outcomes may be moderated by granting visibility to "counter-knowledges": Boden draws on South Africa's experiences in importing cheap generic drugs to fight HIV/AIDS to illustrate how the ethos of economic morality may be contested.

Section two provides critiques of governance models in the following nations: South Africa, China, Austria-Europe, Canada, Philippines, and Australia-New Zealand. Before embarking on country-specific analyses, it is useful to stand back and reflect on the effectiveness of regulations governing transnational corporations (TNCs): Abrahams (2004) identifies 20 industry self-regulations, 32 multilateral regulations and 24 civil regulations initiatives that administer "the working activities of TNCs that affect social, environmental, and human rights" (p. 1). This list does not include regulations specific to different nations. Governance of TNCs has always been problematic because their operations cut across several national boundaries. Nevertheless Abrahams' (2004) industry-mutilateral-civil categorization of regulations reflects the networked workings of these bodies. Networked communities represent the future means of managing organizations because globalization has reduced the influence of nation states in controlling corporate activities that extend beyond national boundaries (Utting, 2000; Bendell, 2004). However, we must continue to be cautious of unproblematically accepting its governance vocabulary because it has the potential to obscure contradictions that could jeopardize attempts to ascertain the rights of the other in a just and equitable manner: the second question that has been raised earlier.

Is it possible to overcome the dilemma created by the contradictions above through governance regimes? Gandhi (2001) and Parekh (1991) assert that such governance will be coercive in nature, as a dominant interest group imposes its priorities on weaker ones. Capitalist relations are by definition violent and undermine individual freedom because it coerces consent to unjust processes of accountability and distribution. Arundathi Roy, an Indian novelist and activist, extends this dilemma to the tension between injustice and peace by asserting, "What we call peace is little better than capitulation to a corporate coup":

> Sometimes there's truth in old cliches. There can be no real peace without justice. And without resistance there will be no justice. Today, it is not merely justice itself, but the idea of justice that is under attack.
>
> The assault on vulnerable, fragile sections of society is so complete, so cruel and so clever that its sheer audacity has eroded our definition of justice. It has forced us to lower our sights, and curtail our expectations. Even among the well-intentioned, the magnificent concept of justice is gradually being substituted with the reduced, far more fragile discourse of "human rights".
>
> This is an alarming shift. The difference is that notions of equality, of parity, have been pried loose and eased out of the equation. It's a process of attrition. Almost unconsciously, we begin to think of justice for the rich and human rights for the poor...
>
> It is becoming more than clear that violating human rights is an inherent and necessary part of the process of implementing a coercive and unjust political and economic structure on the world. Increasingly, human rights violations are being portrayed as the unfortunate, almost accidental, fallout of an otherwise acceptable political and economic system (Source: November 4, 2004, Sydney Morning Herald, Australia, available at http://smh.com.au/articles/2004/11/04/1099362264349.html).

Arundathi's concerns about how justice is being compromised in the larger societal arena have implications for corporate governance: we should ask whether the ideal of inclusive, fair and equitable governance is in danger of being subsumed under the rhetoric of corporate governance? Section 2 of this issue sheds more light on this tension: it provides insights into corporate governance concerns in six nations before teasing out their impact on the universal notion of governance.

Lawrence and Samkin (this issue) draw on the South Africa's experiences in grappling with the social cost of HIV/AIDS virus to argue that there cannot be a single institutional response to this problem (or its underlying concept of sustainability) because its causes are interconnected and interdependent. The HIV/AIDS pandemic has been associated with migrant labor policies of the apartheid era and it has, in turn, resulted in poverty, violence and racism. The authors evaluate the implications for corporate governance by referring to South Africa's institutional responses which encourage companies to account for the health of their stakeholders. They manifest as the King Reports, compliance with the Global Reporting Initiative (GRI) and the requirements of the Johannesburg Securities Exchange. The GRI in particular attempts to provide (evolving) social reporting guidelines to improve corporate accountability and transparency. The South African experience reveals that the GRI's step-by-step implementation of accountability enables management to reflect on policies adopted to tackle the HIV/AIDS problem. It raises senior management's awareness of socio-ecological issues. In keeping with the spirit of evolving standards of reporting, King's second Report emphasizes the human aspects of corporate governance: i.e. it reflects the inclusive nature of governance ethics.

Loong Wong (this issue) revisits governance concerns in Mainland China that have been initially raised by Yu (this issue). Despite the seemingly unstoppable global integration of markets and economies, Wong argues that it is not advisable to replicate the dominant Anglo-American governance model universally. He asserts that a governance framework should reflect the home country's prevailing institutional arrangements and socio-economic realities. The Anglo-American model is out of sync with China's socio-economic context because the Anglo-American framework is orientated towards large public companies; it is based on the presumption that the corporation is a separate legal entity that privileges shareholders. This presumption belies the fact that small, interlocking oligarchic power groups influence the behavior of large companies. On the other hand, the purpose of corporate governance in China is intertwined with economic modernization aimed at generating higher rates of growth (relative to its Anglo-American counterparts). Furthermore, China's financial systems are not sophisticated (and despite reforms, banks continue to dominate its financial system); and it has a substantial number of inefficient and unprofitable state-owned enterprises (SOE) which remain a significant provider of urban employment. Regardless of these underlying differences, China has, since 1993, subscribed to the assumption that nation states are ineffective means of regulating the economy, and that the global market should discipline the economy instead. Consequently, China has attempted to create a modern corporate system by corporatising SOEs and clarifying property rights. The Anglo-American model has been embraced because it appears to be based on laws, rules and regulations. It does not complement China's broad and diverse range of institutional structures and social practices. Wong argues that the attempt to reduce China's multiple enterprises into a formal governance framework may stifle their growth and contribution to the national economy. Transplanting the best Anglo-American practices into China is tantamount to positing these practices in a social and cultural vacuum. Corporate governance should instead be a means of enabling new ideas to emerge from the relationship between corporate practices, business systems and the notion of governance itself.

Bickley and Nowak (this issue) compare and contrast the European approach to corporate governance with the dominant Anglo-American paradigm. The latter is founded on the notion of agency (that grants primacy to the shareholder) whilst the European corporate law tradition of multiple property rights provides for corporate accountability to multiple stakeholders. Under the European approach, stakeholders are entitled (legislatively) and enabled (practically) to voice their views on the management of the corporation: there is a two-tiered board system, an internal Management board and an external Supervisory board. Whilst senior management make up the Management board, the Supervisory board is comprised of representatives of employees, unions or work councils. The latter is in essence a manifestation of Stewardship Theory, which theorizes organizational interaction in terms of collective trust-based relations undertaken in the interest of the organization. It is in direct contrast to antagonistic relations that underpin Anglo-American agency theory. Bickley and Nowak use their qualitative study of Austrian directors' perceptions of corporate governance to explain how managers discharge their responsibilities under the European framework before drawing the following conclusions about the two approaches vis-à-vis sustainability: the Anglo-American primacy of the shareholder implies that the case for sustainable development hinges on the construction of a business case that promotes the corporation's narrowly defined interests. Alternatively, it will have to be imposed on corporations legislatively. On the other hand, the stakeholder approach implicit in the European approach is built on trust between organizational constituents that inherently allows it to develop in a more sustainable manner.

Green and Graham (this issue) use Canada's orientation towards voluntary reform in corporate financial disclosure as backdrop to their study of accountability and independence in the boardroom: i.e. the relationship between corporate governance disclosures and related regulations is examined through disclosure theory and discourse analysis. Even though the Toronto Stock Exchange has standard corporate reporting formats, the choice to comply and to disclose such adherence, is in itself voluntary. The authors problematise disclosures of boardroom responsibilities, roles and practices by arguing that companies have not adhered to the Stock Exchange's suggestion that these representations should reflect a behavioral emphasis. Leading Canadian companies do not describe how Boards function. Firms that comply, disclose its "form" rather than "function". Furthermore, information that is not disclosed serves to increase the "black box around broad practices", or its impenetrability. Therefore, voluntary compliance with guidelines is a weak means of ensuring good governance and the prevention of future financial scandals.

Mendoza et al. (this issue) assert that Human Resource Management (HRM) should play a key role in implementing governance and risk management strategies because "people-risk" is central to strategy implementation in general. The authors define people-risk as the risk of not meeting business needs because of inappropriate policies, motivational problems and fraud. A questionnaire survey of HRM managers in Manila, Philippines, had been conducted: the authors conclude from their analysis of 36 respondents that HR involvement in governance and risk management at board level has not been developed; HR functions have not been significantly aligned with governance-risk management objectives; HRM involvement has been concentrated in the processes that formalize and implement governance-risk strategies. Even though the study did not find any relationship between the variables representing HRM, governance and risk management mechanisms, and organizational performance, the authors assert that the moderating role of these variables should be further studied.

Lockhart and Taitoko (this issue) return to the underlying tension between shareholders and stakeholders in concluding the section on governance issues within a national context. They examine the collapse of an Australian airline company, Ansett, which had significant repercussions for Air New Zealand. Relying on the benefit of hindsight, they analyze decisions made by the players in the (Ansett-Air New Zealand) alliance and conclude that the failures are related to the actions of the Board in privileging the interest of a major shareholder over the interests of the organization. That is, ownership structures will influence strategy and governance and hence, organizational outcomes.

It appears that the capacity for contemporary governance models to protect the interest of larger community interests is at best, cosmetic, and at worst, misleading (even deceptive). Perhaps like Arundathi's injustice and peace analogy, business responsibility cannot be assured as long as the corporate veil remains. Responsibility is intrinsically based on the presumption of caring for the other – a concept that is at odds with a notion of an insentient corporate entity seeking to maximize returns whilst placating socio-environmental interests. The remaining three papers suggest challenging perspectives of ethical corporate relations based on moral agency that upholds the principles of democracy. Roberts (this issue) interrogates the assumption of self-interested opportunism in agency theory that plays a significant role in the construction of contemporary frameworks: he challenges the individualist stance of agency theory and acknowledges the disciplining aspect of governance frameworks. By contrasting the current ethic of shareholder value with a Foucauldian view of governance he is able to argue that governance ethics should be understood in terms of Levinas' responsibility for one's neighbor. On the other hand, as it is implicitly based on presumptions of sentience and proximity, its role will be limited to local influences.

Flanagan, Little, and Watts (this issue) apply the above-mentioned sentience perspective to shed more light on the cultural and decision making aspects within the boardroom decision-making processes. They return the Latin etymology of the term "governance" which refers to firstly the driving force behind management behavior, and secondly, the systems by which the firm's activities are controlled. The authors agree with the Cadbury Committee's recommendation that management should be free to drive their companies but argue that management discretion should be exercised within a framework of effective accountability: that is, a behavioral corporate governance approach. Governance through a system of rules is unlikely to be effective because it is based on the agency theory presumption that actors act out of self-interest. Effective governance requires a more fundamental approach in which directors and other executives are enabled to develop their own personal governance systems and superimpose it on the corporate governance structure. It should embrace shared personal values in constructing collective ones as a means of overcoming the notion of "juridic persons" (or the construction of the corporation as a legal construct). However, as little is known about how directors actually arrive at decisions, the authors provide a framework that is intended to enable actors to gravitate towards ethical conduct by understanding the relationship between personal character, decision-making, leadership and public outcomes of governance. Their model theorizes behavior as emanating from the interplay of self-interested and ethical stances. It moves away from a structural analysis of governance towards a social one based on trust and respect among members, which in turn should be gained by critically reflecting on fundamental presumptions such as: who controls the company, for whom control is exercised, and how accountability is to be achieved. Hence, accountability has to take cognizance of the fact that organizational leadership should not be motivated by economic value alone because other aspects such as knowledge, skilled performance, cooperation and practical reasoning may be sacrificed in the process.

Holloway and van Rhyn (this issue) address the question of legitimacy of governance formulations which prevails in the aftermath of financial failures around the world. In essence, it is a question of securing public confidence that "reformist" governance mechanisms will prevent senior management misbehavior or corporate failure. They propose a two-fold approach to governance reform: firstly, there should be cultural change at the boardroom level to encourage the development of the team approach. It is based on the premise that governance should be effected through the way in which people work together (hence culture), rather than the imposition of rules and regulations. Its culture should enable constructive conflict in decision-making processes as a way of engendering trust and openness in the boardroom. Secondly, this socially structured governance framework should be extended beyond the boardroom: organizational pluralism that requires rethinking leadership roles, from a command-and-control to a coaching-and-guiding behavior.

The prescriptions advocated by Roberts, Flanagan et al., as well as Holloway and van Rhyn (this issue) are at odds with the aims of maintaining the corporate veil that (more often than not) obscures rights and obligations of the insentient entity. As the effects of climate change from decades of unrelenting economic growth repeatedly lash through our constructed environment, we should ask ourselves whether the corporate structure has outlived its relevance in the 21st century. Instead of trying to constrain ethics in the corporate mould, it may be time to reconsider the way in which the business structure is constructed in the light of sustainable and ethically responsible business practices.[3] There can be no sustainable outcomes without ethical practices that extend beyond narcissistic concern for me and mine.

NOTES

1. Seed capital for the conference was provided by the New England Business School (University of New England), Macquarie Graduate School of Management (Macquarie University), and the Faculty of Economics, Business and Management (University of New England). CPA Australia was the official sponsor.

2. I thank my colleague John Whitman for securing this quotation.

3. This radical approach regarding the corporate structure is attributed to Paul Williams' suggestion that the solution may lie in thinking outside the square.

ACKNOWLEDGMENT

Special thanks to Ross Bennetts for graciously setting up and maintaining websites for the conference as well as the special issue. I thank Geeta Singh and Cheryl Lehman for their constructive comments on this Introduction-editorial and support in compiling this Special Issue.

REFERENCES

Abrahams, D. (2004). *Regulating corporations. A resource guide*. The United Nations Research Institute for Social Development, Geneva. Available at http://www.unrisd.org/ Accessed on Nov 10, 2004.

Bendell, J. (2004). Barricades and boardrooms: A contemporary history of the corporate accountability movement. Programme paper Number 13, June. United Nations Research Institute for Social Development, Geneva. Available at http://www.unrisd.org/ Accessed on Nov 10, 2004.

Berle, A., & Means, G. (1967). *The modern corporation and private property*. New York: Harcourt, Brace & World Inc. (1st ed. 1932).

Fama, E. F., & Jensen, M. C. (1983). Separation of ownership and control. *Journal of Law and Economics, 26*, 301–325.

Gandhi M. K. (2001). *India of my dreams*. (Compiled by R. K. Prabhu) Ahmedabad: Navajivan Publishing House.

OECD. (1999). *Principles of Corporate Governance*. Paris: OECD.

Parekh, B. (1991). *Gandhi's political philosophy. A critical examination*. Houndsmills: Macmillan.

Subcommittee on Oversight and Investigations of Committee on Energy and Commerce, House of Representatives (2002) Hearing on The Financial Collapse of Enron- Part 4, One hundred and seventh Congress, Second Session, March 14, Serial no. 107-90. Available via http://www.access.gpo.gov/congress/house Accessed in August 2003.

Tricker, R. I. (1994). *International corporate governance: Text, readings and cases.* New York: Prentice Hall.

Utting, P. (2000). Business responsibility for sustainable development. Occasional Paper No. 2. United Nations Research Institute for Social Development, Geneva. Accessed on July 23, 2004 at http://www.unrisd.org/

PART I:
PROBLEMATISING GOVERNANCE

CORPORATE GOVERNANCE: A CASE OF 'MISPLACED CONCRETENESS'? ☆

Frank Clarke and Graeme Dean

ABSTRACT

Whitehead's notion that if you say something for long enough, it will be believed, aptly describes the development of the latest corporate govern-ance regimes. Curbing managerial opportunism is the current focus, but the regimes contain only more of what has failed in the past. Inexplicably, at a time when reformers are declaring their allegiance to principles over rules, long-standing principles are being by-passed and more rules im-posed. Whereas much of what the rules address is contestable, the fre-quency with which it is proclaimed has been seductive – it is being accepted as if it were true, not by virtue of either convincing evidence or argument, but through the power of repetition. Stock options in executives remuneration packages are to be expensed, not because they satisfy ex-pensing criteria, but because of the penetration of the mantra that they are expenses; independence is being accepted as the consequence of not being in particular relationships, not because that will change one's state

☆ Based on a paper presented by Frank Clarke at the *Corporate Governance and Ethics: Beyond Contemporary Perspectives* Conference, Macquarie Graduate School of Management, 28–30 June, 2004.

Corporate Governance: Does Any Size Fit?
Advances in Public Interest Accounting, Volume 11, 15–39
ISSN: 1041-7060/doi:10.1016/S1041-7060(05)11002-5

of mind, so much as it will appear likely to have done so; and impairment calculations are being declared superior to conventional amortization techniques, not because of any demonstration that they better indicate the decrease in the market price of a physical asset, but because of the repetition of the impairment litany. Corporate governance is being perceived as a set of processes, rules to be complied with, rather than the desired outcome of them – that is, the authority exercised with probity and unquestionable integrity over corporations' affairs, for the public good. There is a less than clear explanation of whether or how the separate governance processes mesh with one another. The governance miasma confuses rather than clarifies corporate activity. Underpinnings of the mechanisms in the governance regimes have achieved a false status of concreteness. Contrary to the universal indoctrination, the case is stronger for fewer, rather than more, governance rules.

IF YOU SAY IT OFTEN ENOUGH…

Casual observation shows that if one says or even implies something long enough, many will treat it as if it were true. Of course, repetition may be indicative of truth. But the phenomena we wish to discuss are those myriad instances when the force of repetition deludes. That aptly describes the discussion of corporate governance. First, is the impression that the current corporate governance prescriptions are new; second, the implication that the opportunistic self-interest of managers, auditors and the like, cannot be engaged for the shareholders' benefit; and third, that the more the system of internal corporate governance is specified, failures of the kind that have attracted public outrage in the recent past, will be avoided.

Whereas there are elements of likely validity in each of those presumptions, the collective focus of them diverts attention from the most insidious aspect of many of the larger corporate failures – the element of surprise when an apparently stable company crashes. That is the most damaging to public trust and confidence in the corporate way of engaging in commerce,[1] and the most damaging to the pursuit of an orderly commercial setting.

Spawned in the maelstrom of public outcry following unexpected corporate collapses, corporate governance reform has centre stage. Myriad proposals have emerged for better controlling the activities of those given the responsibility for the management corporate resources. They are mechanisms intended to monitor and control the undesirable aspects of the *agency* problems arising, as predicted by Berle and Means[2] over 70 years ago, in consequence of the separation of ownership and control of modern corporations.

It is worth contemplating the corporate world when *The Modern Corporation and Private Property* was written. Berle and Means had noted the emergence of the professional agent-manager in the aftermath of the large consolidation of corporate activity through the activities of the *robber barons* at the turn of the century.[3] It is debatable how prescient they were – whether they possibly sensed the manner in which corporate activity would develop, especially since World War II. In the current setting, global corporations are the norm, rather than the exception. In contrast, the multiple and dual listings of company shares, the number of significant international mergers and acquisitions of the magnitude of, for example, the mergers of AOL and Time Warner, or Daimler Benz and Chrysler, are less likely to have been envisaged. Nor is it likely corporations of the size of Enron, WorldCom, Sunbeam, Tyco, Waste Management, or Vivendi could have been in Berle and Means' focus. Collapses of the kind that shook public confidence in the proportions following the fall of Vivendi, Enron and WorldCom, or that rattled the insurance industry in Australia as did the fall of HIH, how losses of the magnitude incurred by the National Australia Bank in its Homeside investment in the United States could be followed so quickly by the losses in its forex "rogue trading" affair, or that the sixth largest company in Italy, Parmalat, could fall from grace in such a way,[4] were possibly outside their thinking. Even more unlikely is that they would have had in their minds the possibility that the sudden failures[5] in the latest spate of collapses could have come after similar recurring spates of unexpected crises of household corporate names in preceding decades.[6] But those outcomes are not inconsistent with the potential implications of the separation between ownership and control that they noted.

Most importantly, we might reasonably wonder what Berle and Means would have made of almost all of these waves of corporate collapses being accompanied by alleged malpractice by directors, managers of one kind or another, accountants and auditors – arguably all agents in place to advance the interests of their principals. We might likewise ponder their likely surprise at the regulators' slow learning in the wake of successive failures of (what in current terms amounts to) corporate governance revisions that for the most part merely increased the specificity of what already existed – in reality, perhaps more tweaking than reforming.

Few commentators seem to see the recent focus on corporate governance as a replay. Few recall the circumstances that prompted President Roosevelt to use *truth in securities* as the poster theme for part of his *New Deal* programme entailing the passing of the Securities Act of 1933 and the Securities and Exchange Act of 1934 as the platform for his agenda to reform corporate affairs. The *Sarbanes–Oxley Act* (SOX) has that heritage – it is simply the latest revision of the U.S. corporate governance mechanisms that stress disclosure as the panacea. The U.K.'s *Combined Code* is merely the latest in the follow-up from the 1992 U.K. Cadbury Code following the Maxwell and the Polly Peck scandals. For Australian companies, Statement 9 of the Commonwealth Government's Corporate Legislation Economic Reform Program (CLERP9) and the Recommendations of the Australian Stock Exchange Corporate Governance Council (ASXCGC) merely thump more heavily themes that had their early exposure in the responses (especially by the accounting profession[7]) to the Australian failures in the 1960s – essentially in each case, more of the same. That is to be expected, for the prevailing view has been that the problem lies solely with the individuals who manage corporations, rather than the fundamentals of the corporate system and with the way in which the outcomes of company affairs are communicated to the market.

Continuous incantations implying that the corporate system is sound, have paid off.

MANAGERIAL OPPORTUNISM

That the corporate structure has nurtured an opportunity for management to act more in its own interest than in the interest of the shareholders had been noticed long before the genesis of the modern corporation in the Companies Act of 1844. Adam Smith 1994/1776 implied the likelihood of the conflict of interest when ownership and control of property were separated in his concept of the *invisible hand of self-interest* (Colley, Doyle, Logan, & Stettinius, 2003). That self-interest, a dominant force in human behaviour, fuelled the specialization and division of labour, of which the separation of the ownership and control of property was a financially driven consequence. Despite possible contrary interpretations, we might reasonably imagine that Adam Smith perceived the invisible hand of self-interest functioning in a positive manner, despite moral hazard.

It was not accidental that the 1844 Companies Act required annual accounts, and that they be audited by a *shareholder*. Who would better protect shareholders' property, than one who shared a common interest in it? In contrast, once there is a separation, once a steward is appointed, mechanisms have to implemented, inducements held out, to forge common interests between the owner of property and the stewards of it. Ideally, effective stewardship relies upon justified trust of the owners in, and in the probity of, the stewards. In reality, inducements have been the mechanism. Perceptions of how those inducements have had an opposite effect to what was intended, evoked and exacerbated self-interest rather than captured and exploited it, not aligned managers' self-interests with those of the shareholders,[8] under-pin a considerable part of the current corporate governance regime.

Nor is it accidental that over the past 160 years the regulatory mechanisms have been increased – company law reform committees have topped-up governance regimes through successive companies legislation, gradually specified the form and the content of financial disclosures, the audit of them, and the duties of company directors and other officers. Each has been injected after a series of corporate collapses evidencing wrongdoing, market disruptions and a loss of confidence. We might take those increments to governance mechanisms to be indicative of the failure of each addition to the regulatory armory to curb managerial opportunism in the way intended.

It does not appear to have evinced an understanding that perhaps curbing managers' self-interest is mission impossible. For, managerial opportunism is endemic of the corporate system, and the battle being waged to align managers' interests to those of the shareholders is an integral facet of the corporate game.

GOVERNANCE AMNESIA

Whereas it is often said that the lessons of past corporate scandals are being ignored, it is just as likely that insufficient is known of them to be learned. *Success* stories and success recipes dominate the business literature. It is doubtful whether any books on commercial disasters have received the attention of the likes of Peters and Waterman's *In Search of Excellence*, and Kaplan and Norton's *The Balanced Scorecard*.

Criticisms of the *Do It Yourself* (DIY) success recipes such as McGill's *American Business and the Quick Fix* (1988), and critiques of the corporate world such as Korten's *When Corporations Rule the World* (Korten, 1995) and his *The Post-Corporation World* (Korten, 1998), or Monks' *The Emperor's Nightingale: Restoring the Integrity of the Corporation* (1998), *rarely* find their way into university business curricula. And interestingly, when the examples used in the *DIYs* fall over, as did most of Peters and Waterman's 1982 "exemplars", they pass mostly without comment.

There is a longstanding love affair with success. Enron was perceived to be the very paragon of innovation in its pre-scandal days. Little is said about the poor judgement of those who previously eulogized Enron in the many commentaries on its collapse[9] Bernie Ebbers' WorldCom received glowing accolades before the rot set in. Its grab for bandwidth capacity in the United States in grossly over-priced acquisitions was seen to be indicative of great foresight. Here in Australia a team evaluating company performance placed National Australia Bank in its *First Eleven*[10] – a place in Australia's top corporate team, on the basis of those virtues of management acumen, risk management, and the like, soon after shown to be lacking in the U.S. Homeside loss, and the losses in the alleged forex "rogue trading" affair.

That is curious; for success and failure find their financial expression in measures on the same economic continuum. Miller's *Icarus Paradox*[11] aptly captures that in his analogy of corporate success containing the seeds of corporate destruction, meltdown, and Icarus' high soaring towards the sun melting its wings of wax, with the inevitable outcome. Perhaps success and failure are not perceived to be part of the same process. A focus on the negative aspects of managerial opportunism permeates the corporate governance literature. Positive facets rarely rate a mention. Certainly, most of the corporate governance literature presents the various proposals as sets of constraints to corral rogue corporate directors, executives and auditors. Even when the case is made that a company "with good corporate governance" – that is, one that pursues the current recommendations in vogue – will be successful, invariably it is in terms of those practices preventing malfeasance rather than avoiding misfeasance. We might consider what underpins this state of affairs.

Avoiding Managerial Opportunism

A central theme coursing through the Berle and Means thesis is that:

> The separation [in the modern corporation] of ownership and control produces a condition where the interests of the owners [of the enterprise] and of [the enterprise's] ultimate manager may, and often do diverge.

Of course, their assessment came against the backdrop of the fallout from the corporate and individual excesses of the three decades prior to the 1929 crash, especially the proliferation of share ownership leading to it, the practices of the share-hawkers, and the exposure of the false impressions financial statements had given of the wealth and progress of companies that failed. That evaluation was of the hazards attending the pursuit of commerce, indeed of western capitalism, through the medium of the relatively primitive corporate structures of the time. The extensive legislation and other matters of company regulation that have emerged since on a frequent catch-up basis are suggestive of an underlying awareness of a possibly intractable problem.

In the context of their concern for the problems arising from the separation of ownership and control, Berle and Means'assessment that large public companies were the *dominant institution in the modern world*, might (perhaps with hindsight) be taken as a warning that the modern corporation could become ungovernable. If we read into their assessment a prediction of how corporate matters would eventuate over the next 70 years, they were extremely prescient. For, arguably, the problem Berle and Means posited underpins most of what the current corporate governance push is directed to changing.

That connection has not been missed by some observers of the fallout from the most recent of U.S. "corporate scandals". Culp and Niskanen in their *Corporate Aftershock* (2003), for example, note how the reliance upon an "independent board" emerged as the favoured governance mechanism to protect the shareholders. They allude to that *consensus view* of corporate governance having failed on some notable occasions. And observe how U.S. interest in governance and corporate propriety in particular, emerged in the wake of the Lockheed, Northrop, Gulf Oil, and other foreign payments scandals, the inquiry into which also exposed illegal political donations by companies, such that in 1973 117 of the *Fortune 500* U.S. companies were found to have engaged in serious misconduct. These were mainly accounting irregularities, despite having audit committees. Audit Committees had been viewed with approbation by the U.S. Securities and Exchange Commission, as a possible governance panacea, as long ago as 1939 and by the New York Stock Exchange in 1940. A curious aspect of Culp and Niskanen's enquiry is that they appear to live in the expectation that the system will mend, that it will become operational and effective. Yet, outside of the commercial setting a diagnosis exposing those and the similar events recurring on a progressively grander scale over the next 30 years, would have prompted serious questioning of whether the remedy was exacerbating the problem, and whether the problem was avoidable. Virtually none of the public brouhaha following the recent collapses has questioned whether the modern corporation is governable,[12] or at least governable through the governance rules continuously being reshaped.

Because it has been said as often as possible that we need more governance rules, it has become dogma. But many of the governance *rules* proposed in response to the alleged abuses of managerial opportunism are contestable. Consider the following examples.

Wrong Option?

There are few better examples of how repeated ideas become "set in concrete" than the pay-off from the repetitive claims that the "stock options" included in executive remuneration packages should be *expensed*. The International Accounting Standards Board, SOX and CLERP 9 have declared that the "costs of options" are expenses of the issuing companies and must be treated as such in their financials.[13] Many companies issuing options have cowered under the barrage. But, again, the loudness of *expensing* assertions has drowned out contrary analyses.[14]

Emotion attaching to the spectre of disgraced executives receiving huge sums from cashing in options in happier times, and of "dismissed" executives receiving payouts arguably disproportionate to their companies' performances, has been substituted for scientific enquiry. The public and private debate over executive share options has been seduced by the temptation to translate a get-tough attitude to disclosure, into a compulsory accounting technique. History, legal and financial facts, have fallen victim to the options verbiage.[15]

It is interesting to note that few of the pro-expensing advocates deny the virtue of the strategy underpinning the issue of options – to align the presumed interests of the agent executives with those of company owners, maximize corporate wealth,[16] to harness managerial opportunism rather than to curb it. Equally interesting is how few of them allude to evidence of successful uses of options in the past – how options substituted for cash components of salary permitted high-tech startups to recruit the best of graduates from MIT, Stanford, Harvard, and fuse their futures with those of the companies they were developing. Nor do they refer to the studies[17] indicating that the general body of shareholders benefited in companies issuing options to employees, though primarily to executives. They refer to the experiences of companies, especially to those involved in the recent scandals, in which contiguity has been noted between options vestings and poor performance.

The pervading implication is that the inducement did not work for the benefit of the shareholders. But, association, correlation, does not prove causation. So, those linking options with poor performances ought to make a corresponding mistake of linking them to good performance. That does not appear to happen.[18] Nor is it usually noted that stock options have not been given exclusively to executives, though undeniably they have been the major recipients.[19] Even so, it is noticeable that the complaints from, or on behalf of, shareholders have come almost exclusively only following the reports of notable poor performances. An inference might be drawn that shareholders are not averse to the options being granted in good times, and were they more directly linked to performance.

The current furore and resurrection of the call to expense options has arisen only following notable collapses in which executives had received massive option inducements – Sunbeam, Enron, Waste Management, Tyco, Adelphi, WorldCom, for example. There was no outcry when the options inducements were accompanied by buoyant share prices; when Enron's stock was in excess of \$US90[20] or when WorldCom's in excess of \$US64, for example. Nor, for example, was there any outcry of "foul play" when Australia's AMP Ltd., was riding high. The quest for accounting transparency, a legitimate concern at all times, appears more potent in bad times!

Issuing options to various categories of employees has a long history in the United States. It dates back to the 1920s and 1930s. It lost momentum (in the United States at least) with the 1929 crash. Unquestionably in the United States, *post* World War II, it has been a primary means employed to mitigate the agency problem. Its capacity to induce performance, without incurring a cash payout has had obvious attractions. An early illustration of its potency as an aligning inducement was well illustrated in the rewards to Charles Lazarus to return to and turnaround the ailing *Toys "R" Us* he had founded.[21] U.S. governments have given the inclusion of options in remuneration packages implicit encouragement.[22] Quick talking regarding the downside of stock options has been peppered with drama-ridden disclosures of the extent to which companies' bottom-lines would be reduced were options to be expensed. Standard and Poors', for example, estimated a 17% negative impact on U.S. companies in 2002. Spurred on by such "revelations", spurious accounting arguments have been used to make options unattractive by hitting companies' bottom line.[23]

Reformers have not seen it necessary to establish "causation" between the issuing of options and the accounting scandals, they have merely asserted it. Nor have they established that the cost of the options is an expense *of the company*, they have asserted that, too. Contrary to the financial characteristics attributed to expenses elsewhere in conventional accounting – a diminution of assets or an increase in liabilities – the costs of options are deemed expenses because the company receives (or has the potential to receive) the benefit of increased executives' efforts without any decrease in its assets or increase in its liabilities.[24]

Several questions need answers: is the current disclosure of share options in executive remuneration packages adequate? Do the options entail a cost and if so, to whom? Should granting companies expense them?

Possibly "not"! Possibly "yes"! "The existing shareholders"! And, unquestionably "no!"

Non-disclosure of the options granted possibly has driven the push for expensing. Disclosure, of course, does not necessitate inclusion in the formal accounts as the expensing *solution* prescribes. Specific disclosure within the information relating to executive remuneration would be adequate disclosure to drive any market efficiency impact.

In the executive options debate metaphorical allusions that the "shareholders 'are' the company", have underpinned confusion between the company and its shareholders. The *Saloman v. Saloman* dictum (and similar dicta before it in the area of company law and trusts) that companies are separate entities, have separate legal personalities, separate property rights, and separate obligations, enjoy separate benefits and incur their own separate costs, is swept aside by the option-expensing advocates.[25] Yet, the legal status of companies is the commercial reality that counts, not the misleading impressions evoked by the repetitive use of imprecise language.

Certainly, when executives exercise share options they receive money's worth. But the critical point is *at whose expense*? Whose financial welfare changes as a consequence when the options are exercised?

Arguably, the exercising of executive stock options dilutes the holding of the other shareholders. On the face of it, that possibly entails a loss *to them*. First, once the options are granted there is the potential that existing shareholders' proportions of the issued share capital will be diluted. Accordingly, when exercised, they are diluted. Second, quite possibly the inflow of capital at the exercise price will be less than had the shares been allotted in a public issue at that time. Whether the other shareholders individually or the company are better or worse off "financially" depends upon whether the share price after the exercise of the options and the consequential capital inflow offset the aggregative financial effects of the dilution. Shareholders potentially stand either to gain or to lose from the dilution. But the shareholders are not the company!

Only the second leg of that scenario entails what might be viewed a potential cost to the company – an *opportunity cost* occasioned by the difference between the strike price and what could, *cet. par.* have been received in the ordinary course of events from a public issue.

But, if the increase in the price of the shares to the strike price is deemed to be the consequence of option recipients achieving the performance benchmark, then an opportunity to make a public issue at that share price must also be considered a function of that performance. So, if an excess of the then current price over the strike price is regarded an *opportunity cost* incurred by the company, then the inflow of cash from exercising the options must also be regarded an immediate *opportunity gain*, available for offset against the presumed opportunity cost. And, once caught in that entanglement, any other net increase in the company's wealth attributable to the achievement of the benchmark might likewise be attributed, and offset.

Governance reformers have campaigned on the platform that because the stock options are valuable and given in lieu of cash salary components, they are a *cost to the company* and must be expensed in the same manner as a cash salary component. That argument cannot be sustained – for there is neither a diminution in the issuing company's assets nor an increase in its liabilities; not when the options are vested – for nothing has changed, other than to make what was hypothetical more likely; and similarly not when they are exercised – for ordinarily the company's net assets will be increased rather than diminished at that point. The "company" stands to gain.

Perversely, potential costs and benefits accrue to shareholders – potential costs, from the diminution of their proportional shareholdings, – potential benefits, by virtue of increased company net wealth from the additional capital inflow when the options are exercised.

Whereas the debate has been heated, no case for expensing the options has been made that is consistent with the realities of the legal or financial settings in which companies operate.

Arguably, the governance prescriptions that set the expensing options rule in concrete have the potential to disadvantage shareholders: expensing does not reduce the cost of any dilution of their investment, reduced earnings (from expensing the value attributed to the options) may adversely impact the share price, and an inducement to offset the agency cost is removed.

Independence – a Slippery Obsession

Contrary to the strategy of aligning management's and shareholders' interests (perhaps now "stakeholders" interests, most of the governance codes focus strongly on the idea that the greater the independence of company officers, the better stakeholders' interests) are served. An independent Chairman, independent non-executive directors, independent auditors, an audit committee comprised of independent non-executive directors, and a likewise independent remuneration committee, are the call. Usually that is backed up with rules for the rotation of auditors (audit firm or lead partner), prohibition on the provision of most non-audit-services by the audit firm, and time constraints between an ex-member of the audit firm exiting the audit and entering employment of an ex-client. Whereas the ASXCGC's Recommendations, CLERP9, the Combined Code and SOX vary in detail, the overall intention is identical.

Curious in those prescriptions for independence is the absence of any clear explanation of what being *independent* entails. Commentaries accompanying the regimes mostly give examples of circumstances in which independence will be presumed to not exist. This is consistent with most of the governance regimes requiring as much attention to be given to the *appearance* that the various individual non-executive directors, the auditors, those comprising the remuneration and audit committees, are independent, as actually being so. It is highly questionable whether appearance has anything to do with the protection of stakeholders' interests.

In the corporate governance literature the notion of *independence* has been subjected to a negative, rather than to a positive focus. No longer, in that literature, does it refer to a *state of mind* driven by an admirable underpinning ethos of probity and integrity, truth and fairness, but to the absence of an assumed force to act improperly that would be fuelled by the strength of personal social and financial relationships. That belief also has been entrenched by its continuous allegation. In Australia the 2001 Ramsay Report advanced that perception, as did much of the evidence before the 2002 JCPAA enquiry into the Independence of Registered Company Auditors. It was inevitable that Australian prescriptions would pick up the prohibition on most non-audit services and restraints on the employment of ex-auditors – ASXCGC both and CLERP the latter. That Arthur Andersen earned about equal from providing non-audit services to Enron as it did from the audit, and the presence of an *ex* Andersen lead partner in past audits of HIH on the HIH Board, were presumed to have at least tempted audit malfeasance. "Association" has been misrepresented as "causation".[26]

That misrepresentation courses through the current corporate governance regimes. It undergirds not only the issues pertaining to audit, but also to Board structure, the call for "independent" non-executive directors, and the composition, functions of audit and remuneration committees. Understandably, it has common appeal – for, if individuals appear to not have anything to gain from decision, there is no self-interest to influence judgment, evaluation or assessment. But that denies the existence of integrity. It also presumes that the separation from potential to gain ensures that decisions, judgements, evaluations and assessments are "value free". Is that likely to be so? Is independence really attainable? Indeed, is it what is required?

Arguably, "No", is a reasonable answer to each of those questions. For, neither executive and non-executive directors, nor auditors, are either financially or professionally independent of their companies and company clients. Each receives financial rewards, each stands to gain commercial and social status, and each may enhance business networks, by virtue of their positions and appointments. So, most of the independence rules in the current governance are mere window dressing, more for the appearance that they achieve what is being sought.

An "independent state of mind" is not reliant upon financial, familial and social relationships. It is a matter of being well-informed, personal commitment to the matter at hand, and the exercise of individual trust and integrity.

CLERP9, the ASXCGC's Recommendations, the Combined Code, and SOX substitute defective organizational structures for a lack of personal character attributes as the core of the governance problem. Yet, curiously they do not inject any measures to change the organizational structural source of the agency impasse – the structure and operational mechanisms of the modern corporation.[27] Rather, they ignore the structure and place all their focus on the functioning of directors, auditors, and the like.

The serviceability of the governance rules as a whole, and in particular the prohibitions and constraints relating to Board structures and compositions, the rotation of audit firms or partners, the provision of non-audit services by the audit firm, composition and functions of audit committees, employment of ex-auditors, and the necessity and functions of non-executive directors, are contestable.

Nobody, however, has established causation between familial, social or financial relations, and corporate failure. Contiguity of corporate failure and circumstances in which the lack of independence is deemed to exist, is taken to be "good enough" evidence. Andersen's substantial fees from non-audit services is presented as if it were enough to justify the presumption of acquiescence to Enron's dubious application of the rules relating to the reporting of its Special Purpose Entities (SPE) and its accounting for the SPEs to get debt off its balance sheet. Guilt by association? Yet, the possibility that the quality of its consulting may have been compromised to retain its audit fee income does not appear to cross the minds of Andersen's detractors.[28]

Guilt by association also arises in the presumption that because ex Andersen auditors were on the HIH Board the probity and integrity required of them was at risk. There also appears to be a questionable linkage drawn between Andersen's alleged misdeeds in other audit engagements and its alleged lack of professional propriety; for example – in the Enron, Sunbeam and WorldCom, and in the HIH audits. Guilt by association is facilitated by the negative image the regimes have on independence. As things stand, the negative focus will remain as long as independence is said to refer to social and financial relationships, rather than to the *state of mind*[29] that directors, auditors, and the like, are to bring to their respective tasks in corporate settings.[30]

Neither directors (executive and non-executive) and managers or other employees, nor auditors can be free of financial dependency – in one way or another they all get paid by "their" company. Pay packets and fees, large and small, are all financial inducements. A functional notion of independence based on the criteria so often repeated in support of the governance regimes now in force, does not exist.

Perversely, *dependency* – in the sense of forging a greater linkage between the corporation's wealth and progress and the personal wealth and progress of the individuals managing and reporting on it – is more consistent with the longstanding desire to frustrate the ill effects of the separation of ownership and control.

The Poverty of Corporate Communication

Continuous assertions to the effect that manipulation of sound Accounting Standards underpins the breakdown in reliable communication of companies' financial affairs, have also paid off.

Whereas it appears to be generally accepted that accounting is "the language of business", its capacity to communicate reliable information about the wealth and progress of companies seems to be disregarded. In its communicative role, accounting has a critical corporate governance function. But conventional accounting in accord with the various national accounting standards is a flawed instrument of corporate governance. Argument is advanced that corporate officers and auditors have manipulated the financials of their company to bolster its reported performance: for example, HIH's under provisioning for claims, Enron's exploitation of SPEs and its use of mark-to-model accounting, WorldCom's capitalizing of expenses, Waste Management's reduction of its amortization charges, and (say) Freddie Mac's and Fannie Mae's classification of its investments.

It may well be that those practices were deliberately tuned to produce desired outcomes. But it should be noted that the opportunity to manipulate the Standards arises because the embedded flaws in the basic mechanisms and other prescriptions equally facilitate both the alleged improper and deceitful interpretations and applications for personal gain, *and* the making of genuine error of equal or greater magnitude without any intention to deceive.

HIH's accounting complied, in principle, with the Accounting Standards.[31] Both the relevant regulatory agencies (the Australian Securities and Investments Commission and the Australian Prudential Regulation Authority) appear to have been (for the most part) satisfied with HIH's accounting practices prior to its collapse. Enron's use of the SPEs had SEC approval: the SEC regulated and controlled of their use; whether the SPE ownership and control conditions were being satisfied, whether the transactions they entered into genuine or merely "wash sales" to create an image of growth and activity. SEC action implied that Enron's practices were in order. Enron's adoption of the *mark-to-model*[32] to value its gas contracts was approved by the SEC in 1992; the SEC's oversight implied approval when the practice was extended to contracts covering other commodities, derivatives of all descriptions[33] up to the time of its failure.

WorldCom's alleged capitalization of expenses Jetter (2003) and Malik (2003) arose by virtue of conventional (FASB variety) accounting being, in essence, an expense capitalization system. Whereas it is generally accepted that WorldCom's application was quite likely a deliberate ruse to increase its earnings, exactly the same "error" could have arisen through genuine misjudgment in identifying how much of the expenditure was linked to "future benefits".

Waste Management's alleged under-amortization of the costs of its garbage truck fleet was, likewise, facilitated by the existing accounting rules that implement the notion that "depreciation" is the "amortization of the cost of an asset over its useful life". Yet, in almost every financial setting outside of accounting depreciation is understood to be a decrease in price – *de pretium*. Were the depreciation of Waste Management's fleet to have been estimated by reference to the observable changes in the market prices for its trucks, Waste Management would have been unable to manipulate the calculation by merely changing the estimated life of its fleet. Again, the prescribed practice equally facilitates genuine error. The frequency of such "depreciation" errors is borne out by the instances and magnitude of "gains and losses on the sale of fixed assets" reported annually in companies' financials – each being attributable to under- and overestimates of amortization charges over the assets' lives and the non-reporting of appreciation (*a pretium*) in their market prices (see Clarke et al., 2003, especially Chap. 2).

Neither Freddie Mac nor Fannie Mae could have manipulated their results with the apparent ease they enjoyed had the values placed upon financial instruments and changes therein not turned upon whether the assets were classified as "available for sale". Virtually nowhere outside of accounting would the money's worth of a security be dependent upon how it was classified. Once again, error equal to Freddie Mac's and Fanny Mae's alleged manipulations could have occurred through compliance with the prescribed practices without any intention to deceive. The *system* is defective. Arguably, those who devised and those who enforce compliance with the current Accounting Standards are as responsible for the outcomes complained of, as are those alleged to have exploited them for their own benefit.

As an instrument of corporate governance, as the means by which the financial outcomes of whatever a company's managers have done and however they have done it is communicated, accounting complying with the prescribed rules has failed miserably. Justice Owen's assessment that there was not any large-scale fraud or embezzlement in the HIH collapse, where there was an approximate $5.3 billion asset shortfall between what was reported and the actual, is indicative of the extent to which conventional accounting in the absence of fraud can deceive. One would reasonably expect a sound system accounting to require fraud for it to be able to produce deceptive information on such a grande scale. Not so in the case of HIH, and arguably equally not so in respect of much of Enron's, Waste Management's, WorldCom's, Freddie Mac's or Fannie Mae's accounting. Yet the habitual rhetoric of the governance reformers, has entrenched the belief that accounting is in good order.

GOVERNANCE OVERLOAD?

Despite the flurry of knee-jerk responses to the so-called corporate scandals, evidence that they were caused by a lack of compliance with governance rules of the kind contained in the current governance regimes, has not been forthcoming. Allegations of responsibility have rained on corporate governance, but causal connections have not been established. There has been considerable debate on whether a "one size fits all" governance regime is possible. In contrast, that perhaps "one size does not fit any" has not been canvassed widely. It is implied that had the current regimes been in place, the unexpected collapses and the accounting scandals would not have occurred. That implication deserves examination.

A most noticeable feature of many of the provisions contained in the Combined Code, CLERP 9, ASXCGC Recommendations, and SOX is that they, arguably, are merely reformulations of what existed previously. Most of the key mechanisms already existed in one form or another prior to the recent crop of failures. Tweaked, specified in additional rules, but a lot has been lost in translation.

Not only is independence of the kind being promoted through the governance regimes impossible to achieve, but also its desirability in many settings is highly contestable. In contrast, the necessity that auditors maintain an independent mental attitude when forming their audit opinion clearly has been a fundamental theme coursing through the principles of company audit practice for over 150 years; and if *independence of mind* is equated with acting with great probity, integrity, honesty as a fiduciary, it has long been understood to be a fundamental ethos for directors and senior executives, too. Most companies have had audit committees for a substantial period of time – nothing new in that, and their perceived functions have been much the same as those implied in the current governance bromides. And if we take the push in (say) CLERP9 for the adoption of the International Financial Reporting Standards (IFRS) to be the *modus operandi* for achieving *comparability* in financial statement data, that too reflects a long-established pursuit. Nor is the oversight of financial communication by the Financial Reporting Council (FRC) new in concept – FRCs and the oversight boards in the United States are merely new versions of similar bodies that previously existed. Little is really new – perhaps some of the labels are, in some instances legal status has changed, compositions and functions expanded, operational issues given more detailed articulation – overall, however, it is simply more of the same.

Revamping and rebadging existing arrangements is a common political ploy by professional bodies, governments and their agencies, in crisis. It gives the appearance of a positive response to public discomfort.

In taking the current push at face value we are justified assuming that those promoting governance matters of the kind just noted believe in the prospect that they will provide a commercial setting less likely to house corporate misbehaviour of the kind criticized. We are equally justified in presuming that those driving the reform proposals are cognizant of the abject failure in the past of most of what they now propose to strengthen, reinforce – in effect to double-up on. That invites the inference that a strong belief prevails to the effect that the proposed governance mechanisms are sound – that the problem lies only in their implementation.

That the improper behaviour of a few "corporate bad eggs" – a few imperfect individuals messing up a perfect system – has caused the problems is the implicit message of the tacit endorsement of the regulatory mechanisms in the governance discussion.[34] Accordingly, whether the collection of regulatory measures has been coordinated, or indeed can be coordinated, to bring about an orderly corporate commercial environment, does not appear to be on the radar of the company-watchers', professional bodies, regulators, or government.[35]

Contrary to the way in which those in other disciplines, medicine for instance, might have addressed the perceived breakdown in governance; corporate reformers do not appear to have considered whether *less, rather than more*, of the current regulatory measures might be the answer. In medicine, if a therapy does not work, thought would normally be given not only to increasing dosage, but also to decreasing it, the manner in which it is administered, and its functioning within the combination of therapies of which it is part. It may be, for example, that there have been too many governance mechanisms in place. It may also be that the different governance mechanisms were not coordinated so as to avoid frustrating and negating the functioning of one another.[36]

Fewer Rules, More Governance?

It is to be noted that none of the new wave of corporate governance regimes rests upon or introduces governance *principles* that were not already woven into the companies legislation, the common law, and stock exchange listing rules. Those fundamental principles of directors' fiduciary duties, auditor independence, and that the financials disclose a "true and fair view" of a company's financial performance and financial position, are promoted in the current governance rhetoric as if new found revelations.[37] Perversely, at a time when principles rather than rules-based regulation is being promoted, the principles already in place go unnoticed. Yet the prescription is for *more rules*. Perhaps the plethora of rules obscures the principles. The answer might be to have fewer rules, rather than more, coupled to an accounting system that promptly "tells it as it is".[38] That we move to have fewer governance rules and mechanisms may not be a popular suggestion. It certainly goes against the worldwide trend, and in particular against the current endorsement by the professional bodies in Australia to give the CLERP9 proposals legislative backing. It may be that the prevailing view in this regard is a popular delusion.

Viewed against the background unrelenting popularizing and entrenching of preferred perceptions of good corporate governance and how to achieve it, perhaps it is not surprising that the current governance regimes contain more of what has failed in the past. For there, failure of the regulatory processes has been mistaken for failure of governance, per se. Despite numerous prescriptions of how to obtain it, those promoting the regimes have not explained what good corporate governance *is*, except for the implication that apparently it is what we do not have! They have presented neither evidence nor argument that the only way to achieve good governance is through a miasma of even more specific rules, or why more of the same that failed in the past will achieve whatever it is they desire. This may be because, generally, government agencies and professional associations have been endorsing processes without any explicit consensus on the commercial condition to which the processes are directed.

Consider the definitions of (implied to be *good*) corporate governance in the ASXCGC's Recommendations, and Justice Owen in his Report into the collapse of HIH:

> Corporate governance is the system by which companies are directed and managed. It influences how the objectives of the company are set and achieved, how risk is monitored and assessed, and how performance is optimized. (ASXCGC *Principles of Good Corporate Governance and Best Practice Recommendations*, p. 2)

> The governance of corporate entities comprehends the framework of rules, relationships, systems, and processes within and by which authority is exercised and controlled in corporations. (*The Failure of HIH Insurance*, Report of the Royal Commission, Volume 1. 6.1, p. 101, The Hon. Justice Neville Owen, Commissioner)

The ASXCGC present good governance as if it were a set of processes. Justice Owen perceives it to be a *framework* created by similar processes. Both, perhaps the former more so than the latter, entail the substitution of the processes by which governance is to be achieved, for governance itself. Justice Owen comes close to declaring corporate governance the concept of an ideal commercial environment in which *company managers exercise authority* with absolute probity with regard to the welfare of corporate stakeholders in general and the shareholders in particular, rather than a set of processes. For, the essential "essence" of governance lies not in any set of processes, but in the ethical and commercially prudent *steering* coming from company executives' exercise of the authority delegated to them.

Looking at governance as the absolute, uncompromising, probity with which that authority is exercised in respect of corporate affairs, places in focus the objective rather than the processes by which to achieve it. In contrast, the promoters of the various governance regimes have committed the fallacy of substituting the "means" for the "end" in mind. Perhaps, were they to have distinguished the desired end from those preferred processes, they may well have seen that the former and the latter are not necessarily linked in the way the conventional and repetitive rhetoric assumes.

Again, repetitive explanation of and allusion to corporate governance in terms of the processes by which it is to be achieved have had their way.

THE FALLACY OF MISPLACED CONCRETENESS[39]

Alfred North Whitehead's description of how repetition entrenches notions to the point at which they are accepted as unquestionable dogma, is an apt explanation for the curious way in which corporate governance is perceived, the features attributed to it, and the continual allegiance given to processes that have failed to deliver in the past. Whitehead's *fallacy of misplaced concreteness* offers an explanation of why a questionable focus on individuals has been allowed to divert attention from the objective, assurance of a commercial environment in which corporate affairs are orderly and predictable; why, in the examination of corporate distress, failures and collapses, processes have been accorded more attention than their objective; and why, in those enquiries well-established understandings of fundamental concepts have been replaced with perversions of them.

We do not appear to have learned much from successive episodes of corporate collapse. Enthusiastic, repetitious, and increasing support for contestable notions of what corporate governance entails has replaced observation and reason throughout those episodes. Corporate governance reformers appear to labour under the popular delusion that if you say something long enough it will become a commercial truth.

NOTES

1. See Brewster (2003) for the argument that over a long period accounting manipulations have sapped trust from accounting data and the accounting profession. Much the same theme underscores the argument in *The Number*, Beresen (2003) – see Chapter 8 "Accountants at the Trough," pp. 111–128.

2. Berle and Means (1932).

3. It is arguable that the outcomes of the operations of the Vanderbilts and J. P. Morgan were relatively as significant in their time as globalization has been in the recent past.

4. See Franzini (2004) for the outline of events up to February 2004.

5. See Smith and Emshwiller (2003) for example, for a description of the essence of the surprise element of Enron's unwinding over 24 days.

6. The recurring episodes of collapses in Australia during the 1960s, 1970s and 1980s are chronicled and discussed in Clarke, Dean, and Oliver (2003). These should be considered against the background of the failures elsewhere over the same period – of the Maxwell insurance empire: (see Thompson and Delano (1991)); the crisis at Lloyd's insurance (see Gunn (1992); Polly Peck in the U.K., BCCI worldwide (see Beaty and Gwynne, 1993; Olympia and York in Canada (see Foster 1993); Prudential Insurance (see, Eichenwald, 1995; the Savings and Loans affair in the United States: (see Pizzo, Fricker, and Muolo, 1989; Robinson, 1991); and, for example, in Italy the Banco Ambrosiano (see DiFonzo, 1983; Almerighi, 2002, I *banchieri di Dio; il caso Calvi*).

7. See, for example, Australian Society of Accountants (1966).

8. See Haigh (2003) for a balanced discussion of CEO's *invisible handouts*, and Flanagan (2003) for a more vitriolic discussion.

9. Most offer no comment on the amount of wisdom after the event. Nor do they comment usually on the mainly unequivocal support for the companies when they were the darlings of the market.

10. Hubbard, Delyth, Heap, and Cocks (2002).

11. Miller (1990).

12. We refer here to the comments emerging from the public enquiries, committees and commissions that have debated governance issues, for they are the means of shaping public understanding. This is particularly so in respect of the manipulative nature of corporate *group structures*. The James Hardie asbestos compensation affair supports the arguments put by Clarke et al. (2003), Chaps. 16 and 17 that the current corporate group structure is possibly ungovernable.

13. Support of that proposition in the United States by Warren Buffett seems to have taken on the mantle of the official voice from commerce, and by Arthur Levitt, the authoritative voice of securities regulation.

14. We should note the confrontations between the SEC, the FASB and the corporate community in the early 1990s regarding the expensing of stock options. Lobbyists on Capital Hill won out in the end. Levitt and Dyer (2002, pp. 11–12) notes how Congress "turned on him" when he was pushing for the expensing of stock options in the early 1990s. Congress has had its day again rejecting the compulsory expensing of *all* stock options on 15 June 2004. The House of Representatives Financial Services Committee approved a bill to restrict any FASB option expensing standard to options granted to the top five officers of a company. This legislation will create the ridiculous situation in which the value of stock options will be an *expense* and *not an expense* depending on who receives them.

15. This is a curious recourse to *substance over form* argument – the *substance* has been wrongly identified as the *form*, and the form as the *substance*.

16. We say *presumed*, for that view tends to ignore the current affinity with corporate *stakeholder* theory that asserts that corporations have obligations to a

considerably wider constituency than merely shareholders. It also draws upon neo-capitalism perceptions of the purpose and means of commerce. Nonetheless, the legal obligation of companies, in contrast to their now claimed social obligations, is to the shareholders.

17. See Blasi, Kruse, and Berstein (2003), Parts I and II, for the general argument and references to studies supportive of the positive benefits claimed of issuing stock options to employees.

18. As part of his allegation that "the Stock Option: [was] The CEO's license to Steal", Flanagan (2003, p. 39), is a good example – whereas he implies a connection between the *poor* performances Enron and WorldCom disclosed once the accounts were adjusted for the alleged manipulations, in contrast he begrudgingly notes that in respect to Citicorp – whilst Citicorp did well in 2001 "...Weill did a lot better".

19. See Blasi et al. (2003, pp. 85–88).

20. This is the *effective* price for stockholders who participate in stock splits in 1993 and 1999. The *actual* price topped at around $US50 in 2000.

21. For illustrations of this kind see, Blasi et al. (2003, pp. 79–153).

22. In 1981, President Reagan increased the differential between capital gains tax and income tax, making the capital gains from options trading an attractive tax alternative, especially for those with options in their 401(k) pension portfolios. In 1993, President Clinton indirectly increased that differential by capping the tax deduction for cash components of salaries at $US1 million.

23. That *ploy* has contributed to the notion that the stock options included in executives' remuneration packages *are* an expense of the issuing company. The argument has been seductive. Of course, the bottom-line would be reduced whenever an amount is deducted – but that does not legitimize the deduction, per se.

24. Curiously, that would seem to be a stronger argument for declaring the value of options "revenue" to the company, rather than an expense.

25. This aspect is discussed in Clarke, et al. (2003), especially Chaps. 16 and 17.

26. The applications of the independence notion are very wide. Accounting firms are reported (e.g. *AFR*, 27 May 2004) to have not only located their "consulting" activities and their "audit" activities in separate companies, but now also their "corporate turnaround" and "insolvency" practices.

27. It has been argued elsewhere, for example, in *Corporate Collapse* ... (Clarke et al., 2003; pp. 247–288) that the parent/subsidiary company structure now in increasingly complex arrangements has been a major vehicle for corporate malpractice, and in particular for the transfer of resources from companies in which the public have investment to the private companies of promoters and executives. Related party disclosures are designed to frustrate that, but their ineffectiveness is well illustrated by the transfers effected by Andrew Fastow through his management of Enron's SPEs. See, for example, Fox (2003); Partnoy (2003); Smith and Ermshwiller (2003), regarding Fastow's involvement with the Chewco, LJM1 and LJM2 partnerships.

28. It is not suggested that this was Andersen's strategy. It is documented that the expectation that non-audit service fees could rise to $US100 million influenced the firm's decision to retain the Enron audit. Point is, however, in other circumstances, any allegation that the Andersen firm consulted with the protection of the *audit* fee in mind, is just as plausible as the inferences habitually drawn regarding fees for non-audit services underpinning a loss of independence.

29. See submissions to the JPCAA Inquiry into the Independence of Registered Company Auditors and Hansard (2002) transcript of evidence (www.aph.gov.au) and to the HIH Royal Commission (*Report of the Royal Commission*, Vol. II) by Clarke, Dean and Wolnizer (2002a,b); and a submission by Clarke, Dean and Hansard transcript of evidence to the Senate Enquiry into the CLERP9 Bill, 2004 (Clarke & Dean, 2004). (www.aph.gov.au)

30. The alleged misdeeds of the Andersen firm appear to be central to the case of those pressing the conventional independence line of argument. The circumstances surrounding Andersen's forced retirement from practice are less clear than usually presented. As early as May 2002 Washington Post journalist Jackie Spinner "explained" how the remaining Big Four representatives agreed with Senator Billy Tauzin that Andersen had to be "cut loose"; see "Sullied accounting firms regaining political clout", *Washington Post*, 12 May, 2002, p. A01; see also Clarke et al. (2003, p. 216). More on the same issue appears in Morrison (2004), Rush to Judgment: The lynching of Arthur Andersen & Co. *Critical Perspectives on Accounting*, Vol. 15, No. 3, pp. 335–375.

31. See Clarke et al. (2003), for a discussion of HIH's accounting – especially Chap. 15.

32. There has been considerable misunderstanding regarding both the term and the practice as Enron applied it. In many commentaries this is referred to improperly as *mark-to-market*. But no market existed for the gas supply contracts for which Enron first gained explicit approval to use the technique. Fusaro and Miller (2002) note that the proper term is *mark-to-model* in which for similar no-price contracts the finance industry developed *models* by which to estimate (what we might call) *synthetic prices*. Enron's use of the *mark-to-model* technique is also properly described, and practice criticized, by Fusaro and Miller (2002, pp. 35–36), Swartz and Watkins (2003, p. 94) and Cruver (2003, p. 79). Other commentators, e.g. Fox (2003), Krugman (2003) and McLean and Elkind (2003), appear to miss the point and the subtleties of the labels. In contrast, Partnoy (2003, p. 159), notes the impact of computer-generated valuations for derivatives, though does not relate this to Enron's activities.

33. These included the widest imaginable contracts, including such instruments as *weather futures*.

34. *Discussion* rather than *debate* in this context, for there has not been any real debate as to why the similar measures failed to effect good governance in the past, other than to imply that the fault lies with recalcitrant directors, other executives, and auditors. This focus is consistent with most of the comment surrounding corporate malpractice. It is what we labelled the *cult of the individual* – a focus on the individuals, the consequence of which is to divert public attention from the systemic defects in corporate regulatory mechanisms – in *Corporate Collapse* ... (Clarke et al., 2003, pp. 14–20).

35. It is worth noting how quickly after the HIH collapse Australia's Federal Government set up the enquiry into Audit Independence, with what appears to have been absolute endorsement from virtually all parties interested in corporate affairs. Perhaps it is not surprising that the necessity for auditor independence almost passed without dissent – what dissent there was arose more from differences of opinion regarding how to achieve it, and even more so, perhaps, regarding how to have it

appear to prevail. Submissions and evidence before the Joint Parliamentary Committee enquiring into the Independence of Registered Company Auditors (Hansard www.aph.gov.au) reveal the common perception of how independence is to function as a governance mechanism.

36. The enquiry into terrorism shows how what might well be worthwhile activities can become dysfunctional when they lack coordination. There seems to be some strong evidence from the 9/11 Commission in the United States, for example that the different intelligence and other agencies did not know what intelligence on terrorism and Iraq's WMDs had been gathered by each other, were unsure of with whom they were to share intelligence, who "owned" the various bits of intelligence, who was following-up which leads, and the like. Corporate governance intelligence gathering and coordination seems to have malfunctioned in like fashion. "Who knew what" about HIH's affairs prior to its collapse, and what actions were being contemplated, appear to have lacked any semblance of coordination.

37. It is interesting to note that the Senate Committee on CLERP9 in its Report No. 2 (June 2004) recommends that directors have greater obligations regarding the "true and fair view" criterion.

38. Though perhaps not for the same reasons, this proposition finds some consonance with the theme pursued by Turnbull (2004).

39. For a discussion of Alfred North Whitehead's notion of *misplaced concreteness* see, Fernside and Holther (1959).

REFERENCES

Amerighi, M. (2002). *Il banchieri di Dio*. Roma: Editoru Ruiniti.

Australian Society of Accountants. (1966). *Accounting principles and practices discussed in reports of company failures*. Melbourne: ASA General Council.

Beaty, J., & Gwynne, C. G. (1993). *The outlaw bank*. London: Macmillan.

Beresen, M. (2003). *The Number*. London: Simon & Shuster.

Berle, A., & Means, G. (1932). *The modern corporation and private property* (reprint ed.). Macmillan: London.

Blasi, J., Kruse, D., & Berstein, A. (2003). *In the company of owners: The truth about stock options*. New York: Basic Books.

Brewster, M. (2003). *Unaccountable: How the accounting profession forfeited an public trust*. Hoboken, NJ: Wiley.

Clarke, F. L., Dean, G. W., & Wolnizer, P. P. (2002a). Submission to JPCAA Inquiry into the Independence of Registered Company Auditors; Hansard.

Clarke, F L., Dean, G. W., & Wolnizer, P. P. (2002b). Submission to the Royal Commission into the collapse of HIH.

Clarke, F. L., Dean, G. W., & Oliver, K. (2003). *Corporate collapse: Accounting, regulatory and ethical behaviour*. Melbourne: Cambridge University Press.

Clarke, F. L., & Dean, G. W. (2004). Submission to the Senate enquiry into the CLERP9 Bill, Hansard.

Colley, J. L., Doyle, J., Logan, L., & Stettinius, W. (2003). *Corporate governance*. New York: McGraw-Hill.

Cruver, B. (2003). *Enron: Anatomy of greed*. London: Arrow.

Culp, C. L., & Niskanen, W. A. (2003). *Corporate aftershock*. Hoboken, NJ: Wiley.

DiFonzo, L. (1983). *St. Peter's banker*. New York: Franklin Watts.

Eichenwald, K. (1995). *Serpent on the rock*. New York: HarperBusiness.

Fernside, W. W., & Holther, W. B. (1959). *Fallacy: The counterfeit of argument*. New York: Prentice-Hall.

Flanagan, W. G. (2003). *Dirty Rotten CEOs: How business leaders are fleecing America*. Rowville: The Five Mile Press.

Foster, P. (1993). *Towers of debt: The rise and fall of the Eichmanns*. London: Hodder & Stoughton.

Fox, L. (2003). *Enron: The rise and fall*. Hoboken, NJ: Wiley.

Franzini, G. (2004). *Il crac Parmalat: storia del crollo dell'impero del latte*. Roma: Editori Ruiniti.

Fusaro, P. C., & Miller, R. M. (2002). *What went wrong at Enron*. Hoboken, NJ: Wiley.

Gunn, C. (1992n). *Nightmare on Lime Street*. London: Smith Gryphon.

Haigh, G. (2003). Bad company: The cult of the CEO. *Quarterly Essay, 2*, 1–97.

Hubbard, G., Delyth, S., Heap, S., & Cocks, G. (2002). *The first XI: Winning organisations in Australia*. Milton: Wiley.

Jetter, L. W. (2003). *Broadbandits*. Hoboken, NJ: Wiley.

Krugman, P. (2003). *The great unravelling*. London: Allen Lane.

Korten, D.C. (1995). *When corporations rule the world*. San Francisco, CA: Berrett-Koehler Publishers, Inc. and West Hartford, CT: Kumarian Press Inc.

Korten, D.C. (1998). *The post-corporation world: Life after capitalism*. San Franscisco, CA: Berrett-Koehler Publishers, Inc. and West Hartford, CT: Kumarian Press Inc.

Levitt, A., & Dyer, P. (2002). *Take on the street: What Wall Street and corporate America don't want you to know*. New York: Pantheon Books.

Malik, O. (2003). *Disconnected: Inside the $750 billion telecom heist*. Hoboken, NJ: Wiley.

McGill, M. E. (1988). *American business and the quick fix*. New York: Henry Holt and Company.

McLean, B., & Elkind, P. (2003). *The smartest guys in the room*. London: Viking.

Miller, D. (1990). *The Icarus paradox*. New York: HarperBusiness.

Monks, R. A. G. (1998). *The emperor's nightingale: Restoring the integrity of the corporation*. Oxford: Capstone.

Morrison, M. A. (2004). Rush to judgment: The lynching of Arthur Anderson & Co. *Critical Perspectives on Accounting, 15*(3), 335–375.

Partnoy, F. (2003). *Infectious greed*. London: Profile Books.

Peters, T. J., & Waterman, R. H., Jr. (1982). *In search of excellence: Lessons from America's best run companies*. Sydney: Harper and Row.

Pizzo, S., Fricker, M., & Muolo, P. (1989). *Inside job*. Harmondsworth: Harper Perennial.

Robinson, M. A. (1991). *Overdrawn*. New York: Plume.

Smith, A. (1994). *An inquiry into the nature and causes of the wealth of nations* ([1776], reprint version). New York: Random House/Modern Library.

Smith, R., & Emshwiller, J. R. (2003). *24 Days*. New York: HarperBusiness.

Swartz, M., & Watkins, S. (2003). *Power failure: The rise and fall of Enron*. London: Aurum Press.

Thompson, P., & Delano, A. (1991). *Maxwell: A portrait of power*. London: Corgi.

Turnbull, S. (2004). Agendas for reforming corporate governance, capitalism and democracy. *Corporate governance and ethics conference*, Macquarie University, June.

DOES ONE SIZE FIT ALL? TRANSPLANTING ENGLISH TAKEOVER LAW INTO CHINA [☆]

Guanghua Yu

ABSTRACT

Corporate governance has attracted enormous attention both in the area of law and in the area of financial economics. In comparative corporate governance studies, many people have devoted their energy to find a best corporate governance model. I argue that a functional analysis does not support the view that there is a single best corporate governance model in the world. I further use the transplantation of an English style takeover law into China to show that the importation of foreign law is not always based on careful analysis whether the imported foreign law is the best in the world. Furthermore, I use the subsequent adjustment of the transplanted English takeover law in China to show that the imported foreign law is subject to local political and economic conditions. If there is no best corporate govern model and the transplantation of foreign law into other countries with different social and political background does not achieve similar objectives, the search for a best corporate governance model is misguided. Just as tort law or constitutional law regimes may have

[☆] Research support for this project was provided by the University of Hong Kong.

Corporate Governance: Does Any Size Fit?
Advances in Public Interest Accounting, Volume 11, 41–70
Copyright © 2005 by Elsevier Ltd.
ISSN: 1041-7060/doi:10.1016/S1041-7060(05)11003-7

diversified models, so do corporate governance regimes in countries with different historical, social and political backgrounds.

1. INTRODUCTION

The problem of separation of corporate control and residual claims documented by Berle and Means has attracted considerable attention in the United States.[1] The early economic explanation of the cause of the problem of separation of corporate control and residual claims focuses on scale of economics and specialized knowledge of managerial experts. If the economic explanations were true, competitive economic forces would drive nations towards a single best model of corporate governance. Roe's pioneering works, however, find that similar matured economies have widely diversified corporate governance regimes.[2] Roe's research suggests that there are alternatives. Despite the differences in corporate governance regimes around the world, considerable research is still focused on the issue whether there is a best corporate governance model in the world. I argue from a functional approach in Section 2 that there might be no single best corporate governance model in the world. If there is no single best corporate governance model, the search for a single best model is largely misguided. I examine in Section 3 the transplantation of an English style takeover law into China and the subsequent adjustment of the transplanted takeover law in China under a different social and political background. This section tries to show that similar legal provisions may lead to different outcomes in different countries. I conclude in Section 4 that even a functional analysis shows one corporate governance model does not fit all. This is compounded by the inclusion of large social and political considerations.

2. THE SEARCH FOR A BEST MODEL

2.1. Corporate Finance and Governance Regimes

The formation and growth of corporations require capital. Capital may be raised through equity financing or debt financing. Both methods of corporate finance result in frictions between users and suppliers of capital. Equity financing gives rise to the agency costs of equity financing while debt-financing gives rise to the agency costs of debt financing.[3] As the methods of financing corporate projects through either debt or equity are not mutually exclusive,[4] most companies adopt both debt financing and equity financing. Differences, however, do exist. Corporations in the United States and the United Kingdom rely far more heavily on the securities market than corporations in Germany and France. For instance, while the United Kingdom has 36 listed firms per million citizens and the United States has 30, France and Germany have only eight and four, respectively.[5] Similarly, the ratio of total stock market capitalization to GDP contracts sharply between Germany on the one hand and the United Kingdom and the United States on the other. In Germany, stock market capitalization was 17% of the GDP at the end of 1990s, but the corresponding ratio was 132% in Great Britain.[6] In the United States in 1995, the stock capitalization of the New York Stock Exchange and NASDAQ was around 87% of the total GDP.[7]

Different corporate finance methods create different sets of conflict of interest problems. The solutions to these different problems call for different corporate governance regimes. Corporate governance is defined as ways designed to make the management work for the best interest of the corporation and to assure a reasonable return to the suppliers of capital. In the United States, the supply of capital is dominantly from the securities market. In such an economy, the growth of corporations under competitive conditions is mainly determined by scales of economics,[8] shareholder diversification,[9] reduction of transaction costs,[10] and special knowledge of managerial experts.[11] According to Demestz and Lehn, share ownership concentration levels are inversely related to the aggregate size of the corporation.[12] This relationship holds because as the value-maximizing size of firm increases, the cost of acquiring a control block will also rise, deterring control accumulation. In addition, when the benefits from control transactions are smaller than the benefits resulting from share diversification, people will choose the latter. Berle and Means documented the phenomenon of widely dispersed shares in the United States.[13] Within a regime where corporate finance is mainly from the securities market and shares are widely dispersed, the costs of equity financing would be higher if the corresponding corporate governance regime did not respond to agency problems well. As a matter of fact, the product market, the stock market, and the takeover market play important roles in the United States in solving the problem of conflict of interest between the management and the shareholders.

In Germany, initial public offerings historically have been rare, only 10 in all of 1994.[14] The stock markets are famously illiquid[15] and volatile.[16] Generally speaking, debt financing plays a much more significant role than equity financing in Germany.[17] Debt financing creates the problem of conflict of interest between a borrowing corporation and the creditor. The corporate governance regime in Germany was very responsive to the agency costs of debt financing. German banks' historical and significant roles in debt financing, without political and legal constraints, make it desirable for them to have the option of holding shares in the debtor corporations.[18]

In debt financing, creditors normally can intervene in the debtors' business only after debtors' default. As bankruptcy generally diminishes claims of general creditors, creditors prefer early exit if they do not have sufficient control of the debtor. If a creditor is also a major shareholder, it may deter wealth-transfer transactions. Ex ante, the creditor–shareholder may prevent wealth transfer transactions being adopted by the management of the borrower. Such intervention is normally done by the creditor–shareholder's representative on the supervisory board. The supervisory board can always ask the management board for reports. The supervisory board may also ask the management board to obtain its approval before important transactions, such as credits above a certain amount.[19]

Ex post, the creditor – shareholder may penalize managers through the supervisory board. Significant shareholding in the debtor corporation makes voice more important than exit; otherwise the creditor–shareholder will suffer both on equity investment and on credit investment. Thus, it is not surprising to see that German banks often take over the reorganization of corporations in distress.[20] Empirical studies show that there is a significant involuntary "fluctuation" of management board members not only in cases of serious problems within the corporation but also in less serious cases in which the supervisory board was displeased with the performance of individual managers or with the management board as a whole.[21] Hence, creditor–shareholders' active participation in corporate governance in Germany reduces both the agency costs of debt financing and the agency costs of equity financing.

2.2. Is there a Best Corporate Governance Model in the World?

The search for a best corporate governance model has been in existence since the beginning of 1990s. Porter argued that the Anglo–American pattern of dispersed ownership was clearly inferior to the bank-centered capital markets of Germany and Japan, because the latter enabled corporate executives to manage for the long run, while United States managers were allegedly forced to maximize short-term earnings.[22] Grundfest argued that the United States regulatory regime systematically subordinated investors desire to resolve agency problems to managers' desire to be protected from capital market discipline.[23] He states:

> As a consequence of the harmony of interests created by joint equity and debt holding position, Japanese firms have to compensate lenders less to induce them to bear the risks associated with potential bondholder – stockholder conflict. Thus, all else being equal, Japanese capital structures reduce agency costs and allow investors to monitor management more effectively than in the United States. In particular, the amelioration of agency problems allows Japanese firms to invest more in research and development and to maintain more liquid and flexible asset structures than their comparably leveraged American counterparts.

Similar criticisms of the American corporate governance regime can be found in the political theories. Political theories explain the dispersed share ownership in large American corporations as the product of political forces and historical contingencies as well as economic efficiency.[24]

Doubts were soon raised concerning whether the corporate governance regime in the United States is inferior to their counterparts in Japan and Germany. Macey and Miller argue that powerful banks in corporate governance carries with it an entirely new set of conflicts between the risk-averse claimants who make loans and the residual claimants who invest risk capital, preventing the equity claimants from undertaking socially optimal risks.[25] The argument of Macey and Miller is not entirely satisfactory, however. The conclusion that powerful banks as fixed claimants care far less about maximizing their firms potential upside performance than about minimizing potential downside performance ignores a major fact that German universal banks sometimes do hold substantial shares in the borrowing corporations. For instance, in 1986 the Deutsche Bank held 41.8% of the shares in Daimler-Benz, 30.82% shares in Bayer and 17.64% of the shares in Siemens.[26] Presumably, the Deutsche Bank would also be able to share a high proportion of benefits from the optimal risk taking activities in these borrowing corporations.

Neoclassical economists have long argued that efficiency considerations ultimately prevail and determine corporate structure. Stigler and Friedland criticize the main theme of Berle and Means on the ground that empirical evidence available at the time when Berle and Means wrote their book was not able to establish any effect of different type of control on profits.[27] Demsetz views the ownership structure of the corporation as an endogenous outcome of a maximizing process.[28] While agency costs may be higher in corporations with dispersed shareholding structure, their higher costs may be more than offset by the reduction in risk-associated capital cost, benefits from economic scales and specialized knowledge of managers.[29]

Recent studies also raise doubts whether institutional investors would play useful roles in corporate governance even if legal barriers were removed. Romano has shown that public pension funds face political constraints that are likely to prevent them from serving very effectively as monitors of corporate management.[30] Coffee has argued that the long-term relational investing by institutional investors may be too costly to such investors because it will require them to sacrifice liquidity.[31] Macey has explained that the public goods nature of institutional investors,' particularly mutual funds', active participation in corporate governance makes it difficult for institutional investors to actively participate in corporate governance in the corporations in which they have invested in.[32] An institution that invests a great deal in efforts to increase the performance of one firm has to share the benefits with other passive institutional investors who own the same stock whereas the cost of monitoring has to be borne entirely by such an active institutional investor. Furthermore, it is not clear that the human capital skills needed to be a successful institutional investor are the same as the skills necessary to provide management advice to the corporations in which the fund is invested.[33] Empirical evidence in the United States also suggest that institutional investors do not have a skilled pool of employees capable of offering suggestions and advice that would improve corporate performance.[34] In addition, active roles played by institutional investors may not create net wealth. Smith has argued that institutional investors cannot acquire large shares in fewer corporations without significantly compromising diversification and thus increasing the risk of their portfolio.[35] He has also observed that under the condition of imperfect information large-scale activities in corporate governance inevitably entails a great deal of risk, and puts activist institutions at a disadvantage to their more passive competitors.[36] Empirical evidence has partially supported Smith's position. After assessing the finance literature on institutional investors' activism in corporate governance, Romano has found that it has an insignificant effect on targeted firms' performance.[37] Proposals by institutional investors calling for limits on executive compensation produce even negative price effects in the target corporations.[38] Similarly, proposals of institutional investors to increase the number of independent directors in target corporations result in negative price impact.[39]

Recently, the focus of studies is on the relationship between a jurisdiction's ability to finance economic development and growth and its legal system.[40] As previously discussed, United States and United Kingdom have strong stock market while Germany and France have relatively weak stock market. Financial economists in this school argue that only those legal systems that provide significant protection for minority shareholders can develop active equity markets.[41] Coffee raises the point that, if this explanation from financial economists is accepted, it amounts to a rejection of the political theory of American corporate finance offered by Roe and others.[42] This is so because dispersed share ownership may be the product not of political constraints on financial institutions. Instead, it is strong legal protection, which encourages investors to become minority owners.[43] This point is not new. Demsetz once said that in a world in which self-interest plays a significant role in economic behavior, it is foolish to believe that owners of valuable resources systematically relinquish control to managers who are not guided to serve the interests of owners.[44]

Regardless whether the dispersed ownership structure in the United States is a function of legal restrictions on financial institutions, the explanation that concentrated ownership becomes the consequence of weak legal protections for public or minority investors[45] is not entirely satisfactory. It is true that the premium for control blocks in Italy is much higher than that in the United States,[46] but it is still difficult to come to the conclusion that the concentrated ownership structure is worse than the dispersed ownership structure. Shareholders with concentrated ownership have both the incentives and ability to monitor the management team. The higher share premium for control is a reward of their monitoring activities. It is very difficult to argue that a system linking monitoring efforts with reward is defective. Although the share premium for control is low in the United States, compensation to the managers is much higher in the United States than in Germany and Japan.[47] For instance, in the year before the merger the Chrysler Chief Executive Officer (CEO) received cash compensation of US$ 6 million and stock options worth US$ 5 million while the Daimler CEO received approximately one-eighth of that amount.[48] A plausible explanation is that minority shareholders in countries with dispersed ownership have to provide the managers and CEOs with greater remuneration to motivate the managers to maximize the shareholders wealth. These differences are, however, not able to suggest which system is better from a contractual perspective. The ability to survive in a large number of countries indicates that concentrated ownership is also consistent with efficiency given the relevant constraints in these economies. Concentrated ownership, however, may also occur in a country with good legal protection to minority shareholders. For instance, entrepreneurs prefer to have control when venture capitalists exit from successful firms.[49] Leveraged buyouts provide another example that just as dispersed ownership in the United States is consistent with efficiency,[50] so is concentrated ownership in the United States. Shleifer and Vishny point out that LBOs are efficient organizations as large investors reduce agency problems.[51]

So far, there is no clear evidence to show whether the corporate governance system in the United States is better or worse than the corporate governance system in Japan or Germany. Claims that one corporate governance system is better than the other are largely influenced by the prosperity of the economy in that country compared with the economy in another country. For instance, when the Japanese economy was very successful until at least the beginning of 1990s, many people expressed their preference to the Japanese corporate governance system.[52] The economic performance in the United States in the 1990s has, however, changed the tide in the corporate governance literature. Soon people voiced their views that the corporate governance system in the United States may be actually better than that in Japan and Germany.[53] Linking the performance of a particular corporate governance system with the success of the economy can further be found from persons who were once quite cautious with comparative corporate governance studies. For example, Romano once stated:

> While we cannot predict whether the United Stated will be surpassed as the economic leader, the key factors that economists believe affect absolute productivity performance are the national savings rate (investment), the labor force's education, and the magnitude of efforts devoted to basic and applied research. There is no theory or evidence relating any of these factors to corporate governance arrangements. It is telling that commentators who are concerned about the effect of corporate governance on comparative economic performance do not mention these key factors; the probable explanation is that it is extremely difficult to relate such fundamental factors to corporate governance patterns.[54]

Recently, Romano has stated:[55]

> Commentators have, in general, commended institutional shareholder activism, at least in part from a belief that it would replicate the block holding-backed governance systems of Germany and Japan and thereby fill the void in managerial monitoring which occurred at the end of the 1980s with the decline in hostile takeovers in the United States (although the bloom now is off Germany and Japan's corporate governance systems given far superior United States economic performance for more than a decade and the increase in hostile takeover activity in recent years)....

Since it is difficult to use the connection between corporate governance and economic performance to establish the claim that a particular corporate governance system is superior than another, we are still further away from discovering the best corporate governance model. The major difficulty with connecting corporate governance systems with economic performance is that the approach fails to measure the substitution effects and the effects of complementarities of the different diversified subsystems in different corporate governance systems.

3. TRANSPLANTATION AND ADJUSTMENT OF AN ENGLISH STYLE TAKEOVER LAW IN CHINA

In Part (1) of this Section, I try to explain that the transplantation of a foreign law may be quite accidental rather than based on careful cost and benefit analysis of the best law among available options. The adoption of an English style takeover law at the beginning of 1990s in China can be explained by Chaos theory. I analyze further in Part (2) and Part (3) that the subsequent adaptation of the transplanted foreign law is path dependent. The use of the transplanted English style takeover law in China provides good evidence that adaptation of the transplanted foreign law in a different country is subject to local, social and political forces. This also shows that there are diversified corporate governance subsystems because of local adaptation and innovation.

3.1. Chaos Theory and the Importation of Takeover Law

China's company law and the stock market were mainly designed to improve the performance of the inefficient State-owned enterprises.[56] As a part of the company law, the law of takeover has similar concerns for State-owned enterprises. This Part will discuss the poor performance of State-owned enterprises and banks until the beginning of the 1990s. The inefficiency of the State-owned enterprises called for a major change of corporate finance from bank loans to issuing shares to the public through the stock exchanges both in China and outside of China, particularly in Hong Kong. The listing of shares of Chinese enterprises in Hong Kong gave great leverage to the regulatory agencies in Hong Kong to persuade the Chinese Government to adopt laws similar to those in Hong Kong, which are of English origin.

Although reform of State-owned enterprises started in 1978, performance of State-owned enterprises and banks remained poor in 1980s and at the beginning of 1990s. In 1987, losses incurred by State-owned, economically independent industrial enterprises amounted to 6.1 billion yuan.[57] Losses increased to 34.8 billion yuan in 1990 and to 45.2 billion yuan in 1993.[58] During the first four months of 1994, 50.1% of these enterprises were running at a loss.[59] Although things improved slightly in the later half of that year, 34.4% of these State-owned enterprises were still running at a loss at the end of 1994.[60] Overstocking of products, chain defaulting of debts and poor management of funds have taken an increasingly heavier toll on the economic performance of enterprises. For instance, stockpiled products were valued at 412.4 billion yuan at the end of 1994.[61] Most of these loans resulted from medium to large-sized State-owned enterprises.

Despite the reform of the financial sector, performance of the banks remained poor at the beginning of the 1990s. Overdue payments and non-performing loans were high. While official reports indicate that overdue payments and non-performing loans accounted for 15% of all credit offered by banks in 1992,[62] unofficial estimates show that overdue payments and non-performing loans were close to 40% of all outstanding loans.[63] The continuation of the dominant means of financing State-owned enterprises by loans from State banks would generate political risks when banks were unable to tighten the soft budget constraints of various loan users.[64]

Soft budget constraints and the legal prohibition against banks from owning shares in non-financial companies require the use of alternative means of financing corporate activities. The stock market was a natural selection. It is argued that if share prices reflect enterprise profitability, capital markets will channel investment funds to the most efficient enterprises as investors seek to maximize their returns.[65] It is further argued that capital markets create a market for corporate control. The reformers believe that market mechanisms are more efficient at rationalizing productive assets than the powers given to banks.[66] Moreover, the creation of a stock market gives enterprises more financial autonomy (since they no longer have to rely on the governments for funds), which also gives them more freedom to respond quickly to market opportunities, cutting through the regional, departmental and bureaucratic ties that continue to bind banks.[67]

Under the support of reformers, two stock exchanges respectively opened in Shanghai in 1990 and in Shenzhen in 1991.[68] Raising capital domestically was not the only objective. The Government was also active to utilizing foreign capital, particularly through Hong Kong. The demand of raising foreign capital mainly through Hong Kong at the beginning of the 1990s gave the regulatory experts in Hong Kong the opportunity to persuade the relevant authorities in China to adopt certain necessary laws and regulations similar to those used in Hong Kong.

The regulations passed in that period provides some evidence that China was keen in using Hong Kong as a base for the purpose of raising foreign capital. Before the Company Law was enacted in 1993, the State Economic

Restructuring Commission issued the Opinions on the Standardization of Joint Stock Companies (Standardization Opinions)[69] in 1992 to facilitate the conversion of State-owned enterprises to joint stock companies. Soon after the issuance of the Standardization Opinions, the State Economic Restructuring Commission issued the Supplementary Measures Concerning the Implementation of the Opinions on the Standardization of Joint Stock Companies by Companies Seeking a Listing in Hong Kong (Supplementary Measures).[70] This Supplementary Measures was designed to adapt the listing in Hong Kong by companies incorporated in China.

As the Standardization Opinions and the Supplementary Measures do not contain detailed provisions for the protection of minority shareholders, the concern about the extent of the protection of minority shareholders in Hong Kong has to be addressed. For this purpose, the Mainland and Hong Kong Joint Working Committee on Securities Affairs was established with the approval of the State Council. The Essential Clauses of the Articles of Association of Companies Seeking a Listing in Hong Kong proposed by this Committee was endorsed by the State Economic Restructuring Commission (Articles of Association).[71]

In the Articles of Association, typical English company law provisions, among other things, on the duty of directors[72] and remedies of a company in case of breach of duties[73] can be found. The Standardization Opinions were replaced by the Company Law enacted in 1993 and the Articles of Association were replaced by the Prerequisite Clauses of the Articles of Association of Companies Seeking a Listing Outside the PRC (Prerequisite Clauses) in 1994.[74] In 1993, the State Council also promulgated the Tentative Regulation on the Administration of the Issuing and Trading of Shares (ITS).[75] These laws and regulations provided the legal infrastructure for the issuing and trading of shares both on the stock exchanges in China and the stock exchange in Hong Kong by companies incorporated in China.

In the ITS, provisions on takeovers are very similar to the Hong Kong Code on Takeovers and Mergers,[76] which was itself based on the London City Code on Takeovers and Mergers.[77]

Chaos theory shows that some phenomenon is extremely sensitive to the historical conditions.[78] According to that theory, accurate predictions about where a system is headed are hard. Applying the theory to China, the adoption of an English style takeover law at the beginning of the 1990s is closely related to the need of raising foreign capital through the capital market in Hong Kong. The greater influence of continental law on the law making in China after 1840 provides further evidence of this random factor. The Chinese legal system is closer to the continental legal system. In the late

Qing Dynasty, several legal experts from Japan and Germany were actively involved in the law making process in China.[79] The draft Civil Law of the late Qing Dynasty was mainly based on the Japanese Civil Code and with reference to the German Civil Code.[80] The structure of the current General Principles of Civil Law cannot escape the influence of the Japanese and German Civil Code. In the area of securities regulation, both the United States and the United Kingdom have relatively satisfactory takeover law. The size of the United States economy and its influence in the world should better influence the law makers in China. Nevertheless, the English style takeover law was transplanted into China via Hong Kong at the beginning of the 1990s. The transplantation of the English style takeover law is accidental rather than based on careful cost and benefit analysis that the English takeover law is the best in the world.

3.2. The Law and Adjustment

As discussed previously, China's early takeover transactions were regulated by the Tentative Regulations on the Administration of the Issuing and Trading of Shares (ITS).[81] While there are only seven articles on takeovers in the ITS, the key provision is based on the London City Code.[82] According to this provision, within 45 working days after any legal person's (other than a promoter's) direct or indirect holding of outstanding common shares in a listed company reaches 30% of such company's total outstanding common shares, such legal person shall make an offer of takeover to all the shareholders of such company, offering to purchase their shares through cash payment.[83] If a takeover is made, the higher of the following two prices should be adopted as the offer price: (i) the highest price paid by the offeror for the purchase of such shares during the 12 months proceeding the issuance of the takeover offer; or (ii) the average market price of such shares during the 30 working days proceeding the issuance of the takeover offer.[84] I will call this provision the mandatory purchase provision and further discuss it later.

A few other provisions are related to fair treatment of minority shareholders and are much easier to justify. For instance, all the conditions contained in a takeover offer shall apply to all the holders of the same kind of shares.[85] If the total number of shares that the maker of a takeover offer prepares to buy is less than the total number of shares for which the offer is accepted, the offeror shall purchase shares from the offeree shareholders on a pro rata basis.[86] In the event of a change in any of the main conditions of offer after a takeover offer has been issued, the offeror shall promptly notify all offerees.[87] Such notice may be made in the form of a press conference or newspaper announcement or by another means of dissemination. During the term of a takeover offer and for a period of 30 working days thereafter, the offeror may not purchase the shares in question on any conditions other than those set forth in the offer.[88]

Still other provisions are related to disclosure and the facilitation of potential competing takeover offers. If a legal person holds, pursuant to the disclosure provision, directly or indirectly, more than 5% of the common shares of another listed company, a public announcement shall be made and a written report disclosing the fact shall be sent to the listed target company, the relevant stock exchange and the China Securities Regulatory Commission (CSRC) within three working days from the date of acquisition.[89] In addition, any change of the above acquired shares of such a legal person reaching 2% will again trigger the reporting duty.[90] Such a legal person shall not directly or indirectly buy or sell shares of the target company for two working days from the date when it makes the announcement and submits the report and before the submission of the report.[91] According to another provision for the purpose of facilitating takeover offers, the takeover offer period, calculated from the date of issuing the offer, shall not be less than 30 working days.[92] Offerors shall not withdraw their takeover offer during the offer period.[93] Furthermore, the offeree shareholders have the right to withdraw their acceptance during the offer period.[94] As will be discussed later, the political goal of maintaining control over the large state-owned enterprises makes the disclosure provision and the provision for facilitating competing takeover offers irrelevant in the 1990s.

The mandatory purchase provision is critical to the English style takeover law. The takeover law in the United States does not have such a provision. The rationale behind such a provision is the equality of treatment of minority shareholders. If an acquiring company pays a premium to the majority, block or some shareholder(s) in a target when purchasing their shares, the acquiring company shall also be required to extend the same premium to the minority shareholders in the target company. An introductory provision in the London City Code reflects that policy concern. The provision stipulates that the Code is designed principally to ensure fair and equal treatment of all shareholders in relation to takeovers.[95] This rationale, however, is based on an unrealistic assumption that whatever the law, the number of takeovers will not be reduced. The provision takes the ex post view that the gains,[96] once a takeover takes place, from the takeover should be shared equally by all the shareholders in the target.

The mandatory purchase provision can be evaluated by the autonomy and the welfare value. Neither criterion can justify this premium sharing provision. On a Nozickian right-based approach, a distinction is made between threats and offers.[97] Threats reduce the possibilities open to the recipient of an offer whereas offers expand them. From that perspective, takeovers would seem properly to be viewed as offer rather than as threat. The possibility of having a new management team indicates that takeovers increase target shareholders' possibilities relative to their position prior to their interaction with the acquirer. Even the threat of takeovers disciplines managers in a potential target company.

Despite the conclusion that takeover transactions enlarge shareholders' contractual possibilities and despite the overwhelming empirical evidence that shareholders of target companies receive abnormal returns resulting from takeover transactions, an enormous body of academic writing has focused on the problem of coercion in takeovers, particularly in partial bids.[98] Coffee notes that demonstrated examples of coercion remain as rare as confirmed sightings of the Loch Ness monster.[99] The ex ante Nozickian rights-based approach provides hardly any justification for the mandatory purchase provision. If takeovers enlarge the opportunities of the target shareholders as they are considered as offers rather than threats, mandatory purchase provisions cannot be justified. Even from the perspective of the remaining target shareholders, mandatory purchase provisions may reduce their contractual opportunities as the heavy burden of the provision on the acquirer could result in few takeovers ex ante. Ex post, mandatory purchase provisions may be viewed as offers to particular offeree shareholders in the target as they can choose either to sell their shares to the acquirer with the premium or to remain in the target and expect the improvement of the target by the acquirer. Mandatory purchase provisions, however, are certainly threats to the acquiring company and the shareholders in the acquiring company. If takeovers do not create third party effects of coercion on the remaining shareholders in the target, it is not clear why the contractual relation between the acquirer and part of the shareholders in the target should be restrained. As this rights-based approach objects interpersonal utility comparison, no clear conclusions can be drawn.

The autonomy value provides little support for such a provision. Welfare value would also object to the mandatory purchase provision. Mandatory purchase provisions increase the cost of acquiring the control of target companies. The harmful effects of the mandatory purchase provision are obvious. In the first place, mandatory purchase provisions reduce the number of offers by making targets more expensive to acquire. According to the economic law of demand, the higher the price, the lower the demand from purchasers. Lower demand in the context of takeovers means fewer takeovers, hence, possibly a smaller pie for society. Secondly, the philosophy of sharing the gains from takeover transactions contained in the mandatory purchase provision reduces the return of investment on the part of the acquirer. The inability of acquirers to appropriate the full value of their investment will lead them to undertake too few takeovers. This is the classic public good problem.[100] The proper management of an inefficient target company is a public good to all the shareholders of the target. Grossman and Hart have pointed out that there are significant costs in ensuring that directors/managers act in the interest of the shareholders.[101] If one shareholder (acquirer) devotes resources to improving management, then all the shareholders benefit.[102] The mandatory purchase provision exacerbates the externality problem by allowing even the remaining shareholders of the target company to share equal gains from takeovers. This severe externality problem indicates that it cannot be assumed that a company which is not being run in the interests of shareholders will always be vulnerable to a takeover bid. An antidote of this externality problem is to exclude the remaining shareholders in the target from sharing equal gains resulting from takeovers ex post, hence, an argument for abolishing the mandatory purchase provision at least at the low threshold of 30%.

To understand how the imported takeover law adjusts to China's local conditions, we need to understand the ownership structure of the listed companies on the two stock exchanges. As discussed previously, the development of China's corporate law and the establishment of the stock market at the beginning of the 1990s were closely related to the reform of the State-owned enterprises. A survey in May 1999 reveals that among the 862 listed companies on the two stock exchanges, State shares exist in 541 listed companies, accounting for 62.76%.[103] Among the 541 listed companies, State shares account for 45% of the total issued shares in these companies.[104] In 312 listed companies, the State shareholder is the only shareholder with more than 5% of the shares, representing 57.67% of the 541 companies.[105] In 473 listed companies, the state shareholder has either absolute or relative control[106] of the company, occupying 87.43% of the 541 listed companies.[107] The State shares are mainly held by State asset administration bureaus, State investment companies or the parent companies of the State-owned listed companies.[108] To be sure, the percentage of State ownership is much higher as State ownership may be held by legal persons of State-owned companies.[109] In 70.79% of the 541 listed companies, State shares range from 30 to 80%.[110] Different from the shares held by individuals, which are traded at the two stock exchanges, State shares and legal person shares of State-owned enterprises are not traded. Another piece of statistics shows that traded shares owned by individual investors in most listed companies are only between 25 and 40%.[111]

The structure of shareholding in most listed companies makes it impossible for an acquiring company to accumulate control through buying shares on any stock exchange. So far, there has been no successful acquisition of control of a listed company by purchasing shares on the stock market. To acquire sufficient percentage of shares in a target listed company, instead, requires the purchase of part of the non-traded shares owned by the State or other companies. This makes the negotiated takeover the preferred method of takeovers in China. Under this method, an acquiring company negotiates with a majority or block shareholder and enters into a share transfer agreement with that shareholder in the target listed company.

Negotiated takeovers in China, however, have to overcome some procedural and legal hurdles. On the procedural side, acquiring State shares or legal person shares of State-owned enterprises requires approval by the relevant authority. Article 29 of the Provisional Measures on the Administration of State-owned Shares of Joint Stock Companies provides that the transfer of State-owned shares need the approval of the State Asset Administration Bureau and the provincial government.[112] Transferring more than 30% of the State-owned shares in a listed company requires the joint approval of the State Asset Administration Bureau and the State Economic Restructuring Commission.[113] The approval procedure is consistent with the goal of the Government to maintain control of the large State-owned enterprises on the stock market.

In addition to overcoming this procedural hurdle, negotiated takeovers have to comply with the requirement of the mandatory purchase provision, which is central to the London City Code. The cost of following such a mandatory purchase provision is well recognized by regulators in China.[114] The practice of dealing with negotiated takeovers and the adjustment of the English style takeover law to the Chinese takeover market reflect the concern that strictly following the mandatory purchase provision is inefficient.

The first negotiated takeover took place in 1994 under the early takeover regime.[115] Hengtong Investment Ltd (Hengtong) was incorporated in Zuhai in 1981. Focusing on real estate development, Hengtong has also developed into areas of shipping, communications, textile and electronic products. To market its electricity meters in Shanghai, Hengtong planned to acquire a property development company in Shanghai. Search efforts revealed that Shanghai Lingguang Ltd (Lingguang), which produces glass and electronic components, is a suitable target. Lingguang issued 33.8 million shares in total. Among all the issued shares, Shanghai Construction Ltd held 55.26% of the shares on behalf of the State, while individual investors and legal person investors accounted for 32.55 and 11.89% of the shares respectively. Shortly before the transfer of control, the price of the shares of Lingguang was trading around 13 yuan per share on the secondary market. Hengtong's motivations of acquiring a controlling block of the shares of Lingguang were two folds: (i) mainly to rely on Shanghai Construction Ltd's connection with the property market in Shanghai, and (ii) partly to take advantage of Lingguang's technology. The deal was encouraging news to Lingguang and Shanghai Construction Ltd based on the information available then as Lingguang was short of funds to carry out ambitious development projects. An agreement was reached among Hengtong, Shanghai Construction Ltd and Lingguang to transfer 35.5% of the shares held by Shanghai Construction Ltd to Hengtong at the price of 4.3 yuan on April 28, 1994. Transferring more than 30% of the shares of a target, however, triggers the mandatory purchase provision. To avoid the high cost of mandatorily purchasing the rest shares of Lingguang, Hengtong applied to CSRC for an exemption from the mandatory purchase requirement. The CSRC granted its permission mainly on the ground that the transferred shares are the non-trading State-owned shares.

The Hengtong case raises a number of questions. Could the CSRC approve the transfer price of 4.3 yuan when the individual shares traded on the secondary market were around 13 yuan? Is the significant discount of control shareholding able to ensure that the productive resources of the target would move towards a more efficient purchaser? Another question is the legal ground that the CSRC gave the exemption from the mandatory purchase obligation when the ITS contains no legal provision, which confers the discretion to the CSRC. The lack of legal provision of course did not constrain the CSRC when the rule of law is not deeply entrenched in China. Finally, should China follow the United States approach by exempting transfer of control through agreement under the need of protection test[116] if it is well recognized that the cost of following the English mandatory purchase provision is too high?

Later development of the takeover law partially addressed the issues that arose from Hengtong. The Securities Law[117] modifies the mandatory purchase provision and deliberately gives the CSRC the discretion to exempt acquirers from following the mandatory purchase requirement if they acquire shares through any stock exchange.[118] The modified mandatory purchase provision now provides that if an investor holds 30% of the issued shares of a listed company and continues to buy such shares through a stock exchange, the investor shall make a takeover offer to all the shareholders of the target listed company.[119] The Securities Law seems to make a difference with respect to negotiated takeovers. Article 89 of the Securities Law stipulates:

> In the case of takeover by agreement, the acquirer may execute the equity transfer by entering into an agreement with shareholders of the target company as prescribed in laws and administrative regulations.
>
> When a listed company is taken over by agreement, the acquirer must, within three days after the agreement is reached, submit a written report on the takeover agreement to the State Council's securities regulatory authority and the stock exchange, and make an announcement.

The above article seems to be based on the need of protection test in United States securities regulation on the ground that selling shares by sophisticated investors does not need the protection of law.[120] It is relatively clear that the article does not expressly compel the acquirer to make an offer to all the shareholders in a negotiated takeover. Nor does the article require the acquirer to obtain approval from the CSRC for such a negotiated takeover except for the compliance of the reporting and announcement requirement. The article seems to recognize the high cost of the mandatory purchase provision and the need of a corporate control market to improve the inefficient State-owned listed companies. This article, however, has not been used in that way. The CSRC's position is that, whatever the method of acquiring control, the mandatory purchase provision must be complied with unless it granted the acquirer a waiver. This position is consistent with the practice of negotiated takeovers in China. By the end of 2000, all the 121 negotiated takeovers had followed the pattern of Hengtong in that a waiver is obtained from the CSRC.[121]

As discussed previously, most of China's State-owned enterprises on the stock market are not very efficient. A study has found that there is a negative correlation between firm performance and the percentage of State-owned shares.[122] Empirical evidence in another study also suggests that takeovers in China are largely efficient.[123]

The inefficiency of the State-owned listed companies and the need of an active takeover market to facilitate the reallocation of productive resources requires that China should modify the English style takeover law in the Chinese takeover environment. This objective has led the CSRC to reconsider its position on negotiated takeovers. In 2002, the CSRC issued the Procedures on the Administration of the Takeover of Listed Companies (Takeover Procedures).[124] While the Takeover Procedures reaffirm the position of the CSRC that, whatever the method of acquiring more than

30% of the shares in a target listed company, the mandatory purchase requirement must be complied with unless exemption from the CSRC is obtained.[125] The Takeover Procedures have provided numerous ground upon which the CSRC is prepared to grant a waiver.

Among the exceptions, some are related to debt restructuring and insolvency reorganization. For instance, a waiver will be given if the transfer of shares is applied for on the basis of a court ruling and results in the percentage of shares held or controlled by the purchaser exceeding 30% of the listed company's issued shares.[126] A waiver will also be provided if a bank engaging in the normal business has acquired more than 30% of the issued shares of a listed company but the bank has no intention or taken no action to actually control such a listed company and has made arrangements to transfer the excess shares to non-affiliated parties.[127] The waiver on insolvency is provided to an acquirer who takes over a listed company in financial distress in order to rescue it and has proposed a feasible restructuring plan.[128]

Other exceptions are based on the ground that no shareholder in a target listed company has received any takeover premium. For example, when an acquirer accumulated more than 30% of the shares of a listed company resulting from the company's issuing new shares.[129] Another exception is if the acquisition of more than 30% of the issued shares of a listed company is caused by the reduction of the capital of the company.[130]

In the past, the CSRC frequently gives waivers if the administrative transfer of State-owned shares has caused the transferee to hold or control more than 30% of the issued shares of a listed company. This exemption is still kept.[131] Finally, the Takeover Procedures have added a catch all provision, giving the CSRC the discretion to waive the mandatory purchase provision if the CSRC considers it necessary to meet the needs of the development and changes of the securities market and the need to protect the legitimate rights and interests of investors.[132] The transfer of control through administrative means as practiced in the past has made the mandatory purchase provision largely irrelevant. If the catch all provision is also liberally used, the mandatory purchase provision will also be made partly irrelevant.

3.3. Does One Size fit?

The discussion of the adjustment of the English style mandatory purchase provision clearly shows that application of the provision in China is path dependent. The political goal of maintaining control of the State-owned listed companies has completely changed the rationale of using such a provision.

The past socialist system of public ownership of the means of production created interested parties which controlled both the political and economic resources. These interested parties will try to protect their vested rights and interests. A very important way of continuing their control is to maintain the control of the large State-owned listed companies. The insistence of this political goal requires a different way of using the law of takeovers. I echo the view of Art and Gu that China's developing securities market can be properly understood only in the context of its underlying motivation, by carefully avoiding the mistake of assuming that adoption of western-style structures and laws implies movement toward western goals.[133]

If we take the ex ante efficiency view discussed previously, the adjustment of the imported takeover law is very positive in the sense of achieving the primary goal of improving the large number of inefficiently run State-owned listed companies. Another positive use of the English style takeover law is the adoption of the position of non-frustration on the part of the directors in a target listed company when facing a takeover offer.[134] Article 33 of the Takeover Procedures provides that the decisions made and measures taken by the directors, supervisors and senior management of the target company with respect to the takeover offer made by an acquirer may not prejudice the legitimate rights and interests of the company or its shareholders. More specifically, the said article prohibits the adoption of measures of issuing new shares or convertible bonds, the repurchase of its own shares, the amendment of articles of association, and the signing of contracts, which could have a major effect on the company's assets, liabilities, rights, interests or business outcome except in the ordinary course of business, after an acquirer has announced its takeover intention.

In the United States, whether the board of directors of the shareholders should be given the ultimate power to decide whether the corporation should be sold to a bidder that offers to buy all the corporation's shares at a substantial premium above the current stock market price is very controversial. Easterbrook and Fischel argue that the management should remain completely passive in the face of a takeover bid.[135] Their argument is based on the assumption that most takeovers are efficient in that they discipline non-performing managers in the target. When non-performing managers are facing a takeover bid which tends to remove them, it is unlikely that their action of defeating the takeover will be for the best interest of the corporation.[136] Bebchuk argues that once mechanisms to ensure undistorted shareholder choice are in place, boards should not be permitted to block offers beyond the period necessary for putting together alternatives for shareholder consideration.[137] In contrast, Lipton argues against a regime of shareholders voting and no board veto.[138] According to Lipton, there are significant costs to corporations in being managed as if they were constantly for sale.[139]

The Delaware General Corporation Law (DGCL) takes a middle ground. The DGCL gives the board of directors a central role in corporate decision-making,[140] but it also requires stockholder assent for many fundamental transactions.[141] The DGCL is, however, silent on the most contentious question in the debate: in what circumstances, and to what extent, are directors empowered to prevent shareholders from accepting a tender offer? The Delaware judicial view is similar. While in principle Delaware case law holds that the purpose of the corporation is to maximize the wealth of its stockholders,[142] Delaware decisions also give directors substantial authority to deploy the powerful weapon of a poison pill[143] and to block takeover offers that appear to be in the best interests of the current array of stockholders.[144] The Delaware courts, however, have subjected defensive measures to a heightened form of judicial review under which directors must prove the reasonableness and good faith of their actions.[145] The result is a regime in which directors are given substantial authority to forge corporate strategies while leaving room for stockholders to vote down management preferred directors and to use the election process to avail themselves of a tender offer.[146]

The accidental adoption of the English style mandatory purchase provision at the beginning of 1990s has educated regulators in China relatively well on other parts of the London City Code. When the CSRC issued the Takeover Procedures in 2002, it again chose the English position of non-frustration over the Delaware type of takeover law on the proper role of the target board when the target is facing a takeover offer. The choice is largely satisfactory in the context of China. There are at least two reasons. Delaware law is very complicated. At this stage, regulators and judges in China are still not sophisticated in takeover law. To expect them to administer the Delaware type of takeover law when even the judges in other parts of the United States are not able to do well is likely to be counterproductive. Second, directors in the United States are subject to greater constraints by very strict fiduciary duties, derivative suits and various market mechanisms which are not available in China.[147]

While the adoption of the English style takeover law and the adjustment of the law in China are in the right direction, negotiated takeover transactions in China have a serious defect. As discussed previously, only shares held by individuals in listed companies are traded on the two stock exchanges. State shares and legal person shares of State-owned enterprises are not traded on the stock exchanges. This raises the issue of pricing the control block of State-owned shares. In the Hengtong case, the control block was priced at 4.3 yuan per share when the shares traded at the stock exchange were around 13 yuan per share.[148] The Opinions Concerning the Exercise of State-owned Shares in Joint Stock Companies[149] dictate that the lowest transfer price of State-owned shares is the net asset value per share.[150] In Hengtong and all the other cases before 2004 when the control block of State-owned shares was transferred, the price of the shares of the block was several times lower than the price of the shares traded on the stock market. In a few cases, even the requirement of the lowest transfer price of net asset value per share is not followed.[151] The practice of nego-tiated takeovers in China also indicates why the mandatory purchase pro-vision, which is central to the London City Code, is not followed in China. The mandatory purchase provision is based on the premise that the acquirer has to extend the same premium to all other shareholders in the target if it buys shares at a price higher than the market price from the majority, block or some shareholders, who are more likely to get the benefits because of their position. This ensures the equality of treatment of all shareholders in the target. In China, when the control block is priced at a much lower price than the market price of other shares traded on the stock market, the man-datory purchase provision lost its rationale. Obviously, the CSRC and the Government are more interested in the facilitation of the reallocation of the productive resources of State-owned listed companies. The interest of the minority shareholders is to a large extent ignored. This again leads to the conclusion that the political goal of maintaining the control of State-owned listed companies has made the imported law considerably irrelevant. While not following the mandatory purchase provision can be justified on effi-ciency ground, cheap transfer of control block in China left minority share-holders with no adequate protection.

In the United States and United Kingdom, the concern of takeover law is to ensure the minority shareholders a premium over the market price if the acquisition of control is at a premium. Because of the benefits of control, the price of control block is normally higher than the price of the shares of a target on the secondary market. The higher price of control block is a basic market mechanism to protect the minority shareholders in that only those who are able to manage the target better dare to obtain the control given the constraints. There might be mistakes in prediction or judgment on the part of the acquirer and the effect of takeover may be disastrous. The market in the long run will correct the mistake. The cheap transfer of control in China, however, is not able to ensure that acquirers are necessarily better than the existing management in targets. Furthermore, the discount of share price of the control block creates serious risks of exploitation of minority share-holders. Recently, the State Asset Administration Bureau and the Ministry of Finance jointly issued the Provisional Measures on the Administration of the Transfer of State-owned Shares in January 2004 (Provisional Measures).[152] The Provisional Measures now permit but do not compel the use of auctions or biddings in takeovers in addition to negotiated takeovers. Similar to other administrative rules, this Provisional Measures are more interested in ensuring that the State-owned assets are not depleted in low price transfer of control to private enterprises.

While auctions and biddings in takeovers will alleviate the problem of cheap transfer of control in listed companies in China, the move towards an efficient takeover market requires a radical reform of large-scale exit of State-owned enterprises in many sectors of the economy. Only when the governments are serious in thinking exit from most listed companies will the regulators pay more attention to the protection of rights and interests of the minority shareholders in listed companies in China. The interest of the minority shareholders can be better advanced if the Government is serious on this issue. State-owned enterprises are unlikely to be efficient. As Trebilcock has persuasively argued that there are not adequate means to motivate the agents in State-owned enterprises and there are not adequate means to discipline such agents in State-owned companies compared with the means available to private firms.[153] To realize the goal of achieving efficiency through corporate law in general and takeover law in particular, the Chinese Government must abandon the concept of controlling the State-owned listed companies for the purpose of political control. Only then can the law of takeover fully realize its efficiency goal.

The discussion in Part (2) shows that the use of the transplanted English style takeover law has been significantly affected by China's social and political factors. The adaptation of that law in China is not only path dependent but also very local in nature and with legislative and administrative innovations. This again raises serious doubt whether a single corporate governance model fits all countries.

4. CONCLUSION

Corporate governance has attracted enormous attention both in the area of law and in the area of financial economics. In comparative corporate governance studies, many people have devoted their energy to find a best corporate governance model. I argue that a functional analysis does not support the view that there is a single best corporate governance model in the world. I further use the transplantation of an English style takeover law into China to show that the importation of a foreign law is not always based on careful analysis that the imported foreign law is the best in the world. Furthermore, I discuss the subsequent adjustment of the transplanted English takeover law in China to show that the transplantation of foreign law is subject to local political and economic conditions. If there is no best corporate governance model and the transplantation of foreign law into other countries with different social and political background does not achieve similar objectives, the search for a best corporate governance model is misguided. Just as tort law or constitutional law regimes may have diversified models, so do corporate governance regimes in countries with different historical, social and political backgrounds.

NOTES

1. See Adolf Berle and Gardiner Means, Jr., The Modern Corporation and Private Property (1932). George Stigler and Claire Friedland, "The Literature of Economics: The Case of Berle and Means" 26 *Journal of Law and Economics* 237 (1983); Harold Demsetz and Kenneth Lehn, "The Structure of Corporate Ownership: Causes and Consequences" 93 *Journal of Political Economy* 1155 (1985).

2. Mark Roe, "A Political Theory of American Corporate Finance," 91 *Columbia Law Review* 10 (1991); Mark Roe, "Some Differences in Corporate Structure in Germany, Japan, and the United States" 102 *Yale Law Journal* 1927 (1993).

3. Michael Jensen and William Meckling, "Theory of the Firm: Managerial Behavior, Agency Costs and Ownership Structure," 3 *Journal of Financial Economics* 305 (1976).

4. Frank Modigliani and Merton Millars, "The Costs of Capital, Corporate Finance, and the Theory of Investment," *American Economic Review* 48 (June 1958) (arguing that in the absence of bankruptcy costs and tax subsidies on the payment of interest the value of the firm is independent of the financial structure); but see Jensen and Meckling, supra note 3, at 33 (arguing that, if agency costs are taken into consideration, the value of the firms is not independent of the capital or ownership).

5. Rafael La Porta et al., Legal Determinants of External Finance, 52 *Journal of Finance* 1131, 1137 (1997).

6. Jeffrey Gordon, "Corporate Governance: Pathways to Corporate Convergence? Two Steps on the Road to Shareholder Capitalism in Germany," 5 *Columbia Journal of European Law* 219, 223 (1999).

7. See Roberta Karmel, "Italian Stock Market Reform," *New York Law Journal* Aug. 20, 1998, at 3.

8. Eugene Fama and Michael Jensen, "Agency Problems and Residual Claims," 26 *Journal of Law and Economics* 327 (1983).

9. Kenneth Arrow, "The Role of Securities in the Optimal Allocation of Risk Bearing," 31 *Review of Economic Studies* 97 (1964).

10. Ronald Coase, "The Nature of the Firm," 4 *Economica* 386 (1937).

11. See Fama and Jensen, supra note 8.

12. Harold Demstz and Kenneth Lehn, supra note 1, at 1158.

13. Berle and Means, supra note 1.

14. See Gordon, supra note 6, at 220.

15. The top six firms accounted for almost 50% of the volume in public markets. Ibid.

16. See Stefan Prigge, "A Survey of German Corporate Governance" in Klans Hope et al., *Comparative Corporate Governance – The State of the Art and Emerging Research* 943, 998–990 (1998).

17. D. Neuberger and M. Neumann, "Banking and Antitrust: Limiting Industrial Ownership by Banks? *Journal of Institutional and Theoretical Economics* 147, 188–199 (1991) (reporting an average of 40% as compared to about 9% in the UK).

18. For more information, see Theodor Baums, "Corporate Governance in Germany: The Role of the Banks," 40 *American Journal of Comparative Law* 503, 508 (1992).

19. *Ibid.* at 510.

20. *Ibid.* at 512.

21. *Ibid.* at 515–516.

22. See Michael Porter, "Capital Disadvantage: America's Failing Capital Investment System," *Harvard Business Review* 65 (Sept.- Oct., 1992).

23. Joseph Grundfest, "Subordination of American Capital," 27 *Journal of Financial Economics* 89 (1990).

24. See Roe, supra note 2; John Pound, "The Rise of the Political Model of Corporate Governance and Corporate Control," 68 *New York University Law Review* 103 (1993); also see Grundfest, supra note 23.

25. Jonathan Macey and Geoffrey Miller, "Corporate Governance and Commercial Banking: A Comparative Examination of Germany, Japan, and the United States," 48 *Stanford Law Review* 73, 77–81 (1995).

26. See Roe, supra note 2, at 1937 (1993).

27. Stigler and Friedland, supra note 1.

28. Harold Demsetz, "The Structure of the Ownership and the Theory of the Firm," 26 *Journal of Law and Economics* 375 (1983).

29. *Ibid.* at 386.

30. Roberta Romano, "Public Pension Fund Activities in Corporate Governance Reconsidered," 93 *Columbia Law Review* 795 (1993).

31. John Coffee, Jr., "Liquidity Verses Control: The Institutional Investor as Corporate Monitor," 91 *Columbia Law Review* 1977 (1991).

32. Jonathan Macey, "Measuring the Effectiveness of Different Corporate Governance Systems: Toward A More Scientific Approach," 10 *Journal of Applied Corporate Finance* 16, 24 (1998).

33. Ronald Gilson & Reiner Kraakman, "Reinvesting the Outside Director: An Agenda for Institutional Investors," 43 *Stanford Law Review* 863, 880 (1991).

34. Robert Vanecko, "Regulations14A and 13D and the Role of Institutional Investors in Corporate Governance," 87 *Northwestern University Law Review* 376, 406–408 (1992).

35. Thomas Smith, "Institutions and Entrepreneurs in American Corporate Finance," 85 *California Law Review* 1, 18–27 (1997).

36. *Ibid.* at 35–44.

37. Roberta Romano, "Less is More: Making Institutional Investor Activism a Valuable Mechanism of Corporate Governance," 18 *Yale Journal on Regulation* 174 (2001).

38. *Ibid.* at 201.

39. *Ibid.* at 195.

40. See Rafael La Porta et al., supra note 5; See also Asli Demirguc – Kunt & Vosislav Maksimovic, Law, Finance and Firms, 53 *Journal of Finance* 2107, 2134 (1988) (arguing that firms in countries with active stock market and well-developed legal system were able to obtain greater funds to finance growth).

41. See La Porta et al., supra note 5; see also Andrei Schleifer & Robert Vishny, A Survey of Corporate Governance, 52 *Journal of Finance* 737 (1997).

42. John Coffee, Jr., "The Future as History: the Prospects for Global Convergence in Corporate Governance and Its Implications," 93 *Northwestern University Law Review* 641, 644 (1999).

43. *Ibid.*

44. See Demsetz, supra note 28, at 390.

45. See La Porta et al., supra note 5, at 1132.

46. See Luigi Zingales, "The Value of the Voting Right: A Study of the Milan Stock Exchange Experience," 7 *Review of Financial Studies* 125 (1994) (finding a high 82% premium for control blocks on the Milan Stock Exchange, against an international average of 10 to 20%, and a United States average of 5.24%).

47. Steven Kaplan, "Top Executives, Turnover, and Firm Performance in Germany," 10 *Journal of Law, Economics, and Organization* 142–59 (1994); Steven Kaplan, "Top Executive Rewards and Firm Performance: A Comparison of Japan and the United States," 102 *Journal of Political Economy* 510–546 (1994).

48. Gordon, supra note 6, at 236.

49. Douglas Smith, "The Venture Capital Company: A Contractual Rebuttal to the Political Theory of American Corporate Finance?" 65 *Tennessee Law Review* 79 (1979).

50. See Demsetz, supra note 28, at 386.

51. See Shleifer and Vishny, supra note 41, at 776.

52. Masahiko Aoki, "Towards an Economic Model of the Japanese Firm," 28 *Journal of Economic Literature* 1 (1990); Joseph Grundfest, supra, note 23; Jonathan Charkham, Keeping Good Company: a Study of Corporate Governance in Five Countries (1994); Michael Porter, "Capital Disadvantage: America's Failing Capital Investment System," *Harvard Law Review* 65 (1992).

53. Macey and Miller, supra note 25; Curtis Milhaupt, "The Market for Innovation in the United States and Japan: Venture Capital and the Comparative corporate governance Debate," 91 *Northwestern University Law Review* 865 (1997); Rafael La Porta et al, supra note 5 (arguing that countries with poorer investor protections have smaller and narrower capital markets); Asli Demirguc–Kunt & Vosislav Maksimovic, "Law, Finance and Firm Growth," 53 *Journal of Finance* 2107, 2134 (1998) (finding that firms in countries with active stock market and well-developed legal system were able to obtain greater funds to finance growth).

54. Roberta Romano, "A Cautionary Note on Drawing Lessons from Comparative Corporate Law," 102 *Yale Law Journal* 2021, 2025 (1993).

55. See Romano, supra note 37, at 176.

56. Robert Art and Minkang Gu, "China Incorporated: the First Corporation Law of the People's Republic of China", 20 *Yale Journal of International Law* 273, 274–275 (1995).

57. Project Group of the Chinese Academy of Social Sciences, "Several Problems Related to the Establishment of a Modern Enterprise System", 17(4) Social Sciences in China 19, 20 (1996). One US dollar equals to roughly 8.2 Chinese yuan.

58. *Ibid.*

59. *Ibid.*

60. *Ibid.*

61. *Ibid.*

62. *Ibid.*

63. Zhou Zhengqing, "Explanations Concerning the Commercial Banking Law of the PRC', a speech delivered at the Thirteenth Session of the Eighth Standing Committee of the National People's Congress; interview with Mr Cai, a middle level manager with the Bank of China in Hangzhou on May 25, 1993.

64. See generally Janos Kornai, Economics of Shortage (1980) for a discussion about soft budget constraints; for a discussion on the difficulty of enforcing the Bankruptcy Law in China in the 1990s, see Guanghua Yu, "The Relevance of Comparative Corporate governance Studies for China", 8(1) *Australian Journal of Corporate Law* 49, 79–80 (1997).

65. See Xu Jingan, "The State-share System: A New Avenue for China's Economic Reform", 11 *Journal of Comparative Economics* 509, 514 (1987).

66. *Ibid.*

67. *Ibid.*

68. Andrew Xuefeng Qian, "Riding Two Horses: Corporatizing Enterprises and the Emerging Securities Regulatory Regime in China", 12 *University of California at Los Angeles Pacific Basin Law Journal* 62, 63 (1993).

69. The Standardization Opinions appeared in the Collection of the Laws of the PRC 650 (1992).

70. The Supplementary Measures were issued by the Commission on May 24, 1993 and available online at ⟨http://www.chinginfobank⟩.

71. This mandatory model Articles of Association was issued by the State Economic Restructuring Committee on June 30, 1993 and appears at ⟨http://www.chinainfobank⟩.

72. Articles of Association, Art. 4.4.

73. Articles of Association, Art. 4.8.

74. The Prerequisite Clauses were issued by the Securities Office of the State Council and the State Economic Restructuring Commission on September 19, 1994. An English translation appears at *China Law & Practice* 19 (May 1995).

75. An English translation of this Regulation appears at *China Law & Practice* 23 (August 1993).

76. The Code is available online at ⟨http://www.hksfc.org.hk⟩.

77. London City Code on Takeovers and Mergers (7th ed 2002), available online at ⟨http://www.thetakeoverpanel.org.uk⟩.

78. For more information on Chaos, see James Gleick, Chaos: Making a New Science 8 (1988); for an application of chaos theory to corporate law, see Mark Roe, Commentary: "Chaos and Evolution in Law and Economics", 109 *Harvard Law Review* 641 (1996) (arguing that chaos theory, path dependence, and modern evolutionary theory together provide a richer understanding of how legal and economic institutions arose and survived).

79. See Li Guilian, "Participation of Foreigners in Legislative Activities in the Late Qing Dynasty", 1(1) *Journal of Chinese and Comparative Law* 145 (1995).

80. Zhang Jinpan, *The Tradition of Chinese Law and Its Modern Transition* (Beijing: Law Press, 1997) at 450.

81. ITS, supra note 75.

82. London City Code, Art. 9.1.

83. ITS, Art. 48.

84. *Ibid.* The current price provision in the Procedures on the Administration of the Takeover of Listed Companies issued by the China Securities Regulatory Commission on September 28, 2002 follows the higher of the following two: (i) the highest price the acquirer paid during the six months prior to the date of public announcement; and (ii) 90% of the arithmetic mean of the daily weighted average prices of the target company's listed shares of that class during the 30 days prior to the date of public announcement. Infra note 77.

85. ITS, Art. 50.

86. ITS, Art. 51(3).

87. ITS, Art. 52(1).

88. ITS, Art. 52(2).

89. ITS, Art. 47(1).

90. ITS, Art. 47(2). The current position is 5% under the Securities Act of 1998 instead of 2%.

91. ITS, Art. 47(3).

92. ITS, Art. 49(2).

93. *Ibid.*

94. ITS, Art. 52(3).

95. London City Code, supra note 77, Section 1(a)

96. For empirical evidence that takeovers are more likely to produce social gains, see Gregg Jarrell et al., "The Market for Corporate Control: The Empirical Evidence Since 1982", 2 *Journal of Economic Perspectives* 49 (1988); Michael Jensen & Richard Ruback, "The Market for Corporate Control: The Scientific Evidence", 11 *Journal of Financial Economics* 5 (1983).

97. Robert Nozick, *"Coercion"* in Philosophy, Science, and Method (Sindey Morgenbesser et al. eds, 1969).

98. Louis Lowenstein, "Pruning Deadwood in Hostile Takeovers: A Proposal for Legislation", 83 *Columbia Law Review* 249 (1983); Michael Bradley and Michael Rosenzweig, "Defensive Stock Repurchases", 99 *Harvard Law Review* 1377 (1986).

99. John Coffee, "The Uncertain Case For Takeover Reform: An Essay on Stockholders, Stateholders and Bust-ups", *Wisconsin Law Review* 435, 459 (1988).

100. For a discussion of the nature of public goods, see Paul Samuelson, "The Pure Theory of Public Expenditure", 36 *Review of Economic Statistics* 386 (1954).

101. Sanford Grossman and Oliver Hart, "Takeover Bids, the Free-Rider Problem, and the Theory of the Corporation", Vol. 11, No. 1, *Bell Journal of Economics* 42, 59 (1980).

102. For a similar discussion of the problem of freerider and externality in the context of freezeout, see Frank Easterbrook and Daniel Fischel, "Corporate Control Transactions", 91 *Yale Law Journal* 698, 705–706 (1982).

103. Zhang Zongxin and Sun Yewei, "The Optimization of Shareholding Structure and the Improvement of Corporate Governance in Listed Companies", *Economic Review* No. 1, 36 (2001).

104. *Ibid.*

105. *Ibid.*

106. Absolute control means that the State controls more than 50% of the issued shares and relative control means that the State controls more than 30% of the issued shares.

107. Zhang and Sun, supra note 103.

108. *Ibid.*

109. *Ibid.*

110. *Ibid.*

111. Zhang Rui, "An Legal Analysis of Negotiated Takeovers of Listed Companies", Jilin University Journal (Social Sciences) 108, 109 (July 2003).

112. These administrative rules were jointly issued by the State Asset Administration Bureau and the State Economic Restructuring Commission on November 13, 1994. The document can be found in the legal database available online at ⟨ http:// www.chinainfobank⟩.

113. *Ibid.*

114. Zhang Xin, "Legislation and Regulation of Takeovers of Listed Companies", Securities Market Herald 12 (August 2003).

115. Chen Gong et al., eds, Principles and Cases of Corporate Mergers and Takeovers 63 - 68 (Beijing: Renmin University Press, 1996).

116. Hanson Trust v SCM, 774 F. 2d 27 (2d Cir. 1985).

117. This Law was promulgated on December 29, 1998 and became effective on July 1, 1999. An English translation appears at *China Law & Practice* 25 (February 1994).

118. Securities Law, Art. 81.

119. *Ibid.*

120. Kennecott Copper Corp. v Curtiss-Wright Corp., 584 F. 2d 1195 (2d Cir. 1978); Hanson Trust v SCM, 774 F. 2d 27 (2d Cir. 1985).

121. Li Bingan, "A Discussion of the Exemption from the Mandatory Purchase Provision", 18(6) *Legal Forum* 50 (November 2003).

122. He Xiaogang, "Management Buyouts: the Status Abroad, Research, and Development in China", 4 *Reform* 54 (2003).

123. Fei Yiwen and Cai Mingchao, "An Analysis of the Takeover Effects of Listed Companies on the Shanghai Stock Exchange", 5 *World Economics* 64 (2003).

124. An English translation of the Takeover Procedures can be found in *China Law & Practice* 43 (November 2002).

125. Takeover Procedures, Arts., 13, 14 and 23.

126. Takeover Procedures, Art. 49(4).

127. Takeover Procedures, Art. 51(4).

128. Takeover Procedures, Art. 49(2).

129. Takeover Procedures, Art. 49(3).

130. Takeover Procedures, Art. 51(2).

131. Takeover Procedures, Art. 51(5).

132. Takeover Procedures, Art. 49(5) and Art. 51(7).

133. Art and Gu, supra note 56 at 139.

134. General Principle 7 of the London City Code. Supra note 77.

135. See Frank Easterbrook and Daniel Fischel, "The Proper Role of a Target's Management in Responding to a Tender Offer", 94 *Harvard Law Review* 1161 (1981).

136. For a similar view, see Alan Schwartz, "The Fairness of Tender Offer Prices in Utilitarian Theory", 17 *Journal of Legal Studies* 165 (1988).

137. Lucian Bebchuk, "The Case Against Board Veto in Corporate Takeovers", 69 *University of Chicago Law Review* 973 (2002).

138. Martin Lipton, "Pills, Polls, and Professors Redux", 69 *University of Chicago Law Review* 1037.

139. *Ibid.* at 1078.

140. See, for example, 8 Del. Code Ann. § 141 (2001).

141. See, for example, 8 Del. Code Ann. § 251 (2001) (mergers), § 271 (2001) (sale of substantially all the assets of the firm).

142. See, for example, Cede & Co v Technicolor, Inc, 634 A2d 345, 360 (Del. 1993).

143. See, for example, Unifrim, Inc v American General Corp., 651 A 2d 1361, 1390 (Del. 1995).

144. Paramount Communications, Inc v Time Inc., 571 A 2d 1140, 1150.

145. Moran v Household International, Inc, 500 A 2d 1346, 1356 (Del. 1985).

146. For a discussion of the theoretical debate on takeovers in the U.S. and the current status of the Delaware law on takeovers, see William Allen et al., "The Great Takeover Debate: A Mediation on Bridging the Conceptual Divide", 69 *University of Chicago Law Review* 1067 (2002).

147. For a regulator's view, see Zhang Xin, supra note 114, at 15–17.

148. Hengtong, supra note 68.

149. The Opinions were jointly issued by the State Asset Administration Bureau and the State Economic Restructuring Commission on 29 August 1997 and available online at ⟨ http://www.chinainfobank ⟩.

150. *Ibid.*, Art. 17.

151. Wang Huacheng and Tong Yan, "Management Buyouts in China: The Case of Media", 10 Economic Theory and Management 66 (2002); An Chunmei and Dou Zhanguo, "An Analysis of Benefits and Risks of Management Buyouts in Listed Companies", 7 *Finance and Accounting Research* 52 (2002).

152. This Provisional Measures are available online at ⟨ http://www.chinainfobank ⟩.

153. Michael Trebilcock and Edward Iacobucci, Commentary: "Public Values in an Era of Privatization: Privatization and Accountability", 116 *Harvard Law Review* 1422 (2003).

SED QUIS CUSTODIET IPSOS CUSTODES?: GOVERNMENTALITY, CORPORATE GOVERNANCE AND ETHICS

Rebecca Boden

ABSTRACT

This paper seeks to challenge a tacit, but nevertheless prevalent, notion that a robust corporate governance framework will, as a matter of course, engender good corporate social responsibility and, thereby, 'ethical' decision-making. It does so by drawing, in the first instance, on an example of apparent good corporate social responsibility and exposing the possibly unethical dimensions of the incident. The paper suggests that corporate governance always has a subjective ethical dimension and that such regimes are best understood as 'regimes of practice' – actions, actors and discourses – that shape and mould both thinking and action. Such regimes, it is posited, can best be explored by looking at actual instances or events of significance and analysing these. The paper then offers the example of international pharmaceutical companies' HIV/AIDS drugs pricing policies, especially in South Africa, as such a critical incident and interrogates it using the 'analytics' approach outlined by Dean (1999). The principal aims of the paper are to demonstrate that corporate social responsibility and corporate governance regimes are not neutral processes

Corporate Governance: Does Any Size Fit?
Advances in Public Interest Accounting, Volume 11, 71–94
Copyright © 2005 by Elsevier Ltd.
ISSN: 1041-7060/doi:10.1016/S1041-7060(05)11004-9

but aspects of 'governmentality' and to offer a technique, analytics, by which such processes can be explicated.

1. INTRODUCTION

In March 2004 *The Guardian* (a major UK daily newspaper) carried a feature from an undercover reporter (27 March, 2004). Passing herself off as a migrant Chinese labourer, with clearly faked papers and permits, called 'Chen Min', the reporter sought and obtained work at a food processing plant in Norfolk in the UK (*The Guardian*, 27 March 2004). The gangmaster[1] who facilitated her employment had formerly been involved in the cockle picking business in Morecambe where, in February 2004, at least 21 'illegal' Chinese cockle pickers were drowned whilst working at night on a treacherous beach. The gangmaster introduced Chen Min to Pertemps, a well-known major employment agency. Allegedly often in return for bribes, Pertemps allocated work to labourers at a nearby processing plant owned by Grampian Country Foods, a major supplier to UK supermarkets. Chen Min's work at Grampian included processing and packing meat for Sainsbury's, one of Britain's largest supermarket chains and a firm long-associated with philanthropy.

Her story documented, in distressing detail, the abuse, privations, exploitation and corruption of the sizeable labour market for casualised migrant labourers in Britain, many of whom are deemed 'illegal'. Chen Min was part of a labour supply chain that included three well-known UK firms. Sainsbury's (the largest of the firms) official response to *The Guardian's* story was:

> Whilst we do not employ these workers directly we take this issue extremely seriously. We have worked very closely with all of our suppliers, including Grampian, to ensure that they are aware of the potential issues surrounding temporary labour.
>
> Sainsbury's is a responsible employer and would terminate contracts with any supplier proved to have seriously breached employment law.
>
> (*The Guardian*, 27 March, 2004)

Supermarkets in the UK are currently involved in a battle to the death to cut prices to win customers. In the same week as *The Guardian* story, Sainsbury's had announced very disappointing quarterly results indicating a diminishing customer base and the price of its shares slid by 6% in 1 day in response.

Such stories go to the very heart of issues of corporate social responsibility, ethics and governance. Sainsbury's had a long history as a family firm with a clear philanthropic tradition. Additionally, given the state of competition for the customer base between supermarkets, it can ill-afford to lose customers because of a poor reputation for the treatment of workers in its supply chain. At the same time, the primary emphasis in the supermarket war is on product price and everyone's margins are being squeezed. Sainsbury's can therefore also ill-afford to increase its costs by insisting on better employment standards amongst suppliers.

Caught in this dilemma, Sainsbury's response to *The Guardian* report was predictably equivocal. It stressed that, in law (as is true) the company did not actually employ Chen Min or her fellow workers. That said, it affirmed its own commitments and values and explained that it also educated its suppliers on these issues. The company also averred that, should it be 'proved' that any supplier has seriously broken the law, it would terminate the contract.

What the Sainsbury's statement did not say was that it *required* suppliers to adhere to employment law or to avoid the 'potential issues surrounding temporary labour'. Nor did the company give any explanation of what constituted 'proof' of employment law breaches or any indication as to how and by whom the newspaper's report might be tested.

Thus, Sainsbury's distanced itself from the apparent perpetrators of the ill-treatment of the workers (Grampian, the agency that hired them and the gangmaster) whilst not acknowledging that it also indirectly benefited. It made strong statements about what it would do if presented with proof, but explained no processes by which such situations might be audited or investigated. The statement does not indicate that any procedures are in place for ensuring or requiring the proper treatment of workers, or that such systems have failed.

Assuming that Chen Min's report is true and accurate, we can ask the question 'is there evidence of a corporate governance failure on the part of Sainsbury's here?' On the one hand, Sainsbury's has satisfactorily acquitted itself in corporate governance terms in that it has sought to demonstrate, and arguably has demonstrated, that it deals competently with these issues and that its systems are robust and intact. There has been no systems failure *if* corporate governance systems are seen entirely self-referentially. Alternately, Sainsbury's might be seen as experiencing a major corporate governance failure with severe ethical consequences in that it has benefited from the exploitation of vulnerable workers.

The purpose of this paper is to begin pulling at the thread that that this story presents us with in order to unravel the meaning of 'corporate governance' and the manner in which it is connected to ethics and morality. My purpose is not to suggest tougher standards, more processes and such like. Rather, it is to interrogate the concept of corporate governance as it relates to ethical, socially responsible behaviour.

In Section 2, which follows this, I demonstrate how corporate governance regimes must always incorporate some ethical dimension. In Section 3, I explore the genealogy of corporate governance as a 'regime of practice'. In particular, I discuss how such regimes can be seen as aspects of contemporary 'governmentality' – that is, how we think about what Foucault called the 'conduct of conduct'. Section 4 presents a discussion of the possible advantages of empirically exploring critical episodes in acts of government as a means of understanding *how* governmentality and regimes of practice work. The paper then offers, in Section 5, such a critical episode – the attempts by South Africa to import cheap generic anti-retroviral drugs to combat HIV/AIDS, as a means of exploring the utility of this approach. In the concluding section this critical episode is analysed to expose the corporate governance regime of practice at work in this critical episode. The aim in sum is not to identify 'solutions' to such failures, but to better understand how such systems work and therefore why they have the consequences that they do.

2. CORPORATE GOVERNANCE AND ITS ETHICAL DIMENSIONS

Few terms can have become so ubiquitous in the UK in recent years than that of 'corporate governance'. And 'governance' is now a watchword of virtually every non-corporate organisation as well, be they hospitals, governments, schools or universities. 'Good' governance is now deemed the key to ensuring ethical conduct and socially responsible behaviour.

Definitions of corporate governance are heterogeneous. For instance:

The public sector health service. Governance is defined by the Audit Commission, in its paper *Corporate Governance in Health Organisations – April 2002* as 'The systems and processes by which local authorities and health organisations lead, direct and control their functions to achieve organisational objectives; develop the capacity for improvement; and relate to their partners and the wider community' (Gloucestershire NHS Trust, 2004).

The private sector company. ITC[Ltd] defines Corporate Governance as a systemic process by which companies are directed and controlled to enhance their wealth generating capacity. Since large corporations employ vast quantum of societal resources, we believe that the governance process should ensure that these companies are managed in a manner that meets stakeholders aspirations and societal expectations (ITC, 2004).

The OECD. Western experience has taught corporations the need for transparency and these experiences have slowly shaped the internal framework of corporations into internal policy guidelines that are being increasingly developed by companies in OECD countries – guidelines that are commonly referred to as corporate governance.

Although there is not one form of corporate governance, there are internationally accepted principles that underlie sound business structures, including those developed by the OECD. These principles put forth the concept that within each company corporate leaders should be not only accountable for the economic but also for the ethical behaviour of the enterprise (OECD, 2004).

In general then, governance is a term used to refer to the systems by which organisations govern themselves or are governed – how the conduct of an organisation is conducted. Some ethical dimension is implicit in all understandings of corporate governance. Even Milton Friedman, in defining corporate governance as the conduct of business in accordance with owner or shareholders' desires (usually to show the highest financial returns possible), required that organisations at the same time conform to the basic rules of society as embodied in law and local customs. Such a convergence between governance and ethics is inescapable – plainly, the conduct of conduct will always involve explicit or implicit decisions between right and wrong acts or good or bad behaviour.

Questions of ethical behaviour generally relate to how one regulates oneself. With regard to *corporate* governance, such regimes are supposed to ensure the correct comportment of the organisation. That is, corporate governance regimes are avowedly meant to sculpt, mould and shape corporate behaviour in certain ways that will be deemed and accepted as what is usually termed 'ethical'. Of course, what constitutes ethical behaviour is ultimately subjective.

It is but a short elision from understanding that corporate governance regimes embody ethical and moral choices to assuming that they will provide the solution to everything that we might see as unethical corporate behaviours. The reasoning seems to be that if only we can get the right systems of corporate governance, and get organisations to comply with them, then the world will inevitably be a better and more ethical place. Similarly, it may be convenient for corporations to let people believe that ethical issues are satisfactorily dealt with by virtue of the simple fact that they have a corporate governance system, policies and procedures.

Given the inherent subjectivity of ethical questions, the dangers in such thinking are immediately apparent. The development of corporate governance regimes may involve no or very little overt and explicit consideration of what is or is not ethical. This suggests at least two variations of corporate governance 'failure': either the system fails to operate as intended or some event occurs that illustrates some very serious ethical issue. In the case of Sainsbury's above, the supermarket chose to stress that its systems were in good working order at the expense of addressing the substantive ethical issue raised.

In order to gain a deeper understanding of the role of corporate governance in ethical and moral matters then, it is necessary to problematise this simplistic notion that 'good' corporate governance flows inevitably from 'good' corporate governance systems. In the next section I trace the genealogy of corporate governance in order to gain a deeper understanding of its significance and role in how we are governed and govern ourselves.

3. THE GENEALOGY OF CORPORATE GOVERNANCE

Although corporate governance is a neologism, the appropriate regulation of corporate activity is not a new preoccupation: indeed, it has been a central concern of liberalism and its derivatives for some time. The early modern era of eighteenth and early nineteenth century Europe saw the shift from agricultural capitalism and absolutist rule to the start of the development of the modern 'state'. These early states relied heavily on notions of 'policing' (Dean, 1999). Policed states sought to replace the absolutist rule of kings, where temporal authority was derived from spiritual authority, with systems of knowledge and surveillance. Attempts were made to 'know' every aspect of every citizen's life in order that they could be better controlled and directed. Such control, the argument ran, could enable states with newly emerging economies to shape the whole towards their aims of achieving wealth greater than that of their competitors.

Police states in turn provoked the development of ideologies of liberalism. The developing liberal critique of the police state was that the state was inherently incapable of being all-knowing and that the economic reality of market exchanges was such that the 'unseen hand' had to be allowed to guide economic activity. Indeed, the argument of classical liberalism continued, the state would, by its interventions, actually cause fatal failure in the realm of the economy that it sought to control (Burchell, 1996). The liberals argued that the key to national wealth lay, in contradistinction to the police state strategy, in governing *less*. Thus Rousseau was to write that the problem of post-absolutist government was to:

> find a form of association which will defend and protect with the whole common force the person and goods of each associate, and in which each, while uniting himself with all, may still obey himself alone, and remain as free as before.
> (Rousseau, 1762, Part 1, Chap. 6)

Such sentiments lay at the heart of the early liberal endeavour. Thus the liberal states that developed from the mid-nineteenth century onwards were characterised by attempts to provide the minimum amount of government conducive to facilitate the free operation of the economy. The aim was to liberate the economic free-market spirit free citizens from the heavy hand of regulation so that they would make the country rich. Liberalism contended that, in some natural or innate way, 'man' was an economic individual and needed only the minimum government to allow his true self to shine forth.

However, as the less desirable consequences of industrialisation took root, certain aspects of the resulting explosion of economic activity began to be seen as problematic (Rose, 1996). In response, governments and wider society began to develop interventionist expertise in key areas such as public health (see, for instance, Ciancanelli, 2004), science (see, for instance, Boden, Cox, Nedeva, & Barker, 2004a), medicine and political economy. The institutions of government began to utilise such knowledges to enhance 'the social' aspects of countries. That is, professionals started to act for government to ameliorate the worst social effects of free market economic activity (Rose, 1996). As expertise grew, so the institutions of government became more interventionist. Some writers have thus drawn German National Socialism, Keynesian economic interventionism and Soviet socialism together as exemplars of this interventionist approach by the state (Dean, 1999). In the UK, the apex of such governmental concerns with the social came with the establishment of the Welfare State after the Second World War.

The past 50 years has witnessed the rise of a fundamental critique of this 'social' state. Initial concerns centred around the supposedly onerous

burden that such states placed on public finance. But the attack subsequently broadened and deepened to include criticism of the social state for
allegedly undermining individual rights and responsibilities (Rose, 1996).
Such critiques are often characterised as *neo-liberalism*.

Authors such as Rose (1996), Dean (1999) and Burchell (1996) describe
and analyse neo-liberalism and the governmental regimes it generates in
detail. They all conclude that in the neo-liberal state the processes and
practices of government are concerned with shaping human conduct in a
rational and calculative manner towards economic goals. 'Rational' in the
sense that the actions of the state embody some form of thinking that seeks
to be explicit, clear, planned, purposive and justified. 'Calculative' in the
sense that the actions of the state are supported by calculative techniques
and technologies – most notably, I would argue, accounting and associated
audit practices. Dean (1999) calls these rational, calculative governmental
practices, 'regimes of practice'. Regimes of practice are more than the actual
actions; they also include their sustaining discourses.

Most importantly then, and in major contrast to classical liberalism, neo-
liberal governmental practice is not about containing regulation in order to
free 'economic man', thus facilitating economic prosperity. Rather, it is
about moulding individuals and organisations into activity that shapes and
sustains economic development. The population is now a resource that can
be deployed to enhance the economy – something that Dean (1999), after
Foucault, calls *biopower*. In the UK such a shift is evidenced in successive
government policy choices since 1979, when Thatcher came to power, and
that have continued under Blair's leadership. Dean (1999) notes how
Thatcher's governments were committed to the development of an 'entrepreneurial society', while Blair, for instance, deploys discourses of exhor-
tation to self-improvement in education, emphasising self-investment by
students in higher education.

Dean (1999) and others argue that because we still have human agency –
the capacity to think and act as we wish – neo-liberal government has to
attempt to shape our activities *through* our freedom to think. That is, it
has to shape how we think. Government is less easily thought of in neo-
liberal states as a set of institutions and organisations. Rather, government
is an act or series of acts exercised through bodies of knowledge, belief and
opinion that combine into a collective mentality about how we should and
do rule ourselves, or conduct our conduct. Foucault defined this as 'governmentality'.

Our governmentality is therefore constituted of a complex, polymorphous
and interlocking/interacting set of organised, rational routines – particular

ways of doing things or '*regimes of practice*'. We perform these regimes of governance practice to create not only acts of government but also 'truths' about social, cultural and political practices. Governmentality is therefore the relationship between government and thought.

Regimes of practice are informed by knowledges or expertise, such as medicine, accounting, audit (Power, 1997) or management skills. In turn, it is through such expertise or knowledges that regimes of practice generate *programmes* to effect action on the population. These programmes are intrinsic to the regimes of practice; they are not the reason for the existence of the regimes (Dean, 1999).

It follows from this that government in the sense of the conduct of conduct must have a plurality of ends, agencies, actors, authorities, norms outcomes and consequences (Dean, 1999). Dean rejects, as a consequence, classical political science that seeks to represent the state and government as a single unified actor or to locate key indiviuals or groups that 'hold' power. Rather, we have to understand government as a diverse matrix of thought, beliefs, knowledges and expertise that conduct our conduct.

The neo-liberal state as described by authors such as Rose (1996) strikes many resonances and is a convincing and persuasive account of our new forms of governmentality. This in turn leads to consideration of where corporate governance fits in with such systems. It can be argued that corporate governance regimes possess all of the qualities of regimes of practice. They are certainly directly concerned with the conduct of conduct. They are rational and calculative and rely heavily on techniques and technologies such as accounting and management generally. They are there to shape behaviour in a moral, ethical way (given that what is moral and ethical is contingent and subjective). They attempt to govern behaviour without force of law as such, acting through the mechanisms and techniques of accountability and transparency. In the remainder of this paper I argue that perceiving of corporate governance regimes as regimes of practice can provide useful insights into and understandings of the nature of corporate governance and its ethical dimensions.

We can see these characteristics of regimes of practice in Chen Min's story, as described above, and in the response from Sainsbury's. Sainsbury's affirms its commitment to good employment practices and that it is a responsible employer. The company explains that it works with suppliers to ensure that they understand the issues. It further explains that it would take action when presented with proof. Notions of expertise and knowledge underpin the company's actions – it educates its suppliers on the potential problems of employing temporary labour. It is rational and calculative – it will respond to 'proof'. The very fact that it responded, with some care and in this manner, indicates that the company regards itself as accountable for the social consequences of its actions. In many senses, Sainsbury's response is a model of good corporate governance practice and will have been carefully constructed to shape our thinking about the story and the company – an unreflective reader might well be left with a positive image of the company and give little consideration to the very serious underlying issues, highlighted at the start of this paper.

As well as moulding our behaviour (for instance, readers might well continue to shop at Sainsbury's with confidence), the regime of corporate governance here also shapes the actions and thinking of the company. An aspect of governmentality is that the governors are also governed. Sainsbury's points out first that it has no direct legal responsibility – it does not directly employ the workers. That said, it implies that notwithstanding any lack of compulsion or regulation, it takes such matters seriously and will act. That is, this act of corporate governance enables the company to explain that it is governing itself into correct and moral behaviour. This may have a number of motivations: the company has philanthropic origins and may be genuinely concerned; it may be worried about further losing customers as a result of consumer boycotts (Baskaran & Boden, 2004b) or it may be seeking a competitive advantage over other supermarkets (the following day, Tesco, the sector leader, was identified as having benefited from the labour of foreign 'indentured' workers denied full employment rights (*The Guardian*, 28 March, 2004)).

Thus corporate governance as a regime of practice, in this instance at least, can be seen as rational, calculative, underpinned by expertise and formative of the behaviour of individuals and corporate entities. It is also an intensely moral activity. Yet such an analysis feels like a rather insubstantial meal. Plainly there is the exercise of much (economic) power in Chen Min's story, and we are able to challenge it and think about it in detailed and interrogative ways. Thus we have agency here. But, nothing has changed and the moral problem still exists and is unresolved – Chinese workers in the UK are still experiencing these conditions and I benefit from their labour when I buy cheap food from a supermarket. Corporate governance as a regime of practice has shaped my fellow citizens' thinking – there is no mass boycott of Sainsbury's, no calls for government inquiries. Rather, the articulations of corporate governance practices have served to distance and assuage. What is plainly, in moral terms, a complex and distressing issue is not cast as a corporate governance failure. Herein lies perhaps the distinction between seeing corporate governance failures as systems failures (that is, there is only something wrong when the system as defined fails) and seeing corporate governance failures as ones which result in unpalatable moral outcomes. Of course, if ethics are subjective yet implicit to corporate governance regimes and if such regimes form our governmentality and therefore exercise power over us, then failure can only be seen in terms of systems failure for there are no other standards by which to judge things.

Such a depressing conclusion need not lead to nihilism. If neo-liberal government exercises power through regimes of practice supported by and sustaining specific knowledges, then a way to challenge the exercise of such power is by making rendering such regimes highly visible. I turn my attention to this in the following section.

4. DIGGING DEEPER: INTERROGATING CORPORATE GOVERNANCE

Corporate governance regimes represent the exercise of power in that, in combination with other regimes, they combine to shape our thinking into a particular form of economic morality. The question then becomes on of how we might view the operation of this power.

Lukes (1974) three-dimensional analysis of power has value here. He described one-dimensional power by reference to the work of Robert Dahl (e.g. Dahl, 1961). Dahl's behaviourist stance asserted that power can only be analysed in operation, by looking at the outcomes of decision-making processes. Lukes concludes that this one-dimensional view of power

> involves a focus on *behaviour* in the making of *decisions* on *issues* over which there is an observable *conflict* of (subjective) *interests*, seen as express policy preferences, revealed by political participation (p. 15).

Dahl's approach presupposes that an absence of observable conflict over decisions signals an absence of conflict per se and that, therefore, no power has been exercised. This analysis of power can offer little by way of meaningful explanation of corporate governance regimes of practice because such regimes represent a collective mentality, and thus it will be difficult to observe conflict of the type needed for such an analysis of power.

Lukes explains how Bachrach and Baratz (1962) refute Dahl's one-dimensional view of power, arguing instead that power in fact has 'two faces'. The first relates, as Dahl reasoned, to the observable operation of power when decisions are made. The second is when power is exercised in such a way as to inhibit issues from being raised or discussed openly in the first place, leading to 'non-decisions'. In Schattschneider's (1960) famous phrase, 'organisation is the mobilisation of bias'. Lukes notes that this two-dimensional view of power still involves the observation of overt conflict and (non)decision-making. But he ultimately rejects the two-dimensional view of power as an unsatisfactory critique of behaviourialism, rooted as it is in the notion of observable phenomena.

Lukes finally develops his own, third dimension, analysis of power. This power involves preventing the recognition by others of their needs and interests such that they never emerge for discussion or decision in the first place. That is, power can be seen as the ability to shape the very consciousness and critical awareness of people and organisations.

Lukes explores the visibility, or otherwise of the exercise of power. He rejects Dahl's simplistic and positivistic notion that the exercise of power only occurs when there are observable phenomena. Similarly, he finds Bachrach and Baratz's second dimension unsatisfactory in this regard because it still rests on the notion of the observable phenomena. His own, third, dimension escapes these behaviourist traps, but necessitates consideration of how the operation of power might be identified and examined.

Lukes argues that third-dimension power can be identified by the careful analysis of discourses, ideas and such like and their subsequent critique. He acknowledges that such approaches lack the objective truth claims of Dahl's methodology, but that such claims are in any case a chimera. The difficulty of verifying the operation of the second and third dimensions of power lies in determining that there is a counterfactual – power only exists where it has produced an outcome that would not otherwise have occurred. Lukes advocates close examination of events and episodes for indications of counterfactuals. In search of the second dimension of power, there will be observable (albeit not measurable or quantifiable) phenomena. In looking for counterfactual evidence of the third dimension of power, 'by nature of the case, such evidence will never be conclusive' (p. 50).

However, there are means by which the exercise of power in regimes of practice might be explored and analysed. In his work *Governmentality*, Dean (1999) argues for what he calls an 'analytics' of government as a technique to understand how governmentality is formed, sustained and transformed. He defines analytics as being concerned with the examination of

the conditions under which regimes of practices come into being, are maintained and are transformed (p. 21)

Because regimes of practice are the means by which power is exercised, an analysis of them should reveal greater understanding of how they work and therefore of how power operates. The process of analytics, Dean states, often begins with the examination of programmes. He continues

> An analytics of government takes as its central concern *how* we govern and are governed within different regimes, and the conditions under which such regimes emerge, continue to operate, and are transformed (p. 23).

Dean (1999) identifies a number of elements in the analytics of regimes of government. The first is *problematisation*. This is the 'identification and examination of specific situations in which the activity of governing comes to be called into question' (p. 27). Dean asserts that such episodes are rare, have a temporal and geographical or organisational specificity. So, rather than starting with the analysis of a theory about how government works, analytics starts with specific instances of it being challenged or questioned.

The second element is the *prioritisation of 'how' questions*. Rather than being simple description, this implies a detailed analysis of the exact working of regimes of practice, the better to explicate the operation of power.

Finally, Dean stresses that we must see government as *assemblages* or *regimes*. That is, we have to understand government as a complex whole consisting of many intermeshing regimes – a 'matrix of ends and purposes' (p. 22).

Following Deleuze (1991), Dean advocates examining regimes in four dimensions. First, the visible aspects of practice need to be examined. Second, investigators should examine the technical aspects of government that sustain the regimes of practice. This would include mechanisms, procedures and such like which sustain the regime. Third, government has to be seen as a rational and thoughtful activity. This entails an examination of the knowledges and expertises that sustain regimes. Fourth, Deleuze would argue that an analysis of governmentality requires attention to how governmental processes encourage us to align ourselves with certain identities (consumer, taxpayer, stakeholder), the better to shape our conduct.

Such an approach may provide a useful way of interrogating what is happening with corporate governance systems and how they represent the exercise of power because they are regimes of practice. To ascertain the potential value of this, the next section describes a case study from a paper on the commodification of science (Baskaran & Boden, 2005), which involves a number of complex corporate governance issues. In Section 6, I subject this case study to Dean's 'analytics' approach.

5. HIV/AIDS: PHARMACEUTICAL FIRMS AND THE PANDEMIC

The global market for pharmaceuticals is now dominated by a small number of extraordinarily powerful drug giants for whom scientific knowledge is a key commodity. While scientific research and development on drugs *is* highly speculative and costly, there is also evidence that the global pharmaceutical companies effectively deploy these justifications in support of their pricing policies in situations where these factors are not significant. This legitimates high prices for new drugs. The drug companies also practice 'market segmentation' pricing policies, fixing the price of their drugs at different levels in different countries according to local ability to pay.

Poorer countries have resorted to two forms of action in response to high prices and market segmentation pricing. First, they have used 'generic substitution'. This is where copies of off-patent medicines are made or where the manufacture of patented medicines is undertaken under a 'compulsory license' without the payment of royalties. Governments issue compulsory licenses using enabling state legislation to meet national emergencies. The second strategy is to make 'parallel imports'. Here the producer is deemed to have ceded ownership of the product to the first purchaser. That first purchaser (in a low-price country) may then sell the product on in a different (higher price) segment of the global market, undercutting the original producer.

Pharmaceutical firms expend much effort in defending their prices and markets from the producers of cheap generics and from parallel imports. The legal tools used are the World Trade Organisation's patent rules governing trade-related intellectual property rights (TRIPS). Articles 30 and 31 of TRIPS provide exceptions to patent rights and theoretically allow countries to procure drugs from cheap sources, that is, to make 'parallel imports' or to make generic versions under 'compulsory licensing', in cases of national emergency (WTO, 2001). However, what constitutes a national emergency is a moot point. Individual states may also have their own national legislation which permits the setting aside of TRIPS in certain circumstances. In practice, TRIPS can be used effectively to ban countries in need from buying medicines from cheap sources. Attempts to use the exceptions on the grounds of national emergency have been vigorously challenged.

HIV/AIDS is now a global pandemic. More than 90% of people living with HIV/AIDS are in developing countries. By 2000, some 15 million people had died of AIDS, 2.8 million in 1999 alone (*The Independent*, 9 July, 2000).

A further 30 million people in Africa are expected to die by 2020: that is, more people are expected to die of AIDS than from war or famine (*The Independent*, 5 September, 1999).

South Africa faces one of the most serious HIV/AIDS problems. By 2001, there were 4.2 million HIV+ people, the majority with fully developed AIDS. A 2001 report by the South African Medical Research Council (MRC) estimated that 40% of South African deaths between the ages of 15 and 49 were due to AIDS. The disease is widespread among women in their late 20s and men in their 30s. Figures suggest that HIV affects women much more than men. It is anticipated that the average life expectancy will fall to 41 years by 2010 from 54 years in 2001 (life expectancy has fallen from 69 to 44 in Botswana and from 65 to 43 in Zimbabwe) (*The Guardian*, 27 April, 2001; *The Guardian*, 17 October, 2001). This means that a significant percentage of the younger and most economically productive population will die early, leading to serious socio-economic and political consequences for many African countries. The problem of large number of AIDS orphans is already extreme: nearly all the world's 11 million AIDS orphans live in sub-Saharan Africa (*The Independent*, 20 July, 2000).

The pharmaceutical firms have made significant progress in developing drugs such as AZT, 3TC and protease inhibitors which, when taken long term in 'cocktails' can substantially delay the onset of AIDS in HIV+ people. The advanced scientific knowledge embodied in these drugs is the intellectual property of pharmaceutical firms. As part of their corporate (profit-motivated) strategy, they aim to maximise the profitable commercial exploitation of their intellectual property assets. This profit motivation has driven the annual cost of patented HIV/AIDS drugs per patient up to somewhere between £6,700 and £10,000. Due to the high cost, only a tiny minority of people in developing countries can afford these drug therapies.

The pharmaceutical firms who own the HIV/AIDS drugs now face two acute and linked pressures. First, there is competition from the suppliers of cheap generic drugs that use the pharmaceutical firms' intellectual property. Second, the size of the HIV/AIDS pandemic is such that the corporations face strong demands to exhibit a greater sense of corporate social responsibility and drop their prices.

In response, the pharmaceutical companies and their strong backer – the US government – produced proposals to supply HIV/AIDS drugs at discounted rates between £670 and £1,340 per patient per year (*The Independent*, 20 July, 2000). However, even this discounted price is beyond the financial capabilities of developing states. Simultaneously, and with strong support from the US, the drug multinationals have been fighting hard to prevent poorer countries from importing cheap substitutes or making their own generic equivalents.

In response to its domestic public health crisis, South Africa tried to use the national emergency clause in TRIPS to procure cheap generic drugs for AIDS. In 1999, the government decided to use the National Medicines and Related Substances Control Amendment Act 1997 to achieve a substantial cost reduction with regard to HIV/AIDS treatments.

In response, the drug multinationals reported South Africa to the US and the US threatened trade reprisals (Bond, 2001). The US placed South Africa on its '301 Watch List' of countries that might be close to contravening (by the US definition) TRIPS. The UK and the EU also cautioned South Africa against undermining the *status quo* of TRIPS. Despite these cautions and in response to severe financial pressures on its health system, South Africa proceeded with its decision to procure cheap generic copies of HIV/AIDS treatments from alternate sources such as India.

The Indian generic drug manufacturer, Cipla, offered a three-drug combination cocktail to treat HIV/AIDS for £250 per year. The same combination from patent protected sources would cost about £10,000 per year per patient in developed countries. Alarmed by this development, 39 pharmaceutical companies, including GlaxoSmithKline, Merck & Co. Bristol-Myers Squibb, Roche and Boehringer Ingelheim, acting under the banner of Pharmaceutical Manufacturers Association (PMA) filed a lawsuit against the government of South Africa for violating their patent rights. Their case sought to invalidate the provisions of the South African enabling legislation. The combined market capitalisation of these companies was ten times greater than South Africa's GNP (*The Independent*, 19 April, 2001).

The court case opened in the Pretoria High Court in March 2001 after 2 years of negotiation between the drug companies and the South African Government. The drug companies appear to have misjudged the consequences of their decision to resort to legal action. The case generated worldwide attention and a public outcry. Oxfam, an NGO, accused drug multinationals of charging poor developing countries more than they charged Western countries and called the legal action against South Africa 'the shadowy side of globalisation' (*The Independent*, 12 February, 2001). Both Oxfam and the international medical charity Medecins Sans Frontieres (MSF) warned of worldwide demonstrations against 'the callousness and bullying' of the drug multinationals (*The Independent*, 5 March, 2001). Protest marches in several South African cities heralded the opening of court proceedings.

Nelson Mandela criticised the companies for 'exploiting the situation that exists in countries like South Africa in the developing world' and charging 'exorbitant prices which are beyond the capacity of the ordinary HIV/AIDS person.' (*The Guardian*, 16 April, 2001). He also condemned them for their decision to take the South African government to court. The World Health Organisation joined the fray against the companies. The media in the US and Europe criticised the firms for exaggerating their research and development costs and overcharging developing countries. Central to the case made by the drugs companies was that their prices merely reflected essential R&D costs and the necessity of generating and retaining capital to fund future research. That is, the prices were the result of financial pressures.

The Treatment Action Campaign (TAC), a well-organised South African lobby group, succeeded in getting itself accepted as a friend of the Pretoria court – giving it the right to introduce evidence. It filed an affidavit in which leading industry researchers swore that a third of life-saving drugs developed by pharmaceutical companies in the US received significant amount of government funding. TAC argued that the R&D cost for all five of the main anti-AIDS drugs had been met by American universities or by the US National Institute for Health (NIH), not the drug companies. TAC maintained that the drug companies had deliberately underplayed the role of public institutions such as NIH in developing new drugs. The role of the NIH in the invention of two of the key drugs in the triple therapy for AIDS and its conduct of clinical trial for a number of other drugs were highlighted. These arguments seriously weakened the drug companies' case by undermining the financial justifications for their pricing policies.

These revelations fuelled further global protest. European countries such as Germany, France and the Netherlands, and the European Parliament called on the drug companies to withdraw their legal action. Even the UK, which strongly supported the industry at first, quickly realised that the case was generating strong adverse public reaction against both the drug companies and the WTO regulations and changed its position. UK ministers called on the companies to respond to public pressure by providing discounted drugs to help eradicate disease and poverty. Pharmaceutical companies had previously argued that countries in the sub-Saharan Africa were so poor that they would be unable to buy drugs even at discounted rates (*The Guardian*, 31 May, 2001).

The drug companies came to appreciate that 'fighting this sensitive battle does nothing for their image as a caring, sharing industry' (*The Economist*, 10 March, 2001). GlaxoSmithKline and Merck approached the United Nations Secretary General, Kofi Annan and asked him to arrange a compromise deal with South Africa. In return, they wanted South Africa to amend its disputed Medicines Act that enabled it to override the WTO's intellectual property right agreement. South Africa refused to accede to this demand.

A final blow was delivered to the drug firms' case when the trial judge ordered them to respond point-by-point to TAC's detailed affidavits on their pricing, costs and profitability. This would have necessitated the production of detailed and commercially sensitive financial information relating to R&D subsidies, R&D costs and their global pricing strategies (*The Guardian*, 7 March, 2001). The case was adjourned to allow the production of the information.

When the court reconvened 6 weeks later in April 2001, the pharmaceutical firms withdrew their case. This was in return for an agreement that a joint working committee between the South African government and the industry would draw up regulations governing the use of the Medicines and Related Substances Control Amendment Act and that South Africa would abide by the TRIPS agreement under WTO (*The Observer*, 22 April, 2001).

The pharmaceutical corporations' decision to withdraw from the joint action appears to have been motivated by a number of reasons. First, they were concerned about the adverse publicity generated by their case throughout the world. Second, they were concerned that the South African courts would require them to reveal the amount of funding they have received from various governments to support R&D activities. Third, they would be forced to disclose the details of development costs, profit margins and their international pricing strategies (*The Observer*, 22 April, 2001). Fourth, it is reasonable to speculate that a victory for the South African government would have holed TRIPS beneath the waterline with regard to the definition of a national emergency, setting a precedent that would have allowed other poor countries to follow South Africa's lead.

Subsequently, the British pharmaceutical company GlaxoSmithKline, which had vehemently opposed the South African Government's decision to procure cheap generics, gave a voluntary license on its patents to Aspen Pharmacare, a South African manufacturer of generic drugs. It also waived royalties in exchange for Aspen paying a 30% fee on net sales to non-governmental groups fighting HIV/AIDS in South Africa.

Bond (2001) argues that episodes such as these are skirmishes in long-running battles between poorer countries and global pharmaceutical firms backed by Western governments (and especially the US). Although the drug companies were apparently routed, withdrawing their case and, in many instances, selling their patented medicines at discounted prices to developing nations, the long-term benefit to these countries is more ambiguous. South Africa agreed to form a joint committee with the industry to formulate regulations governing its national law. It also agreed to abide by the TRIPS agreement under the WTO: an agreement that largely favours global corporations. That is, the action left TRIPS itself largely unchallenged.

Following the withdrawal of the legal action in South Africa, 80 developing countries, led by African states, called for a special session of WTO to discuss their concerns over drug patents. They sought a relaxation in the interpretation of WTO rules, especially when serious public health issues were involved. A number of developed countries, led by the US and the European Union, opposed any modifications to TRIPS and continued to support the drug companies' patent protection rights. The resulting Doha Declaration in November 2001 did not amount to the clear commitment to the prioritisation of public health and access to medicines over commercial concerns. 'This is a serious flaw since TRIPS as it is currently written can serve as the basis for future legal challenges to countries that override patents in the interest of public health' (Bello & Mittal, 2001).

Thus, the South African case amounts to little more than a one-off concession rather than setting a precedent for the restructuring of international regimes in this area. Indeed, developing countries are likely to find it increasingly hard to get cheap drugs from 2005, as new drugs will increasingly enjoy more rigorous patent protection following the implementation of tougher intellectual property laws under TRIPS (*The Economist*, 30 September, 2000). Sadly, the story from South Africa is not unique.

6. CONCLUSIONS: HIV/AIDS AND CORPORATE GOVERNANCE FAILURES

There can be little question that the HIV/AIDS pandemic represents a crucial moral, ethical issue at the centre of which lie questions of corporate action. Yet corporate governance, as the OECD (2004) suggests, should embody principles of transparency and that:

> although there is not one form of corporate governance, there are internationally accepted principles that underlie sound business structures, including those developed by the OECD. These principles put forth the concept that within each company corporate leaders *should be not only accountable for the economic but also for the ethical behaviour of the enterprise.*

> (2004, emphasis added)

In this section, I provide a brief exercise in 'analytics' (Dean, 1999) of this South African episode in order to explore the regime of corporate governance practice in evidence here. The corporate governance aspects of this story concern the explicit decisions that the pharmaceutical firms made with regard to the provision or non-provision of HIV/AIDS drugs to countries in dire need. Thus they were presented with a clear ethical choice and it is reasonable to assume that their implicit or explicit corporate governance frameworks (that is, how they conduct their conduct) informed the decisions that they made.

Turning first the Dean's (1999) issue of *problematisation*, we have in this story a clear example of a specific situation where a governing activity (in this case, the way in which the drug firms were conducting their own conduct) can be brought into question or problematised. It is through such powerful examples that the operation of regimes can be exposed.

Looking next at questions of *how* this corporate governance regime worked and was challenged, the details of the actions taken are readily discernible. But of greater interest are the insights that can be gained regarding sources of corporate power and the accountability pressues to which the firms were exposed.

The primary source of corporate power was that the companies had succeeded in commodifying specific R&D-based knowledge under a system that gave valuable property rights to those who 'owned' such knowledge. A system of intermeshing regimes supporting global capitalism rewarded the companies for apparently taking risks by guaranteeing their rights economic exploitation and protecting these rights. Thus, the companies' regimes of governance were also interlocked with a globalised set of regimes including the WTO and international law. Together, these property rights and global systems facilitated the companies' actions.

The visible aspects of these regimes reveal much useful data. Thus specific international agreements exist, even the most cursory examination of which reveals that the systems actively support and sustain the profits of pharmaceutical firms via a system of international property rights. The pricing policies of the firms also make their operations highly visible. And there were in addition the court papers filed in pursuit and defence of the case. Thus in a very real way, the nature of this set of relationships is laid open for examination.

The technical aspects that sustain the regime of practice are also clearly visible here – the procedures and mechanisms used. Thus a framework of law and international agreements shaped the whole event. There were procedures to be followed by lawyers, defendants and other organisational actors. The companies bonded together in an organised way and launched a joint action against the South African government.

Different types of knowledge and expertise also were at the heart of the incident. Thus the crux of the matter concerned ownership and deployment of scientific knowledges (and indeed a contest about who had the right to use them). A second important area of technical knowledge was accounting itself – used to sustain the companies' decisions with regard to pricing and availability. Indeed, science and accounting were heavily intermeshed knowledges at this juncture, with one determining the access to the other.

And finally, there were matters of identities. Most interestingly, governments of developed countries around the world, but notably the US and UK, at first closely aligned themselves with the pharmaceutical firms. But later, as the incident unfolded, they shifted their allegiances and began to identify with the opposition to the firms. The identification of the protestors around the world was plainly with campaigners in South Africa.

A vexing and innocent question arising from this episode might be 'How can it be that global firms nested within systems of corporate governance that place emphasis on social well-being reach decisions that plainly endanger the lives and well-being of millions of people?' In short, if we have corporate governance systems, how can immoral decisions be reached and actions taken?

The corporate governance regimes in place were very rational: the firms owned assets (knowledge) that, because of the profit maximisation imperatives of the firm, it was essential to defend. The companies operated within a system of international law to defend those economic rights and engaged in the procedures in a clear, planned and (within the paradigm in which they were operating) wholly justifiable way. An intermeshing set of regimes of practice – international law, the South African court system and other government systems and so on – combined to enhance the perceived rationality and correctness of the firms' case. That the firms should have chosen to go to court in the first place is possibly indicative of their own belief in the rationality of their cause.

Moreover, this rationality was calculative in nature. It was supported by calculative techniques – most notably here by resort to accounting arguments to sustain the case on financial points. Thus it was by reference to accounting information that the companies sort to justify their pricing policies. What we see in operation therefore is a rational, calculative regime of practice that is intermeshed with other, supporting, regimes.

What that rational, calculative corporate governance regime of practice produced was a fundamentally amoral set of initial decisions and actions on the part of the firms. It may be that the reason for this lie in the entirely self-referential nature of the rationality of such regimes and their complete capture and control of the calculative practices that sustain them.

Thus, this should have been a straightforward court case the likely outcome of which would have been victory for the pharmaceutical firms. Yet, without any legal compulsion or any other specific sanction, the pharmaceutical firms, to a certain extent, backed down in this case. The story makes clear how this regime of practice operated and was sustained, but what led to its transformation?

Possible factors that contributed to the outcome include visibility and the deployment of counter-knowledges. Certainly, the involvement of high profile figures such as Nelson Mandela together with the media coverage that attended the episode made the operation of power here very visible indeed. This exposed the amorality of the companies' actions to public scrutiny, undermining their self-referential rationality. This in itself would not have changed things but for the consequential shift in identifications – especially as governments began to exert pressure on the firms.

There were two important counter-knowledges, both employed in very visible ways. Firstly, the action of TAC in seeking out alternative scientific authority on who had done the work was highly influential in shaping the outcome. And second, the challenge on the basis of the accounting information was perhaps the final straw in a teetering attempt at defending corporate privilege. Thus the calculative basis of the regime's decisions was thoroughly undermined. Interestingly, these two counter-knowledges were deployed through the judicial system – itself a regime of practice.

Of course, this was far from a resounding victory for the campaigners and similar struggles continue elsewhere. But if politics is the continuation of war by other means, then this was a significant battle. What the story shows us is how regimes of practice (in this case, that of the corporate governance of the pharmaceutical firms) emerge, develop and are transformed. It also shows how all of these aspects of governance are intermeshed and impact on each other. It also demonstrates how visibility and the identifications that actors make are central to the unfolding drama. And finally, it shows the central role of expertise and its deployment.

This paper has sought to demonstrate that corporate governance is just one part of a system of interlocking regimes of practice that shape our thinking and lead to the exercise of power in contemporary societies. As such, it is not really possible or indeed helpful to conceptualise events such as those described here as 'failures'. Rather, it is more useful to use such events as the means by which to peer beneath the surface of 'corporate governance' and to explore how it is a regime of practice that is influential in the exercise of power and an element in the assemblage that constitutes our 'governmentality'. Of course, after Foucault, we know that no power is absolute (for power to be exist it must be exercised). It is episodes such as the South African case described in this paper, where regimes of practice are challenged and made visible that permit us some insight into how such regimes are constructed, deployed and transformed. Most importantly, such approaches can assist in exposing how decisions with ethical consequences for corporate social responsibility are made and legitimised.

NOTES

1. 'Gangmaster' is the term employed to describe those who procure gangs of temporary labourers on behalf of the primary employer. The term is often used in the agriculture sector for people who organise, say, gangs of fruit pickers. Gangmasters may be either part of the formal or informal economy.

REFERENCES

Bachrach, P., & Baratz, M. S. (1962). The two faces of power. *American Political Science Review, 56*, 947–952.

Baskaran, A., & Boden, R. (2004b). Science – a controversial commodity? *Science, Technology and Society, 9*(1), 1–21.

Baskaran, A., & Boden, R. (2005). Globalising science. *Futures*, forthcoming.

Bello, W., & Mittal, A. (2001). The meaning of Doha. Commondreams News Center. 16 November, 2001; see < www.commondreams.org/views01/1116-07.htm >

Boden, R., Cox, D., Nedeva, M., & Barker, K. (2004a). *Scrutinising science*. London: Palgrave.

Bond, P. (2001). *Global apartheid*. Cape Town: University of Cape Town Press.

Burchell, G. (1996). Liberal government and techniques of the self. In: A. Barry, T. Osborne & N. Rose (Eds), *Foucault and political reason*. London: UCL Press.

Ciancanelli, P. (2004). Public sector accounting and accountability: The case of public health. Unpublished manuscript.

Dahl, R. (1961). *Who governs? Democracy and power in an American city*. New Haven: Yale University Press.

Dean, M. (1999). *Governmentality: Power and rule in modern society*. London: Sage.

Deleuze, G. (1991). What is a dipositif? In: T. J. Armstrong (Ed.), *Michel Foucault philosopher*. New York: Harvester Wheatsheaf.

Gloucestershire NHS Trust. (2004). http://www.partnershiptrust.org.uk/partnership/partnership39267.html. Accessed February 2004.

ITC. (2004). http://www.itcportal.com/our_values/corp_governance.html. Accessed February 2004.

Lukes, S. (1974). *Power: A radical view*. London: MacMillan.

OECD. (2004). http://www1.oecd.org/daf/nocorruptionweb/Business_Integrity/corpgov.htm. Accessed February 2004.

Power, M. (1997). *The audit society*. Oxford: Oxford University Press.

Rose, N. (1996). Governing "advanced" liberal democracies. In: A. Barry, T. Osborne & N. Rose (Eds), *Foucault and political reason*. London: UCL Press.

Rousseau, J. J. (1762). *The social contract*. London: JM Dent 19773.

Schattschneider, E. E. (1960). *The semi-sovereign people: A radicalist's view of democracy in America*. New York: Holt, Rinehart and Winston.

The Economist, 30 September, 2000.

The Economist, 10 March, 2001.

The Guardian, 7 March, 2001.

The Guardian, 16 April, 2001.

The Guardian, 27 April, 2001.

The Guardian, 31 May, 2001.

The Guardian, 17 October, 2001.

The Guardian, 27 March, 2004: Inside the grim world of the gangmasters.

The Guardian, 28 March, 2004.

The Independent, 5 September, 1999.

The Independent, 9 July, 2000.

The Independent, 20 July, 2000.

The Independent, 12 February, 2001.

The Independent, 5 March, 2001.

The Independent, 19 April, 2001.

The Observer, 22 April, 2001.

World Trade Organisation. (2001). Declaration on the TRIPS agreement and public health. WT/MIN(01)/DEC/2, 20 November, 2001.

PART II:
GOVERNANCE ISSUES

ACCOUNTING FOR INCLUSIVENESS: THE CORPORATE RESPONSE TO THE CHALLENGE OF HIV/AIDS IN SOUTH AFRICA

Stewart Lawrence and Grant Samkin

ABSTRACT

This paper examines the corporate and institutional responses to the challenge of HIV/AIDS in South Africa. The circumstances of South Africa have demonstrated the need for new ways of governance if businesses and society are to be sustainable. A confluence of historical, political and social factors in the 21st century, has produced the circumstances for new corporate principles, practices and reporting. The paper investigates the impact of institutional initiatives on corporate practices. Based on semi-structured interviews, the influences of the Global Reporting Initiative (GRI), the King Report, the Johannesburg Securities Exchange (JSE), and trade unions on corporate practices are explicated. There is no single path to a solution. What is clear is that firms cannot be uni-dimensional in the pursuit of profits, but have to be more 'inclusive', and not only in South Africa, but everywhere.

Corporate Governance: Does Any Size Fit?
Advances in Public Interest Accounting, Volume 11, 97–116
ISSN: 1041-7060/doi:10.1016/S1041-7060(05)11005-0

The 19th century saw the foundations being laid for modern corporations: this was the century of the entrepreneur. The 20th century became the century of management: the phenomenal growth of management theories, management consultants and management teaching (and management gurus) all reflected this pre-occupation. As the focus swings to the legitimacy and effectiveness of the wielding of power over corporate entities worldwide, the 21st century promises to be the century of governance.

(Institute of Directors in South Africa (IODSA), 2002, p. 14)

1. INTRODUCTION

Social, political and economic circumstances sometimes conspire to produce new forms of governance. Out of a new consciousness of the importance of social relationships and the need for sustainable communities come forth new structural arrangements. Such an example, it is argued in this paper, is that of South Africa. The specific confluence of historical forces has produced an approach to corporate governance that has lessons for all countries. This paper will not only explain these specific circumstances but also reflect on their significance for other places and times and how they are affecting global reporting initiatives.

After many years of apartheid, the election in 1994 of Nelson Mandela and the African National Congress (ANC) marked a new era in government in South Africa. It was also a landmark year for corporate governance in South Africa. South African businesses underwent a more subdued but highly significant transition (Barrier, 2003). Mervyn King, a corporate lawyer and former High Court judge, headed a committee which produced the "King Report on Corporate Governance" (IODSA, 1994). This was a significant document which incorporated a code of corporate practices and conduct that looked beyond the corporation itself, taking into account its impact on the larger community. It preceded by several years the groundswell of public opinion that resulted in the more general, global, movement towards corporate social responsibility. A second King Committee report published in 2002 (IODSA, 2002) captured the inclusive approach:

There is a growing weight of expectation on organizations to operate as good corporate citizens. This is because of the influence they exercise on the lives of so many individuals. Each organization is the sum of its stakeholders, such as its shareowners, customers, employees, suppliers, and the communities within which it operates. It depends on them, individually and collectively, for the goodwill required to sustain its operations.

(IODSA, 2002, p. 97)

Recently, South Africa has been facing a challenge that according to Makuto Lennox, National Union of Mineworkers, is greater than the struggle against apartheid (interview, July 2003). It is the challenge of HIV/AIDS. The research reported here is about the historical conditions of possibility that led to the principles of inclusivity being enunciated as the basis of corporate governance. It focuses on the HIV/AIDS pandemic and the corporate response, to illustrate the potential and the challenges to the wider concept of corporate governance than offered in mainstream management, finance and accounting texts.

2. PHILOSOPHICAL FOUNDATIONS

The concept of "sustainability" has become a commonplace in recent years. As argued by Visser and Sunter (2002) its philosophical groundings lie in the holistic movement towards understanding phenomena. Everything is connected and interdependent and part of a complex set of relationships. In South Africa, a far-sighted Prime Minister, Jan Smuts, wrote of such a philosophy under the title "Holism and Evolution" in 1926, before its current populism (Smuts, 1926).

According to Smuts, there is a common driving force in all creation and evolution – a common explanatory force that he termed *holism*. It refers to a fundamental tendency in all nature to form *wholes* of ever greater synergy. Synergy is the well-known concept of the whole being greater than the sum of the parts. What characterises these wholes is increasingly complex relationships between diverse elements, resulting in progressively higher levels of intelligence and creativity. The relationship between things is therefore more important than the things themselves. This reflects the Nietzschian conception that there is no such thing as "Das Ding an Sich" but only a set of dynamic relations between things.

Smuts demonstrated the working of holism in basic mineral and chemical elements, through to organisational level of plants, animals and humans. According to his theorising, the greatest scope for creativity is where fields overlap – where the outer edges of different wholes mingle (perhaps if he were alive today he would see great possibilities in the post-apartheid society – the overlapping of once-segregated white and black communities in South Africa).

Holism has been taken up widely as a theoretical organising principle. A well known example is that of the Gaia principle popularised by James Lovelock (1987), named after the Greek Goddess of the Earth, Gaia.

Physicists such as Fritjof Capra (1997) have applied the holistic concept to "living systems theory", which includes the social sphere. Human intelligence acts like a global brain of a living, self-regulating and self-sustaining earth system. In business, Peter Senge (1992), applied living systems theory and popularised the phrase "the learning organisation." Learning organisations understand that they not only impact on the environment but the external environment impacts on them. Only by gaining knowledge of the interactive processes between the self, other interested parties, the markets and the physical universe, can sensible decisions be made. Even then decisions will probably be wrong because of the complexity of the situation and the interdependency of so many variables. Decisions have to involve a process of continual learning.

The tendency towards more complex systems, and complex relationships, has been very apparent over the last century. Technological developments have made the peoples of the Earth into an interconnected whole, the "global village" concept. There are almost instantaneous communication networks and increasingly rapid transportation systems. There are developing common economic structures inhabited by multinational corporations and lubricated by international financial markets. It may reflect a holistic evolution in progress.

Yet there are danger signals to the idea of expanding progress. The Earth, we are constantly reminded, may not be able to sustain the increasing demands of a global market place. We may need new forms of governance to prevent damage to and depletion of the Earth's human and environmental resources. Corporate behaviour often illustrates examples of myopic behaviour threatening social and environmental systems. The pursuit of self-interest, so sanitised by Adam Smith, may no longer be a feasible model for business enterprise. Complex relationships demand a more inclusive model for the interests that business people have to take into account in decision making.

The circumstances of South Africa have demonstrated the need for new ways of governance if businesses and society are to be sustainable. Threats to sustainability are numerous. A glaring example today, in South Africa and much of the developing world, is that of HIV/AIDS. The circumstances of its rapid growth in South Africa are described in the following section. After that the corporate response to the pandemic is examined. The inclusive principles enunciated for governance processes in South Africa are explained, and it is suggested that such principles may be applicable more widely in an interconnected world.

3. BACKGROUND – THE SOUTH AFRICAN PREDICAMENT

The social and political conditions prevalent in South Africa in the late 20th century offered fertile ground for the spread of poverty and disease among much of the population. The policy of apartheid segregated races for the benefit of the minority white population. Blacks were not allowed to live in the same areas as whites. It was in the 1980s that opposition to apartheid in South Africa began to acquire momentum. This was evidenced through internal opposition and externally through international sanctions and boycotts. In 1990, the then-president, F.W. de Klerk, unbanned all political parties and released from prison the political leadership of the ANC and other political parties set up during the liberation struggle. After decades of apartheid, democratic elections based on a universal franchise were held in South Africa in May 1994 with the ANC winning the first election. The legacy of apartheid soon became apparent. Even as Nelson Mandela celebrated his inauguration as President of South Africa, the interconnected social problems of violence, poverty, racism and HIV/AIDS challenged the sustainability of the democratic state and its economy.

The reasons for the spread of HIV/AIDS in South Africa are both numerous and complex. They have been considered by Smith (2000) and in more detail by Barnett and Whiteside (2002). In order to appreciate the complexities associated with HIV/AIDS it is instructive to consider certain of the factors that contribute to the spread of HIV/AIDS. These conditions are reflected on below, before the response from the corporate institutions is examined. The response includes the expression of the principles through the King Report, the Global Reporting Initiative and the Johannesburg Securities Exchange, and how these principles affected corporate governance, if at all.

3.1. Migrant Policies

The apartheid period created a context for the rapid spread of AIDS. Its associated migrant labour policies contributed to the problem. By forcing black labour to migrate from their "homelands", the absence of male role models from the nuclear family contributed to the risk of breakdown of family structure and resulted in dysfunctional families (Smith, 2000).

Many men joined the ranks of migrant labour, living in single-sex hostels and using the services of commercial sex workers. In the Carletonville study reported on by Barnett and Whiteside (2002), 60% of adolescent girls in the study area were infected with HIV, while 50% of the women admitted to being commercial sex workers. When the men return home, sexually transmitted infections and HIV/AIDS are transmitted to their partner/s. It is this migration and mobility that creates patterns of sexual behaviour and mixing which are perfect for the spread of sexually transmitted diseases (Barnett & Whiteside, 2002). A World Vision spokesperson, Ken Casey (2003, p. 4) states:

> The majority of 16-year-old girls in South Africa today will die of AIDS-related illness before they get a chance to celebrate their 25th birthday.

Extreme poverty and inequality have also contributed to the spread of HIV/AIDS (Barnett & Whiteside, 2002; Smith, 2000). Following the collapse of apartheid, the institution of a democratically elected government and the relaxation of certain laws previously in pace, large informal settlements or squatter camps, developed on the periphery of major towns.

3.2. Poverty and Inequitable Wealth Distribution

Wealth distribution in South Africa remains largely skewed. The majority of the country's wealth remains in an exclusive and small number of hands with some estimates being 10% of the population controlling 80% of the wealth. The poorest 40% of households receive only 11% of total income, while the richest 10% receive 40% (Whiteside & Sunter, 2000, p. 92). A significant number of black South Africans continue to experience homelessness, degraded neighbourhoods and unemployment. In September 2002 Statistics South Africa placed the unemployment rate at 30.5%. A number of analysts however believe that the unemployment rate is higher than that published. In addition to the unemployed, a significant number of individuals are underemployed and uneducated.

3.3. Crime and Violence

Crime and gang violence is endemic in South Africa. Barnett and Whiteside (2002, p. 154) claim that rape and gang rape are potent methods of spreading HIV. They provide figures of 54,310 sexual crimes officially reported in

1998. Rape is an efficient means of HIV transmission because of the trauma it inflicts.

Barnett and Whiteside (2002, p. 153) suggest that the violence that accompanied the end of apartheid contributed to a widespread philosophy of fatalism.

> This perception that "what will be, will be" in turn diminished individual worth, responsibility and accountability. The feeling is still prevalent and makes people live for today without valuing tomorrow. It can be summed up in a shrug of the shoulders and the response: "If AIDS kills me in five years' time, so what?"
>
> (Ibid., p. 153)

3.4. Current Perspective

In 2000, UNAIDS estimated that 19.9% of the population were infected, up from 12.2%, 2 years previously (Dorrington, Bourne, Bradshaw, Laubscher, & Timaeus, 2001, p. 7). More recently Dorrington, Bradshaw, and Budlender (2002, p. 28) have used an AIDS and demographic model developed by the Actuarial Society of South Africa (ASSA) to project the impact of the disease. The most recent indicators for total population and numbers of HIV positive, AIDS sick and cumulative AIDS deaths is shown in Table 1.

This table is consistent with the Arndt and Lewis (2000, p. 856) expectation that by 2015, the number of deaths from AIDS is likely to be more than 10 million. As the number of deaths increase, so will the overall life expectancy decrease with overall life expectancy expected to fall from its pre-epidemic high of 65 years to 40 years by 2008.

Dorrington et al. (2002) consider that in South Africa, the HIV epidemic is entering its mature phase. This means that in a worst case scenario, with no changes in behaviour, and no interventions, the ASSA model estimates that 6,558,628 people are infected with HIV on 1 July 2002. For an epidemic to reach its peak, the number of new infections must slow down because those who are infected are dying. Dorrington et al. (2002, p. 2) consider that the number of new infections peaked in 1998 and has since begun to decrease (Whiteside (2003) does not consider HIV infections in South Africa to have peaked yet). The number of individuals dying from AIDS on an annual basis has only recently started to increase. Dorrington et al. (2002) argue that without interventions to reduce mortality, the number of deaths will peak in 2010 with one of its consequences, the number of children who are orphaned peaking in about 2015.

Table 1. Total Population, Number of HIV Positive, AIDS Sick People
and Cumulative AIDS Deaths.

Year	Total Population	Total HIV+	Cumulative AIDS deaths	Total AIDS sick
1990	35,783,975	48,818	242	394
1991	36,513,522	106,732	648	974
1992	37,422,066	218,197	1,606	2,258
1993	38,375,873	412,674	3,725	4,922
1994	39,375,664	727,452	8,139	10,085
1995	40,410,256	1,203,847	16,817	19,519
1996	41,452,486	1,864,140	32,954	35,714
1997	42,489,541	2,684,545	61,410	61,996
1998	43,439,051	3,578,195	109,043	102,097
1999	44,298,552	4,457,033	184,624	159,180
2000	45,078,805	5,236,841	298,645	236,228
2001	45,768,984	5,968,521	462,642	334,253
2002	46,361,337	6,558,628	688,428	453,352
2003	46,848,269	7,027,931	987,061	591,088
2004	47,223,831	7,373,071	1,367,429	742,519
2005	47,485,369	7,594,403	1,834,484	899,071
2006	47,635,680	7,697,600	2,387,587	1,049,742
2007	47,683,822	7,695,201	3,019,659	1,182,710
2008	47,645,665	7,605,111	3,717,519	1,287,844
2009	47,540,955	7,449,678	4,463,489	1,358,743
2010	47,392,059	7,252,801	5,237,867	1,393,926

Source: Dorrington et al. (2002, p. 28).

A breakdown detailing the various significant groupings of the number of
people living with HIV/AIDS is detailed in Table 2.

What is significant about the figures shown in Table 2 is that of the
approximate 6.5 million people living with HIV/AIDS, 6.1 million (95.1%)
are in the 18–64 age group. This age group, most likely to form part of the
labour force, is the most productive, and is responsible for raising the next
generation. It is the extent of the potential problem that has enabled Bell
Devarajan and Gersbach (2003, p. 9) to argue that:

> By killing off mainly young adults, AIDS also seriously weakens the tax base, and so
> reduces the resources available to meet the demands for public expenditures, including
> those aimed at accumulating human capital, such as education and health services not
> related to AIDS.

Dorrington et al. (2002, p. 4) also estimate that 3.2 million women of child-
bearing age (15–49) were living with HIV/AIDS. However in the age group
15–24, four women were infected over one male. Smith (2000, p. 8) identifies

Table 2. People Living with HIV.

Total HIV infections[a]	6,461,372
Adult men (18–64)	3,016,080
Adult women (18–64)	3,125,498
Total Adults (18–64)	6,141,578
Child-bearing age women (15–49)	3,199,493
Male youth (15–24)	263,069
Female youth (15–24)	947,680
Total Youth (15–24)	1,210,749
Children (0–14)	205,134

Source: Dorrington et al. (2002, p. 4).
[a]The ASSA model when summed across total HIV infections over all provinces provides a slightly different figure for HIV-infected people than when the model is applied to the country as a whole.

a possible reason for the significant difference in the HIV infection rates in this particular age group which exists until the late 20s to early 30s. This difference, Smith argues, reflects the preference shown by young women for older male partners, and the preference for younger female partners on the part of males.

HIV infected people typically move through four stages. While many in the first two stages of the infection will be relatively asympamatic, those in stage three typically suffer from weight loss and illnesses associated with opportunistic diseases such as tuberculosis. Stage four is full blown AIDS. If a person at the full blown AIDS stage does not receive any treatment, it is likely that they will die within 1 year to 18 months. In Table 3, the percentage of the HIV infected people at each stage of the infection.

It is clear that in the next few years businesses will be losing a large number of skilled and experienced employees. How these impacts will be assessed and reported is what our research project wanted to discover.

4. REPORTING AND CORPORATE ACCOUNTABILITY

Increasingly, firms are expected to be accountable for more than financial performance. The term *corporate social responsibility (CSR)* refers to the obligations of the firm to society, or more specifically, the firm's

Table 3. Percentage of HIV Infections at Each Stage of Infection.

No. of Stages	%
Stage 1	55
Stage 2	20
Stage 3	18
Stage 4	7
Total	100

Source: Dorrington et al. (2002, p. 4).

stakeholders – those affected by corporate policies and practices. This new responsibility is reflected in influential documents produced in the South African context, the King Report and the social reporting requirements, especially in relation to HIV/AIDS, of the Global Reporting Initiative (GRI) both of which are discussed below. The position of the South African Chartered Institute of Accountants (SAICA) is also examined.

4.1. The King Report

A very influential document in South Africa is called the King Report on Corporate Governance. The King report was developed as an initiative of the Institute of Directors of South Africa (IODSA), with input from a variety of stakeholders. It was acknowledged that a novel concept of corporate governance which recognised the increasing involvement of previously excluded black citizens in business and society would be required in the new democratic South Africa. The first King report was issued in 1994 and a revised version (King II) was published in 2002. The report argues that an inclusive approach to corporate governance requires that the purpose of the company be defined and the values by which the company will carry on its daily life should be identified and communicated to all stakeholders. The Report expresses in a uniquely South African way the basic purpose of corporate activities. The report includes the following words at the beginning of the section on integrated reporting (Section 4, p. 96):

Umuntu ngumuntu ngabantu
(I am because you are; you are because we are)

The words express the sense of the interdependence and interconnectivity of humanity. The King report reflects on South African values and culture especially that of Ubuntu. Ubuntu means "being human"; "humanness" or what it means to be human. It involves qualities such as cooperation; supportiveness; togetherness or "solidarity". We are interdependent and interconnected. What matters most is the quality of our relationships with others. This idea of interdependence and quality of relationships is used in a corporate context. What would a truly human business organisation have as its purpose?

> Corporate citizenship is the commitment of business to contribute to sustainable economic development, working with employees, their families, the local community and society at large to improve their quality of life.
>
> (IODSA, 2002, p. 96)

The 2002 King report recommends that every organisation should take into account all threats to the health of stakeholders, including that of HIV/AIDS. It imposes a responsibility on directors of companies to ensure that they understand the economic impact of HIV/AIDS on business activities, and have a strategy in place to manage the impact. Moreover, it advises that companies should monitor and measure performance and report on the health and well-being of employees to stakeholders on a regular basis.

The King Report has no regulatory backing. The Report offers a challenge to the corporate community which has voluntarily offered little by way of public accounting and reporting on its strategies and actions for combating the social and economic impacts of HIV/AIDS (IODSA, 2002, p. 117). A recommended way forward was that companies report in accordance with the GRI, for which South Africa has been requested to develop a resource document on reporting on HIV/AIDS.

4.2. Global Reporting Initiative (GRI)

The Global Reporting Initiative (GRI) was first published in June 2000. It represents an international cooperative effort to establish *Sustainability Reporting Guidelines* for voluntary use by organisations worldwide. It develops ways of reporting on economic, environmental and social dimensions of companies' activities, products and services. As Mike Murphy, a representative of GRI in South Africa, says of the general principles of GRI:

> It is to ultimately make social and ecological reporting as normal and in a sense as expected as financial reporting.
>
> (Interview, June 2003)

The mission is to provide a framework for disclosure which will result in a new level of accountability and transparency.

Among the driving forces for the development of the GRI have been the expansion of a global capital market and developments in information technology. These developments not only offer opportunities for wealth creation, but also provide a widely voiced scepticism that such wealth will help to decrease social inequities. Demonstrations throughout the world have made it important that transnational corporations become more accountable for the consequences of their business operations wherever, whenever and however they occur.

Public demonstrations have drawn attention to problems of governance; to the capacity of existing national and international institutions to govern or regulate corporate activity. There is a need for borderless governance structures to ensure corporate activity results in environmental and social as well as economic benefits. Global standards of reporting are needed, as represented by the GRI.

According to the King report (IODSA, p. 96) increasingly corporate social accountability is now expected not just for multi-nationals but has become a broader movement for all sizes of organisations around the world. Companies of all sizes are facing new expectations from informed consumer groups for sustainability practices. The news media and other information technologies make people more aware of such issues.

Financial markets are recognising the long-term benefits of sustainability practices and placing a premium on companies with sound environmental and social strategies and policies (Spiller, 2000). New measures of "social responsibility" are emerging and linkages between corporate sustainability practices and brand image, reputation and future asset valuation are capturing the attention of mainstream financial markets. Sustainability reporting, according to an internationally accepted framework, like the GRI, would assist the better understanding of such linkages. The movement to harmonise financial accounting standards now encompasses the broader reporting of an integrated set of performance indicators.

The GRI is an evolving set of guidelines. The contribution of South Africa has been to develop a set of guidelines for a particular set of social performance indicators, specifically on HIV/AIDS reporting (Global Reporting Initiative, 2003). The guidelines were in the eighth draft early in 2003 and were exposed for global comment and for pilot testing by South African Companies.

The GRI's general guidelines on social reporting drew heavily on the ILO Tripartite *Declaration Concerning Multinational Enterprises and Social Policy*, and the OECD's *Guidelines for Multinational Enterprises* (GRI, 2002, p. 51). More controversial than environmental disclosure, many of the social issues are non-quantifiable. So the indicators are often of a qualitative nature dealing with measures of the organisation's systems and operations, such as the existence of policies, procedures and management practices.

So it is with the HIV/AIDS. The guidelines take an incremental approach recognising that organisations face different operational situations, reporting capacities and stakeholder pressures. So it is acknowledged that different amounts of disclosure will be relevant to different organisations. The guidelines provide a full and detailed suite of reporting recommendations, from very broad to very specific. The aim is to allow experimentation by reporting entities.

There are a set of "basic level indicators", and an exceedingly detailed decomposition of the basic indicators for those wishing to engage in "full disclosure". As Brad Mears of the Durban Chamber of Commerce said:

> You have got to achieve a balance between making sure those requirements (for reporting) help that individual business in managing HIV/AIDS, and doesn't overwhelm it with just copious amounts and screeds and screeds of reports that never ever get put into action., and never result in anything.
>
> (Interview 6 July 2003)

Several interviewees expressed similar views concerning the amount of detail required. A common view was that level one, the barest qualitative information about the existence of relevant policies and practices, is the most valuable.

> One approach I did like is the incremental approach, saying. Well, here's the first stage. A company should start somewhere; just go through the first basic level indicators.
>
> (C. Hundermark, Alexandre Forbes and adviser to GRI, July 2003)

The basic level indicators are listed below. Apart from "Measurement, and monitoring and evaluation", the first level requires no quantitative information, but descriptions of any policies and practices the firm has under each heading. For that reason, it was suggested by C. Hundermark that the "Measurement" indicator was an anomaly and should have been introduced only for the more detailed levels when firms had had perhaps a few years experience with the process. He suggested the question could have been re-phrased: "Has the organization considered the financial costs, or calculated, or estimated the financial costs?". For each indicator, the guidelines provide more detailed instructions and specific indicators for companies wishing to comply with "full" reporting requirements. The following guidelines shows the basic level requirements rather than the detailed indicators.

(a) Good governance – describe the HIV/AIDS policy; describe overall strategy for managing the risk; describe contingency planning in light of likely impacts.
(b) Workplace management and conditions – describe how stakeholders are involved in policy formulation; describe HIV/AIDS intervention programmes; indicate total allocated budget dedicated to HIV/AIDS.
(c) Depth/quality and sustainability of HIV/AIDS programmes – detail support and counseling programmes; education and training programmes; condom distribution; general healthcare and wellness provision, additional benefits and support for employees sick, dying or dead.
(d) Measurement and monitoring and evaluation – prevalence and incidence of HIV/AIDS and estimated costs and losses (current and projected prevalence among workforce, service providers, surrounding communities, target customers, direct suppliers; estimate of current costs and losses; estimated and predicted future costs and losses).

4.3. Evidence of Extent of Reporting

The GRI guidelines are demanding reporting requirements. Few companies could meet the full reporting requirements including detailed measurements and indicators in all the areas above. However, many firms were making progress and had knowledge of the incidence and consequences of HIV/AIDS within their organisation.

As a representative of SAICA stated:

> I know there are a lot of companies that are really proactive; to manage the problem as it is and (institute) preventative steps for their employees; to educate their employees....
>
> From our side, the financial side, the reporting side, our responsibility is to work with other people to create awareness among companies to put processes in place, and the way in which we can do that, is to actually force them to start reporting on it.
>
> (SAICA, Interview, June 2003)

SAICA was in favour of minimal compulsory reporting, but was cautious of expecting companies to report on detailed quantitative measures before they were adequately prepared to do so. The representative pointed out that incorrect information could be more dangerous than no information. Moreover, for such a sensitive issue with negative connotations, there was a concern that those reading HIV/AIDS reports may not fully understand the information being provided. So there was an educational process necessary before requiring reporting compulsorily.

Maybe for this reason, since our interview, The Johannesburg Securities Exchange (JES) has decided not to make full reporting, a requirement for listing on the JES (Wessels, 2003, p. 10). This is contrary to the recommendations of the GRI that the extent of the epidemic and the potential cost to a company be incorporated into financial statements. The listing requirement will not require companies even to report on the prevalence of HIV/AIDS. The accuracy of the determination of such rates and their auditability was the reason provided for this change in stance. It would be counter productive if inaccurate or false information were reported. Companies would, however, still have to disclose how HIV/AIDS was being managed.

There are several companies, which have attempted to report fully. A reported business case example is Anglo Gold (www.weforum.org/global-health).

At the time of writing Anglo Gold reported:

- a prevalence rate of between 25 and 30% of the workforce.
- expenses related to HIV/AIDS calculations put the expenses of HIV/AIDS between 8 and 17% of payroll based on (different) actuarial estimates.
- because of the difference in actuarial estimates, the company is to develop its own actuarial model.
- the cost of intervention programmes is reported to be a budget in 2002 of $US 743,000 ($US 17 per employee).
- the company offers antiretroviral drugs to infected employees and their families.
- the cost of highly active antiretroviral drugs is reported as $US244 per patient per month ($US2,928 pa).
- There were 410 patients in 2002 estimated to rise to 820 by December 2003.

Anglo-Gold has established a combined worker-management project team to devise ways of improving working conditions. Among the improvements has been the provision of married quarters in place of single sex hostels (Representative of SA Mine Workers' Union, interview, July 2003). The benefits are obvious.

There are other large South African companies which have trialed the reporting guidelines of the GRI. For example, South African Breweries gathered all the information necessary for reporting but has not yet published all the detail (interview, July 2003). The KPMG survey of sustainability reporting in South Africa (KPMG, 2001), indicated that 57% of the top companies report to some extent on sustainability issues. However,

HIV/AIDS is one of the issues least reported (across all sectors, an average of 32% of companies mention HIV/AIDS in their annual reports). Interviewees indicated that the detail of reporting required was possibly too revealing for external reporting

> It just becomes too difficult to do business if you have to report to that level [of detail]....
> Some of the information may contain some proprietary information so it shouldn't
> necessarily be made available to all and sundry. It is important that a company should
> disclose that they have documented to that level, but the next level of detail nobody is
> actually going to read it.
>
> (Interview, Manager in Financial Services Sector, 24 June 2003)

So the objections to the GRI are that it is relevant for internal reporting and managerial action but with the current level of knowledge may lead to reports too inaccurate for external purposes.

5. INTERNAL RESPONSES TO THE REPORTING AND PREVENTATIVE MEASURES ADOPTED

Though reporting is not extensive, many interviewees reported that companies were well aware of the extent of the problem and the financial implications. Representatives from various companies stated that intervention was a more economic option than non-intervention.

Because of privacy requirements surrounding HIV/AIDS, medical intervention programmes are usually conducted through third-party health providers. Such private-sector providers offer different programmes and range of services. There are private health service providers, which offer the full range of services. For example, a consulting firm called Lifeworks offers the following service (interview, July 2003):

HIV prevalence measurement
Using either (i) salivary testing or (ii) actuarial modelling
↓
Sick rate and death projections
Impact assessment based on applied projections
↓
Financial risk assessment
Calculation of impact on future profitability
Impact on insurance, recruitment, absenteeism, training costs
Pre- and post-medical intervention scenarios

The risk assessment is based on a detailed model developed by Lifeworks in conjunction with several client companies. The Directors of Lifeworks expressed the conviction in an interview (July 2003) that the model demonstrated without doubt the economic (as well as humanitarian) benefits of companies having proactive management interventions.

Lifeworks offers a range of services including reporting packages, medical interventions and management programmes, the latter including administration of antiretroviral drugs. They have modelled the costs before and after medical intervention and claim that it is cost effective to have an intervention programme, i.e., doing nothing will cost companies.

Various models have been developed to assess the impact on a company's costs of HIV/AIDS. The estimates of this cost vary – some estimate that within a few years it could be as high as 54% of payroll (W. Myslik, Sowetan Sunday World, 2001). Wayne Myslik believes that without an appropriate managerial strategy South African firms will not be able to compete globally.

Costs incurred have been categorised for analytical purposes (Whiteside & Sunter, 2002, p. 112):

5.1. Direct Costs

Benefits package – health clinics, disability and pension insurance, funeral expenses, subsidised loans.

Recruitment – advertising, recruitment, covering vacancies.

Training – pre-employment and in-house training costs.

HIV/AIDS programmes – prevention programmes, educational programmes.

The direct costs are relatively easily recorded and reported. In addition there are indirect costs.

5.2. Indirect Costs

Absenteeism – sick leave, bereavement and funeral leave, leave to take care of dependents with AIDS.

Morbidity – reduced performance due to sickness.

Management resources – responding to workplace impacts, planning programmes, training, covering for absentees.

Such indirect costs are less easily identifiable and recordable. On top of direct and indirect costs, a third category of costs, systemic costs, have been identified.

5.3. Systemic Costs

Loss of workforce cohesion – reduction in morale, motivation and concentration, loss or disruption of teamwork/units, breakdown of discipline.

Workforce performance and experience – reduction in skill levels, performance institutional memory and experience.

The total costs of HIV/AIDS would be the aggregate of all such costs for a company. Few companies are able or willing to devote resources to finding out the costs.

Wayne Myslik (*ibid.*) an actuary, finds it ironic that in South Africa, the HIV/AIDS pandemic has highlighted the greatest need of management is for strategic foresight, but he witnesses management myopia. Making reporting, at least to a minimum standard, compulsory could be the way forward to protect investors, workers and communities. The representative of SAICA certainly supports this approach. More and more countries may consider the wisdom of making external reports include triple-bottom-line content. This is a way to bring to management's consciousness the deeper ecological and social issues for long term sustainability.

6. REFLECTIONS

Increasingly, the debate about CSR is no longer about whether to make substantial commitments to CSR, but how to implement it? (Smith, 2003, p. 55). South Africa provides a case study of responses to a crisis evident in one country. There are signs of shifts in consciousness that could provide new structural possibilities. In an interconnected global community, the problems of South Africa are symptomatic of more widespread challenges to global sustainability. The response locally provides a basis for international action. It requires a transformation in thinking on the part of the drivers of economic and social and environmental impacts – businesses large and small. The GRI provides guidelines, which are voluntary. From our research in South Africa, it seems the most significant aspect of the GRI is that it raises awareness of social and ecological issues among senior management of companies. The incremental approach encourages companies to self-reflect on the policies and programmes they have in place for dealing with a potential threat to their long-term sustainability. Reporting internally is the first step. External reporting need not be quantitative but could be simply informing interested stakeholders and potential investors of the preparedness of the company to tackle the problems they confront through the HIV/AIDS pandemic. The GRI guidelines allow an incremental approach starting with self-awareness. They stand on the premise that corporations worldwide need to rethink their activities and encompass a new vision of purpose. Corporations are the only organisations with the resources, technology, and global-reach to facilitate sustainability (Cooperrider & Dutton, 1999). Companies may have to rethink their prevailing views about strategy, competition and cooperation if the world's resources are to be sustainable. This is reflected in the Global Compact initiative of the United Nations launched in the new Millenium, together with other cooperative agreements in addition to the GRI, such as Accountability 1000 (Institute of Social and Ethical Accountability) and ISO 14001 (International Organisation for Standardisation). There are international agreements concerning climate change, i.e. the Bonn agreement on the Kyoto protocol. The financial markets are drawing attention to the need for sustainable practices, witnessed by the FTSE 4 Good Index (U.K.), the Dow Jones Sustainability Index (USA). In South Africa KPMG is developing a sustainability index for rating and ranking South African companies. International investors will be attracted to companies that report active social and environmental programmes to enhance the well-being of their communities and employees.

7. CONCLUSION

It is significant that in the study of practices concerning the corporate response to HIV/AIDS in South Africa, one of the most influential documents, King II, speaks of corporate governance in human rather than economic terms. Economic performance is important, but it is a means not an end. There is a need for a more inclusive approach. The example of South Africa could be an exemplar. There the crisis represented by the HIV/AIDS disease has forced a re-think of corporate objectives. Though actions are still embryonic, a change in consciousness is evident. The inclusive philosophy of corporate governance reflected in the King Report is a start. The new re-visioning of corporate purpose implicit in the Global Reporting Initiative is another major influence. The Global Compact incorporates a new ethic. The confluence of social, economic and political circumstances are such that a more inclusive ethic could come to permeate perceptions of business responsibilities in South Africa and affect business practices everywhere.

REFERENCES

Arndt, C., & Lewis, J. D. (2000). The macro implications of HIV/AIDS in South Africa: A preliminary assessment. *Journal of South Africa Economics, 68*(1), 856–887.

Barnett, T., & Whiteside, A. (2002). *AIDS in the twenty-first century: Disease and globalisation.* Basingstoke: Palgrave Macmillan.

Barrier, M. (2003). Mervyn king: principles, not rules. *The Internal Auditor, 60*(4), 68–73.

Bell, C., Devarajan, S., & Gersbach, H. (2003). *The long-run economic cost of AIDS: Theory and an application to South Africa.* World Bank Report, June.

Capra, F. (1997). *The web of life.* London: Harper Collins.

Cooperrider, D. L., & Dutton, J. E. (1999). *Organizational dimensions of global change.* Thousand Oaks, CA: Sage Publications.

Dorrington, R., Bradshaw, D., & Budlender, D. (2002). *HIV/AIDS profile in the provinces of South Africa – Indicators for 2002.* Centre for Actuarial Research, Medical Research council and the Actuarial Society of South Africa.

Dorrington, R., Bourne, D., Bradshaw, D., Laubscher, R., & Timaeus, I.M. (2001). *The Impact of HIV/AIDS on adult mortality in South Africa.* Technical Report. Burden of Disease Research Unit Medical Research Council.

Global Reporting Initiative (2002). *Sustainability Reporting Guidelines.* GRI.

Global Reporting Initiative (2003). *Reporting Guidance on HIV/AIDS: A GRI Resource Document* (8th draft for public comment), GRI, February.

Institute of Directors in Southern Africa (IODSA) (1994). King Report on Corporate Governance. Johannesburg: IOD.

Institute of Directors in Southern Africa (IODSA) (2002). King Report on Corporate Governance for South Africa – 2002. Johannesburg: IOD.

KPMG. (2001). *Survey of sustainability reporting in South Africa* (4th ed.). Johannesburg, South Africa: KPMG.

Lovelock, J. E. (1987). *Gaia: A new look at life on earth.* Oxford: Oxford University Press.

Myslik, W. (2001). *AIDS: Exposing strategic myopia in SA business.* Soweto Sunday World, 9 September.

Senge, P. (1992). *The fifth discipline: The art and practice of the learning organization.* Sydney, Australia: Random House.

Smith, A. (2000). HIV/AIDS in Kwa Zulu-Natal and South Africa. *AIDS Analysis Africa* 11 (1), June/July, pp. 6–9.

Smith, N. C. (2003). Corporate social responsibility: Whether or how? *California Management Review, 45*(4), 52–76.

Smuts, J. (1926). *Holism and Evolution.* New York: Macmillan & Co.

Spiller, R. (2000). Ethical business and investment: A model for business and society. *Journal of Business Ethics, 27*, 149–160.

Visser, W., & Sunter, C. (2002). *Beyond reasonable greed: Why sustainable business is a much better idea.* Cape Town, SA: Human & Rousseau Tafelberg.

Wessels, V. (2003). *JSE will not demand HIV disclosure.* Natal Mercury Business Report, 4 July, p. 10.

Whiteside, A. W. (2003). *Health, economic growth, and competitiveness in Africa.* Paper originally developed for the AGOA meeting in Mauritius in January 2003.

Whiteside, A., & Sunter, C. (2000). *AIDS: The challenge for South Africa.* Cape Town, SA: Human & Rousseau Tafelberg.

CORPORATE GOVERNANCE IN CHINA: A LACK OF CRITICAL REFLEXIVITY?

Loong Wong

ABSTRACT

*Recent spectacular collapses globally have sparked renewed public inter-
est in corporate governance and the pursuit of a new global model. The
prevailing dominance of an American model has overshadowed constructive attempts to derive a model that is more appropriate for 'non-western'
and developing countries. In this paper, I examine the discourse of corporate governance in China. I argue that rather than being a mere captive
of the American model, it could have crafted and developed an alternate
and more appropriate model that takes into account the economic and
social needs of China instead of a corporate governance model developed
for other countries.*

INTRODUCTION

The issue of governance has become a fashionable concern over the past few
years. It became mandatory in developmental aid calculations and has been
blamed for the Asian financial crisis of 1997. Of late, it has enveloped the

Corporate Governance: Does Any Size Fit?
Advances in Public Interest Accounting, Volume 11, 117–143
ISSN: 1041-7060/doi:10.1016/S1041-7060(05)11006-2

globe as the public watched the spectacular collapses of Enron, MCI and others in the United States of America; in Australia, we have HIH, OneTel and Harris Scarfe and more recently, NRMA, among others. Governments globally have responded and sought to re-engineer new measures of good governance to ensure continuing growth and economic success.

In Asia, corporate governance policies clearly showed the marked influence of western traditions; a 'cultural hegemony' exists, persists and remains dominant. In part, this is due to the colonial heritages of many Asian societies, e.g. in Singapore, Hong Kong, Malaysia, Philippines and India, where laws and statutes resemble those of their former colonial masters. In others, for example in Japan, China and Taiwan, the transfusion of European ideas, laws and practices have been significant nation-building artefacts. The singular most important factor, however, has to be the growth of, and the need to attract, international capital.

Be that as it may, the issue of which model of corporate governance to adopt is, however, not so apparent. The suggestion that there is only one approach to corporate governance is clearly not tenable. Its history and genealogy suggests that conceptually, corporate governance is ambiguous, contentious and evolutionary. Its intellectual roots similarly suggest that the 'one size fits all' approach is not sustainable – various disciplines emphasise and privilege different insights and lead to varying analytical insights. Moreover, different legal systems, business cultures and corporate structures further complicate the picture (Whitley, 1999; Albert, 1993). This is even discernible in American and western traditions.[1] For example, there is a profound difference in corporate structures and practices between and within Europe and the U.S.A. (Hampden-Turner & Trompenaars, 1993; Thurow, 1992; Chandler, 1990; Herrigel, 1996), and even in highly individualistic, capitalistic, democratic and liberal societies like Australia and the U.S.A., corporate governance practices are different. Indeed, this has been widely recognised and acknowledged. The OECD (Organisation for Economic Co-operation and Development), for example, boldly proclaims in the preamble to its 'Principles of Corporate Governance', that 'There is no single model of good corporate governance' (www.oecd.org/daf/governance/principle.html).

Despite this claim and recognition that there are diverse business systems, academics and analysts alike have sought to maintain the fiction that there is only one route to good corporate governance. This is most marked in the literature and criticisms of corporate and corporate governance practices in developing and transitional economies. China, for example, has been regularly castigated for its record and performance and yet businesses have scrambled for access to its large emerging market. Because of this, the Chinese government has sought to reinvent itself and embrace corporate governance as a means of developing its rapidly emerging private sector. The Chinese approach to corporate governance, as Tam (1999) argued, is flawed and has certainly not been effective. In transplanting a stylised American system into China, it is unnecessarily top-down, legalistic and fails to come to terms with China's economic institutions and history.

This paper seeks to contribute to an understanding of the issue of corporate governance in China. It seeks to challenge the monolithic and one-dimensional proclaimed truth of the 'one true road' to corporate governance. The paper begins with a genealogical discussion of the concept of corporate governance. It argues that current approaches to corporate governance are culturally specific and is rooted in an idealised 'American' view of the world. The paper points to other possible constructions of corporate practices; in particular the institutional settings through which corporate structures and practices have evolved in different economies and societies. It next examines the Chinese approach to corporate governance in its emerging corporate sector. In the process, it seeks to highlight some of the critical and salient issues impacting on Chinese enterprises. The paper also suggests some possible directions, which China and its corporate sector might take as it seeks to maintain its sustainable economic development and reform.

CORPORATE GOVERNANCE: AMBIGUOUS AND CULTURALLY CONSTRUCTED

Over the last 20 years, the term 'corporate governance' has gained greater currency (Hopt, Kanda, Roe, Wymeesch, & Prigge, 1999; Shleifer & Vishny, 1998; 1997). The global drive towards privatisation opened up new arenas for concern, but the Asian financial crisis of 1997 propelled the idea of corporate governance to the frontline of change and soon, it dominated business discourses globally. 'Cronyistic and corrupt' Asia was beseeched to emulate the 'clean, ethical, accountable and robust' corporate systems in western societies (Backman, 1999; Delhaise, 1998) but as recent events in the U.S.A., Australia, Japan and elsewhere have shown, the issues of the reliability, credibility and efficacy of clean and transparent corporate systems and practices are not confined to Asia, but also to western, advanced industrial economies (Chew, 1997; Clarke, Dean, & Oliver, 1997).[2]

Emanating from the U.S.A., corporate governance has now become part of the business lexicon. Although it has become very much voguish, it is nevertheless rather ambiguous in both its intent and practice (Keasey, Thompson, & Wright, 1997; Manne, 1982). As Farrar (2001, p. 3) points out, 'it (corporate governance) has been used to refer to control of corporations and to systems of accountability by those in control', and is capable of being subsumed under broader concepts of contractual and social governance. It refers to legislations impacting on corporations, but has become increasingly expansive and now incorporates practices and arrangements of *de facto* control of companies, including self-regulatory codes of practices and business ethics. In a wide sense, it encompasses 'the entire network of formal and informal relations involving the corporate sector and their consequences for society in general' (Keasey et al., 1997, p. 2). Clearly then, corporate governance is not only an evolving concept, but is also tied in with the notion of corporations and their practices within the wider society.

Corporations do not exist in a vacuum; they develop within society, its laws and its practices. Historically, corporations were social organisations established to pursue the 'public benefit', however defined (Hurst, 1970; Monks & Minow, 1995); over time, they evolved into associations of individuals and became viewed as separate legal entities, enjoying its own sovereignty (Samuels, 1987; Fama, 1980; Demestz & Lehn, 1985). Of late, because of the changing nature of share ownership (including the role of institutional shareholders) and growing public interest, there has been a clear shift to see corporations as embedded within an elaborate nexus of contracts. This suggests a shift in locus of power and accountability and that shareholders do not necessarily and uniformly share interests and objectives e.g. between individual and institutional shareholders. It also points to a more complicated set of arrangements which while maintaining and privileging the shareholders (owners), point to the web of existing relationships between corporations and different stakeholders (including creditors, employees, consumers and even local communities).[3] The *telos* of corporate governance has accordingly shifted and to suggest therefore that there is only one form of corporate governance practice that is clearly not borne out by its historical evolution. Indeed, as numerous writers have pointed out, corporate structures depend in part on the structures with which the economy evolved (Whitley, 1999; OECD, 1999; Hollingsworth & Boyer, 1997; Roe, 1997; Bebchuk & Roe, 1999).[4] These structures also shape and affect the parameters in terms of engagement with and within the economy, in particular, the various interest groups that determine the rules of practices (Unger, 1976; Domhoff, 1979; Dan-Cohen, 1986; Kelsey, 1995).

As companies developed and adapted to the corporate form, shares were issued, traded, and increasingly, the ownership and control became de-linked. This gave management great power and provoked public wariness (Berle & Means, 1968; Hurst, 1970; Williams, 2000). In order to ensure that there were no systemic abuses by managers, legislations on fiduciary restraints, disclosure regimes and directors' duties were developed, and the notion of corporate governance gained greater circulation, salience, credibility and eventually, entrenched as part of corporate practices of public-listed companies in 'advanced', sophisticated market economies. In these economies, the proportion of shares held by intermediaries/institutions were generally small, both for fiduciary reasons and to retain liquidity, so that they are not locked into the fate of particular firms and as such, exposed only to limited risks. Since the end of the Second World War, this changed and fund managers and related institutions grew in numbers and strength; they also increasingly began to realise, assert and exercise their powers (Gates, 1998; Stapleton, 1998; Lazonick & O'Sullivan, 1996; Stapleton, 1996; Baum & Stiles, 1965). These institutional arrangements are often significant, as they set *de facto* performance standards, particularly via growth and financial indicators and also affect long-term relationships resulting in elaborate cross-holdings and interlocking directorships, which enable them to exercise considerable power and influence at board levels (Herman, 1981). Potentially, these relationships engender conflicts of interest in group transactions. These images, commonly associated with crony capitalism in 'third world' countries, are surprisingly also common in many western countries, including Australia, France, New Zealand, Canada and the U.S.A. (van der Berghe and de Ridder, 1999; Stapleton, 1998; Farrar, 1987; Daniels & Morck, 1995). Corporate governance principles and practices, as such, became a *de facto* vehicle for protecting minority shareholders' interests.

Clearly, the idea of a corporate governance, where all shareholders have an equal voice and vote, has some way to be realised in either 'western', sophisticated markets or the 'wild capitalist' transition and emerging economies; the volume of shares held are still determinative and in the hands of institutional voters and proxies, often decisive in effecting strategies, policies and outcomes. As a concept, corporate governance as such, is more an ideal rather than a reality in most economies.

THE NORTH AMERICAN HEGEMONY

Ronald Coase's paper 'Nature of the Firm' sets the agenda for much of the reworking of corporate governance (Coase, 1937). According to him and his followers, the corporation is a distinct species of firm, which carried out production in modern western economies. It is also a method of raising substantial amounts of capital, enabling both an elaborate organisation and a team of professional management to pursue growth economies in transaction costs. In conjunction with the growth of limited liability, corporate firms grew rapidly; management and ownership diverge and evolve into separate spheres of specialisation. Via the elected board of directors, owners exercise their control internally (Fama & Jensen, 1983; Lazonick & O'Sullivan, 1996; Williams, 2000) while the market flexes its control externally. This is usually manifested in the firms' capacity to attract investment capital which rewards management efficiencies (which in turn affects their competitiveness and survival prospects as take-over bids) and capabilities (via reward systems and also as in the articulation and circulation of management as a resource and a commodity). Auditors and other fiduciary statutes augment these control measures.

In its current form, corporate governance is both influenced and shaped by a North American ethos and a focus on large public-listed companies. There is the notion of a triumphalist, universalising and civilising influence of North American governance and governing practices replicated on a global scale.[5] But as Bebchuk and Roe (1999) so perceptively and cogently argue, despite the forces of globalisation and the quest for greater global efficiency, key differences have persisted and could well continue in the future, the evidence clearly supports that. In the 'west', there are a range of business organisations – ranging from public-listed companies to small and medium-sized enterprises and the private limited liability companies to public corporations. The notion and the practices of corporate governance therefore differ accordingly, but most analyses have approached the issue of corporate governance in a uncritical and undifferentiated manner. This has meant a narrowing of the terms of the debate and a failure to understand the different cultural logics of different businesses (Clarke & Clegg, 1998; Kristensen, 1997; Clarke & Bostock, 1994; Best, 1990; Chandler, 1990).[6]

Moreover, the concept of the corporation as a separate legal person and the privileging of shareholders are clearly not universally shared.[7] Moreover, empirical evidence does not validate its efficacy (Clarke & Clegg, 1998; Clarke et al., 1997). In Europe, corporate practices have tended to recognise a broader range of stakeholders interests and sought to incorporate employees' interests into its business calculus (Freeman, 1984; Balling, 1993; Charkham, 1994; Clark & Bostock, 1997; Plender, 1997; Hopt & Wymeersch, 1997; Waddock & Graves, 1997; Franks & Mayer, 2001).[8] In Japan and parts of Asia, duties and responsibilities of corporations towards society are also given due emphasis (Charkham, 1994: chapter 3; Gerlach,

1992; Westney, 1996; Kanda, 1997) and business groups (*keiretsus*) play important roles in corporate governance (Sheard, 1994; Berglof & Perotti, 1994; Prowse, 1992; Hoshi, Kashyap, & Scharfstein, 1991; Aoki, 1990; Nishiyama, 1984). Kenichi Ohmae (1982) for example, suggests that in Japan, the concept of a corporation is fundamentally different. According to him, 'Japanese chief executives, when asked what they consider their main responsibility, will say that they work for the well-being of their people. Stockholders do not rank much higher than banks in their list of concerns' (Ohmae, 1982, pp. 218–219, see also Kang & Shivdasani, 1995). These varying practices have prompted some writers to suggest that economic and legal practices are rooted, shaped and affected by prevailing social and cultural institutions and cannot simply be wished away (North, 1990; Whitley, 1992; Wheeler, 1994; Orru, 1997; Hollingsworth & Boyer, 1997; Whitley, 1999).

Colin Mayer (1994) has suggested that there are broadly two clearly discernible systems – the outsider-based system epitomised by the 'American' strand (including the U.K., Australia and New Zealand) and the insider-based strand, exemplified by Germany, Japan and other West European countries. The former works through an active 'external' market for shares which moderates, monitors and evaluates the corporations and their systems of governance. The latter, on the other hand is characterised by long-term stable relationships and cross-shareholdings. Concerns have, however, been expressed that these 'ideal-types' neglect many other emerging and transitional economies (Tam, 1999). Tam, in fact, argues that it is possible to delineate other possible systems – that of the insider control system and dominant in Eastern Europe and a complex, emerging system in China (Tam, 1999, p. 32; see also Whitley, 1999). Recent research had not only validated these observations, but they go further. They point out that the commonly held view of the separation between ownership and control in public listed corporations is a myth. Many of the largest corporations are family controlled and there is very little distinction made between ownership and management (La porta, Lopez-de-Silanes, Shleifer, & Vishny (1998a); La Porta, Lopez-de-Silanes, Shleifer & Vishny (1998b); La Porta, Lopez-de-Silanes & Shleifer, 1999).[9] Despite popular perception, Demestz (1983) and La Porta et al. (1998a, b, 1999) also found that concentration of ownership and control exists in western developed countries, including among the largest American corporations. Similar trends are discerned in Australia. These research findings are of grave concern for they suggest that contrary to the popular public view of greater public regulation, accountability and control, many large contemporary businesses are in fact governed by a small, interlocking oligarchic elite (Lazonick, 1991). As such, calls for reforms are largely ineffectual.

A related concern of current systems of governance is the issue of regulation. Present systems of corporate governance are essentially self-regulatory regimes despite the misnamed 'outsider-based system' of the 'American' model. Ostensibly market-derived and driven, this model privileges the discipline of market forces, which it argues is both flexible and the most efficient method of regulation and governance. Its roots lie in the notion of the corporation as a private person and as such, its affairs are self-regarding and should be autonomous and independent of the heavy hand of the state. The state (and governments) play minimal roles; essentially, they ensure and maintain law and order and enable market conditions to flourish. According to this minimalist view, the privately elected board of directors, because of their skills, expertise and knowledge, should be left free to tend to, manage and exercise their powers; all other considerations are superfluous. The market is supreme, but as has been pointed out, there is the question whether self-regulation can be adequate especially when there is an oligarchic elite and where the power of stakeholders, society, and other groups, cannot be exercised directly, and where prudential and regulatory bodies find themselves unequal to the task of implementing controls effectively (as is evident in recent corporate collapses in many western democratic countries). The debate still rages on and remains unresolved. Defendants of the market will, of course, rationalise and argue that these very collapses demonstrate the veracity and truth claims of market forces at work. In the meantime, however, stakeholders are adversely affected and often pay the penalty of 'moral hazards', in the form of levies and taxes.[10]

CORPORATE GOVERNANCE IN CHINA:
AN OVERVIEW

The Chinese notion of corporate governance is intricately linked to and dictated by the economic modernisation of China. Since 1978, China has been moving from a planned to a market-oriented economy. Reforms introduced have been gradual, incremental and even experimental in contrast with the 'big bang' approach of Eastern Europe. The reform process often utilised intermediate mechanisms to minimise disruption and to effect a smooth transition,[11] and also gradually increasing market channels and practices (e.g. in market determination of prices and allocation of resources and via the dual track system). Economic decision-making has been progressively decentralised to local authorities and the state has actively (and rather successfully) promoted the development of the non-state sector (Perkins, 1994; Naughton, 1996; World Bank, 1997; Steinfeld, 1998; Nolan, 2001; Chang, 2002; Chow, 2003). Managers, since the introduction of the Enterprise Laws in 1988, can now even be elected, although more often are appointed (Simon, 1996). These managers are also given more autonomy and made responsible for decision-making. This has led to extensive investment in the industrial sector and the economy has registered average growth rates of and above 10% over the last 20 years. Today, even as the economy slows, growth rate is steady and remains relatively high at around 8%.

Despite these impressive figures, reform outcomes have been mixed. At the macro-level, China has experienced strong growth with burgeoning exports, high domestic demand and improved technology (Naughton, 1996). At the micro-level, state-owned enterprises (SOEs) seemed to have improved their productivity and economic efficiency (Jefferson & Xu, 1991; McMillan & Naughton, 1992; Jefferson, Rawski, & Zheng, 1994; Groves et al., 1994, 1995). China continues to suffer from a rather 'under-developed' financial system and a need to transform its predominantly State-Owned Enterprises (SOEs) into more efficient and profitable market-oriented enterprises. Financial reforms in China have tended to focus on institutional development (including liberalisation of the operations of financial institutions) and creating (new) markets (Mehran, Quintyn, Nordman, & Laurens, 1996; Qi, Wu, & Zhang, 2000).[12] The reforms have not changed the fact that the financial system remains dominated by banks, particularly state-owned institutions, which have often been directed to lend funds to inefficient state enterprises, resulting in non-performing loans (Chang, 2002; Li, 1994). Besides, there are serious questions regarding the efficacy of loan portfolios, supervision and regulation of the banking sector. Apart from seeking to develop more efficient financial markets and new financial institutions to take on the responsibility of ushering in reforms, the state in China has to develop systems and practices to replace direct administrative economic control mechanisms with more market-oriented macroeconomic levers.

Similarly, the concerns over SOEs range over its operational effectiveness, performances and its transparency. Although the relative size of the SOE sector has decreased considerably (in 1978, it accounted for about 78% of the gross value of industrial output), it is still by far the most significant urban employer in China. It is also closely linked to the banking sector through the credit plan, accounting for well over two-thirds of domestic credit. It features prominently in budgetary operations, providing one-fourth of the state's revenues and receiving substantial operating subsidies (Chang, 2002; Naughton, 1996). The overall financial performance of the SOE sector has remained weak, and has caused grave concerns within China.[13]

In order to satisfactorily resolve the need for more reforms and the demands for a more open and friendly market, the Chinese government in the mid-1990s sought to establish a system of corporate governance to woo international capital and investment. It reasoned that with the development of this 'new' system, confidence and credibility could be built up and maintained, and recent policy pronouncements have made corporate governance a key plank in the country's reform and transformation agenda.

Since 1993, the Chinese government has sought to develop a modern corporate system. Via the 14th Congress of the Chinese Communist Party (CCP), decisions called for the establishment of modern corporation as a key enterprise reform measure. It also placed emphasis on reorganising SOEs into legal entities through corporatisation[14] and the need to clarify property rights.[15] This reform agenda (*zhua da fang siao*) further developed into the adoption of a more liberal and open interpretation of public ownership reform at the 15th Congress in 1997. It now includes a mix of state and collective (group) ownership.[16] Significantly, it signals the critical import of ownership, control and rights,[17] and was reaffirmed and further enlarged in 1999. In *Some Important Decisions on the Reform and Development of State Owned Enterprises*, the Chinese government argues that the state via its ownership as a shareholder, can still maintain control over enterprises (McGregor, 2001).

These reforms have shaped the development of China's regulatory framework and are enshrined in China's Company Law. This Law provides a relatively clear set of specifications for the distribution of decision-making powers among shareholders, board of directors and managers, thus institutionalising shareholder control in the shareholding companies (Tam, 1999; You, 1998; World Bank, 1997). Tam has argued that in doing so, the Chinese government conveniently ignores history and the structural outcomes and interplay of forces between investors, owners and control. It is also highly prescriptive, and critically fails to recognise the import of such legislation – that other critical elements of this system – an independent legal system, competitive markets for corporate control and self-regulation – are absent and are not actively developed or fostered.

CONVERGENCE CONFUSION AND A LACK OF REFLEXIVITY?

China's recent entry to the World Trade Organisation (WTO) is a most significant event. It marks the integrative forces of economic globalisation. The principal driving forces of this global change (on China and other countries in the world) have been: capital market imbalances, innovations in information and computer technologies, a global push towards deregulation and a new emphasis on business management, risk management and flexible practices (including networks, joint ventures and strategic alliances) (Castells, 2000; Child & Faulkner, 1998; Thurow, 1999; Clarke & Clegg, 1998; Nalebuff & Branderburger, 1996; Ohmae, 1995; Reich, 1992). These forces prompt financial investors, national governments and regulators to seek a new, more effective and comprehensive economic architecture to facilitate and improve greater transparency, accountability and more effective regulation of economic, business and financial markets.[18] This of course led to a revamping of GATT (General Agreement on Trade and Tariffs), giving birth to the WTO and its attendants' agreements and protocols, including the General Agreement on Trades and Services (GATS).

It has been claimed that nation states are not effective in regulating their own economic activities and that they are further subjected to the disciplining logic of the competitive global capital market. Managerial practices, accordingly have converged to realise the most efficient and uniform form of practice. Corporate governance is similarly affected by this same set of considerations, and not surprisingly, the American model, with its emphasis on laws, rules and regulations, is privileged and embraced. This model has a tendency to be reductionistic and confines itself to questions of method, housekeeping practices and maintaining a minimalist obligatory business ethical practice. In an otherwise perceptive analysis, Michael Backman (1999) has extended and applied this model to the 1997 Asian financial crisis. According to him, the crisis arose due to poor prevailing corporate governance practices. His prescriptions for change, not surprisingly, articulated the 'American' mode as a panacea, which ironically, in 2001 and 2002, has seen spectacular corporate collapses. Minimalist legislative changes clearly are not effective; the spirit and substance of good corporate practice is elusive and may not be attainable – standards and practices will differ from persons to persons and organisations to organisations. Indeed, in so far as the international economy does continue to become more integrated, it can be argued that societies with different institutional arrangements will continue to develop and reproduce varied systems of economic organization with different economic and social capabilities (Orru, 1997; North, 1990).[19]

Studies of cross-national variations in governance mechanisms in nine industries reveal considerable national differences in the prevalence of markets, hierarchies, networks, states and associations as institutions regulating economic exchanges. Such variations reflected longstanding contrasts in the characteristics of national legal systems, political and financial systems (Hollingsworth, Schmitter, & Streeck, 1994). Therefore, despite legislations, formal compliance of corporate governance regulations will not be effected unless these 'ethereal' and substantive issues are resolved.

In the case of China, this manifests itself in the different meanings of corporate governance in China, its scope and its contents, making operational decisions difficult. It has, in public pronouncements, been variously seen as a new and modern way of management while for some, it is a set of procedures and structures enabling owners and regulators to supervise managers. This confusion, Tam suggests, is because of the Chinese language itself. There are no precise terms in the Chinese language for corporate governance but the preferred current nomenclature, *farenzhilijiegou* (which has been officially adopted by the CCP in 1999) is more suggestive of administering and supervisory roles. More critical is the lack of reflexivity, that is, the term is used without an appreciation of its context and evolution. Corporate governance does not arise in a vacuum – it has an accompanying history and is shaped by institutional thinking and practices.[20]

The Chinese model of corporate governance as it stands, fails to contextualise and appreciate this critical institutional insight. As such, it is a historical, stylised, highly prescriptive, legalistic and partial. It originated as a tool used in reforming SOEs through corporatisation and *de facto* privatisation (both partial and complete) of these enterprises, but its effects have yet to be clearly thought through. Operationally, it has not been effective and has not achieved its desired objectives: the Chinese government confuses form with substance – installing the nominal structures of governance is not synonymous with that of a fully functioning system. Prevailing social structures and conventions not only have consequences for the ways that particular systems of economic coordination and control develop, but also greatly influence the 'rules of the game' according to which individuals and organisations make 'rational' decisions about investments and compete (North, 1990; Orru, 1997). In embracing the 'American' orthodoxy, the Chinese government has in effect, elevated and privileged a particularistic view. Market forces have taken on a *deux ex machina* role operating in a social and cultural vacuum. Moreover, this view is essentially static ignoring dynamic costs and learning; the rules and practices of governance have to be learnt, tested, refined, internalised and seemingly 'naturalised'.

Be that as it may, the Chinese government needs to push on for greater reforms. As indicated above, there are varying practices in governance and they have evolved historically. Adopting what is seemingly imported 'best practices' simply does not work. For example, in the west, a plethora of measures aimed at improving corporate governance – separation of the position of board chairman and the CEO, increasing the proportion of non-executive directors on the board, providing share options, increasing disclosure and 'transparency' etc., have all not met with the unmitigated success they are supposed to deliver. Recent corporate failures clearly attest to doubts over the effectiveness and rationale of these measures.[21]

In promoting enterprise reforms, the Chinese government should be aware that even in the American tradition, governance for financial firms and non-financial firms have trekked substantively different paths and if they are not expected to converge even in the American model (Chandler, 1990; Fligstein, 1990; Campbell & Lindberg, 1991; Dobbin, 1994), the Chinese should seriously question the 'one size fits all' model articulated by investors and enthusiastic proponents of corporate reform.

Moreover, a concentration on SOEs reforms fail to recognise that the non-state sector, particularly the private enterprises sector (comprising small and medium-sized enterprises) are now significant economic and industrial agents within China's economic transformation. China's present economic landscape is too heterogeneous with a broad range of organisational forms, practices, activities, scale and scope. Corporate reforms instituted needs to recognise that these firms have varying needs and practices and the formalistic and unitary corporate (governance) model could effectively stifle their growth and participation in modern China's economic, business and financial transition and development. The danger is that these 'intermediaries' may be too active in corporate governance within these firms, obviating any perceived and real advantages; it would be business as usual.[22]

This is not to argue that there is no need for reforms. The contrary is true especially in the current context when the government is seeking to offload the state banks' bad debts through various schemes of debt-equity swaps and the establishment of financial intermediaries to help state-owned financial assets from the corporatisation and privatisation of SOEs. This has led Gordon Chang (2002) to caution the one-dimensional and enthusiastic response to China's ascension to the WTO; the 'barbs' are there and one can readily be choked and lacerated in the process.

WHERE TO NOW?

van der Berghe and de Ridder suggest that another model of corporate governance is possible. According to the authors, this new model must take cognisance of changes in our industrial and working practices and lives. We have, as they argue, evolved into a post-industrial society characterised by knowledge work. In this new economy, employees will be empowered and there will be a corresponding shift of power towards knowledge workers. They also point to the centrality and import of shared corporate values (van der Berghe & de Ridder, 1999, chapter 4, see also Clarke & Clegg, 1998, chapter 6; Child & Faulkner, 1998; Wheeler, 1998; Plender, 1997; Aoi, 1997; Teubner, 1997). While useful, their suggestions need to be more expansive – institutional investors and their roles and duties must similarly be interrogated for they are important players in effecting change and practices.[23] Notwithstanding these remarks, adopting a universal and uniform model of corporate governance is not recommended. Like the OECD (1998), we need to recognise that practices will not be static but evolving and will vary in and between countries and cultures. Moreover, institutional settings and arrangements are critical variables as they impact on ownership structures, market conditions, corporate life cycle and business practices, which all impact directly on corporate governance practices. However, as a minimum, good corporate governance practices must embrace:

1. An alignment of shareholder and other stakeholder interests;
2. Increased transparency and independent oversight of management by an independent and accountable board of directors;
3. An adoption of universal rules in certain areas for example, accounting and disclosure requirements;
4. The need for independent, sound and transparent audit practices made readily and publicly available;
5. The equitable treatment of shareholders;
6. The recognition of societal interests and the definition and transparency over firms' non-economic objectives; and
7. The need for effective compliance and enforcement mechanisms.

Because the Chinese economy is growing and increasingly dependent on foreign capital investment, the Chinese government has sought to soothe over concerns of international investors by moving from a credit-based financial system (with its large, dominant long-term credit banks and financial institutions) towards that of a capital-market based financial system (Zysman, 1983; Cox, 1986).[24] The Chinese authorities clearly recognise that capital shortages during high-growth periods, and state control of interest rates to support economic development are often inadequate to meet the demand for investment fund and can be detrimental to the state's own economic agenda. Moreover, in such a system, since shares are not easily traded, owners, bankers and managers become locked into particular borrowers' fates and so have to be more involved in decision-making and the detailed evaluation of investment plans than they have to do in capital-market-based systems.

To address the issue of corporate reform, as it pertains to large public-listed corporations in China,[25] corporate governance practices in China need to deal with two special problems – the issue of manager's capabilities, capacities and discretion and that of raising badly needed external capital to effect technology upgrades, financial restructuring and corporate transformations. It has recognised the problem of transition economies and 'insiders' control of enterprises, and has sought to achieve a separation of ownership and regulatory functions of the state from the management of the enterprises. While a useful and critical first step, the government needs to push this reform agenda further. It needs to promote greater economic efficiency, and this could be done through legislative changes requiring portfolio diversification and greater competition.[26] In the process, this could unwittingly graft a new and different corporate practice,[27] and thus serve as an effective response in a globalising economy characterised by a unifying and singular practice populated with dense, global networks and alliances.

As China searches and seeks to introduce corporate governance arrangements into its present regulatory framework, it is imperative that it takes stock of possible effects of similar measures in an environment with vastly different institutional practices and arrangements. The environment could foster 'feral' and even fatal responses and China can learn much from the evolution of corporate governance. Corporate governance announced and proclaimed by *fiat*, does not necessarily work and can be counter-productive. Institutional arrangements and practices are critical and shape the way in which corporate governance is thought of, conceived and practised. In particular, the extent to which property rights' owners, and the economic actors they control, feel able to rely on impersonal institutionalised procedures when making business commitments is a crucial factor in the establishment of collaborative relations within and between firms. It also affects the perception and management of risk and trust.

In the Chinese case, the Chinese state like many late industrialising economies, continues to play a major role in coordinating economic development and market regulation. Business development tends to be highly dependent on the state. However, the degree of state involvement is neither prescribed nor guaranteed. Where the state is less directly involved in the economy through ownership and credit allocation, businesses can be more autonomous. This is certainly true for the SMEs sector in China. Conversely, when the state is more involved in regulating market entry and exit and is promoting partnership arrangements, there is often a lot more bargaining and negotiation with strong institutionalised procedures limiting opportunistic behaviour. Indeed, SOEs and other market reforms seem to suggest that China is heading down this route, particularly as it seeks to woo foreign investment (in capital-intensive industries) and accordingly, recalibrate its corporate governance procedures and mechanisms. In implementing and embracing these 'new' procedures, the Chinese government is seeking to engender trust and to signal, its continual evolution to a market economy, albeit one with Chinese characteristic, conducive to collaboration between economic actors where the Chinese government could and promote itself as a major (outside) institutional and block shareholder and investor.[28] While there may be a greater level of risk than fund managers in highly liquid capital markets and less likely to delegate high level of strategic control to managers, they will be more inclined to intervene directly in managerial matters when performance drops significantly. In a developing economy, this could stabilise entry and exit options, foster greater cooperation, collaboration and interdependence within particular sectors, and therefore, potentially mutually advantageous.

CONCLUSION

Contemporary discussions on corporate governance are steeped in the 'American mode' and typically, it posits the view that mechanisms of governance are necessary where capital raising extends beyond the immediate capacity of management. In other words, corporate governance is derived from the separation of ownership and management. As this paper has pointed out, this is one view and does not correspond with corporate realities in many parts of the world – indeed, corporate governance practices are not homogenous but the American model is dominant. The reality is different e.g. in Europe, U.K., Australia, Japan and myriad other countries, and that the much touted 'American' model of corporate governance is in actuality, an idealised form. Clearly then, the options for a more engaged and critical corporate governance regime exist and the case of China, with an emerging market economy and different organizational forms, offers the

Chinese government an opportunity to reshape corporate governance practices and principles. Instead, they have adopted an expedient programme of change and confined themselves to the corporate model of separation of ownership and management, thus missing the opportunity to develop a far broader understanding and practice of governance, particularly as it relates to emerging entrepreneurial firms in the Chinese economy.

From the foregoing discussion, I have argued that good corporate governance systems and practices cannot be merely legislated for nor is there a singular model. There is no perfect or best system; it involves tradeoffs between competing goals and as such, can only involve 'second best' options. Moreover, institutional arrangements are all-pervasive and highly influential in effecting economic directions and outcomes (Roe, 1994). Therefore, despite the global economy, a singular mode of governance is unlikely. A singular mode of corporate governance would require a reorganisation of central institutional structures and relationships, as well as a restructuring of interest-group relations and perhaps, of their constitution and organisation. This is unlikely to be realised given the different social and economic histories of countries and very strong held beliefs of political arrangements e.g. sovereignty, individualism, liberalism and collectivism, and that adoption of specific corporate governance practices may be politically driven (Sternberg, 1994). The diversity, interactions and changes in the increasingly complex global economic system will also engender different adaptations ensuring varying practices and arrangements. Thus, rather than proclaiming 'the end of history' and a universal mode of corporate governance, we need to be more circumspect and seek to locate our understandings of particular economies within their specificities (O'Sullivan, 2000). In the context of corporate governance, this means a move away from abstract, idealised forms and a commitment to historical and institutional contexts and realities. This would require us therefore, to undertake the task of continually and constantly developing, adapting and rewriting corporate governance practices capable of meeting our new needs and challenges.

In this paper, in critically examining the discursive practices imbricated with the notion of corporate governance, I have sought to employ it as a foil to facilitate, stimulate and hopefully, engender new thoughts on the relationships between corporate practices, business systems and governance, rather than seeing the notion of corporate governance as a mere disciplining economic tool preoccupied solely with the profit margins. The structures, practices and systems engendered through a reworking of corporate practices (including corporate governance) could lead to significant qualitatively different workplaces, work and social values.

NOTES

1. Despite claims of a growing convergence of 'global capitalism', the ways in which economic activities are organised in different economies suggest different systems of economic organisation persists and exist (Kristensen, 1997). Indeed, even in the U.S.A. there is the recognition that American capitalism is uneven and manifests different characteristics (Hollingsworth, 1991; Lindberg & Campbell, 1991; Chandler, 1990; Fligstein, 1990). Dobbin (1994) has also demonstrated the importance of state actions in the development of different economic ideologies and coordination systems. Herrigel (1996) has also shown that in Germany, different kinds of industrial order have characterised different regions of Germany and accordingly, impacted on regional forms of production and development. Lazonick, in his formulation of a more general approach to economic development and competitiveness, for example, suggests that there are at least three varieties of capitalism: proprietary, managerial and collective.

2. Clarke et al. (1997) have consistently raised these issues of credibility and reliability pointing out that the charter of accounts and financial statements do not reflect real-time transactions.

3. In Australia, this is perhaps best seen in the corporate collapses of Ansett Airlines, HIH Insurance and OneTel. Of course, there were the earlier cases of Alan Bond, Laurie Connell and Christopher Skase of the 1980s. Clarke et al. (1997) have argued that corporate collapses in Australia results from poor professional regulations and standards, particularly in accounting and auditing procedures, practices and education (for a critique of corporate excesses and practices, see Tomasic & Bottomley, 1993). In a 1997 study, Australian directors overwhelmingly consider shareholders as their first priority (74%) in their consideration of stakeholders. Employees were not part of their deliberations and the company featured over 20% while customers rated less than 5% (Francis, 1997, pp. 353–354). The evidence on stakeholders interests and financial performance have been mixed.

4. Clearly, there are numerous examples globally. See van der Berghe and Ridder (1999) but in Australia, one can also discern similar forms of evolution. For example, in the 19 century, 'banking capitalism', where banks finance businesses usually through debt financing, was a common practice atleast until the 1930s (Ma & Morris, 1982; Sykes, 1988; Bryan & Rafferty, 1999). This then shifted to a period of public ownership with its concomitant legislations on fiduciary restraints and directors' duties. The opening up of the Australian financial markets in 1983, the rise in institutional strengths and the crash of 1987 saw a shift towards corporate reform. Corporate governance, with an emphasis on self-regulation, became widely articulated. One could have cynically argued that this was a pre-emptive strike against new and possibly more restrictive legislations.

5. It must be pointed out that the U.S.A. does not have a uniform approach to corporate laws although much of securities regulation is federal (Jordan, 1997). States in the U.S.A. each have their own separate law jurisdiction and its own business corporations act and tend to adopt a competitive approach towards legislative control, compliance and penalties.

6. For a discussion of the issues of SMEs, see Dugan, McKenzie and Patterson (2000) and Neubauer and Lank (1998); non-governmental organisations' issues are

covered in Hirshhorn (1995); McGregor-Lowdes, Fletcher and Sievers (1996). Public corporations and their governance are discussed fairly extensively. For some examples, see Duncan and Bollard (1992); Ashburner (1997); Collier and Pitkin (Eds) (1999); Joint Committee of Public Accounts and Audit Report (1999); Konig and Siedentopf (1988).

7. Williams (1999, p. 82), however, suggested that recently, both the west European and Japanese model are now changing and appear to be heading down the road of privileging shareholders value over and above stakeholders and other considerations.

8. The case of U.K. is particularly interesting as it seeks to 'harmonise' its laws and practices as required and provided for in the Treaty of Rome. There are and have been numerous studies on these aspects of integration – see Edwards (2001); Sugarman and Teubner (1990); Buxbaum and Hopt (1988) among others.

9. Among the more interesting findings, La Porta et al. (1998a, b, 1999) found globally were: many of the largest firms are controlled by families; in family-controlled firms, there is very little separation between ownership and control; family control is more common in countries with poor shareholder protection; state control is common, particularly in countries with poor shareholder protection; deviations from one share, one vote are most common in countries with poor shareholder protection; and corporations with controlling shareholders rarely have other large shareholders.

10. This is certainly true for Australia where levies have been introduced to meet the claims of 'stakeholders' arising out of corporate collapses, as a result of management and directors' decisions. While claiming to consider stakeholders' interests, American legislations and practices have largely been dismissive of stakeholders' claims; shareholders' interests have remained their primary (and almost exclusive) concern.

11. This has involved implementing the dual track system to improve the allocation of resources at the margin; establishing a swap market in foreign exchange retention rights to improve the use of foreign exchange; establishing special economic zones; using contract responsibility systems to stimulate market behaviour and practices and enabling local governments to enact and implement market-oriented programmes and legislations.

12. China's financial system can be characterised as a bank-dominated system, as much as Asia is. Typically, there is an absence of a well-developed capital market, and banks remain the dominant player within the system. They also tend to systematically under-price loans and to lend excessively to government-linked firms. The state is able to effect allocation decisions and thus able to intervene and influence the economic development path for the country (Drake, 1980).

13. SOEs employ a significant proportion the workforce and reforms inevitably will lead to greater and more efficient use of resources. This will result in retrenchment and the growing pool of unemployed could turn out to be a significant political problem. Gordon Chang (2002) suggests that in many instances, SOEs have often been playing 'musical chairs' – they are re-tagged private enterprises and sold off and thus appears to be off the public books. Chang claims that this sale is a mere transfer process and the same people and operations persist.

14. This involves transforming SOEs into profit making firms with share capital, initially held by the state. Managers were given decision-making powers, although they had no ownership stake in the firms. A significant numbers of these corporatised SOEs were later listed and traded on the stock exchanges; it was hoped that this

would allow for great managerial autonomy, discretion and accountability as managers were issued issues.

15. Reforms have included: the establishment of enterprises groups where some groups have been required to take over loss-making enterprises to help rationalise their operations; restructuring of SOEs via joint ventures with foreign direct investors and the introduction of corporate forms of ownership and management (including shareholding and the establishment of limited liability companies) (Naughton, 1996; Xu & Wang, 1999; Harvie & Naughton, 2000).

16. This collective (group) ownership includes partially privatised companies and joint ventures.

17. There was no equivalence for the term corporate governance in the Chinese language when it was first introduced and debated within China.

18. George Soros, a financial speculator and investor, one charged as the cause of the 1997 Asian financial crisis, has been vociferous in calling for a re-regulation of the global financial markets. According to him, the present system is inherently unstable and that more appropriate and rigorous supervisory practices and systems with enforcement powers need to be developed (Soros, 2000). The debate on international corporate governance has traditionally been dominated by concerns over transnational corporations and their practices. This has led the UN to develop and proclaim various codes of conduct but there was clearly no possible consensus. Since then, professional and non-governmental bodies (for example, the International Federation of Accountants, the International Accounting Standards Committee and the International Organisation of Securities Commission), have taken the lead and been active in pushing for new similar international standards and practices. Of course, the WTO and its various committees have now taken over this drive for global standardisation.

19. Firms are by no means the same sorts of economic actors in different economies – the ways in which private ownership is organized and connected to authority hierarchies – as well as how these latter hierarchies are structured – are able to delimit production and pricing levels and coordinate investment decisions of legally autonomous entities (Hamilton & Feenstra, 1997).

20. Indeed, the many myths surrounding the robustness of the American model has also been subject to critical scrutiny and debates in recent years. The journal, *Corporate Governance: An International Review*, for example, has in various issues canvassed the adequacy of the prevailing model.

21. Indeed, there is much that can be discussed but this would be beyond the purview of this paper. For example, the links between the proportion of non-executive directors and firms performances; the efficacy and the economic rationale of stock option as a method of executive compensation, among others.

22. Various studies have suggested that despite reforms, shareholder controls in China's listed companies remain weak; this is due to political control which negatively impacts on economic performances. See for example, Shleifer and Vishny (1994); Shleifer (1998); for the Chinese case, see the discussions in You (1998); Tam (1999); Xu & Wang (1999); McGregor (2001); Chang & Wong (2002).

23. Indeed, institutional investors can play critical role in effecting some form of change in corporate practices. Examples include the case of thalidomide, the case of apartheid and investment in South Africa and more recently, the concerns and

shareholder activism over Burma Nigeria and its abuses of human rights. Typically, institutional shareholders, usually behind the scenes, seek a change of corporate practices to offset risks to investment performance, failing which they will sell. While economically rational, it has the effect of disassociating itself from any responsibility, either as duty to other fellow shareholders and other groups, including the public, employees and consumers, and as such, it still maintains a minimal obligatory thrust. For discussion of their roles, see, Brancato (1997).

24. Although a number of financial systems do not fit into this broad dichotomy, this basic contrast has strong implications for firms and businesses and is a critical feature of the institutional context of business systems and practices (Iterson & Olie, 1992).

25. In the context of China, it is very hard to disentangle the public-private mix. Stat-owned enterprises (SOEs) have been publicly listed and many public-listed corporations similarly have significant state involvement, particularly through nominated individuals, organisations and share ownership.

26. This would not be unlike practices in some market economies e.g. Japan and even western Europe, where institutional ownership in corporations (such as financial intermediaries) is a common feature of major corporations. This does not mean that corporate governance is relinquished. For example, in Japan, a typical corporation is controlled by insiders because all board members are managers but managers can be replaced by the main bank when the corporation is in financial trouble.

27. In the American model, outsiders are typically active in corporate governance through their representations on the board while in other market economies, a typical corporation is controlled by insiders who can be replaced by the main financial investor (intermediary) when the corporation is in financial strife. In many transition economies, insiders (usually managers) have obtained substantial control of enterprises because of privatisation schemes or because of weak government supervision, and as such adversely affect their performances. In the case of China, China could therefore, have created a hybrid form of corporate governance where it marries the western European and Japanese models with its particularistic characteristics of 'state socialism'.

28. This would certainly be consistent with corporate experiences and practices in continental Europe, Japan and 'free market and transparent' Singapore.

ACKNOWLEDGMENT

I would particularly like to thank Kala Saravanamuttu and James Lockhart for their comments and the comments of other contributors at the Corporate governance conference.

REFERENCES

Albert, M. (1993). *Capitalism vs. capitalism: How America's obsession with individual achievement and short term profit has led it to the brink of collapse.* New York: Four Walls Eight Windows.

Aoi, J. (1997). To whom does the company belong? A new management mission for the information age. In: D. H. Chew (Ed.), *Studies in international corporate finance and governance systems*. New York: Oxford University Press.

Aoki, M. (1990). Toward an economic model of the Japanese firm. *Journal of Economic Literature, 28*, 1–27.

Ashburner, L. (1997). Corporate governance in the public sector: The case of the NHS. In: K. Keasey, S. Thompson & M. Wright (Eds), *Corporate governance – economic, management and financial issues*. Oxford: Oxford University Press.

Backman, M. (1999). *Asian eclipse: Exposing the dark side of business in Asia*. New York: Wiley.

Balling, M. (1993). *Financial management in the new Europe*. Cambridge, MA: Blackwell.

Baum, D. J., & Stiles, N. B. (1965). *The silent investors*. Syracuse, New York: Syracuse University Press.

Bebchuk, L. A., & Roe, M. J. (1999). A theory of path-dependence in corporate ownership and governance. *Stanford Law Review, 52*, 127–170.

Berglof, E., & Perotti, E. (1994). The governance structure of the Japanese financial keiretsu. *Journal of Financial Economics, 36*, 259–284.

Berle, A., & Means, G. (1968). *The modern corporation and private property* (Revised Edn). New York: Harcourt Brace & World.

Best, M. (1990). *The new competition: Institutions of industrial restructuring*. Oxford: Polity Press.

Brancato, C. K. (1997). *Institutional investors and corporate governance*. Chicago: Irwin.

Bryan, D., & Rafferty, M. (1999). *The global economy in Australia*. Sydney: Allen and Unwin.

Buxbaum, R., & Hopt, K. (1988). *Legal harmonisation and the business enterprise*. Berlin: Walter de Gruyter.

Campbell, J. L., & Lindberg, L. N. (1991). The evolution of governance regimes. In: J. L. Campbell, et al. (Eds), *Governance of the American economy*. Cambridge: Cambridge University Press.

Castells, M. (2000). Information technology and global capitalism. In: W. Hutton & A. Giddens (Eds), *Global capitalism*. New York: New Press.

Chandler, A. (1990). *Scale and scope*. Cambridge, Mass: Harvard University Press.

Chang, E., & Wong, S. (2002). Corporate governance, political interference and corporate performance of China's listed companies (mimeo).

Chang, G. (2002). *The coming collapse of China*. London: Arrow.

Charkham, J. (1994). *Keeping good company – A study of corporate governance in five countries*. Oxford: Clarendon Press.

Chew, D. H. (Ed.) (1997). *Studies in international corporate finance and governance systems*. New York: Oxford University Press.

Child, J., & Faulkner, D. (1998). *Strategies of cooperation – managing alliances, networks and joint ventures*. Oxford: Oxford University Press.

Chow, G. (2003). *China's economic transformation*. Princeton: Princeton University Press.

Clarke, F., Dean, G. W., & Oliver, K. G. (1997). *Corporate collapse: Regulatory, accounting and ethical failure*. Cambridge: Cambridge University Press.

Clarke, T., & Bostock, R. (1997). International corporate governance: Convergence and diversity. In: T. Clarke & E. Monkhouse (Eds), *Rethinking the company*. London: FT Pitman.

Clarke, T., & Clegg, S. (1998). *Changing paradigms*. London: HarperCollins Business.

Coase, R. (1937). The nature of the firm. *Economica, 4*, 387–405.

Collier, B., & Pitkin, S. (Eds) (1999). *Corporations and privatisation in Australia*. Sydney: CCH Australia.

Cox, A. (1986). State, finance and industry in comparative perspective. In: A. Cox (Ed.), *State, finance and industry*. Brighton: Wheatsheaf.

Dan-Cohen, M. (1986). *Rights, persons and organisations – A legal theory for bureaucratic society*. Stanford: Stanford University Press.

Daniels, R., & Morck, R. (Eds) (1995). *Corporate decision-making in Canada*. Calgary: University of Calgary Press.

Delhaise, P. F. (1998). *Asia in crisis: The implosion of the banking and finance systems*. New York: Wiley.

Demestz, H., & Lehn, K. (1985). The structure of corporate ownership: Causes and consequences. *Journal of Political Economy, 93*, 1155–1177.

Demestz, H. (1983). Corporate control, insider trading and rates of return. *American Eonomic Review, 86*, 313–316.

Dobbin, F. (1994). *Forging industrial policy: The United States, Britain and France in the railway age*. Cambridge: Cambridge University Press.

Domhoff, G. (1979). *The powers that be*. New York: Random House.

Drake, P. J. (1980). *Money, finance and development*. London: Wiley.

Dugan, R., McKenzie, P., & Patterson, D. (2000). *Closely held companies – legal and tax issues*. Auckland: CCH, New Zealand Ltd.

Duncan, I., & Bollard, A. (1992). *Corporatisation and privatisation – lessons from New Zealand*. Auckland: Oxford University Press.

Edwards, V. (2001). *EC company law*. Oxford: Oxford University Press.

Fama, E. F. (1980). Agency problems and the theory of the firm. *Journal of Political Economy, 88*, 288–307.

Fama, E. F., & Jensen, M. C. (1983). Separation of ownership and control. *Journal of Law and Economics, 26*, 301–325.

Farrar, J. (2001). *Corporate governance in Australia and New Zealand*. Oxford: Oxford University Press.

Farrar, J. H. (1987). Ownership and control of listed public companies – revising or rejecting the concept of control. In: B. Pettet (Ed.), *Company law in change*. London: Stevens & Sons.

Fligstein, N. (1990). *The transformation of corporate control*. Cambridge: Mass., Harvard University Press.

Francis, I. (1997). *Future directions – the power of the competitive board*. Melbourne: FT Pitman.

Franks, J., & Mayer, C. (2001). Ownership and control of German corporations. *Review of Financial Studies, 14*, 943–977.

Freeman, R. E. (1984). *Strategic management: A stakeholder approach*. Boston: Pitman.

Gates, J. (1998). *The ownership solution – towards a shared capitalism for the twenty-first century*. London: Penguin Books.

Gerlach, M. (1992). *Alliance capitalism*. Berkeley and Los Angeles: University of California Press.

Groves, T., Hong, Y., McMillan, J., & Naughton, B. (1994). Autonomy and incentives in Chinese state enterprises. *The Quarterly Journal of Economics, 109*, 183–209.

Groves, T., Hong, Y., McMillan, J., & Naughton, B. (1995). China's evolving managerial labour market. *Journal of Political Economy, 107*, 873–892.

Hamilton, G., & Feenstra, R. C. (1997). Varieties of hierarchies and markets: An introduction. In: M. Orru, et al. (Eds), *The economic organisation of East Asian capitalism*. London: Sage.

Hampden-Turner, C., & Trompenaars, F. (1993). *The seven cultures of capitalism.* London: Piatkus.

Herman, E. (1981). *Corporate control, corporate power.* New York: Cambridge University Press.

Herrigel, G. (1996). *Industrial constructions: The sources of German industrial power.* Cambridge: Cambridge University Press.

Hirshhorn, R. (1995). The governance of non-profits. In: R. Daniels & R. Morck (Eds), *Corporate decision-making in Canada.* Calgary: University of Calgary Press.

Hollingsworth, J. R. (1991). The logic of coordinating American manufacturing sectors. In: J. L. Campbell, et al. (Eds), *Governance of the American economy.* Cambridge: Cambridge University Press.

Hollingsworth, J. R., Schmitter, P., & Streeck, W. (Eds) (1994). *Governing capitalist economies.* Oxford: Oxford University Press.

Hollingsworth, J. R., & Boyer, R. (1997). *Comparing capitalisms: The embeddedness of institutions.* Cambridge: Cambridge University Press.

Hopt, K. J., & Wymeersch, E. (Eds) (1997). *Comparative corporate governance.* Berlin: Walter de Gruyter.

Hopt, K. J., Kanda, H., Roe, M. J., Wymeersch, E., & Prigge, F. S. (1999). *Comparative corporate governance – The state of the art and emerging research.* Oxford: Oxford University Press.

Hoshi, T., Kashpay, A., & Scharfstein, D. (1991). Corporate structure, liquidity and investment: Evidence from industrial groups. *Quarterly Journal of Economics, 106,* 33–60.

Hurst, J. W. (1970). *The legitimacy of the business corporation.* Charlottesville: University Press of Virginia.

Iterson, A. van, & Olie, R. (1992). European business systems: The Dutch case. In: R. Whitley (Ed.), *European business systems: Firms and markets in their national contexts.* London: Sage.

Jefferson, C., & Xu, W. (1991). The impact of reform on socialist enterprises in transition: Structure, conduct and performance in Chinese industry. *Journal of Comparative Economics, 15,* 45–64.

Jefferson, G. H., Rawski, T. G., & Zheng, Y. (1994). Enterprise reform in Chinese industry. *Journal of Economic Perspectives, 8,* 47–70.

Joint Committee of Public Accounts and Audit. (1999). Corporate governance and accountability for commonwealth government business enterprises. Report 372, Canberra, AGPS.

Jordan, C. (1997). International survey of corporate law in Asia, Europe, North America and the Commonwealth. Melbourne, Centre for Corporate Law and Securities Regulation.

Kanda, H. (1997). Corporate governance, country report: Japan. In: K. Hopt, et al. (Eds), *Comparative corporate governance – The state of the art and emerging research.* Oxford: Oxford University Press.

Kang, J., & Shivdasani (1995). Firm performance, corporate governance and top executive turnover in Japan. *Journal of Financial Economics, 38,* 29–58.

Keasey, K., Thompson, S., & Wright, M. (Eds) (1997). *Corporate governance – economic, management and financial issues.* Oxford: Oxford University Press.

Kelsey, J. (1995). *Economic fundamentalism.* London: Pluto Press.

Konig, K., & Siedentopf, P. (1988). An international perspective II: Privatisation and institutional modernisation in Asia and Europe. In: I. Thynne & M. Ariff (Eds), *Privatisation: Singapore's experience in perspective.* Longman: Singapore.

Kristensen, P. H. (1997). National systems of governance and managerial strategies in the evolution of work systems: Britain, Germany and Denmark compared. In: R. Whitley & P. H. Kristensen (Eds), *Governance at work: The social regulation of economic relations.* Oxford: Oxford University Press.

La Porta, R., Lopez-de-Silanes, F., Shleifer, A., & Vishny, R. (1998a). Corporate Ownership Around the World. National Bureau of Economic Research, Working Paper No 6625, Cambridge, Mass.

La Porta, R., Lopez-de-Silanes, F., Shleifer, A., & Vishny, R. W. (1998b). Law and finance. *Journal of Political Economy, 106,* 1113–1155.

La Porta, R., Lopez-de-Silanes, F., & Shleifer, A. (1999). Corporate governance around the world. *Journal of Finance, 54,* 471–518.

Lazonick, W. (1991). *Business organisation and the myth of the market economy.* Cambridge: Cambridge University Press.

Lazonick, W., & O'Sullivan, M. (1996). Organisation, finance and international competition. *Industrial and Corporate Change, 5,* 1–49.

Li, K. W. (1994). *Financial repression and economic reform in China.* Westport: Praeger.

Lindberg, L. N., & Campbell, J. L. (1991). The state and the organisation of economic activity. In: J. L. Campbell, et al. (Eds), *Governance of the American economy.* Cambridge: Cambridge University Press.

Ma, R., & Morris, R. D. (1982). *Disclosure and bonding practices of British and Australian banks in the nineteenth century.* Sydney: University of Sydney Accounting Research Centre.

Manne, H. G. (Ed.) (1982). *Corporate governance: Past and future.* New York: KCG Publications.

Mayer, C. (1994). Stock markets, financial institutions and corporate performance. In: N. Dimsdale & M. Preveser (Eds), *CapitaMarkets and corporate governance.* Oxford: Clarendon Press.

McGregor, R. (2001). *The little red book of business in China.* London: Financial Times.

McGregor-Lowdes, Fletcher, K., & Sievers, A. S. (Eds) (1996). *Legal issues for non-profit associations.* Sydney: Law Book Co.

McMillan, J., & Naughton, B. (1992). How to reform a planned economy: Lessons from China. *Oxford Review of Economic Policy, 8,* 130–143.

Mehran, M., Quintyn, M., Nordman, T., & Laurens, B. (1996). *Monetary and exchange reforms in China: An experiment in gradualism.* IMF Occasional Paper 141, Washington.

Monks, R. A. G., & Minow, N. (1995). *Corporate governance.* Cambridge, MA: Blackwell.

Nalebuff, B. J., & Brandenburger, A. M. (1996). *Co-opetition.* London: HarperCollins Business.

Naughton, B. (1996). *Growing out of the plan: Chinese economic reform.* New York: Cambridge University Press.

Neubauer, F., & Lank, A. G. (1998). *The family business: Its governance for sustainability.* Basingstoke: Macmillan.

Nishiyama, T. (1984). The structure of managerial control: Who owns and controls Japanese businesses. In: K. Sato & Y. Hoshino (Eds), *The anatomy of Japanese business.* London: Provident House.

Nolan, P. (2001). *China and the global economy.* Basingstoke: Palgrave.

North, D. (1990). *Institutions, institutional change and economic performance.* Cambridge: Cambridge University Press.

O'Sullivan, M. (2000). *Contests for corporate control, corporate governance and economic performance in the United States and Germany.* Oxford: Oxford University Press.

OECD. (1998). *Corporate governance: Improving competitiveness and access to capital in global markets.* Paris: OECD.

OECD. (1999). *Principles of corporate governance.* Paris: OECD.

Ohmae, K. (1982). *The mind of the strategist.* London: McGraw-Hill.

Ohmae, K. (1995). *The end of the nation state.* New York: Free Press.

Orru, M. (1997). The institutionalist analysis of capitalist economies. In: M. Orru, et al. (Eds), *The economic organisation of East Asian capitalism.* London: Sage.

Perkins, D. (1994). Completing China's move to the market. *Journal of Economic Perspectives, 8,* 23–46.

Plender, J. (1997). *A stake in the future: The stakeholding solution.* London: Nicholas Breaery.

Prowse, S. (1992). The structure of corporate ownership in Japan. *Journal of Finance, 47,* 1121–1140.

Qi, D., Wu, W., & Zhang, H. (2000). Shareholding and corporate performance of partially privatised firms: Evidence from the listed Chinese firms. *Pacific Basin Finance Journal, 8,* 587–610.

Reich, R. (1992). *The work of nations.* New York: Simon and Schuster.

Roe, M. (1997). Path dependence, political options and governance systems. In: K. Hopt & D. Wymeersch (Eds), *Comparative corporate governance.* Berlin: Walter de Gruyter.

Roe, M. J. (1994). *Strong managers, weak owners – the political roots of American corporate finance.* Princeton: Princeton University Press.

Samuels, W. (1987). The idea of the corporation as a person. In: W. J. Samuels & A. S. Miller (Eds), *Corporations and society: Power and responsibility.* New York: Greenwood Press.

Sheard, S. (1994). Interlocking shareholdings and corporate governance. In: M. Aoki & R. Dore (Eds), *The Japanese firm – the sources of competitive strength.* Oxford: Oxford University Press.

Shleifer, A., & Vishny, R. (1994). Politicians and firms. *Quarterly Journal of Economics, 109,* 737–783.

Shleifer, A., & Vishny, R. (1998). *The grabbing hand: Government pathologies and their cures.* Cambridge, Massachusetts: Harvard University Press.

Shleifer, A., & Vishny, R. W. (1997). A survey of corporate governance. *Journal of Finance, 52,* 737–783.

Shleifer, A. (1998). State versus private ownership. *Journal of Economic Perspectives, 12,* 133–151.

Simon, W. H. (1996). The legal structure of the Chinese socialist market enterprise. *Journal of Corporate Law, 21,* 267–306.

Soros, G. (2000). The new global financial architecture. In: W. Hutton & A. Giddens (Eds), *Global capitalism.* New York: New Press.

Stapleton, G. (1996). *Institutional shareholders and corporate governance.* Oxford: Oxford University Press.

Stapleton, G. (1998). Australian Sharemarket Ownership. In: G. Walker, B. Fisse & I. Ramsay (Eds), *Securities Regulation in Australia and New Zealand.* Sydney: LBC.

Steinfeld, E. S. (1998). *Forging reform in China: The fate of state-owned industry.* Cambridge: Cambridge University Press.

Sternberg, E. (1994). *Just business: Business ethics in action.* London: Warner Books.

Sugarman, D., & Teubner, G. (Eds) (1990). *Regulating corporate groups in Europe.* Ban Baden: Nomos Verlagsgesellschaft.

Sykes, T. (1988). *Two centuries of panic- A history of corporate collapse in Australia.* Sydney: Allen and Unwin.

Tam, O. K. (1999). *The development of corporate governance in China.* Cheltenham: Edward Elgar.

Teubner, G. (Ed.) (1997). *Global law without a state.* Aldershot: Dartmouth.

Thurow, L. (1992). *Head to head: The coming economic battle among Japan, Europe and America.* Sydney: Allan & Unwin.

Thurow, L. (1999). *Building wealth.* New York: Harper Collins.

Tomasic, R., & Bottomley, S. (1993). *Directing the top 500 – Corporate governance and accountability in Australian companies.* Sydney: Allen and Unwin.

Unger, R. (1976). *Law in modern society.* New York: Free Press.

van der Berghe, L., & De Ridder, L. (1999). *International standardisation of good corporate governance.* Boston: Kluwer Academic Publishers.

Waddock, S. A., & Graves, S. (1997). The corporate social performance-financial performance link. *Strategic Management Journal, 18,* 303–317.

Westney, E. (1996). The Japanese business system: Key features and prospects for change. *Journal of Asian Business, 12,* 21–50.

Wheeler, S. (1998). Inclusive communities and dialogical stakeholder – A methodology for authentic corporate citizenship. *Australian Journal of Corporate Law, 9,* 1–20.

Wheeler, S. (Ed.) (1994). *A reader on the law of the business enterprise.* Oxford: Oxford University Press.

Whitley, R. (1992). *Business systems in East Asia: Firms, markets and societies.* London: Sage.

Whitley, R. (1999). *Divergent capitalisms.* Oxford: Oxford University Press.

Williams, A. (2000). *Who will guard the guardians: Corporate governance in the millennium.* Chalford: Management Books 2000 Ltd.

World Bank. (1997). *China's management of enterprise assets: The state as shareholder.* Washington, DC: World Bank.

Xu, X., & Wang, Y. (1999). Ownership structure and corporate governance in Chinese stock companies. *China Economic Review, 10,* 75–89.

You, Ji. (1998). *China's enterprise reform: Changing state-society relations after Mao.* London: Routledge.

Zysman, J. (1983). *Governments, markets and growth.* Ithaca, NT: Cornell University Press.

THE AUSTRIAN WAY: DIRECTOR CONDUCT IN THE CONTEXT OF LEGAL AND CULTURAL FRAMEWORKS OF CORPORATE GOVERNANCE

Maureen Bickley and Margaret Nowak

ABSTRACT

In recent years there has been considerable discussion of and some move-ment towards, harmonisation of governance structures and processes be-.tween the EU and North America in particular. Multilateral organisations (i.e. World Bank), the USA's Sarbanes Oxley and the expansion of the EU in 2004 have all provided added impetus for a broader focus on harmonisation or convergence. But is convergence pos-sible? Can any 'one size fits all' approach to governance be consistent with divergent national legal and cultural systems? A qualitative study of Austrian company directors is used to investigate whether the recent de-velopment of a more open economy coupled with the global capital market is generating a convergent model of director conduct. It was apparent that a stakeholder approach, where stewardship theory best explains the proc-esses to mediate director conduct, continues to best describe the Austrian way. This contrasts with 'theory in use' in Anglo-American practice which

Corporate Governance: Does Any Size Fit?
Advances in Public Interest Accounting, Volume 11, 145–165
ISSN: 1041-7060/doi:10.1016/S1041-7060(05)11007-4

conforms to the tenets of Agency Theory. We conclude with a discussion of the implications for sustainability management.

Behind Descriptions of market reforms, …and the convolutions of the Dow, I gradually made out the pieces of a grand narrative about the inner meaning of human history, why things had gone wrong and how to put them right. Theologians call these myths of origin, legends of the fall and doctrines of sin and redemption.

Cox (1999)

INTRODUCTION

In April 1999, the OECD issued its "Principles of Corporate Governance", developed by its Ad-Hoc Task Force on Corporate Governance. While these are specifically a "set of non-binding principles," they are presented in the words of the preamble, as "a common basis that OECD Member countries consider essential for the development of good governance practice."(OECD Principles of Corporate Governance, 1999, p. 2). These principles bring a multinational perspective to the principles and practices of corporate governance, which had previously resided within individual state historical, legal, social and cultural contexts. In doing so this document focuses on shareholder interests and rights. While a number of OECD member states specifically recognise stakeholder rights in corporate law and regulation, this document considers stakeholder aspects of governance to be treated elsewhere and not within the document on the Principles of Corporate Governance. A recent report for the European Commission (2002a) also tended to downplay the issue of divergence in governance grounding, structures and processes and seeks to foster convergence.

At the same time, a doubling in the past decade of foreign corporations listed in the USA has increased the reach of the United States Securities and Exchange Commission (SEC). The requirement to conform to Sarbanes Oxley has exerted unilateral pressure on individual corporations world wide. Recent high profile cases which have involved the SEC include the Italian group Parmalat and Royal Dutch Shell Group (Schroeder, 2004, p. 14). Schaub (2004) sees this tendency to force global convergence as an unavoidable regulatory 'spill-over' (Schaub, 2004). This global spill-over is evident in a recent study of 794 firms from 24 countries in Europe and Asia (Khanna, Palepu, & Srinivasan, 2004). They found a positive association between those firms using USA-style disclosure with them having U.S. listing, USA investment flows, exports to and operations in the USA.

More open securities markets are encouraging a convergence that is, in effect, pressure to accept the Anglo-American paradigm giving primacy to the shareholder. However, some European nations hold on to the importance of divergence – the co-existence of a European tradition. As the EU grapples with governance 'harmonisation' issues, these competing paradigms, grounded in different legal and cultural traditions have been debated (see for example, Becht, 1999; Van den Berghe & De Ridder, 1999; Maeijer & Geens, 1990; OECD, 1998, as well as the fora provided by the European Commission's High Level Group of Company Law Experts, 2002b). The Draft Fifth Directive which was under active discussion in the 1990s, and which included a range of proposals to increase shareholder rights, was completely abandoned at the end of the decade (Becht, 1999, p. 1081), while governments continued to develop interpretations of corporation laws consistent with their governance traditions. As an example newly introduced German law regulating takeovers provided that the takeover code specifically protects the interests of employees and continues to make hostile takeovers more difficult (McCathie, 2000).

Branson argues that convergence may occur in discrete areas, such as financial accounting or disclosure but that convergence is far more likely to be regional than global (Branson, 2002). Rather than seek convergence or identical USA/EU approaches, Schaub argues for the recognition of 'equivalence' based on dialogue to preserve the integrity, and avoid dilution, of the internal market. "Regulatory dialogues are evolving and there is no one size fits all framework." (Schaub, 2004, p. 1)

It is argued here that there may be important issues at stake in respect of questions of sustainability and corporate social responsibility which convergence could overrun. In particular we argue that the property rights and enterprise-based approach of the major European tradition may embody important elements required to assure a culture of social responsibility and sustainability.

This paper considers alternate paradigms and competing theories concerning the motivation and behaviour of directors. It looks at how difference in the specification of property rights within corporate law impacts on director motivation and corporate accountability. It concludes with a case study based on Austrian data. Austrian directors' views focussing on director conduct and board dynamics demonstrate that, despite tensions arising from EU integration and globalisation, an "Austrian Way" continues to hold sway. It is firmly based in the Austrian social, legal and cultural context and in a stakeholder approach. It is further argued that such an approach may be more compatible with a culture of sustainability than one perpetuated by the view that, for corporations, the property rights of the shareholder (as financial owner) are dominant.

LEGAL TRADITIONS AND THE CORPORATE LAW

Nowak and Bickley (2004) point out that the differences in legal traditions underlined by Berglöf (1997), which underpin the European as compared to the Anglo-American patterns of corporate law are the basis for differences in the mechanisms for corporate monitoring and accountability. These are summarised in Table 1.

The system typical of traditions based in common law (e.g. Australia, Canada, USA, UK) is based on a nexus-of-contracts with the focus of the law being the analysis of contracts between the various capital providers (Berglöf, 1997, p. 105). The role of public policy is to facilitate such contracts amongst self-interested individuals. In this setting, other legislative constraints are seen as impediments to such contracting and therefore a disadvantage to these individuals. Corporate law is specific about the obligations and accountability of the corporation to the shareholder group as owners and confers on that group-specific powers such as voting at the annual general meeting.

Nowak and Bickley (2004) argue that within this tradition the only property rights which are closely specified in corporate law are the property rights of the shareholder as 'owner'/finance provider. When property rights are incomplete we identify that the market fails to achieve the socially optimal outcome and this failure is analysed using the concept of the

Table 1.   Characteristics of Corporate Law Traditions.

Anglo/U.S.	Continental Europe
Common law system	Codified legal system
Based on nexus of contracts	Based on multiple property rights
Analyses contracts between various investors	Enterprise-based system recognising multiple stakes
Company-based system	Emphasis on the physical entity
Focus on the firm as legal entity	Takes on broader view of stakeholders
Agency theory as theory base	Stakeholder theory
Monitoring and discipline role of securities market	Monitoring and discipline emphasis within enterprise and by stakeholders

Adapted from Nowak and Bickley (2004) and Berglöf (1997).

externality (either cost or benefit). We are very familiar with the use of this concept in the analysis of environmental degradation where incomplete property rights enable business entities to shirk responsibility for pollution. Moves to establish water rights at national government level and carbon credits (rights) at the international level are examples of efforts to internalise these current non-market externalities into the originating business entities. Our understanding of the issues of environmental property rights is growing, although our ability to analyse them has not made it a whole lot easier to manage the issues.

In contrast, the traditions of the European or Continental legal systems (Berglöf, 1997) result in a corporate law tradition which is based on multiple property rights and provides specifically for corporate accountability to multiple stakeholders. Companies are viewed as serving first the 'enterprise' – the wide range of stakeholders including employees, creditors, the economic entity, customers and the national economy. Shareholders are argued to play a secondary role (Wymeersch, 1997, p. 487). "Within the EU, each state member has its own system of corporate governance, reflecting its own cultures and company law structures" (EIU ViewsWire, 2003). In a number of cases (e.g. Germany, Austria) specific voice is given to one group of stakeholders, viz. employees who have the right to representation on the Supervisory Board. Despite moves to convergence the German/Austrian codes for corporate governance continue to explicitly preserve a commitment to worker involvement. In a study of the developing regulatory framework in the EU – characterised by a model of corporate governance based on workplace democracy, Reberioux (2002) rejects national convergence in favour of an approach rooted in institutional complementarities.

Nowak and Bickley (2004) recognised that new models of corporate governance are likely to emerge from transition economies as they undertake significant experimentation. Social norms around legal practice may play just as important a role as law in shaping corporate governance. When emerging economies super-impose either Anglo-USA or European-style laws over local social norms ('Indonesian Patrimonialism' or 'Chinese Confucianism'), dissonance between local legal cultures and 'imported laws' may lead to ineffective legal system implementation (Tabalujan, 2002). This is typical of what Bebchuk and Roe (1999) term path dependent phenomenon also occurring in the transitional economies of the former eastern bloc. In recognising that governance systems in practice are historically and culturally contingent it is clear that social patterns, comparative politics, levels of economic development and structure all contribute to those differences. These national characteristics of corporate governance with unique social and cultural underpinnings are clearly evident in emerging economies such as Indonesia (Lukviarman, 2001) and South Africa (King Committee on Corporate Governance, 2002).

GOVERNANCE THEORY AND POLITICAL/LEGAL TRADITIONS

Whilst we recognise that country-specific variations are to be found, our focus in the discussion below is on the general features or characteristics of each tradition.

The Anglo-American paradigm aligns with the political tradition of economic liberalism (Benn & Dunphy, 2004) and is based on notions and practices of individualism, short-termism, competition and a strong belief in market-oriented capitalism. It identifies 'economic man' – individualist, opportunistic and self serving. The underlying principles of behaviour are modelled by Agency Theory. In the agency relationship the principal (shareholder or owner) engages an agent "to perform some service on their behalf which involves delegating *some decision making authority* on their behalf" (Jensen & Meckling, 1976, p. 308 emphasis added). It has come to mean the shareholder as principal and delegates the *power to maximise return* on financial capital.

Underlying the analysis of behaviour in Agency Theory is the assumption that rational individuals act always and only in their own self-interest. Thus "goal conflict is inherent when individuals with differing preferences engage in co-operative effort" (Bird & Wiersema, 1996, p. 151) as they are required to do in organisations. For example, managers are in a position to create information asymmetries which enable them to expropriate shareholder value. Governance systems are required to "align goals" of the principals/ owners or shareholders and the agents/management (Jensen & Meckling, 1976). A range of internal accountability and incentive mechanisms under the authority of the board of directors (the focus of governance activities) seek to ensure the agents – management – *do* operate in the shareholder's interest and not in their own. This model also places emphasis on market place contestability for control through its facilitation of shareholder exit and takeovers and low levels of intercorporate cross holdings.

It has been argued that this is a far narrower view than originally conceived in this tradition. Clarkson (1994) argues for recognition that the context of the firm is society. He proposes us to view the firm from a systems perspective, with each firm a system of stakeholders within the host society system. The host society provides the infrastructure for the firm's operations. The firm's purpose, he argues, is to convert the 'stakes' into goods and services, thus creating wealth for stakeholders (Clarkson, 1994).

By contrast with the shareholder-centric Anglo-American model, the European tradition has often given specific voice, both legislatively and in practice to a wider group defined in legislation as stakeholders. Maeijer and Geens (1990) term this the institutional view of companies and argue that in this tradition the interests of the company do not only or primarily correspond to the interests of the shareholders. This tradition of company as institution and 'enterprise' is deeply rooted in Germany, Austria and the Netherlands but, they argue is also important in 'Civil Code' countries such as France and Spain (Maeijer & Geens, 1990, p. 5). This may, as in Austria and Germany, include specific board representation of employees. This approach aligns with a political tradition which Benn and Dunphy (2004) term Social Democracy which has a focus on the protection of the collective interests of citizens. While agency theory in capitalist countries viewed the corporate governance problem as that of a conflict between weak dispersed shareholders and self-interested managers, most continental European social democracies were marked by a concentrated or blockholder ownership morphology (Bhasa, 2004).

The European model specifies the two-tiered board system, a management board (internal) and a supervisory board (external). In this tradition management is responsible to conduct the affairs of the corporation with specific recognition of their responsibilities to multiple stakeholders. Senior management comprise the Management Board. Management is not represented on the Supervisory Board. This board, which usually includes employee, union or work council representatives (under codetermination legislation, Maeijer & Geens, 1990) and in some cases government instrumentality representatives, is responsible to hire and fire management and to monitor in the interests of stakeholders. It is interesting to note that corporations in this tradition have in the past made little use of market related executive incentive pay schemes while the market for corporate control is very blunted both by corporate structures and lower levels of share market penetration (Becht, 1999).

The behavioural principles underlying this model align with Stewardship Theory. Stewardship theory depicts organisational participants as potentially collectivists, pro-organisation and trustworthy (Davis, Schoorman, & Donaldson, 1997). It proposes that the interests of stakeholders and management may be able to be aligned through empowerment and trust rather than through monitoring and control. In such a setting, performance pay may be more broadly specified to reflect performance in spheres other than shareholder value.

Albert (1993) argues that a stakeholder model includes the processes to challenge its own sustainability. He contrasts this with "company" in capitalism as epitomised by the Anglo-American model. "Things have come a long way since the word 'company' meant, as its etymology suggests, a community of interest, a mutually beneficial partnership of employers, employees and investors. Gone is the *esprit de corps* implicit in incorporation; companies are now mere cash flow machines, subject to the whims of finance and exposed to the crudest elements of stock market speculation." Albert (1993, p. 75)

SUSTAINABILITY AND PROPERTY RIGHTS

The assumption of optimisation of resource use claimed for the competitive markets is based on completely specified property rights. Where property rights are incomplete (e.g. in water) the market seems unable to achieve this optimisation. We have argued (Nowak & Bickley, 2004) that one of the problems for stakeholders who contribute value to corporate activities (communities, employees and the natural environment) is that their property rights are legally underspecified and lacking in recognition within Anglo-American corporate regulation. The problem of underspecified property rights for the environment has long been recognised by economists but Steadman, Albright, and Dunn (1996) have suggested that community property rights, stemming from the provision of social capital and infrastructure, are also inadequately specified. The rights of future generations, clearly incomplete and underspecified, remain a challenge to either agency or stakeholder traditions.

Anglo-American corporate law specifies the rights of shareholders or fractionated owners and the obligations of the corporate board and management in the protection of shareholder interests. This emphasis on shareholder or stockholder interests results in primacy to these interests in rhetoric and in practice in the Anglo-American paradigm. In this paradigm the interests of employees, customers, suppliers, and the environment are not given voice in corporate law and thus, where protected, this is done through separate legal intervention such as employment law. This separation has the effect of bringing protection of such stakeholders, for example employee property rights, into the adversarial legal system.

Turnbull (1995) proposes new institutional protections for stakeholders such as independently appointed stakeholder councils to advise non-affiliated independent directors on corporate boards.

Stakeholder theory, however, proposes that a broader set of accountabilities exists (Donaldson & Preston, 1995; Preston & Donaldson, 1999; Jones & Wicks, 1999; Dyer & Singh, 1998; Turnbull, 1997). As noted above Albert (1993) argues that originally a 'company' was, "a community of interest, a mutually beneficial partnership of employers, employees and investors." These broader accountabilities implicitly recognise the property rights of participants other than shareholders/owners. Bhasa (2004) contends that central to the pluralist stakeholder-based approach is the creation and distribution of value to each of those entities involved in the corporation's functioning. The issue for stakeholder theory is then posed as 'how do managers manage what may at times be conflicting interests'?

Nowak and Bickley (2003) found that within the EU, Austria provides an example where accountability to multiple stakeholders is internalised to the organisation through corporate law rather than externally mediated either through the adversarial legal system or through additional institutional arrangements as proposed by Turnbull.

We have been able to explore the perceptions of Austrian Board members in the research reported below. We argue that this example of the European enterprise-based model with its recognition of stakeholder rights is more able to encompass the range of societal sustaining property rights than one where corporate law and corporate rhetoric give primacy to recognition of the property rights of the capital provider alone. In doing so within the corporate governance system, it reduces the need for regulatory intervention in the case of market failure to protect property rights while developing a culture more conducive to corporate sustainability.

PERCEPTIONS OF AUSTRIAN CORPORATE GOVERNANCE: THE AUSTRIAN WAY

The study of the perceptions of Austrian directors provides interesting perspectives on the European tradition during a period of economic change which is not well represented in English-language journals.

The Austrian corporate scene at the beginning of 21st century could be described as a mixed private/public system. The private part comprised a high proportion of family owned or dominated firms. Many of these were moving to widen their shareholdings to increase access to capital and assist expansion in the climate of opportunities offered by an expanding European Union (EU). The earlier structure of dominating and complex public ownership of firms (involving city and provincial as well as central government) had been diluted with partial privatisation in the 1990s. A holding company, ÖIAG, was established to manage the remaining central government holdings at 'arms length'.

Doralt (1999) investigated the impact of these changes on Austrian companies and in particular the arrival of USA and UK institutional investors as shareholders. He concluded that institutional investors had an impact on managerial attitudes and behaviour; this could be interpreted as convergence and he noted that companies "could only afford to ignore some key demands (*of institutions*), by responding to others." It was in this climate of pressure for change that in-depth interviews in English with company directors/senior executives of 15 Austrian listed companies along with five executives of large private unlisted companies were conducted in late 1999.

Bank-dominated relationships; pyramidal ownership structures; familial control; illiquid capital markets and a high degree of cross-holding remained pervasive features of the Austrian system. Austrian corporate law epitomises the European tradition described above. It lays down the two-board system, a Supervisory board and a Management board, and sets out the representation of employees on the Supervisory board at one third of membership. It specifies that the company is responsible to act in the interests of stakeholders, not just shareholders. "The management board manages the company on its own responsibility for the company's benefit in consideration of shareholder and employee interests as well as public interests" (Khol, 2002, p. 6). Austria and Luxembourg were the last two countries in the EU to develop codes for corporate governance. The voluntary Austrian Code of Corporate Governance (ACCG) was introduced in 2002 (Khol, 2002).

In the qualitative study of Austrian directors' perceptions about corporate governance (Nowak & Bickley, 2003) the phenomenon of *The Austrian Way* emerged where directors continually referenced their comments to a unique national approach. This approach as described by directors was focussed on "*dividing the world rather than fighting one another*" and developing a tradition of coalitions based on compromise and consensus. We did conclude that there were pressures to increase emphasis on shareholder value emanating from the opening up of the capital market.

One director who had long experience on a number of boards stated "...
[I] *wouldn't say it changed, but has evolved."* As another Director observed
"...[*we*] *know their jargon, language, their fashions and affairs and
everything...".* However the stakeholder approach remained the pervasive
model and director conduct and accountability was mediated by processes
consistent with stewardship theory. What emerged from the analysis of
director interviews was a strong sense that Austrian companies were attuned
to stakeholder power. Director reflections from the study are provided
below as evidence of this approach. We have retained the qualitative nature
of the study by allowing the directors' voices to be heard directly in the
reporting of the data.

---

*"The management board runs the company under its own responsibility in
the interests of the shareholders, the employees and the public. This is the
law. It's Paragraph 70 of our company law..."*
"The company law defines the stakeholder approach..."
*"There is a basic rule in Austrian Company Law and has been originally
in German law which defines for the law the stakeholder approach... So,
but the differences are not as sharp as they are often described in
literature,... but there is a very strong feeling that [holding company
name] must behave as a steward"*
*"...our attitude is not pure shareholder value but [rather that]
shareholders are happy and will stay..."*

EMPLOYEE STAKEHOLDERS AS BOARD PARTICIPANTS

The Austrian directors and executives considered the regulated system of
workplace democracy, providing unions with one-third of Supervisory
Board positions, as reflecting the broader societal approach of a social
partnership (co-determination). This level of worker involvement was yet
another example of the Austrian preference for coalitions of multiple and
potentially competing stakeholders. Austria had survived threats of parti-
tion after World War II by adopting the politically united stance of a
'Grand Coalition'.

> "*Afterwards* [*WW2*] *the two formed a coalition and originally the coalition had about 85/90% of the votes, behind it. Out of this attitude came a very strong parallel system of social partnership between economy and labour. So you have two layers of cooperation, one politically between the Conservative and the Socialist Party and another institutionally, represented through Trade Unions and the parallel Chamber of Labour and various industrial, economic organisations and their parallel Chamber of Industry*"
>
> "*…unions are still strong and we try not to overrule them but to get them into the boat to convince them, to negotiate with them and to find a consensus with them. You have certainly heard about Austrian social partnership and its part of this partnership*"

In general, those interviewed expressed a positive approach to employees as participants in the decision processes of the Supervisory Board. Whilst adversarial agency-based companies in the Anglo-American model are unable to countenance such a union role, Austrians saw this as an effective mechanism to ensure good communication, achieve successful change and enhance company performance. They saw this role as ensuring that unions had a realistic 'stake' in the company's future prosperity. One director did suggest that having unions on the Supervisory board occasionally reduced the frankness of discussion at board level but this was not the general view.

> "*Shop stewards would know the firm is totally dependent on reasonable profit …would be now quite willing to criticise something that is detrimental*"
>
> "*I think that Austrian companies compare quite well with their participation of workers on the board because whatever has to be decided, then the employees and the unions also have to follow. They can't agree to cost cutting and then say the opposite in practice. So basically, I think this one third participation, they were very good and very positive*"
>
> "*Yes, they have seats in the supervisory board. I enjoy very much to have these people on top in this hierarchy because they are growing enormously. They hear all the troubles and all the interesting decisions …in the old days he had only one point to do. He wanted to increase his salary and the income of the workers, nothing else. So if the company*"

> *goes bankrupt or not he does not more or less care. He wants more income. Now it is a really big responsibility and those labour union people who are in the supervisory board, they are changed completely. You have now a partner who really knows that decisions are so important and what a decision may bring your company, the way your company's going will be changed if the wrong decision is taken. If the right decision is taken at the end of the day this leads to jobs which leads to income for the people, this leads to employment or unemployment"*

REGULATION

One of the paradoxes of the Austrian system is that although stakeholders' rights are enshrined in law and regulation, the resultant sense of stakeholder power and power sharing has meant that government intervention as the (external) referee was less evident. In the transition from state-owned enterprises to partial privatisation there had been several significant (by Austrian standards) corporate losses during the early 1990s. It was interesting to note that interviewees were unable to provide an example of supervisory board members being prosecuted – although there were one or two examples given of prosecution of senior management.

> *"Theoretically, very, very strict regulation of responsibility, so theoretically we, I think all of us [supervisory board] could be sued for something. [That] is practically not done, and even in some dubious cases, it is not done because the sums involved are so huge, that it absolutely makes no sense."*
> *"...So the supervisory board should be liable. Ja?[Yes?] They should be held liable but after some weeks it calms down and then it's forgotten. But theoretically yes"*

The securities market role in providing market discipline and control in the Anglo-American model is also less evident in Austria (see Table 1). With a tradition of concentrated ownership and illiquid capital markets typical of continental European countries Austrian firms were certainly not typical of Berle and Means (1932) style firms which underpinned the development of Anglo-American agency theory. In discussing new takeover law in Austria one director sought to differentiate it as having an Austrian flavour

"*...amount of fairness which brings equal treatment of shareholders, not the UK/US [model where it is] necessary to have pressure on the management.*" Another director likened takeovers to the mini skirt: "*We don't need it* (takeover law) *and it's sort of foreign to us....*"

IMPLICATIONS FOR DIRECTOR CONDUCT

Relationships between the management board and supervisory board in this different corporate governance climate were characterised by trust and good information flows, which in turn enabled fast decision making when required. Although most supervisory boards meet infrequently – 4 to 8 meetings each year – most had executive decision-making processes characterised by regular and often informal communication processes.

"*We have a small working committee within this board ...consists only of three people. This is the President/the Chairman and his Deputy Chairman, both coming from the two main shareholders plus the head of our Reps [union] council. These people are available day and night if I like it and this gives us the opportunity of very hard decision making*"

"*we are not around for approval or just clipping some papers. We are informing these three people in advance of the projects. Sometimes a project never becomes reality but they are informed, so we are prepared but if we need a decision we get it very, very quickly because they're informed and they are only three people and they trust us*"

"*There is a good and positive contact to the Chairman and Vice Chairman of the Board. He does not mingle in day-to-day business but there is very good communication. There is mutual trust*"

"*The Austrian system of co-operation is opposed to the US/UK fad of gaining dominant position...*"

Within Supervisory Boards the board dynamics were characterised by consensus seeking, compromise and a broader sense of internal orderliness. Consensus seeking leading to compromises or agreements were key concepts seen as deep-rooted Austrian national characteristics evidenced by the Post World War II grand coalition government structures (see Nowak & Bickley, 2003). The Chairperson's role was to achieve this consensus through compromise and to ensure board processes, including robust discussion, reflected this objective. This not only strengthened the Board but also Austrian society through the consensus of multiple stakeholders.

> *"I insist that in difficult situations and important situations that [our] compromise is written down immediately, that it is copied and that each member gets his copy and then we have the final voting on that and "Have you all read it? Is that our common compromised opinion? Yes. OK. Then we vote""*
>
> *"No, no, no. We don't have cumulative voting. And this is very important to understand. You find consensus and that then is the decision."*
>
> *"But it is impossible that you are a member of both boards because you cannot control yourself"*
>
> *"If you have a spectrum and put on one extreme some US board cultures which can be controversial... and on the other extreme the Japanese who decide everything beforehand.... We are somewhere in the middle. We try to communicate well enough so that I know no great surprises but there is discussion. There's lively discussion. We have a Japanese board member. He's always surprised. He is quite flabbergasted by the frankness of the discussions, especially between employee representatives and ourselves. It's somewhere in between – it is not argumentative and controversial but it is also, it's a lively sort of community structure."*

One chairperson's conclusion of the requirements of best practice was *"to have a certain minimum number of meetings, to have good minutes, to have good reporting, to have good discussion, to have a chance for good preparation."* Whilst this list might appear in many countries, in Austria it is underpinned with trust and communication – directors and managers maintain an internal sense of ethical orderliness.

> *"There is mutual trust... the trust is very big, we trust in what we make and so we don't act all disorderly"*

This stakeholder-based governance system placed employee, social and environmental accountability alongside accountability to shareholders. *"I can't imagine non complying management decisions..."* one director commented in respect of the environment. *"Public concern translates into management concern"* another remarked.

The Austrian stakeholder model, which fits well with the Austrian historical and social environment, illustrates the case for not accepting the 'one size fits all' approach. We argue that particular features of this Austrian style have fostered corporate sustainability which has a very contemporary feel when we consider the triple bottom line and beyond.

MOVING FROM AMORAL TO MORAL

As identified earlier in this paper agency theory and the supporting philosophical framework of economic liberalism treats companies as amoral instruments of commerce, charged with the single responsibility to maximise investor value. In this model the question of ethics is outside the arena of companies' responsibilities although compliance with legal requirements becomes a focus of companies in the quest for maximum profitability. However, increasingly companies are viewed as having responsibilities for their impacts on others. In corporate surveys (see Paine (2003, p. 119) for an analysis of Asian Business, Fortune, Financial Times and other surveys), company performance is defined by multiple criteria including their appeal to investors, employees, customers and communities. Publicity about the impact of companies on 'others', has been felt in many major corporations. Where Nike had argued that supplier labour conditions were 'not their business' in the early 1990s, rapid loss of shareholder value led to them taking a very different stance on working conditions among suppliers by 1998. Shell experienced a similar community backlash over its involvement with the brutal Nigerian regime. James Hardie seems likely to reap a similar backlash from governments and unions in Australia.

Shareholder and activist voices have forced more companies to adopt a voluntary quasi-stakeholder approach as 'good for business'. The debate on triple-bottom-line reporting is an evidence of this move. Paine (2003) argues that the broadening domains of accountability can be seen on two fronts: *accountability for whom* and *accountability for what* as represented in Fig. 1.

She argues that managers and directors find this broadened accountability hard to accept because it adds significantly to the range of issues that demand their attention. Furthermore, accepting wider impacts on 'others', moves them from an amoral instrument role to the moral actor role. Here the company is viewed as a separate entity akin to a 'natural person' and capable of doing either harm or good (Adams, 2002). The increasing attachment of person characteristics to companies can be seen in legal developments where corporate manslaughter has been recorded and directors given custodial sentences for breaching their duty of care (Slapper, 2003).

This renewed Anglo-American interest in what is 'good for business' has led some firms to consider what Jones and Wicks (1999) term an

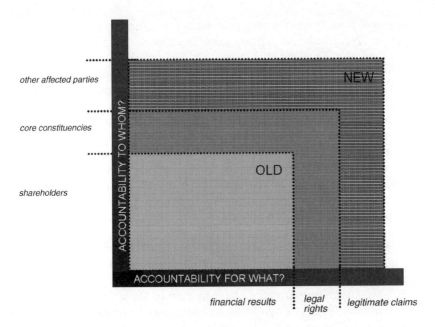

Fig. 1. Domains of Accountability. *Source*: Paine (2003, p. 123).

instrumental stakeholder approach. This approach of minimising the costs of externalities was also evident when Dyer and Singh (1998) endeavoured to account for inter-firm alliances and 'goodwill' by claiming these 'relational assets' as forms of a relational stakeholder approach. These approaches aimed at profit and wealth maximisation via a consideration of the impact of company activities on stakeholder costs or externalities ignore the normative (ethical/moral) dimensions which underpins stakeholder theory and is evidenced in the Austrian approach. They represent an attempt to transplant some of the features of stakeholder theory without the legal and cultural framework to support such an approach.

CONCLUDING COMMENTS

What are the conclusions for corporate sustainability? As Bird and Weirsema point out "economic views of organisations tend to ignore concepts such as norms, trust or tradition" (1996, p. 153). There is a groundswell of comment from corporate players in Australia about the onerous nature of regulation. Nevertheless if our argument is supported, the Anglo-American model logically leads to the need for an enforceable and structured regulatory environment which provides the benchmarks for monitoring and accountable reporting. This provides the external enforcement processes required because when property rights of the investor are contractually complete (and subject to continued strengthening) and the important social and environmental property rights for sustainability are incomplete and not able to be contractually specified in this tight way. Primacy to the shareholder, which is the hallmark of this system, means that the argument for sustainability is seen to depend on the 'good for business' approach or to require specific government (external) regulation to balance the failures of the internal system to take them into account.

In contrast the stakeholder approach produces, via the formal legal recognition and regulation of a range of property rights (even though not fully specified), an 'internal frame of reference', relying on stewardship, judgement and trust – hence the normative basis of the theory. Paradoxically, this alternative provides the opportunity for a less regulated and less adversarial system that embeds consideration of a range of stakeholders including employees and the community. The Austrian Way case study clearly demonstrates this alternative despite the pressure exerted for conformance with the Anglo-American model. With the stakeholder approach the focus switches to choosing management who will act responsibly as stewards for these multiple interests. This obligation for gaining consensus among multiple interests provides internal control requiring an underlying climate of trust. Managers and directors are then charged with accepting the complexity of these multiple claims as moral actors. Carroll, quoted in Vinten (2001), points out that this dictates that managers assess stakeholder interests – legal, moral and ownership rights; this is a process with which Austrian management is well versed by virtue of its commitment to stakeholders. We argue this provides a more sustainable corporate and social future.

Increasingly the push for global convergence is seen as a "Trojan horse for U.S. dominance" (Branson, 2002, p. 403) and an "economic fad" (Bhasa, 2004). Australia has other choices: some of which may be based on its future rather than its past. South Africa to our west has signalled a commitment to travel down the stakeholder path (King Committee on Corporate Governance, 2002). Confucian economies to our north which abnegate individualistic aspirations are unlikely to adopt the individualistically based American model. Australia has the choice of defaulting to the global USA model or choosing, as have the Austrians, to recognise those unique elements of our national culture which we wish to see played out in our Australian boardrooms.

REFERENCES

Adams, M. (2002). The convergence of international corporate governance systems – where is Australia heading? *Keeping Good Companies, 54*(1), 14–21.

Albert, M. (1993). *Capitalism against capitalism.* London: Whurr Publishers.

Bebchuk, L. A., & Roe, M. J. (1999). A theory of path dependence in corporate governance and ownership. *Stanford Law Review, 52,* 127.

Becht, M. (1999). European corporate governance: Trading off liquidity against control. *European Economic Review, 43,* 1071–1083.

Benn, S., & Dunphy, D. (2004). Can democracy handle corporate sustainability? Constructing a path forward. Innovation: Management policy and practice [Special Issue]. *Corporate Sustainability, 6*(2), 141–155.

Berglöf, E. (1997). Reforming corporate governance: Redirecting the European agenda. *Economic Policy, 24,* 91–123.

Berle, A., & Means, G. (1932). The modern corporation and private property. In: J. Beatty (Ed.), *Colossus: How the corporation changed America* (pp. 272–278). Broadway Books: NY.

Bhasa, M. P. (2004). Global corporate governance: Debates and challenges. *Corporate Governance, 4*(2), 5–17.

Bird, A., & Weirsema, M. F. (1996). Underlying assumptions of agency theory and implications for non-US settings: The case of Japan. *Research in the Sociology of Organisation, 14,* 149–180.

Branson, D. (2002). 'Global' convergence in corporate governance. *Keeping Good Companies, 54*(7), Aug. 402–405.

Clarkson, M. B. E. (1994). A risk based model of stakeholder theory. The Centre for Social Performance and Ethics, University of Toronto, Toronto.

Cox, H. (1999). The market as God. *The Atlantic Monthly,* 18–23.

Davis, J. H., Schoorman, F. D., & Donaldson, L. (1997). Toward a stewardship theory of management. *Academy of Management Review, 22*(1), 20–28.

Donaldson, T., & Preston, L. E. (1995). The stakeholder theory of the corporation: Concepts, evidence and implications. *Academy of Management Review, 23,* 660–697.

Doralt, P. (1999). Strong voices for change; How international portfolio managers can affect managerial attitudes – the Austrian case. *Zeitschrift Fur Das Gesamte Bank – Und Borsenwesen* (pp. 366–375). Wien: Bank Verlag.

Dyer, J. H., & Singh, H. (1998). The relational view: Co-operative strategy and sources of interorganizational competitive advantage. *Academy of Management Review, 23,* 660–697.

EIU ViewsWire (2003). *EU regulations: Good governance June 3, NY.* (Accessed ProQuest October 4 2004.)

European Commission (2002a). *Comparative study of corporate governance codes relevant to the European Union and its member states.* Final Report, Brussels.

European Commission (2002b). *Report of the high level group of company law experts on a modern regulatory framework for company law in Europe.* Final Report, Brussels.

Jones, T., & Wicks, A. C. (1999). Convergent stakeholder theory. *Academy of Management Review, 24,* 206–221.

Jensen, M. C., & Meckling, W. H. (1976). Theory of the firm: Managerial behaviour, agency costs and ownership structure. *Journal of Financial Economics, 3,* 305–360.

Khanna, T., Palepu, K. G., & Srinivasan, S. (2004). Disclosure practices of foreign companies interacting with U.S. markets. *Journal of Accounting Research, 42*(2), 475.

Khol, F. (2002). The Austrian code of corporate governance. *Corporate Finance,* London, Sept. 6.

King Committee on Corporate Governance (2002). King Report on Corporate Governance for South Africa. Institute of Directors, Parktown, South Africa.

Lukviarman, N. (2001). *Key characteristics of corporate governance: The case of Indonesia.* Curtin Graduate School of Business Working Paper 01.01.

Maeijer, J. M. M., & Geens, K. (Eds). (1990). *Defensive measures against hostile takeovers in the common market.* Dordrecht: Martinus Nijhoff.

McCathie, A. (2000). Foreign takeover angst spurs tougher new German code. *Australian Financial Review, 15,* 13.

Nowak, M., & Bickley, M. (2003). Corporate sustainability: An Austrian study finds a national approach to an International dilemma. *Presented ANZAM conference.* Perth.

Nowak, M., & Bickley, M. (2004). Does one size fit all? Reflections on the importance of national legal and cultural frameworks for corporate governance. In: G. Callendar, D. Jamieson & C. Williams (Eds), *Governance by accident or design* (pp. 21–32). Perth: Vine Yard Publications.

OECD (1998). *Corporate governance; Improving competitiveness and access to capital in global markets.* OECD Report, France.

OECD (1999). *OECD principles of corporate governance.* Paris: OECD Directorate for Financial, Fiscal and Enterprise Affairs.

Paine, L. S. (2003). *Value shift: Why companies must merge social and financial imperatives to achieve superior performance.* NY: McGraw-Hill.

Preston, L. E., & Donaldson, T. (1999). Dialogue: Stakeholder management and organizational wealth. *Academy of Management Review, 24*(4), 619–620.

Reberioux, A. (2002). European style of corporate governance at the crossroads: The role of worker involvement. *Journal of Common Market Studies, 40*(1), 111.

Schaub, A. (2004). Europe and U.S. must guard against regulatory clashes. *International Financial Law Review,* July 1, 1.

Schroeder, M. (2004). U.S. enforcer has global watch. *Australian Financial Review,* 14.

Slapper, G. (2003). Corporate manslaughter: The changing legal scenery. *Asia Pacific Law Review, 11*(2), 118–125.

Steadman, M., Albright, T., & Dunn, K. (1996). Stakeholder group interest in the new manufacturing environment. *Managerial Auditing Journal, 11*(2), 4–14.

Tabalujan, B. S. (2002). Why Indonesian corporate governance failed-conjectures concerning legal culture. *Columbia Journal of Asia Law, 15*(2), 141–171.

Turnbull, S. (1995). Corporate governance; What is world best practice? *Australian Company Secretary,* Dec. 485–491.

Turnbull, S. (1997). Corporate Governance: Its scope, concerns and theories. *Corporate Governance, 5*(4), 180–205.

Van den Berghe, L., & De Ridder, L. (1999). *International standardisation of good corporate governance: Best practices for the board of directors.* Dordrecht: Kluwer Academic Publishers.

Vinten, G. (2001). Shareholder versus stakeholder – is there a governance dilemma? *Corporate Governance, 9*(1), 36–47.

Wymeersch, E. (1997). *Applied corporate governance.* Australian Company Director, Dec., pp. 485–488.

ACCOUNTABILITY AND INDEPENDENCE IN CORPORATE GOVERNANCE: AN ANALYSIS OF BOARD DISCLOSURES IN CANADA

Duncan Green and Cameron Graham

ABSTRACT

In Canada, companies are focusing on corporate governance as an ethical response to accounting scandals and the resulting crisis of confidence. Although, many aspects of corporate governance remain free from strict regulation, we examine the voluntary changes in the disclosures of the largest Canadian companies. We attempt to understand, through disclosure theory, discourse analysis, and structuration theory, the quality of these corporate governance disclosures. We recognize that much of the disclosure is opportunistic as companies state that they have not only complied with the non-compulsory Canadian guidelines, but have also met and exceeded the requirements of U.S. regulators. This is an important finding that supports the notion that Canadian companies do not need rules and regulations. Instead, a culture of governance is developing at the boards of large companies that encourages voluntary change. Whether this is enough to prevent future accounting scandals is a question for future research.

Corporate Governance: Does Any Size Fit?
Advances in Public Interest Accounting, Volume 11, 167–193
Copyright © 2005 by Elsevier Ltd.
ISSN: 1041-7060/doi:10.1016/S1041-7060(05)11008-6

INTRODUCTION

In recent years, corporate governance has become the "ethical response" to accounting scandals. Following a period of high-profile corporate failures and financial statement restatements, we are witnessing a renewed concern with business ethics and governance practices. The most frequent response is encompassed by the term corporate governance. Presumably, the assumption is that better corporate governance would have prevented these problems.

Although many of the failures were due to poor accounting or managerial fraud, the predominant response has been to focus on corporate governance rather than changes to accounting standards or audit procedures. Many of the proposed corporate governance changes involve improving board practices which provide us with the incentive to examine the disclosures in annual reports relating to the Board of Directors. Considerable attention has been paid to the issue of corporate governance[1] in the popular business press. Cover stories and feature articles have often focused on the roles and responsibilities of boards of directors (e.g. Reingold, 1999; Brooker, 2002; Useem, 2002). For example, on April 1, 2003, Toronto's *Globe and Mail* newspaper devoted a full section to the topic, filled with pronouncements from high-profile corporate directors and quotes from would-be governance gurus. The section was sponsored by large advertisements from consulting firms hoping to cash in on the "corporate governance crisis."

In addition to such press coverage, corporate governance issues have received attention from several high-profile commissions, including the Treadway Commission of 1987 in the U.S., the Macdonald Commission of 1988 in Canada, and the Cadbury Commission of 1992 in the U.K. These reports, following earlier scandals, focused on the financial reporting and internal controls aspects of corporate governance more than the practices of the Board of Directors. In Canada, the Toronto Stock Exchange (TSE – now known as TSX) has joined the debate by striking its own commissions, resulting in the Dey report of 1994, entitled *Where were the directors?*, and a follow-up report in 1999, *Five Years to the Dey*.

These TSE reports have recommended against the regulation of corporate governance practices, and suggest instead that governance is best improved through voluntary adherence to "guidelines." At least one academic study (Bujaki & McConomy, 2002) has looked directly at the TSE guidelines and measured the rate of compliance.

In Canada, the issue of corporate governance has crystallized around the TSE guidelines that were approved in 1994, and whether or not they are sufficient to correct perceived corporate governance problems and avoid the imposition of strict government regulations. A TSX-appointed committee subsequently recommended updates to these guidelines in 2001. However, these were not officially implemented because the Ontario Securities Commission (OSC) began a broader review of governance standards. In January 2004, the OSC announced 18 new corporate governance standards for the boards of publicly traded companies to replace the TSE guidelines. These guidelines are influenced by the Sarbanes–Oxley Act (SOX), enacted in the U.S. in July 2002, and incorporate a number of the rules introduced by the New York Stock Exchange. Such regulatory changes in the U.S. are of great interest to Canadian companies. Canadian regulatory policies in accounting and corporate governance often closely follow U.S. policies, at least in the popular mind (e.g. Kazanjian, 2002). In addition, U.S. regulations directly affect Canadian public companies that are cross-listed on U.S. exchanges.

Despite these new legislative initiatives, most aspects of corporate governance remain free from strict regulation in Canada. The existing TSX guidelines and the proposed OSC guidelines remain voluntary, meaning companies can choose whether or not to comply. As one lawyer and corporate governance expert says: this is the "Canadian way...to move forward with recommended best practices coupled with a disclosure requirement" (Hansell, 2004). However, in the absence of formal regulatory and monitoring mechanisms for corporate governance, neither the TSX nor any other audience can really know the extent of a company's compliance with voluntary guidelines. The problem stems from the unobservability of board practices and the problems of interpreting the board disclosures. Corporate boards of directors meet behind closed doors. Therefore, it is usually impossible to observe board behaviours and practices directly (Leblanc, 2001). As Leighton and Thain (1997, p. xv) state, "...the board of directors remains a kind of 'black box,' whose internal workings can only be surmised from public information about decisions announced and actions taken." While we agree that it would be useful to be able to "surmise" the internal workings of a board from public information sources, we suggest that such sources are not unproblematic. Most information about what goes on inside the boards of public companies comes from the disclosures made by those companies.[2] While the 1999 TSE report says that "the TSE intends to prescribe a standard table format for annual corporate governance reporting" (p. b) to facilitate comparing company compliance with the guidelines, to date such a table has not consistently been included in Canadian annual reports. And even with the availability of standard reporting formats, the choice to disclose compliance would remain as voluntary as the compliance itself.

We attempt to assess and understand the relationship between corporate governance disclosures and corporate governance regulations. Looking at disclosures contained in the annual reports and management proxy circulars of Canada's largest public companies, we seek to develop a descriptive theory of how boards of directors come to disclose their corporate governance practices. We also ask whether written disclosures can really help a financial statement user (such as a shareholder) assess the quality of corporate governance practices of that particular company. Our analysis focuses on two key coordinates of corporate governance, *accountability*, and *independence*. By these terms, we mean the accountability of the board of directors to shareholders and the independence of the board from management. We develop our rationale for selecting these coordinates in our theoretical framing section.

Our analysis draws upon both disclosure theory and discourse analysis. Disclosure theory suggests that statements by companies result from complex processes that mask the actual corporate attributes or actions being disclosed (Gibbins, Richardson, & Waterhouse, 1990). Discourse analysis recognizes that textual sources, such as annual reports, buffer the author from the reader, and in the context of disclosure serve to decouple a corporation's actions from its public image (Neu, Warsame, & Pedwell, 1998).

We find that voluntary disclosures about compliance with voluntary guidelines are weak mechanisms for ensuring good corporate governance. Our results highlight the sometimes tenuous connection between disclosure statements and the actual responsibilities and roles and practices that the statements purport to represent. We are hopeful that by helping to analyse corporate governance disclosure, we contribute toward the ultimate goal of understanding and improving corporate governance itself. Our results help to understand how corporate governance disclosure arises and changes, how it is related to underlying governance practices, and how it is related to the emergence of related regulations. Without such an understanding, one cannot evaluate the claim made by the TSX that guidelines and voluntary disclosure will not only lead to better corporate governance, but will do so more effectively than regulations.

In the next section of the paper, we explain our theoretical framework and show how it links with prior research. We then introduce our coordinates of analysis – accountability to shareholders and independence from management. This is followed by a description of our data sources and methodology, and then by our analysis of the corporate governance disclosures for fiscal years 2000 and 2002. In the penultimate section we discuss the implications of our analysis and consider possible directions for future research. Finally, we offer some conclusions to our research.

PRIOR RESEARCH AND THEORETICAL FRAMING

As previously noted, this paper attempts to improve our understanding of the relationship between corporate governance disclosures, corporate governance practices, and the emergence of corporate governance regulations. We analyse disclosure statements about corporate governance in annual reports and management proxy circulars of Canadian companies, using disclosure theory and discourse analysis.

Disclosure Theory

Disclosure theory indicates that corporate disclosures are complex constructions capable of a variety of interpretations. Corporate disclosures may be regarded as politically constructed messages (Tinker & Neimark, 1987), which by design or otherwise "manage" perceptions of the company's situation and activities (Neu et al., 1998). As Dowling and Pfeffer (1975) suggest, managing an organization's image through communications is an alternative to substantive change in organizational behaviour.

When Neu et al. (1998) explore the construction of environmental disclosures in annual reports, they demonstrate that public disclosures are in fact tailored to various "publics" (Lindblom, 1994) depending on the legitimation needs of the corporation. This dehomogenizing of "the public" is important because it encourages one to ask critical questions about disclosures, such as which audience is being addressed and enlisted by the disclosure.

Watts and Zimmerman (1986) suggest that one such audience is the political environment of the corporation. They argue that disclosure may be undertaken in order to limit political interference, and that larger companies have higher political visibility and will therefore disclose more than smaller companies. Lev (1992) suggests that these disclosure decisions are subjected to cost/benefit analyses, and that disclosures will be made when the benefits (not just deterring political and regulatory intervention, but also correcting stock misvaluations, enhancing financial market liquidity, changing shareholder mix, and gaining competitive advantage) exceed the costs (direct costs as well as various market costs and potential litigation costs).

Gibbins et al. (1990) offer a more complex model of the forces influencing disclosure. They argue that disclosures may be ritualistic (produced because of routine, relatively unthinking behaviour) or opportunistic (made purposively in order to gain corporate advantage). They also suggest that the disclosure practices of companies are mediated by the professional routines of external experts such as auditors and consultants. A firm's auditors, for example, may habitually insist on certain kinds of disclosures from all their clients. Preston, Wright, and Young (1996) and Neu et al. (1998) similarly suggest that public relations consultants hired to produce annual reports have routines and templates that standardize their product.

Discourse Analysis

Discourse analysis has a rich theoretical tradition that includes Saussure (1961); see also Culler (1976), Derrida (1978), and Foucault (1991). Discourse analysis techniques have been used in various strands of empirical accounting research (e.g. Lehman & Tinker, 1987). They have also been used successfully in a number of studies of annual reports (e.g. Tinker & Neimark, 1987; Neu et al., 1998; Craig, Garrott, & Amernic, 2001). A discourse includes the entire stream of documents and commentary and thought in which a document is situated. Discourse analysis deals with the use of language beyond the sentence level (Stubbs, 1983). For Foucault, the boundaries of relevance in discourse analysis are enlarged to take in all the communication that deals with the topic of the discourse, even outside the time or place in which a document was written; hence, every statement in a given discourse shapes the meanings of the other statements at the time of reading, not just at the time of writing. While the scope of the present study is limited by comparison with Foucault's ambitious standards, we attempt, when interpreting a given document, to take into account the context provided by related documents. Thus we interpret statements of disclosure not just within the context of that annual report, but in relation to previous and subsequent disclosures by the company, the disclosures of peer companies, and the statements pertaining to disclosure in the regulatory environment in which the company operates.

As Neu et al. (1998, p. 268) state, "the association between organizational actions and the words used to represent them is often ambiguous." Discourse analysis recognizes this ambiguity as a distance created by the text between the author and the reader. This space permits a variety of interpretations of the text, thereby necessarily buffering the organization-as-author from both scrutiny and external demands.

A key question for our research is the relationship between discursive statements and the social context of the writer. In discourse analysis, the meanings and significance of a statement are often considered to be only tenuously connected with the writer. Rather, the legitimacy or power of a statement "depends on its capacity to enlist, echo, harmonize with, and resonate with other themes prevailing in the discursive environment" (Lehman & Tinker, 1987, p. 509). Foucault (1977) considers a focus on authorship to be misplaced when interpreting texts. This is particularly worth pondering for annual reports. These documents, at least in Canada, are the product of heavy editing by professional public relations (PR) firms. The work of an individual writer is often hard to discern in an annual report. The original text may come perhaps from a leader of the board or management, perhaps from some technical writer within the company or the PR firm. It may pass through many hands, with words, phrases, and nuances changing along the way. The end product is then vetted by the various participants, particularly the board and the company's auditors. This multiple authorship must be kept in mind throughout the present study.

Yet, however cautiously one construes "the author," one quickly comes through usage to mean "the corporation," since multiple authorship is an awkward concept to keep in mind. This shorthand reifies the corporation, but may be impossible to avoid completely. Indeed, notwithstanding the complex process of authorship, annual reports are corporate documents. They are shaped by and serve corporate goals. Understanding the relationship between the statements contained in an annual report and the social, political, and economic situation of the corporation is at the heart of the present study.

As Neimark (1990) observed, some critical accounting research fails to connect accounting to its material social contexts. According to Neimark, such research ignores "the interpenetration of language and materiality" (p. 107), leaving the researchers to play "free-floating language games" (p. 110). Neimark's criticism was directed at Foucauldian accounting research in general, but any discourse analysis such as ours must heed her warnings. In other words, failure on the part of the present study to connect disclosure statements to the structured, material conflicts that condition them would limit both the power and the applicability of the analysis. Worse yet, the study would contribute tacitly to the status quo of institutionalized relationships between power and knowledge in our society.

Structuration Theory

Therefore, in order to elucidate the connection between our textual sources and their social contexts, we draw upon the vocabulary of structuration theory (Giddens, 1984). Structuration theory seeks to explain social actions in the context of a dialectic between social structures and individual agency.[3] People are constrained and enabled in their actions by the formal and informal structures that surround and support them. Their very actions, however, serve to reproduce the structures.

We believe, the use of structuration theory as a framework for discussion is justified. Archer (1982, p. 459) criticizes structuration theory as non-propositional. That is, it does not predict the relative extent of influence that agency or structure will have in any given situation. We accept this criticism, but maintain that even without predictive power, structuration theory serves well as a means of organizing our discussion and revealing conceptual connections in the data. We point to Macintosh and Scapens (1990, p. 469), who explain that:

> ... structuration theory does not provide final answers to the key question in social theory. It does not, for instance, tell us which dimensions of structure are primary and which are secondary, or whether agency has primacy over structure or vice versa. This, however, may be a strength of structuration theory in that it does not attempt to privilege particular theoretical positions. Rather, it permits the researcher to explore the issues in specific time–space locations and to develop theories in relation to particular contexts.

Structuration theory can be seen as an attempt by Giddens to resolve or transcend a polarized sociological debate. Where some prior theorists had structure as autonomous and fully determining of individual actions, and others had individual agency as predominant, with structure a mere social construction, Giddens puts a duality of structure and agency. Each constitutes the other. *Structure* develops across time and space, produced and reproduced constantly through human action. Giddens suggests that structure consists of rules and resources. Rules are things like codes of signification or meaning, and normative sanctions for particular behaviours. He divides resources into "authoritative" and "allocative" types, which provide control over people and things, respectively. *Agency*, the ability to act purposefully, arises from understanding the rules and being able to command resources. The reproduction of structure through agency can be understood psychologically as deriving from the agent's need for ontological security (Macintosh & Scapens, 1990, pp. 458–460). Yet agency is also social in nature. Given that the rules and resources employed by an agent are social, agency involves not just individual action, but the coordination of actions with others. Hence agency can be a collective attribute of a group (Sewell, 1992, p. 21), such as a board of directors.

Structuration, the duality of structure and agency in a reciprocally constitutive relationship, has three dimensions:

- legitimation, having to do with morality, shared values and ideals, normative rules, and rights and obligations,
- domination, having to do with influence, and relations of autonomy and dependency, and
- signification, having to do with meaning, communication, understanding, organized webs of semantic codes, interpretive schemes, and discursive practices.

These dimensions are interrelated. Each influences the other, and cannot have any effect without the others coming into play. This is particularly so on the level of structures, where each conception of structure leads to and implies the others, and on the level of social interaction, where control, communication and sanction are interdependent. In social interaction, the various modalities of legitimation, domination and signification, which are the concrete instantiations of the abstract structures, come into play. People draw upon or pull into action modalities such as written rules, technologies, or weapons.

The notion that structures are constituted constantly through agency (as agency is through structure) suggests that when agents draw upon the structures that surround them, they are implicitly interacting with other agents whose actions also constitute these structures. For example, boards are faced with a number of structures that delimit and organize their practices. But these structures are patterns of action on the part of other agents, such as management and regulators. This opens up for examination the possibility that board members interact with these other agents in multiple ways: on other boards, in social settings such as private parties or golf games, at conferences or government hearings, and so forth. Far from being faceless, the structures that directly affect the practices of board members may well be enacted by friends and colleagues from other social and institutional settings.

In summary, disclosure statements are not transparent windows into corporations. Both disclosure theory and discourse analysis identify that disclosure statements have an implicit intermediation effect, acting more like thick distorting lenses than windows. However, by making use of the vocabulary of structuration theory, we hope to show that the distortions are not merely passive, as in a lens, but are deliberate actions related to the structured social conflicts over corporate power within Canadian capitalism.

COORDINATES OF ANALYSIS

We examine corporate governance disclosures with respect to two primary interfaces of the board of a public company: the one directed to shareholders and the other to management. That is, in our discussion of the disclosure statements we have collected, we focus on (a) the notion that boards ought to be accountable to the shareholders of the corporation, and (b) the notion that boards ought to be independent of management. These two conceptual responsibilities occur frequently in the public discourse on board responsibilities (e.g. Gale, 2002; Gibbs, 2002; Ottawa Citizen, 2002; Rega, 2002). We use the following general definitions of these corporate governance responsibilities.

Accountability to Shareholders

Shareholders at the company's Annual General Meeting legally appoint directors. Therefore, the directors individually and the board collectively should be responsible to the shareholders[4] and answer to them regarding their activities and practices. Further, the board of directors should be willing to act as stewards of the corporation's assets and consequently work to maintain and enhance shareholder value. All of these aspects of accountability are included in this concept.

Independence from Management

Independence is a difficult concept to define because it often refers to a person's state of mind rather than the person's relationship with other parties. Daily, Johnson, and Dalton (1999) show that definitions of board independence that depend on board composition characteristics are problematic. We therefore use a definition of independence that is behavioural. A dictionary definition of independence is "not looking to others for one's opinions or for guidance on conduct" (Webster's Dictionary). This suggests that board members should be willing to express opinions on important company decisions and conduct board business without being unduly influenced by management. In practice, boards of directors are dependent on management for information on key activities. However, an independent board should be willing to question that information and at times request other opinions on the information in order to avoid acting as a "rubber stamp" for management decisions.

These two definitions serve as coordinates in our discussion of corporate governance disclosures. These definitions do not emphasize board composition. Questions, such as, how many "independent" directors are required, is the board chaired by a non-CEO, and are board members required to resign after a set number of years are frequently discussed in other research (e.g. Rhoades, Rechner, & Sundaramurthy, 2000; Prevost, Rao, & Hossain, 2002; Bujaki & McConomy, 2002). While we acknowledge that board composition issues, along with the issue of interlocking directorates (Dooley, 1969; Pfeffer, 1973; Allen, 1974) will influence the actual disclosure outputs via mimetic and normative means, studies that focus exclusively on compositional factors sometimes fail to theorize adequately the relationship between board composition and corporate governance effectiveness (Daily et al., 1999). They also often fail to understand the discursive and institutional nature of their data sources.

DATA AND METHODOLOGY

The disclosures we examine come from the companies that were on the TSE 35 index on 11 May, 2001. Companies were chosen by the TSE to appear on this index because of their relative importance amongst Canadian public companies. Together these companies might be said to have dominated the Canadian economy, not only through their capitalization but through their significant political power. By virtue of their large size, it can be hypothesized that they are more likely to disclose than other TSE companies, due to their political visibility and exposure (Watts & Zimmerman, 1986). They would also have had the resources to make sophisticated corporate governance disclosures. This is not to say that other Canadian companies at that time did not exceed the corporate governance (disclosure) standards exemplified by the TSE 35 companies, but merely that the TSE 35 companies received great scrutiny for all their corporate practices, and possessed the resources to respond to this scrutiny in deliberate and sometimes sophisticated ways. These responses included the actual governance practices of the companies as well as their disclosure choices and mechanisms.

The disclosures we examine come from the annual reports and management proxy circulars[5] of the selected companies. These documents are readily available from corporate and other public websites. We chose to use the annual reports and proxy circulars of these companies for the 2000 fiscal year as our baseline. We extracted from these documents every portion pertaining to the responsibilities of the Board of Directors and the associated Board Committees. We found that only nine companies included a section in the annual report that was clearly devoted to the discussion of corporate governance practices. The remaining companies who provided corporate governance disclosures did so in the proxy circular.

The documents in our data set were first analysed for their content with respect to corporate governance practices. This provided an understanding of the scope of disclosure in each company, and of the patterns of disclosure in various industries. Second, the specific aspects of corporate governance were examined in detail for the manner and wording of disclosure. This provided an understanding of the specific audiences that were addressed by disclosure of corporate governance practices, and the specific messages that were being sent to these audiences.

A content analysis approach was then adopted with an objective coding scheme (Berg, 1989). A list of basic board practices (Appendix 1) was used to analyse the companies' specific disclosures. An initial version of the list was prepared by one of the authors based on a reading of Canadian corporate governance literature, including the 1994 and 1999 TSE reports. The list was then reviewed by the other author, and refined through discussion between the authors to its present form. Three elements or constructs of disclosure were sought in each company's documents: a clear statement that the board of directors is accountable to the shareholders, a clear statement that the board is independent of management, and a clear statement of directors' roles, responsibilities, and inter-relationships. The first two of these constructs are the two board practices defined above, which we referred to as the "coordinates" of our study. The third construct captures aspects of the board's roles and responsibilities, and is included to help the reader relate our analysis to corporate governance studies that look primarily at board organization. Each of these elements of disclosure was coded by a number of more specific items that were used to refine the analysis of the extent of disclosure.

Following Buhr (2002) and other empirical studies discussed above, we then examined our selected disclosures at two levels: the first-order interpretation that they faithfully represent board practices, and the second-order interpretation that they reveal underlying reasons for the particular disclosure choices that were made. By "reasons" we mean something besides the personal rationales that board members may have had for their behaviour. Rather, we mean the connections that may be made to material social contexts and structured social conflict (Lehman & Tinker, 1987).

Following our examination of the 35 companies for fiscal 2000, and presenting the initial results (see Appendix 2), we decided to examine disclosures for the same companies in fiscal 2002. This was considered useful because after the failure of Enron and other high profile companies, many boards of directors, in response to new guidelines and a perceived crisis of confidence, decided to re-examine their corporate governance procedures during the intervening period.

We used the same content analysis and coding scheme to analyse the companies' specific disclosures in the later year. By examining the annual reports and proxy circulars, we were able to confirm what we were hearing from board members that disclosures had been extensively reviewed and in many cases significantly revised. The results for 2002 are included in Appendix 3.

ANALYSIS OF DISCLOSURE OF CORPORATE GOVERNANCE PRACTICES IN 2000

Our sample companies, those on the TSE 35 index on 11 May, 2001, were at that time the largest publicly traded Canadian companies by market capitalization. Due to our selection of only large, prominent companies, we had expected that a study of annual disclosures would reveal a high level of compliance with the TSE guidelines on Corporate Governance. After all, these guidelines have been available since 1994 and have received much attention in the financial press and related media. At the most basic and fundamental level, we were surprised to find how little was actually disclosed, how poorly were the disclosures presented and how difficult it was to compare one company with another. Despite the number of "boxes" we were able to check in our table in Appendix 2, most of the disclosures were cursory, and offered little detail to substantiate the claims made about corporate governance practices. While there were certainly some companies that were more forthcoming than others, the general impression is that corporate governance is a somewhat awkward or embarrassing topic for a corporation to address, and one that is best dispensed with quickly. Alternative explanations could be offered, however: that the market for corporate disclosure does not demand more detail (Watts & Zimmerman, 1986), or that the symbolic function of the disclosure is fulfilled by the cursory disclosures given (Oliver, 1991).

Interestingly, the TSE's own *Final Report of the Joint Committee on Corporate Governance* (November 2001) refers to a survey that found that 51% of Canadian corporations did not report their practices against all the guidelines. This information comes just a few pages before the statement that "disclosure is a much better approach than attempting to regulate behaviour" (p. 10).

The Joint Committee identified one of the major weaknesses of relying on disclosure guidelines – the tendency for "disclosure to degenerate into boilerplate – to become less meaningful as well as less complete" (p. 9). We believe that they were correct on this point. However, their remedy for this weakness that board members should discuss governance practices is inadequate. Shareholders, including large institutional investors, cannot yet consistently identify which companies and boards have followed all the guidelines and which have provided incomplete disclosure. We have offered some theoretical reasons for the common use of "boilerplate" disclosures, including the isomorphic effects of public relations firms in preparing the disclosures (Preston et al., 1996; Neu et al., 1998).

The TSE's Joint Committee suggested that "(w)herever possible, disclosure should be focused on behaviour rather than structure, on function rather than form" (Interim Report, p. 11). We see little evidence that the boards of leading Canadian companies are disclosing information about their behaviour or describing how the Boards and their committees actually function. Indeed, much of the disclosure that is made can only be regarded as "form" rather than "function". Further, the Joint Committee recommends that the disclosure statement "should discuss the processes used by the board to fulfil the functions that the guidelines suggest are important" (Interim Report, p. 16). Our data indicate that the companies in our sample are unwilling to discuss the processes actually followed by the board, are unlikely to disclose non-compliance, and sometimes they simply state that they comply with the numbered TSE guidelines without further explanation.

The results of our content analysis are shown in Appendix 2. Some of the companies made their disclosures in the annual report, but most used the management proxy circular. This raises the question of why a company would prefer to embed an apparently important disclosure in a dense proxy statement strewn with legal jargon, rather than in the more accessible and more attractive annual report. Typically, the proxy statements are at least 20 pages and in some cases over 80 pages long. They contain detailed information about voting procedures, shareholdings, stock options, and other legal requirements. Diligent readers can, of course, take the initiative to acquire and read the proxy circular. However, the glossy magazine-like appearance of the annual reports we examined, compared to the more pedestrian appearance and relative textual density of the proxy circulars, suggests that the annual report is the higher profile site. Disclosures about corporate governance, including information about the Board and its committees, are therefore not given much prominence when they are relegated to the proxy circular.

Our results, compiled from these annual reports and proxy statements, reveal a lack of consistent disclosure and several surprising omissions. We found that most boards do not make a clear statement that they are accountable to the company's shareholders. Further, many boards do not indicate that they are directly involved in developing policies to communicate with the shareholders. For example, the Board of Directors of Shaw Communications does not disclose that it is accountable to the shareholders and does not take responsibility for communication with shareholders. Indeed, a specific disclosure states that the Corporation has this responsibility, with no apparent Board review or monitoring. Specifically, it states that communication with shareholders is the responsibility of the finance department or an appropriate officer.

A further illustration comes from Nexen Corporation. Schedule A of Nexen's annual report claims that the company complies with TSE guideline 1d. This guideline requires the *Board* to specifically assume responsibility for communication policy. Yet in their attached comments they state that the "Board has mandated Nexen's Corporate Planning and Finance Group to disseminate information." However, they also state that this group should "report to the Board on such matters through the Finance Committee." It is not clear whether or not the Board has really *assumed responsibility for a policy* or how it can ensure that management or the Finance Committee provides a complete report of the shareholders' feedback.

One possible explanation for these omissions is that boards are constrained by the structures that have been developed by companies, the regulators, or the accounting profession. Another possible explanation is that boards believe that it is so obvious that they are accountable to shareholders that they do not need to disclose it. Alternatively, these omissions could indicate that directors are in fact more accountable to management, particularly to the CEO who often recommends their appointment to the board, than to the shareholders. Reading through the shareholder resolutions in the proxy statements we examined, one gains the impression that directors are often perceived in this way. This perception is exacerbated by the apparent reluctance on the part of some boards to use direct communication with shareholders, as demonstrated by the disclosure lacunae in many of the documents.

Given the mechanisms by which board members are nominated and elected, the board's "agency" might be apparent in *any* action of a director that was focused on being accountable to the shareholders. In practice, structure intercedes through the development of modalities of legitimation, domination, and signification (Dillard & Yuthas, 2002) that limit or organize the directors' actions. Since the board members have some influence over the modalities that are developed (e.g. the TSE guidelines), agency may influence structure. The direct citation of these guidelines in an annual report can be regarded as both an attempt to gain legitimacy for the board, and as a broader attempt to legitimize the guidelines and reinforce or entrench them as modalities before regulations can be imposed on the board.

Whittington (1992) suggests that one source of agency is the tension that exists between the internal and external structures of a system. For example, the internal logic and the practices of a given board of directors may contradict what is known about boards of directors in other companies. Through interlocking directorates (Dooley, 1969; Pfeffer, 1973; Allen, 1974), directors come to experience a tension between what they know or expect of boards, and what they experience on one particular board. The structural influence of both the norms of legitimation from other companies and the personal stocks of knowledge of the director, itself creates an opportunity for agency. The director can draw upon these sources of legitimation to change the board in question.

We also found that many boards do not clearly state that they operate independently of management. In this section of Appendix 2, we see evidence of a few boards that disclose non-compliance with specific questions. In spite of all the recommendations to have a non-executive chair or lead director and to have a majority of unrelated directors, some companies chose to not follow the majority view. Further, many boards did not indicate that they meet without management present, control the agenda for meetings, or have the authority to hire and fire the CEO. Possible explanations for these omissions parallel those offered above regarding accountability.

An example of a board that is not independent, but is honest enough to make this disclosure is Barrick Gold which states that "the Board of Directors believes that it is desirable for the majority of the Executive Committee to be related to the Company since its mandate requires members to be available on very short notice to deal with significant issues." Apparently, independence is sacrificed for expediency. A more contradictory example is shown by Noranda when they state that "each board meeting includes an in-camera session which excludes all management except the CEO and Corporate Secretary." The problem with the exception is that two key members of top management *are* present which obviously goes against the spirit of the guideline.

With management controlling the preparation and dissemination of all information provided to shareholders, the difficulty of credible disclosure of fully independent actions by the board is apparent. In practice, the discussion of independence is limited to saying how many directors are inside or outside, executive or non-executive, related or unrelated, and with or without potential conflicts of interest.

Analysis of our third construct revealed a higher level of compliance than with the first two categories. However, the disclosure that the board has a mandate, is involved with defining corporate objectives, strategic planning, risk management, and evaluates its own effectiveness does not indicate how well they carry out these duties. Most of the disclosure statements in this category gave no indication of the extent or quality of board involvement in these matters.

Several companies, such as Barrick Gold, Canadian Pacific, Celestica, and RIM, disclose that they do not have a clear mandate for the Board or clear objectives for the CEO. In stating that it does *not* comply with guideline 11a, NOVA comments that "there is no specific mandate for the Board, although the Chairman does have a mandate." This disclosure does indicate that they have considered the issue and since they state elsewhere that there are mandates for each board committee, the deficiency is not significant. More troublesome is the disclosure by Barrick Gold and Celestica that their boards have not developed mandates for themselves or their CEOs because "responsibilities are well understood." If they are so well understood, why not document them?

Overall, we were forced to conclude that the corporate governance disclosures of the largest Canadian companies created a less than reassuring picture. We saw evidence of board structures, but little evidence of actual behaviour or specific practices that would convince most shareholders that boards were operating effectively on their behalf. Considering that almost all companies in our sample indicate that they were following the highest standards of corporate governance, the level of omissions is surprising, particularly because we did not feel we were setting the bar very high. It is questionable, at this time, whether the "guidelines and voluntary disclosure" approach results in companies meeting even a minimum standard of disclosure.

ANALYSIS OF DISCLOSURE OF CORPORATE GOVERNANCE PRACTICES IN 2002

By examining disclosures for a second year, we were able to see greater compliance by many companies in our sample of 35 large Canadian companies. Since no specific rules or regulations were passed during the intervening period, we consider this to be an example of opportunistic disclosure (Gibbins et al., 1990) that demonstrates mimetic isomorphism (DiMaggio & Powell, 1983). We saw more references to SOX, NYSE, and SEC requirements than before and many statements that the companies were following, what they consider to be, the highest standards of corporate governance. We saw much evidence of companies' disclosures imitating formats that had been used by other companies.

However, we are still not convinced that boards are disclosing much about actual behaviour. The TSX guidelines suggest that companies should include a table showing compliance with their 15 guidelines. Our 2002 data show more adoption of this approach[6] and more use of standardized wording that merely claims compliance and indicates nothing about the process followed in order to comply.

The majority of companies in our sample have increased the volume of corporate governance disclosures which indicates that this subject is receiving more attention by boards of directors. However, we are still left with the problem that more disclosure does not necessarily imply stronger corporate governance practices.

IMPLICATIONS AND FUTURE RESEARCH

It is not the disclosure statements themselves that catch the eye in the annual reports and proxy statements we examined. It is what is *not* disclosed. The level of omissions in disclosure of accountability to shareholders and independence from management is surprising. Also surprising is the way in which structures of legitimation, domination, and signification (Dillard & Yuthas, 2002) are drawn upon to create a perhaps even more impenetrable black box around board practices.

As we have seen in the preceding analysis, the guidelines developed by the TSX become boilerplate text that is quoted verbatim in the annual reports and proxy circulars around the time of the 2000 fiscal year. It is unclear whether these represent new practices or simply new disclosures of existing practices. This is similar to changes in financial disclosure, where the appearance of a new detail about inventory valuation may represent a new method of valuation, or a new requirement to disclose existing valuation methods. But where financial disclosure is often mandated by regulators, the disclosure of corporate governance practices is not required. Indeed, there is not even a set of "generally accepted corporate governance practices" that can be attested to by auditors. The quotation of boilerplate text from the TSE guidelines is an interesting development from the point of view of structuration theory (Giddens, 1984). The resource – the guidelines – that boards are drawing upon for their own purposes becomes more concrete, more of a specific facility and less of a vague norm. However, without the coercive force of regulation and an appropriate monitoring agency for these disclosures, the guidelines become less than a minimum standard for disclosure, and perhaps therefore less than a minimum standard for practice.

The TD Bank annual report for 2000 is illustrative: while the bank specifically cites TSE guidelines by number, there are still some portions of the guidelines that remain unaddressed. For example, Guideline 1A states that the board is responsible for the adoption of a strategic planning process. The TD's compliance statement on this says that it is a "main responsibility" of the board to "approve and oversee the implementation of our strategies." This gives no information on the nature of the planning process, and does not even indicate that the board is involved in strategy *formation*. The following year, the bank rearranged its compliance statements to match the order of the TSE guidelines. In some cases, the disclosures statements exceed the guidelines. However, concrete details are still absent in almost every case and the disclosure statements amount to a "trust us" plea. Note, that several items from our disclosure constructs were not to be found in the bank's documents. Despite explicit citation of all the TSE Guidelines, there is no indication in the 2000 TD Bank annual report that the board sees itself as responsible for enhancing shareholder value (A3), that the board controls the agendas of its own meetings (B5), that the board has the authority to hire and fire the CEO (B6), that the board provides any training or orientation for its members (C3), or that the board is responsible for monitoring their code of ethics (C9).

Such specific discrepancies between TD disclosures and TSE guidelines could not even be noted if the new TSE guidelines were not a prominent part of the corporate governance discourse at the time of this annual report. This suggests a partial answer to Archer's (1982) critique of structuration theory (Giddens, 1984), that it is non-propositional. Agency is the ability to act purposefully, but it is sometimes hard to distinguish the agency "signal" from the "structural" noise. When structures like those denoted by the TSE guidelines modality are in flux, as the guidelines were at this time, agents have the opportunity to anticipate the changes or resist them. While this does not yet explain how the flux itself begins, it does help explain how actors can achieve the "critical distance" from structures that they need to exercise agency (Mouzelis, 1989; Whittington, 1992). The changes in the structures – or the attempt by other parties to change them – bring those structures into relief, render them visible, and break their "taken for granted" status. As Whittington (p. 704) suggests, agency springs from the opportunity to exploit the tension between contradictory structures. The advent of the guidelines creates a three-way tension between guideline-based disclosure, the status quo without guidelines, and the potential future of regulated disclosure. This tension creates the opportunity for the agents to be reflexive, and decide how they will act more independently of the structures, at least for a time. This is an example of what Mouzelis (p. 626) calls syntagmatic duality.

This temporary visibility of the structures creates a research opportunity, as well. Mouzelis (p. 617) suggests that dualism, and not just duality, is important for a complete understanding of structuration. This is particularly so for the researcher, who must employ a double hermeneutic, figuratively, and reflexively stepping outside (but nonetheless never escaping) the duality of structure in order to understand it. In this example, with the TSX guidelines coming to the forefront of the corporate governance discourse, a researcher could compare the timing of the adoption of the guidelines in different companies. The researcher could thereby possibly identify both styles of agency, the anticipation and the resistance. Coupled with a textual analysis of the ways that the social actors (the boards) participated in the discourse, this approach could yield a rich analysis. Note that this approach connects the notion of agency to innovation literature (Rogers, 1983), and suggests that both early adopters and laggards may be exercising agency in their own ways.

The present study provides a basis for this future research. Because, however, the documents in this data set that might pertain to active resisters of the guidelines are as silent on the topic as those of what might be termed procrastinators, additional data from the public discourse would be required. These data might include speeches, media interviews, and other such discursive data to supplement the formal documents gathered here.

CONCLUSION

It is uncertain what will happen to the TSE guidelines and OSC standards in the near future. While it is possible that U.S. regulations will force U.S. (and cross-listed Canadian) companies to meet those corporate governance standards, it is also possible that Canadian regulations will change to correspond to the U.S. regulations. The opportunity certainly exists to extend the present study to provide comparisons to U.S. and international companies. It is also possible that corporate governance disclosures will one day be subject to the same sort of auditing that financial disclosures receive. This would go far beyond the mere guidelines and voluntary disclosure now seen in Canada.

Our goal in this study was to examine the relationship between corporate governance disclosures and corporate governance regulations, and the role disclosures play in the emergence of corporate governance standards. We have seen evidence of structuration (Giddens, 1984) in the discourse of corporate governance disclosures. Further qualitative analysis of the data set we have assembled is possible, using techniques other than the content analysis we have used here. However, this study needs to be extended to examine the production of the TSE guidelines themselves, and the production of any related regulations that may arise from them. This would connect more clearly the disclosures we have examined to the emergence of structures and modalities in corporate governance. In addition, there may be ways to conduct interviews and surveys with directors of these companies that would help supplement or corroborate the disclosure statements found in the public documents we already have. We conclude that this alternative research is necessary to develop a theory of how boards of directors actually make choices regarding disclosures.

We recognized in this study that much corporate governance disclosure is opportunistic since Canadian regulations continue to be voluntary. However, various U.S. rules that affect cross-listed companies act as a stimulus to change in all Canadian boardrooms. In 2002, 28 of our sample companies not only refer to the TSX guidelines, but also refer to SOX, NYSE, or SEC rules. This is an important finding that supports the idea that Canadian companies prefer to avoid strict rules and regulations. Instead, a "culture of governance" is developing at the larger Canadian companies, which is driving change. Whether this will be enough to prevent future accounting scandals is a question for further research. We also conclude that financial statement users (such as shareholders) will find it difficult to assess the quality of corporate governance practices of a particular company and that they need to continue to be somewhat sceptical about such disclosures.

NOTES

1. A recent Google search revealed that "Corporate Governance" produces 2,450,000 hits compared to 2,040,000 hits for "Enron" and 284,000 for "Accounting Scandals."

2. Other sources of information would include the occasional journalistic investigation or academic research project. While these can provide vital insights into corporate governance, such observers are seldom invited into actual board meetings. In addition, their coverage is not comprehensive across companies or over time.

3. The use of the word "agency" causes an unfortunate coincidental overlap in terminology with agency theory. By agency in this paper we mean voluntarism, the ability to act purposefully, rather than action on behalf of a principal.

4. Although directors may also be accountable to other stakeholders, we do not attempt to consider corporate governance practices from their perspective in this study. Similarly, while the board may well consider potential investors as an audience for their disclosures, we limit our consideration to the existing shareholders who have a legal vote in the election of the board.

5. The proxy circular, also known as the proxy statement, is a document that public companies in Canada are required to provide to shareholders in advance of the annual general meeting. By regulation it contains, among other things, details regarding the proxy voting procedure for the election of directors.

6. In 2002, 24 of our sample companies use a table or schedule that quotes the TSX guidelines, indicates whether the company's corporate governance practices align with the guidelines, and comments on the specific procedures followed.

ACKNOWLEDGMENT

The helpful comments of colleagues at the Haskayne School of Business and Jean du Plessis of Deakin University are gratefully acknowledged. The authors also thank the Certified General Accountants for their generous financial support for this research.

REFERENCES

Allen, M. P. (1974). The structure of interorganizational elite cooptation: Interlocking corporate directorates. *American Sociological Review, 39*(3), 393–406.

Archer, M. (1982). Morphogenesis vs. structuration: On combining structure and action. *British Journal of Sociology, 33*(4), 455–483.

Berg, B. L. (1989). *Qualitative research methods for the social sciences.* Boston: Allyn & Bacon.

Brooker, K. (2002). Trouble in the boardroom. *Fortune, 145*(10), 113–116.

Buhr, N. (2002). A structuration view on the initiation of environmental reports. *Critical Perspectives on Accounting, 13,* 17–38.

Bujaki, M., & McConomy, B. J. (2002). Corporate governance: Factors influencing voluntary disclosure by publicly traded Canadian firms. *Canadian Accounting Perspectives, 1*(2), 105–139.

Craig, R., Garrott, L., & Amernic, J., (2001). A "close reading" protocol to identify perception-fashioning rhetoric in web site financial reporting: The case of Microsoft®. *Accounting and the Public Interest, 1* [available online: http://aaahq.org/ic/browse.htm]

Culler, J. D. (1976). *Saussure.* Hassocks, Sussex: Harvester Press.

Daily, C. M., Johnson, J. L., & Dalton, D. R. (1999). On the measurements of board composition: Poor consistency and a serious mismatch of theory and operationalization. *Decision Sciences, 30*(1), 83–106.

Derrida, J. (1978). In: A. Bass (Trans.), *Writing and difference: Jacques Derrida.* Chicago: University of Chicago Press.

Dillard, J. F., & Yuthas, K. (2002). Ethical audit decisions: A structuration perspective. *Journal of Business Ethics, 36,* 49–64.

DiMaggio, P., & Powell, W. W. (1983). The iron cage revisited: Institutional isomorphism and collective rationality in organizational fields. *American Sociological Review, 48,* 147–160.

Dooley, P. C. (1969). The interlocking directorate. *American Economic Review, 59,* 314–323.

Dowling, J., & Pfeffer, J. (1975). Organizational legitimacy: Social values and organizational behavior. *Pacific Sociological Review, 18*(1), 122–136.

Foucault, M. (1977). What is an author? (Trans. D. F. Bouchard and S. Simon). In: D. F. Bouchard (Ed.), *Language, counter-memory, practice.* Ithaca, New York: Cornell University Press.

Foucault, M. (1991). Politics and the study of discourse. In: G. Burchell, C. Gordon & P. Miller (Eds), *The Foucault effect: Studies in governmentality* (pp. 53–72). Chicago: University of Chicago Press.

Gale, D. (2002). How to create truly independent boards. *Wall Street Journal, A10.*

Gibbins, M., Richardson, A., & Waterhouse, J. (1990). The management of corporate financial disclosure: Opportunism, ritualism, policies, and processes. *Journal of Accounting Research, 28*(1), 121–143.

Gibbs, L. (2002). Which companies really work for you? *Money, 31*(8), 29–36.

Giddens, A. (1984). *The constitution of society: Outline of the theory of structuration.* Cambridge: Polity.

Hansell, C. (2004). *Quoted in the Globe and Mail, B14.*

Kazanjian, J. (2002). U.S. reforms hit Bay St.: Looking for a new national securities regulator for Canada? We now have one. It's the SEC in Washington, and that creates major policy risks. *National Post, FP11.*

Leblanc, R. (2001). Getting inside the black box: Problems in corporate governance research. Background paper prepared for the TSE *Joint Committee on Corporate Governance.*

Lehman, C., & Tinker, T. (1987). The 'real' cultural significance of accounts. *Accounting, Organizations and Society, 12*(5), 503–522.

Leighton, D. S. R., & Thain, D. H. (1997). *Making Boards Work: What Directors Must Do to Make Canadian Boards Effective*. Toronto: McGraw-Hill Ryerson.

Lev, B. (1992). Information disclosure strategy. *California Management Review, 34*(4), 9–32.

Lindblom, C. K. (1994). The implications of organisational legitimacy for corporate social performance and disclosure. Paper presented at the *Critical perspectives on accounting conference*. New York.

Macintosh, N., & Scapens, R. (1990). Structuration theory in management accounting. *Accounting Organizations and Society, 15*(5), 455–477.

Mouzelis, N. (1989). Restructuring structuration theory. *Sociological Review, 37*(4), 613–635.

Neimark, M. (1990). The king is dead. Long live the king!. *Critical Perspectives in Accounting, 1*(1), 103–114.

Neu, D., Warsame, H., & Pedwell, K. (1998). Managing public impressions: Environmental disclosures in annual reports. *Accounting, Organizations and Society, 23*(3), 265–282.

Oliver, C. (1991). Strategic responses to institutional processes. *Academy of Management Review, 15*, 145–179.

Ottawa Citizen. (2002). TSX wants greater board independence. *Ottawa Citizen, D1*.

Pfeffer, J. (1973). Size, composition, and function of hospital boards of directors: A study of organization–environment linkage. *Administrative Science Quarterly, 18*(3), 349–364.

Preston, A. M., Wright, C., & Young, J. J. (1996). Imag. *Accounting, Organizations and Society, 21*(1), 113–137.

Prevost, A. K., Rao, R. P., & Hossain, M. (2002). Board composition in New Zealand: An agency perspective. *Journal of Business Finance & Accounting, 29*(5/6), 731–760.

Rega, J. (2002). CEOs suggest making boards more independent. *Vancouver Sun, D8*.

Reingold, J. (1999). Dot.com boards are flouting the rules: They're small and packed with insiders Does it matter? *Business Week, 3660*, 130–134.

Rhoades, D. L., Rechner, P. L., & Sundaramurthy, C. (2000). Board composition and financial performance: A meta-analysis of the influence of outside directors. *Journal of Managerial Issues, 12*(1), 76–91.

Rogers, E. (1983). *Diffusion of Innovations*. New York: Free Press.

Saussure, F. (1961). *Course in General Linguistics*. London: Owen.

Sewell, W. (1992). A theory of structure: Duality, agency and transformation. *American Journal of Sociology, 98*, 1–29.

Stubbs, M. (1983). *Discourse analysis: The sociolinguistic analysis of natural language*. Chicago: University of Chicago Press.

Tinker, T., & Neimark, M. (1987). The role of annual reports in gender and class contradictions at General Motors: 1917–1976. *Accounting, Organizations and Society, 12*(1), 71–88.

Useem, J. (2002). In corporate America it's cleanup time. *Fortune, 146*(5), 62–72.

Watts, R. L., & Zimmerman, J. L. (1986). *Positive Accounting Theory*. Englewood Cliffs, NJ: Prentice-Hall.

Whittington, R. (1992). Putting Giddens into action: Social systems and managerial agency. *Journal of Management Studies, 29*(6), 693–712.

APPENDIX 1. BOARD PRACTICES

Accountability to Shareholders

A clear statement that the Board of Directors is accountable to the shareholders evidenced by following:

1. Board is responsible for policy to enable company to communicate effectively with its shareholders
2. Board participates in development of corporate policy regarding communication with external audiences
3. Board is responsible for enhancing shareholder value

Independence from Management

A clear statement that the Board of Directors is independent of management evidenced by following:

1. Non-CEO chair or lead director exists
2. Board is constituted with a majority of unrelated directors
3. Board has procedure by which directors can retain outside advisors
4. Board meets without management present
5. Board controls meeting agendas
6. Board has authority to hire/fire the CEO

Mandate

A clear statement regarding roles, responsibilities, and inter-relationships (i.e. Board Mandate well defined) evidenced by following:

1. Board approves position description for the CEO
2. Board approves corporate objectives which the CEO/top management is responsible for meeting and reviews CEO performance
3. Board provides orientation and education program for board members
4. Board has process for assessing the effectiveness of the board as a whole, the committees of the board, or the contribution of individual directors
5. Board is involved in strategic planning
6. Board is responsible for approving company's risk management practices
7. Board is responsible for succession planning for senior management
8. Board is responsible for the integrity of the company's internal control
9. Board is responsible for monitoring company's code of ethics or conduct

APPENDIX 2. CODING OF FISCAL 2000 DOCUMENTS

Company	A1	A2	A3	B1	B2	B3	B4	B5	B6	C1	C2	C3	C4	C5	C6	C7	C8	C9	Source
Abitibi-Consolidated	✓		✓	✓	✓	✓	✓	✓		✓			✓	✓		✓	✓	✓	A
Alcan			✓		✓	✓	×				✓	✓	✓	✓					P
Bank of Montreal	✓	✓			✓	✓	✓	✓	✓	✓	✓	✓	✓	✓	✓	✓	✓	✓	A,P
Bank of Nova Scotia			✓			✓	✓	✓		✓	✓		✓	✓	✓	✓	✓	✓	A,P
Barrick Gold						×	✓			×		✓	✓			✓	✓		P
BCE	✓	✓		✓	✓	✓	✓			✓		✓	✓	✓	✓	✓	✓	✓	P
Biovail		✓	✓			×	✓			×					✓	✓	✓		P
Bombardier	✓	✓			×	✓	✓	✓		✓		✓	✓	×	✓	✓	✓	✓	P
Canadian Imperial Bank of Commerce		✓		✓		✓		✓			✓		✓			✓	✓	✓	A
Canadian National Railway	✓		✓		✓	✓	✓		×	✓		✓	✓	✓		✓	✓	✓	P
Canadian Pacific Limited	✓	✓	✓		×	✓	✓	✓		×	×	✓	✓	✓	✓	✓	✓	✓	P
Canadian Tire	✓	✓		✓	✓	✓	✓	✓		✓	✓	✓	✓	✓	✓	✓	✓	✓	P
Celestica	✓	✓			×	✓	✓	✓		×			✓	✓	✓	✓	✓		P
Dofasco	✓	✓	✓	✓	✓	✓	✓	✓		✓	✓	✓	✓	✓	✓	✓	✓		P
Husky Energy	✓			✓	✓		✓	✓		✓	✓		✓	✓	✓			✓	P
Inco	✓	✓	✓		×	✓				✓		✓		✓	✓	✓	✓	✓	P
Magna	✓	✓	✓	✓	✓	✓	✓		✓		×		✓		✓	✓	✓	✓	P
National Bank of Canada	✓	✓	✓		✓		✓	✓	✓		✓		✓	✓	✓	✓	✓	✓	A
Nexen	×			✓	✓	✓	✓			×		✓	✓	✓	✓	✓			P
Noranda					✓		×		✓		✓	✓	✓	✓		✓	✓		P
Nortel Networks	✓	✓			✓	✓	✓			×		✓	✓	✓	✓	✓	✓	✓	P
NOVA Chemicals	✓	✓	✓	✓	×	✓	✓			×	✓		✓	✓	✓	✓	✓	✓	P
Petro-Canada					✓	✓	✓			✓	✓	✓	✓	✓	✓	✓			P
Placer Dome	✓				✓	✓	✓			✓	✓	✓	✓	✓	✓				P
Research in Motion	✓	✓		×	×	×	✓			×	×	✓	✓	✓	✓	✓	✓	✓	P
Royal Bank	✓	✓	✓	✓	✓	✓	✓	✓	✓	✓	✓	✓	✓	✓	✓	✓	✓	✓	A,P
Shaw Communications	×	×			×	✓	✓						✓	✓	✓	✓	✓		P
Suncor Energy	✓	✓			✓	✓	✓	✓		✓	✓	✓	✓	✓	✓	✓	✓	✓	P
Talisman Energy	✓	✓		✓	✓	✓	✓			✓	✓	✓	✓	✓	✓	✓	✓	✓	A
Teck	✓	✓	✓	✓		×	✓				✓	✓	✓	✓	✓	✓			A,P
Telus		✓			×	✓	✓	✓		✓	✓	✓	✓	✓	✓	✓	✓	✓	P
Thomson		✓			✓		✓					✓	✓			✓			P
Toronto-Dominion Bank	✓	✓	✓		✓	✓	✓	✓		✓	✓	✓		✓	✓	✓	✓		A
TransAlta		✓	✓		✓	✓	✓			✓		✓	✓	✓	✓			✓	P
TransCanada Pipelines	✓	✓			✓	✓	✓	✓		✓	✓	✓	✓	✓	✓	✓	✓	✓	P

APPENDIX 3. CODING OF FISCAL 2002 DOCUMENTS

Company	A1	A2	A3	B1	B2	B3	B4	B5	B6	C1	C2	C3	C4	C5	C6	C7	C8	C9	Source
Abitibi-Consolidated	✓	✓	✓	✓	✓	✓	✓	✓		✓		✓	✓	✓	✓	✓	✓	✓	A
Alcan	✓	✓	✓	✓	✓	✓	✓			✓	✓	✓	✓						P
Bank of Montreal	✓	✓		✓	✓	✓	✓	✓		✓	✓	✓	✓	✓	✓	✓	✓	✓	A,P
Bank of Nova Scotia	✓			✓	✓		✓	✓		✓	✓	✓		✓	✓	✓	✓	✓	A,P
Barrick Gold				×	×	✓	×			×		✓				✓	×		P
BCE	✓	✓		✓	✓	✓	✓	✓		✓	✓	✓	✓	✓	✓	✓	✓	✓	P
Biovail		✓	✓	×	✓	✓				×				×	✓	✓	✓	✓	P
Bombardier	✓	✓		✓	✓	✓	✓			✓	✓	✓	✓	×	✓	✓	✓	✓	P
Canadian Imperial Bank of Commerce	✓		✓		✓	✓	✓	✓	✓	✓	✓	✓	✓	✓	✓	✓	✓	✓	A,P
Canadian National Railway	✓	✓	✓		✓	✓	✓	✓	✓	✓	✓	✓	✓	✓	✓	✓	✓	✓	P
Canadian Pacific Limited	✓	✓			✓	✓	✓	✓		✓	×	✓	✓	✓	✓	✓	✓	✓	P
Canadian Tire	✓	✓		✓	✓	✓	✓	✓	✓	✓	✓	✓	✓	✓	✓	✓	✓	✓	P
Celestica	✓				✓	✓	✓	✓		✓	✓		✓	✓	✓	✓	✓	✓	P
Dofasco	✓	✓	✓		✓	✓	✓	✓			✓		✓	✓	✓	✓	✓	✓	P
Husky Energy	✓	✓		✓	✓		✓	✓		✓	✓			✓	✓	✓		✓	P
Inco	✓	✓	✓		✓	✓	✓	✓		✓	✓	✓		✓	✓	✓	✓	✓	P
Magna	✓	✓		✓	✓	✓	✓	✓			×	✓	✓		✓	✓	✓	✓	P
National Bank of Canada	✓	✓				✓	✓	✓		✓	✓	✓	✓	✓	✓	✓	✓	✓	A,P
Nexen	✓	✓			✓	✓	✓	✓		✓	✓	×	✓	✓	✓	✓	✓	✓	P
Noranda	✓				✓	✓	✓	✓			✓		✓	✓	✓	✓	✓	✓	P
Nortel Networks	✓				✓	✓	✓				✓		✓	✓	✓	✓	✓	✓	P
NOVA Chemicals	✓	✓	✓	✓	✓	✓				✓	✓	✓	✓	✓	✓	✓	✓	✓	A,P
Petro-Canada	✓	✓	✓		✓	✓	✓	✓		✓	✓	✓	✓	✓	✓	✓	✓	✓	P
Placer Dome	✓	✓	✓		✓	✓	✓	✓		✓		✓	✓	✓	✓	✓	✓	✓	P
Research in Motion	✓	✓		×	×	×	✓			×	×	✓	✓	✓	✓	✓	✓	✓	P
Royal Bank	✓	✓	✓	✓	✓	✓	✓	✓		✓	✓	✓	✓	✓	✓	✓	✓	✓	A,P
Shaw Communications	✓	×			×	✓	✓				×		✓	✓	✓	✓	✓	✓	P
Suncor Energy	✓	✓			✓	✓	✓	✓		✓	✓	✓	✓	✓	✓	✓	✓	✓	P
Talisman Energy	✓	✓	✓	✓	✓	✓				✓	✓	✓	✓	✓	✓	✓	✓		A
Teck	✓				✓	✓	✓	✓		✓	✓	✓	✓	✓	✓	✓	✓	✓	A,P
Telus	✓	✓	✓	✓		×	✓	✓	✓	✓	✓	✓	✓	✓	✓	✓	✓	✓	P
Thomson			✓	✓		✓		✓			✓	✓	✓			✓	✓		P
Toronto-Dominion Bank	✓	✓			✓	✓	✓	✓		✓	✓	✓	✓	✓	✓	✓	✓	✓	A,P
TransAlta	✓	✓			✓	✓	✓			✓	✓	✓	✓	✓	✓	✓	✓	✓	P
TransCanada Pipelines	✓	✓		✓	✓	✓	✓	✓		✓	✓	✓	✓	✓	✓	✓	✓		P

A LOOK INTO THE ROLE OF HUMAN RESOURCE MANAGEMENT IN CORPORATE GOVERNANCE AND RISK MANAGEMENT: THE PHILIPPINE EXPERIENCE

Anna Maria E. Mendoza, Vivien T. Supangco and Maria Teresa B. Tolosa

ABSTRACT

This exploratory study attempted to determine the level of formalization and implementation of corporate governance and risk management practices, and the role of human resource management in the design and formulation of such practices. This study also attempted to derive some patterns of association among the variables studied, including the degree to which specific human resource management practices were linked with the overall corporate governance and risk management objectives. Human resource management was consulted from time to time during the formulation of strategic plan, the design of behavioral control mechanisms, and the development of risk management guidelines and formal corporate

Corporate Governance: Does Any Size Fit?
Advances in Public Interest Accounting, Volume 11, 195–222
ISSN: 1041-7060/doi:10.1016/S1041-7060(05)11009-8

culture programs. However, it was consulted only during implementation of corporate governance structures at the board level. Generally, human resource management involvement in the formulation of corporate governance and risk management mechanisms was related to the degree of formalization and implementation of such mechanisms, but not to the degree of congruence of human resource management functions with corporate governance and risk management objectives. However, the degree of formalization and implementation of corporate governance structures at the board level was related to the degree of congruence of human resource management functions with corporate governance and risk management objectives and the driver measures of performance. The latter was likewise related to mechanisms of behavioral control.

INTRODUCTION

This study aims to explore the state of linkage of human resource (HR) management with corporate governance and risk management practices in selected Philippine organizations. Specifically, it attempts to answer the following research questions: What is the extent of implementation of corporate governance and risk management objectives in these organizations? What is the role of HR in the design and formulation of such practices? To what extent are specific HR practices linked to the overall corporate governance and risk management objectives?

While corporate governance has often been linked with risk management, there has been no empirical research linking either of them to human resource management. Thus far, the relationships have only been described. The linkage or integration among the three practices and its implications on organizational effectiveness present rich research possibilities. This study hopes to contribute by providing directions for future studies in this area.

CORPORATE GOVERNANCE, RISK MANAGEMENT, AND HUMAN RESOURCE MANAGEMENT

Despite the dearth of empirical studies directly linking corporate governance, risk management, and human resource management together, it is recognized that these practices are intertwined.

Traditionally, corporate governance is defined as the management of an organization in the best interest of its shareholders (Tricker, 1994). The OECD principles have expanded the firm claimants to include other stakeholders including employees, creditors, and suppliers (OECD, 1999). However, when the managers are not the owners, agency problem may drag firm performance inasmuch as the managers as the decision makers are not the residual claimants of wealth. As such, these managers may have a tendency to act in their own interests and not of those of the shareholders (Fama & Jensen, 1983). To mitigate such agency problems, it is suggested (Fama & Jensen, 1983) that control (ratifying and monitoring) of decisions be separated from its management (initiation and implementation). Thus modern corporations have board of directors, representing the shareholders, whose main role is to provide the necessary checks and balances. Following poor organizational performance that was characteristic of the 1980s, the 1990s saw more board involvement. In addition, several reforms were initiated including the separation of the positions of CEO and chairman of the board. Critiques claim that the separation of the positions of the CEO and the chairman of the board compromises the authority of the CEO and dampens the entrepreneurial spirit that is so needed for companies to turnaround (Collis & Montgomery, 1998).

In the Philippines, reforms were not ready until 2002. The Securities and Exchange Commission (SEC) guidelines were intended to conform to the OECD principles and specifically provided for the protection of shareholder rights. The SEC required from publicly listed companies the submission of corporate governance manual. These companies are also required to provide members regular and timely information. SEC also requires that companies should have at least 20% independent directors in their board. In addition, several committees are to be in place, namely: audit and compliance committee, nomination committee, compensation committee, and risk management committee (SEC, 2002).

While risk preferences differ among organizations, the introduction of risk management committee at the board level emphasizes the importance of managing risk. Even as the CEO initiates and implements corporate strategy, there is still need for a board to review risk assessment and management. Proponents of this practice argue that because managers cannot diversify employment risk, mechanisms that reduce risk may be pursued, which may not be in the best interest of the shareholders (Collis & Montgomery, 1998).

The literature on corporate governance has focused on board structures, board composition, CEO duality, board actions, etc. (Beatty & Zajac, 1994;

Conyon & Peck, 1998; Finkelstein & D' Aveni, 1994; Johnson, Hoskisson, & Hitt, 1993; Kosnik, 1990; Westphal, 1998; Zajac & Westphal, 1996). On the other hand, the literature on risk management has focused on assessing risk, and providing structure to manage risk (Liebenberg & Hoyt, 2003; Dowd, 1999). There have been studies that look into the link between risk management and corporate governance (Kleffner, Lee, & McGannon, 2003; Bedard & Johnstone, 2004; Beasley, 1996), and some discussions on the link between risk management and human resource management (Le & Kleiner, 2000; Wang & Kleiner, 2000). However, it is argued here that even as governance and risk management structures are in place at the board level, there needs to be a strong link between the board structure and actions, and the implementation of board decisions at the operational level. Because human resources are at the heart of implementing strategies, the Human Resource Management function should play a key role in implementing such strategies. It is argued here that a closer integration among corporate governance, risk management, and human resource management increases an organization's performance.

The experience of HR in the acquisition, development, compensation, and management of performance of employees can become handy in meeting challenges at the board level (Potter, 2003). Beyond experience, however, certain changes must take place in both HR activities and competency of the HR executive in order for HR to fully take part in board selection, development, and evaluation (Fuller, 1999). Even as human resource planning can be made an essential component of corporate strategy, for example, the HR director must have not only a keen understanding of the organization's culture, plans, and policies, but also knowledge of the company's business and market conditions to be able to identify competency requirements for executives to meet new challenges. In global companies, there is also a need to develop skills in international executive recruitment and development.

The organization cannot overemphasize the significance that people-risk plays in strategy implementation. People are a source of risk but at the same time necessary in managing risk (Erven, 2003). There is a human component in every business activity and decision making. It is important that the right people are selected, trained, and rewarded so that they perform their jobs properly and are also able to take steps in handling the risks within their areas of responsibility.

People-risk may be defined as the risk of not meeting business requirements due to improper human resource management policies, motivational issues and fraud (Shimpi, 1999). Some context related to people-risk or employee-related risk include human resources procedures, industrial actions, workers' compensation, and skills and training. In addition, mergers, expansion, and other growth activities of the organization necessarily expose the organization to higher risks including people-risks. Specific consequences of people-related risk include employer's liability, key person loss, employee theft and dishonesty, and costly mistakes that may be due to poor training.

It is recognized that strategic human resource management has not received as much attention at the board level as it should (Pyne & McDonald, 2001). However, this trend is gradually changing as firms witness the collapse of good governance and risk management in some leading companies. The human risk factor has increasingly become a major concern of corporate boards. One of the biggest people-risks is with recruiting and retaining key personnel (Lee, 2000). Choosing the right employee is important in reducing such risks as theft, fraud, embezzlement, pilferage, sabotage, and workplace violence (Wang & Kleiner, 2000). Such potential problems further underscore the importance of exercising reasonable care in pre- and post-selection screening practices.

In the United States, for instance, negligent hiring is one of the legal-risk issues that is causing concern among employers (Le & Kleiner, 2000). Negligent hiring occurs when a company fails to do an adequate background investigation that would have revealed that the candidate was a risk; as a result, an unsuitable or incompetent employee causes harm to a customer or another person. The employer may be held responsible, financially and possibly even criminally, for the actions of its employee because these are done in the interest of the company. In studying Indonesian enterprises, Alijoyo (2002) concludes that a company cannot achieve good corporate governance without installing an effective risk management system. Such a task requires the judicious action of a board that is both independent, and competent in risk management tools and methodologies.

While corporate governance has often been linked with risk management, there has been no empirical research linking either of them to human resource management. Thus far, the relationships have only been described. Despite the dearth of empirical studies directly linking corporate governance, risk management, and human resource management together, it is recognized that these practices are intertwined. Thus this study explores the link among corporate governance, risk management, and human resource management.

Conceptual Framework

The review of literature suggests that human resource management plays a key role in corporate governance and risk management. The effectiveness of human resource management is enhanced when it is integrated with decision making (Erven, 2003). The decision, implementation, monitoring, and gathering of feedback depend on people.

This study looks into three issues in selected Philippine companies:

The level of implementation of corporate governance and risk management: The extent to which corporate governance and risk management are formalized and implemented varies in organizations. Two dimensions are examined: the degree of formalization and the smoothness of implementation. On the higher extreme, an organization may have a formal document, unit or process for such practices and, at the same time, implementation is smooth. On the opposite extreme, these practices do not exist at all. Most firms may fall in between where there might be no formal document but somehow corporate governance and risk management are practiced, or the practice may be formalized in a document but implementation is problematic.

The extent of involvement of HRM in the design and formulation of corporate governance and risk management: There are also different levels at which HRM is involved in a firm's practice of corporate governance and risk management. Two dimensions are likewise considered: involvement in the formulation of the practice and involvement in the implementation of the practice. The most ideal level of involvement would be where HRM is involved from the beginning of any initiative relative to these practices. The opposite situation is where HRM is not consulted at all about the formulation or the design of these practices.

The degree to which HRM practices are linked to the overall corporate governance and risk management objectives: The extent to which HRM practices support corporate governance and risk management also runs along two dimensions: the degree to which governance and risk management guidelines are articulated and the degree to which HRM practices are undertaken to support corporate governance and risk management. The best situation is where the HR executive plays a key role in the formulation of governance and risk management guidelines. The other extreme would be where the organization governance or risk management guidelines are not well articulated and HR practices are completely divorced from these issues Fig. 1.

DATA COLLECTION

The current study is exploratory in nature. It attempts to determine the level of formalization and implementation of corporate governance and risk management practices as well as the role of HRM in the design and

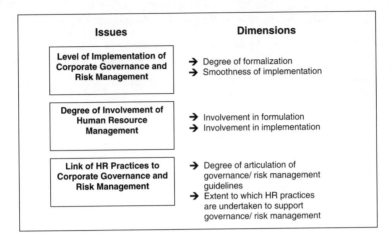

Fig. 1. Conceptual Framework.

formulation of such practices. In addition, this study looks into the degree to which specific HR practices are linked with the overall corporate governance and risk management objectives. Moreover, this study attempts to derive some patterns of association from the variables studied.

A structured questionnaire was sent through email to members of the Personnel Management Association of the Philippines and other human resource managers in August and September 2003. A total of 39 questionnaires were returned; however, three did not fit the criterion of being a corporation so they were not included in the analyses. Thus, results were based on a convenience sample of 36 organizations in Metro Manila, Philippines. Because a convenience sampling was used, the generalizability of results is limited to organizations that participated in the study.

Table 1 below presents the profile of respondent organizations. The average sample was an organization that provided services, was predominantly owned by Filipinos, and was not publicly listed. In addition, the average company had been operating for the past 28.7 years and has employed 1240.7 workers.

MEASUREMENTS

Levels of involvement variables were measured by asking respondents to identify HR's involvement in the design development or preparation of the

Table 1. Profile of Respondent Organizations.

Variable	Mean/Mode	Standard Deviation	N
Employment Size	1240.7	3127.2	34
Years in Business	28.7	20.0	35
Principal Business Activity	Services (75.0%)		36
Characteristic of Organization in Terms of Citizenship of Owners	Filipino-owned (52.8%)		36
Listing with the Philippine Stock Exchange	Not Publicly Listed (72.2%)		36

various elements of corporate governance and risk management practices. (The questionnaire may be obtained from the authors upon request.) The four levels were the following:

1. HRM is not consulted.
2. HRM is consulted during implementation only.
3. HRM is consulted from time to time during formulation.
4. HRM is involved from the start. It is part of the strategic management team.

The same method was used in measuring the level of implementation of corporate governance and risk management practices. Respondents were asked to rate the level of implementation of such practices. The scales used to assess the level of implementation were the following:

1. No formal document/unit/process and not practiced.
2. There is no formal document/unit/process but somehow practiced.
3. There is formal document/unit/process but implementation is problematic.
4. There is formal document/unit/process and for the most part, implementation is smooth.

The following were the scales used in assessing the link between specific HR practices and corporate governance and risk management objectives:

1. The organization does not have a well-articulated governance/risk management guideline, and this HR function/practice is completely

divorced from the company's corporate governance/risk management concerns.

2. The organization has an articulated governance/risk management guideline, but this HR function/practice is completely divorced from corporate governance concerns.

3. The organization has an articulated governance/risk management guideline, and this HR function/practice is undertaken to support such guideline.

4. The HR executive is involved in the formulation of governance/risk management guideline, and this HR function/practice is undertaken to support such guideline.

Inasmuch as the study is exploratory in nature, dependent and independent variables were not identified at the outset. In addition, because the concepts were derived from several sources, there was a need to determine their dimensions empirically (Snell, 1992). Factor analysis was used in order to empirically determine the dimensions of the concepts used in this study. In such cases when the factor loading of an item was not clear, the item was removed and another run of factor analysis was performed until a clear picture of relationships emerged. Consistency checks were performed on the final sets of dimensions identified with each concept.

As noted above, the purpose of using factor analyses was to empirically validate dimensions of the concepts used in this study. Once these dimensions were empirically validated, the average scores of these items were computed. The average scores were used in further analyses, instead of the factor scores, because the former are easier to identify with the original scales. The variables used in the study are described in detail in the Appendix.

RESULTS

Below are results of the study. The first section addresses the objectives of determining the level of formalization and implementation of corporate governance and risk management practices, the role of HR in the design and formulation of such practices, and the degree to which specific HR practices are linked with the overall corporate governance and risk management objectives. The second section discusses results of the analyses that explored some underlying relationships among the key variables in the study.

Corporate Governance, Risk Management, and Role of HR and Linkages

Table 2 presents the means, standard deviations, and internal consistency coefficients (Cronbach's alpha) of selected variables.

In general, HRM was consulted from time to time during the formulation of the strategic plan, the design of behavioral control mechanisms, and the development of risk management guidelines and formal corporate culture programs. However, it was not consulted during formulation but only during implementation of corporate governance structures at the board level. Still, while HRM was consulted from time to time during the development of a formal corporate culture program, the implementation of such was problematic. A similar picture was gathered from the data on the link between the HR functions, practices, and activities, and the corporate governance and risk management guidelines. The link between HR function and corporate governance and risk management objectives was such that HR functions, practices and activities were undertaken to support well-articulated corporate governance and risk management guidelines except for the compensation function where respondents claimed that its implementation was divorced from any corporate governance or risk management guideline.

However, looking at the mean scores alone might be misleading. The above results represented the average scores among those that responded to the relevant items in the questionnaire. Information on the number of respondents providing answers to the questions revealed that only 38.8% responded to the items in the categories of formulation and implementation of corporate governance structures at the board level. The implication is that some 61.2% of the respondent companies did not have those practices in place in their organizations. Based on the number of responses it also appeared that HR involvement in formulation and implementation of corporate governance and risk management mechanisms was pronounced only in the areas of strategic planning and behavioral control mechanisms and was yet quite undeveloped in the areas of corporate governance structures at the board level and risk management guidelines. This pattern of small numbers responding to certain items is repeated in the data that looked into the linkage of HR functions with corporate governance and risk management objectives. The implication was that these items were not applicable to their organization. The more salient aspects were in the areas of compensation and employee relations. Compensation practices that ensured alignment of goals between individuals and the organization, as well as employee relation practices that promoted transparency of management

Table 2. Means and Standard Deviations of Key Variables.

Variable	Mean	Standard Deviation	Cronbach's Alpha	N
HR involvement in the strategic planning process	3.44	0.80	0.92	28
HR involvement in the development of behavioral control mechanisms	3.66	0.67	0.88	29
HR involvement in corporate governance structures	2.62	0.90	0.87	14
HR involvement in risk management guidelines	3.0	1.0	_a	27
HR involvement in formal corporate culture programs	3.35	1.07	_a	23
Level of implementation of the strategic planning process	3.37	0.69	0.86	30
Level of implementation of behavioral control mechanisms	3.51	0.57	0.82	35
Level of implementation of corporate governance structures at the board level	3.08	1.0	0.94	14
Level of implementation of risk management guidelines	3.0	1.04	_a	27
Level of implementation of formal corporate culture programs	2.88	1.03	_a	26
Linkage of governance with acquisition	3.56	0.64	0.79	26
Linkage of governance with development	3.55	0.58	0.86	21
Linkage of governance with compensation	3.39	0.72	0.79	18
Linkage of governance with employee relations	3.53	0.50	0.79	19
Linkage of governance with the management of the HR environment	3.40	0.64	0.75	24
Linkage of risk management with acquisition	3.42	0.84	0.90	24
Linkage of risk management with development	3.41	0.77	0.92	23
Linkage of risk management with compensation	2.80	1.09	0.90	14
Linkage of risk management with employee relations	3.43	0.66	0.89	17
Linkage of risk management with the management of the HR environment	3.19	0.87	0.83	24
Perceived performance (outcome measures)	3.05	0.84	0.78	33
Perceived performance (driver measures)	3.03	0.95	0.86	31

[a]One-item measure.

decisions, were not happening in their organizations. This situation characterized between 47 and 61% of the sample organizations.

Relationships among Variables

Table 3 presents the correlations of the key variables in this study. The first five variables represent measures of HR involvement in the formulation of mechanisms that facilitate the promotion of good corporate governance and management of risk: HRISTRAT, HRICON, HRICGS, IIHRIQ6, and IIHRIQ19 (See Appendix for definition of the variables.) The second set of five variables represents measures of the degree to which these mechanisms are formalized and implemented: PSTRAT, PCON, PCGS, IIPRQ6, and IIPRQ19. The third set of five variables pertains to measures of the degree to which specific human resource management functions are linked with corporate governance objectives:

GACQ, GDEV, GCOMP, GER, and GMHRE. The fourth set of five variables measures the degree to which these human resource management functions are linked to risk management objectives: RMACQ, RMDEV, RMCOMP, RMER, and RMHRE. Variables 21 (PPOUT) and 22 (PPINPUT) are measures of perceived organizational performance while variables 23 and 24 are contextual variables such as organization size and age, respectively.

All significant correlations had positive signs. There was generally high correlation within each group of variables. However, from the first group of variables the degree of HR involvement in the formulation of corporate governance structures at the board level (HRICGS) was not correlated with any variable within this group, but with variables in the second and third groups, namely: the degree of formalization and implementation of corporate governance structures at the board level (PCGS) and the degree of linkage between employee-relation functions and corporate governance objectives (GER). Three variables that captured the level of HR involvement (first group: HRISTRAT, HRICGS, and IIHRIQ6) correlated with two variables (GCOMP and GER) in the third group – the degree to which HR functions were linked with corporate governance objectives. No variable in the first group was correlated with any variable in the fourth group – the degree to which HR functions were linked with risk management objectives.

Although only the degree of formalization and implementation of corporate governance structure at the board level (PCGS) in the second group was correlated with most variables representing linkage of HR function with

Table 3. Correlation Matrix of Key Variables.

	HRISTRAT	HRICON	HRICGS	IIHRIQ6	IIHRIQ19	PSTRAT	PCON	PCGS	IIPRQ6	IIPRQ19
HRISTRAT	1.0									
HRICON	0.72**	1.0								
HRICGS	0.15	0.07	1.0							
IIHRIQ6	0.58**	0.52**	-0.20	1.0						
IIHRIQ19	0.86**	0.54**	0.056	0.206	1.00					
PSTRAT	0.40*	0.02	0.34	0.47*	0.21	1.0				
PCON	-06	0.11	0.43	0.00	-0.20	0.48**	1.0			
PCGS	0.75**	0.57*	0.60*	0.26	0.31	0.73**	0.69**	1.0		
IIPRQ6	0.52**	0.40*	0.20	0.48*	0.37	0.71**	0.38	0.87**	1.0	
IIPRQ19	0.46*	0.37	0.21	0.28	0.56*	0.49*	0.64**	0.69**	0.28	1.0
GACQ	0.03	0.15	0.25	0.26	0.09	0.16	0.33	0.66*	0.02	0.31
GDEV	0.22	0.35	0.56	0.19	0.25	0.02	0.39	0.85**	0.03	0.44**
GCOMP	0.16	0.32	0.25	0.65**	0.43	0.03	0.11	0.46	0.07	0.19
GER	0.52*	0.35	0.64*	0.33	0.42	0.40	0.32	0.93*	0.40	0.33
GMHRE	0.04	0.06	0.19	0.18	0.04	0.20	0.35	0.84**	0.12	0.33
RMACQ	0.10	0.24	0.28	0.39	0.09	0.28	0.45*	0.64*	0.19	0.38
RMDEV	0.02	0.22	0.32	-0.02	0.16	-0.03	0.31	0.65*	0.40	40
RMCOMP	0.15	0.38	-0.01	0.55	0.47	0.30	0.31	0.57	0.50	0.24
RMER	0.36	0.18	0.63	0.38	0.22	0.39	0.45	0.94*	0.40	0.31
RMHRE	0.16	0.36	0.18	0.31	0.10	0.63	0.39	0.45	0.47*	0.40
PPOUT	0.05	0.14	0.47	0.05	0.04	0.30	0.22	0.48	0.20	0.23
PPINPUT	-0.10	-0.01	0.31	-0.22	-0.19	0.45*	0.51**	0.65*	0.14	0.32
SIZE	0.08	0.01	-0.14	-0.03	0.12	-0.04	0.12	0.11	0.09	0.01
COAGE	-0.05	0.14	-0.06	-0.12	0.06	-0.38	0.01	-0.21	-0.26	-0.12

Table 3 (*Continued*)

	GACQ	GDEV	GCOMP	GER	GMHRE	RMACQ	RMDEV	RMCOM	RMER	RMHRE	PPOUT	PPINPUT	SIZE	COAGE
GACQ	1.0													
GDEV	0.87**	1.0												
GCOMP	0.80**	0.74**	1.0											
GER	0.67**	0.67**	0.66*	1.0										
GMHRE	0.66*	0.85**	0.61*	0.73**	1.0									
RMACQ	0.82**	0.69**	0.48	0.50*	0.74**	1.0								
RMDEV	0.75**	0.77**	0.45	0.53*	0.69**	0.94**	1.0							
RMCOMP	0.60*	0.64*	0.79**	0.51	0.56	0.84**	0.82**	1.0						
RMER	0.46	0.42	0.39	0.81**	0.55*	0.74**	0.69**	0.66	1.0					
RMHRE	0.59**	0.71**	0.43	0.57*	0.73**	0.88**	0.82**	0.83**	0.80**	1.0				
PPOUT	0.11	0.09	0.43	0.26	-0.08	0.06	0.06	0.29	0.18	0.09	1.0			
PPINPUT	0.26	0.10	0.16	0.31	0.22	0.36	0.48*	0.57	0.53	0.39	0.44*	1.0		
SIZE	0.20	0.16	-0.03	0.01	0.26	0.14	0.10	-0.10	-0.05	0.22	-0.08	0.06	1.0	
COAGE	0.14	-0.04	0.05	-0.09	0.12	-0.07	-0.07	-0.09	-0.20	-0.25	0.11	0.11	-0.13	1.0

$**p < 0.01; *p < 0.05.$

corporate governance and risk management objectives (third and fourth groups, respectively), the implication of such result may be far-reaching. These indicated that a corporate governance structure at the board level that was formalized, communicated and implemented properly could pave the way for a high degree of linkage between HR practices and corporate governance objectives.

Generally, variables in the third group – linkage of HR functions with corporate governance objectives – and the fourth group (linkage of HR functions with risk management objectives) were highly correlated except for the variable that represented linkage of compensation with corporate governance objectives (GCOMP). The non-correlation of the degree of linkage of the compensation function with corporate governance objectives from the linkages of the other HR functions with risk management was a cause for concern. The role of incentives and rewards has been recognized as significant in shaping organizational behavior. This may be one area that is underutilized by the respondents.

The two measures of perceived performance, outcome measurements and driver measurements were correlated. Outcome measurements indicate the result of a strategy, e.g. increased sales growth, increased market share, and increased operating profits. They are also called lagging indicators (Anthony & Govindarajan, 2001). Driver measures are indicators of progress of key areas in implementing strategy, e.g. new product/service development, human resource development, and market development. They are also called leading indicators.

However, only the driver measures showed any correlation with some variables in the study. Driver measures are important in the sense that they indicate progress in support areas necessary for implementing a strategy (Anthony & Govindarajan, 2001). More specifically, the driver measures of perceived performance was positively correlated with the degree of formalization and level of implementation of the strategic plan (PSTRAT), behavioral control mechanisms (PCON), and corporate governance structures (PCGS). Among the linkage variables, only the link between human resource development and corporate governance was related with the driver measures of performance. Organization size and age were not correlated with any of the key variables in the study. These results implied that formalization and degree of implementation, more than involvement of HRM in designing corporate governance and risk management mechanisms, co-vary with driver measures of performance.

To further explore some relationships among the variables, this study looked into the differences between measures of involvement and implementation and between the degree of HRM linkage with corporate governance objectives and the degree of HRM linkage with risk management objectives. It also analyzed relationships of the key variables discussed above with some categorical variables such as industry, nationality of owners, and the status of listing with the Philippine Stock Exchange.

Table 4 shows the results of tests of means of several pairs of variables. Involvement scores were compared with implementation scores while scores on HRM linkage with corporate governance objectives were compared with scores on HRM linkage with risk management objectives. A difference in

Table 4. Test of Means between HRM Involvement and Implementation in Corporate Governance and Risk Management Objectives and between the Degree of Linkage of HRM with Corporate Governance and Risk Management Objectives.

Variable	Mean	Standard Deviation	N	t
HRISTRAT	3.4296	0.8166	27	
PSTRAT	3.4519	0.6117	27	−0.145
HRICON	3.6552	0.6729	29	
PCON	3.6552	0.4129	29	000
HRICGS	2.5385	0.8823	13	
PCGS	3.2308	0.8675	13	−3.195**
IIHRIQ6	3.0	1.0198	26	
IIPRQ6	3.0769	0.9767	26	−0.386
IIHRIQ19	3.3478	1.0706	23	
IIPRQ19	3.0	0.9045	23	1.785+
GACQ	3.5417	0.6621	24	
RMACQ	3.4167	0.8362	24	1.282
GDEV	3.5583	0.5955	20	
RMDEV	3.4667	0.7406	20	873
GCOMP	3.3056	0.8464	12	
RMCOMP	2.9167	1.0408	12	2.102*
GER	3.5529	0.5269	17	
RMER	3.4353	0.6566	17	1.738+
GMHRE	3.3768	0.6459	27	
RMHRE	3.1594	0.8754	27	−0.145

**p<0.01; *p<0.05; +p<0.10.

mean scores existed in corporate governance structures at the board level where the degree of involvement of HRM was lower than the degree of formalization and implementation of corporate governance structures. Governance structures at the highest level still remained the purview of the board. Although marginally significant, the level of involvement of HRM was higher than the degree of formalization and implementation of a corporate culture program. Thus it appears that HRM had less involvement in the formulation of the more strategic aspects and more involvement in the operational aspects of governance mechanisms. On the other hand, the link of HRM with corporate governance objectives was higher than its link with risk management objectives, and such relationship was significant for compensation and employee relations. This implied that the congruence of compensation and employee-relation practices with corporate governance objectives was more developed than the congruence of these HR practices with risk management objectives.

Table 5 shows the differences of mean scores of key variables in the study. Publicly listed corporations were compared with those that were not publicly listed. In general, publicly listed corporations had higher mean scores in HRM involvement in the formulation and implementation of governance and risk mechanisms compared to corporations that were not publicly listed. This pattern was particularly significant in HRM involvement in strategic planning, in the formulation of behavior control mechanisms and risk management guidelines, and in the degree of formalization and implementation of corporate governance structures. Thus, in comparing publicly listed and not publicly listed corporations, what figured prominently was the degree to which HR was involved in the formulation of corporate governance mechanisms. There were no differences in the degree to which HR functions were linked to corporate governance and risk management objectives and the level of implementation of corporate governance and risk management objectives, except in the degree of implementation of structures at the board level, where publicly listed companies had higher degree of implementation.

Table 6 presents the differences of mean scores of the key variables in the study between organizations in the service sector and those in the non-service sector. In general, those in the service sector had lower mean scores in HRM involvement in the formulation and implementation of governance and risk mechanisms as well as in the degree of linkage between HRM functions and corporate governance and risk management objectives compared to corporations in the non-service sector. This pattern was particularly significant in HRM involvement in the formulation of behavioral control mechanisms and corporate governance structures. Companies that

Table 5. Comparison of Means of Key Variables between Publicly
Listed and Not Publicly Listed Corporations.

Variable	Type of Corporation	Mean	Standard Deviation	N	T
HRISTRAT	Not Listed	3.2737	0.9170	19	
	Listed	3.8000	0.2828	9	-2.283*
HRICON	Not Listed	3.5500	0.7847	20	
	Listed	3.8889	0.1816	9	-1.826^+
HRICGS	Not Listed	2.6852	1.0783	9	
	Listed	2.5000	0.5270	5	0.431
IIHR1Q6	Not Listed	2.7895	1.0842	19	
	Listed	3.5000	0.5345	8	-1.752^+
IIHR1Q19	Not Listed	3.2667	1.0998	15	
	Listed	3.5000	1.0690	8	-0.489
PSTRAT	Not Listed	3.2762	0.7835	21	
	Listed	3.5778	0.3528	9	-1.453
PCON	Not Listed	3.4267	0.6200	25	
	Listed	3.7333	0.3784	10	-1.452
PCGS	Not Listed	2.7222	1.0704	9	
	Listed	3.7333	0.3651	5	-2.577*
IIPRQ6	Not Listed	2.8421	1.1187	19	
	Listed	3.3750	0.7440	8	-1.450
IIPQ19	Not Listed	2.8125	1.0468	16	
	Listed	3.0000	1.0541	10	-0.443
GACQ	Not Listed	3.4375	0.6862	16	
	Listed	3.7500	0.5401	10	-1.220
GDEV	Not Listed	3.3939	0.5882	11	
	Listed	3.7167	0.5558	10	-1.289
GCOMP	Not Listed	3.3000	0.8233	10	
	Listed	3.5000	0.6172	8	-0.570
GER	Not Listed	3.3800	0.6356	10	
	Listed	3.6889	0.2472	9	-1.422
GMHRE	Not Listed	3.2381	0.6971	14	
	Listed	3.6333	0.5080	10	-1.607
RMACQ	Not Listed	3.3214	0.9010	14	
	Listed	3.5500	0.7619	10	-0.652
RMDEV	Not Listed	3.3590	0.7131	13	
	Listed	3.4667	0.8706	10	-0.326

Table 5. (*Continued*)

Variable	Type of Corporation	Mean	Standard Deviation	N	T
RMCOMP	Not Listed	2.5938	1.1014	8	
	Listed	3.0833	1.1143	6	−0.819
RMER	Not Listed	3.3556	0.6839	9	
	Listed	3.5250	0.6585	8	−0.519
RMHRE	Not Listed	3.0238	0.9560	14	
	Listed	3.4333	0.7209	10	−1.140

$*p < 0.05$; $+p < 0.10$.

provided services also had lower scores in the degree of linkage between the compensation function and the corporate governance objectives.

Table 7 presents the differences of mean scores of the key variables in the study. Corporations predominantly owned by Filipinos were compared with multinational corporations. Multinational corporations had significantly higher mean scores in the degree of formalization and implementation of strategic planning and risk management guidelines.

CONCLUSIONS AND MANAGERIAL IMPLICATIONS

This study provided us an empirical assessment of the state of involvement of HRM in corporate governance and risk management in the Philippines. It also revealed some relationships among the elements of corporate governance mechanisms and the congruence of HR practices with corporate governance and risk management objectives.

Companies that had corporate governance and risk management mechanisms – including strategic planning, behavioral control, corporate governance structures at the board level, risk management guidelines, and formal corporate culture program – generally involved HRM in the formulation of these. However, while mean scores revealed a positive state of affairs, the low number of those responding specially in items that pertained to governance structures at the board level indicated that HR involvement in board matters was still undeveloped. It also appeared that the alignment of HR functions with corporate governance and risk management objectives was still insignificant. This is of particular concern in the areas of compensation and employee relations because the results imply that compensation

Table 6. A Comparison of Means of Key Variables between Two
Principal Types of Business Activities.

Variable	Type of Corporation	Mean	Standard Deviation	N	t
HRISTRAT	Service	3.3636	0.8522	22	
	Industry	3.7333	0.5610	6	−0.998
HRICON	Service	3.5761	0.7364	23	
	Industry	3.9583	0.1021	6	−2.403*
HRICGS	Service	2.4545	0.9548	11	
	Industry	3.2222	9.623E-02	3	−2.618*
IIHR1Q6	Service	2.9048	1.0911	21	
	Industry	3.3333	0.5164	6	−0.923
IIHR1Q19	Service	3.2222	1.1660	18	
	Industry	3.8000	0.4472	5	−1.071
PSTRAT	Service	3.3727	0.6363	22	
	Industry	3.3500	0.8734	8	0.078
PCON	Service	3.5128	0.6054	26	
	Industry	3.5185	0.5031	9	−0.025
PCGS	Service	3.0667	0.9169	10	
	Industry	3.1250	1.3428	4	−0.095
IIPRQ6	Service	2.8500	0.9881	20	
	Industry	3.4286	1.1339	7	1.285
IIPRQ19	Service	2.9000	1.208	20	
	Industry	2.8333	1.1690	6	0.136
GACQ	Service	3.5125	0.6613	20	
	Industry	3.7083	0.6003	6	−0.648
GDEV	Service	3.5000	0.6295	16	
	Industry	3.7000	0.4150	5	−0.661
GCOMP	Service	3.2381	0.7559	14	
	Industry	3.9167	0.1667	4	−3.105**
GER	Service	3.4286	0.5483	14	
	Industry	3.8000	0.2000	5	−1.457
GMHRE	Service	3.3333	0.6849	19	
	Industry	3.6667	0.4082	5	−1.031
RMACQ	Service	3.4583	0.8543	18	
	Industry	3.2917	0.8429	6	0.415
RMDEV	Service	3.5000	0.7144	17	
	Industry	3.1389	0.9215	6	0.989

Table 6. (*Continued*)

Variable	Type of Corporation	Mean	Standard Deviation	N	t
RMCOMP	Service	2.5000	1.1456	9	
	Industry	3.3500	0.8216	5	−1.453
RMER	Service	3.4333	0.6080	12	
	Industry	3.4400	0.8414	5	−0.018
RMHRE	Service	3.1930	0.9048	19	
	Industry	3.2000	0.8367	5	−0.016

$**p < 0.01$; $*p < 0.05$.

practices that ensured alignment of goals between individuals and the organization, as well as employee-relation practices that promoted transparency of management decisions, were not present in the majority of the sample organizations.

Generally, HRM involvement in the formulation of corporate governance and risk management mechanisms was related to the degree of formalization and implementation of such mechanisms. However, HRM involvement in the formulation of the various aspects of attaining corporate governance objectives was not related to the degree of congruence of HR practices with corporate governance and risk management objectives. These results imply that despite high involvement of HRM in the formulation and implementation of corporate governance and risk management objectives, the congruence of HRM practices with corporate governance and risk management objectives was not assured. There is, therefore, a need to examine the nature of HR involvement in the formulation of corporate governance and risk management mechanisms to enhance the link among the three aspects: HR, corporate governance, and risk management.

In addition, the more formalized and properly implemented corporate governance structure at the board level was associated with a higher level of HRM congruence with corporate governance and risk management objectives. Some insights may be gained from this result. It appears that there is much to be gained from having a formalized, communicated, and properly implemented corporate governance structure at the board level. This situation was associated with HR practices that were congruent with corporate governance and risk management objectives. More importantly, however, is the pattern showing that the more formalized and properly implemented the corporate governance structure at the board level, the higher the driver

Table 7. Comparison of Means of Key Variables between Filipino-owned Corporations and Multinational Corporations (MNC).

Variable	Type of Corporation	Mean	Standard Deviation	N	t
HRISTRAT	Filipino-owned	3.5077	0.8231	13	
	MNC	3.3000	0.9534	10	0.560
HRICON	Filipino-owned	3.7692	0.3139	13	
	MNC	3.4750	1.0701	10	0.842
HRICGS	Filipino-owned	2.8333	0.9930	5	
	MNC	2.6429	0.8842	7	0.350
IIHR1Q6	Filipino-owned	3.0000	1.0377	14	
	MNC	3.1250	0.9910	8	−0.276
IIHR1Q19	Filipino-owned	3.5000	1.0801	10	
	MNC	3.0000	1.3093	8	0.889
PSTRAT	Filipino-owned	3.1600	0.8526	15	
	MNC	3.7400	0.3534	10	−2.349*
PCON	Filipino-owned	3.3519	0.6414	18	
	MNC	3.6970	0.4334	11	−1.573
PCGS	Filipino-owned	2.7222	1.2413	6	
	MNC	3.4444	0.7794	6	−1.207
IIPRQ6	Filipino-owned	2.6429	1.0818	14	
	MNC	3.7500	0.7071	8	−2.897**
IIPRQ19	Filipino-owned	3.0000	1.0954	11	
	MNC	2.6000	1.0750	10	0.843
GACQ	Filipino-owned	3.5417	0.7449	12	
	MNC	3.5556	0.6821	9	−0.044
GDEV	Filipino-owned	3.5556	0.6614	9	
	MNC	3.5417	0.6409	8	0.044
GCOMP	Filipino-owned	3.5417	0.7333	8	
	MNC	3.3810	0.7052	7	0.431
GER	Filipino-owned	3.3778	0.6438	9	
	MNC	3.7143	0.2268	7	−1.456
GMHRE	Filipino-owned	3.2333	0.8322	10	
	MNC	3.5417	0.5893	8	−0.883
RMACQ	Filipino-owned	3.2500	1.1304	10	
	MNC	3.5278	0.6783	9	−0.657
RMDEV	Filipino-owned	3.4259	0.8503	9	
	MNC	3.3519	0.8954	9	0.180

Table 7. (*Continued*)

Variable	Type of Corporation	Mean	Standard Deviation	N	t
RMCOMP	Filipino-owned	2.5000	1.2247	5	
	MNC	3.0938	1.0517	8	−0.932
RMER	Filipino-owned	3.1750	0.8447	8	
	MNC	3.7333	0.2422	6	−1.775
RMHRE	Filipino-owned	2.8000	1.1353	10	
	MNC	3.4583	0.6156	8	−1.568

$**p < 0.01$; $*p < 0.05$.

measures or the leading indicators of performance. In addition, more formalized, communicated, and implemented strategic plans and behavior control mechanisms also relate to higher driver measures of performance. The results imply that driver measure of performance may be associated with formalized and well-implemented governance structure at the board level, strategic plan, and behavioral control mechanisms.

DIRECTIONS FOR FUTURE RESEARCH

This study presented several concerns and questions that merit further research. HRM involvement in the formulation and design of corporate governance and risk management mechanisms was not related to the congruence of HR practices with corporate governance and risk management objectives, as well as with measures of perceived performance. HRM involvement is related only to the degree of formalization and implementation of the mechanisms of corporate governance and risk management. However, formalization and implementation of corporate governance structure at the board level is one important factor to look into. It appears that organizations that formalize and smoothly implement corporate governance structure at the board level also involve HR in the formulation of corporate governance objectives and mechanisms and tend to have HR practices that are more congruent with more corporate governance and risk management objectives and, hence, are related with the driver measures of organizational performance.

This study did not find any relationship between linkage variables and perceived organizational performance. While they may not have direct effects on measures of performance, their role as moderating variables may be looked into.

Several contextual variables were also tested in this study. Organization size and age were not related to any of the key variables in the study. However, industry and listing in the stock exchange may be used as control variables in looking into relationships pertaining to HRM involvement in the formulation of governance and risk mechanisms. Furthermore, multinational status may be used as a control variable in determining relationships involving the degree of formalization and implementation of these mechanisms.

REFERENCES

Alijoyo, F. A. (2002). Risk management's role in corporate governance, Paper delivered during the *Panel Discussion on Corporate Governance: "Accelerating The Implementation of Good Corporate Governance through Boards Independence*, December 16 and 23, 2002, Indonesia. Retrieved September 2003, from http://www.fcgi.or.od/download-able%20filesFCGI%20article%201320%20Risk%20Management%20Role%20in%20GCG%20versi%20pdf.pdf.

Anthony, R. N., & Govindarajan, V. (2001). *Management control systems*. New York: McGraw-Hill.

Beasley, M. (1996). An empirical analysis of the relation between the board of director composition and financial statement fraud. *The accounting review*, *71*, 443–465.

Beatty, R. P., & Zajac, E. J. (1994). Managerial incentives, monitoring, and risk bearing: A study of executive compensation, ownership, and board structure in initial public offerings. *Administrative Science Quarterly*, *39*, 313–335.

Bedard, J. C., & Johnstone, K. (2004). Earnings manipulation risk, corporate governance risk, and auditors' planning and pricing decisions. *The Accounting Review*, *79*, 277–304.

Collis, D. J., & Montgomery, C. A. (1998). *Corporate strategy: A resource-based approach*. New York: Irwin McGraw-Hill.

Conyon, M., & Peck, S. (1998). Board control, remuneration committees, and top management compensation. *Academy of Management Journal*, *41*, 146–157.

Dowd, K. (1999). Financial risk management. *Financial Analysts Journal*, *55*, 65–71.

Erven, B. L. (2003). The role of human resource management in risk management, Department of Agricultural, Environmental and Development Economics, Ohio State University. Retrieved September 2003, from http://www-agecon.ag.ohio-state.edu/people/erven.1/HRM/Ohio%20Challenges.pdf.

Fama, E. F., & Jensen, M. C. (1983). Separation of ownership and control. *Journal of Law and Economics*, *26*, 301–325.

Finkelstein, S. D., & D' Aveni, R. A. (1994). CEO duality as a double-edged sword: How boards of directors balance entrenchment avoidance and unity of command. *Academy of Management Journal*, *37*, 1079–1109.

Fuller, C. L. (1999). How HR can become a corporate boardroom player. *Workforce*, *78*(1), 40.

Johnson, R. A., Hoskisson, R. E., & Hitt, M. A. (1993). Board of director involvement in restructuring: The effects of board versus managerial controls and characteristics. *Strategic Management Journal, 14*, 33–50.

Kleffner, A. E., Lee, R. B., & McGannon, B. (2003). Effect of corporate governance of the use of ERM: Evidence from Canada. *Risk Management and Insurance Review, 6*, 53–65.

Kosnik, R. D. (1990). Effects of board demography and directors' incentives on corporate greenmail decisions. *Academy of Management Journal, 33*, 129–150.

Le, M. N., & Kleiner, B. H. (2000). Understanding and preventing negligent hiring. *Management Research News, 23*(7/8), 53.

Lee, K. (2000). 'Risk management', Retrieved September 2003 from http://www.hr.com.

Liebenberg, R., & Hoyt, E. (2003). The determinants of enterprise risk management: Evidences from the appointment of risk officers. *Risk Management and Insurance Review, 6*, 37–46.

Organization for Economic Co-operation and Development (OECD) (1999). *OECD Principles of Corporate Governance*, SG/CG 5.

Potter, M. J. (2003). HR's role in improving board effectiveness. Retrieved September 2003 from http://www.hr.com.

Pyne, V., & McDonald, O. (2001). *The competent company in the new millennium*. London: Price Waterhouse Coopers.

Securities and Exchange Commission (SEC). (2002). *SEC Memorandum Circular No. 2: Series of 2002*, Securities and Exchange Commission, Philippines.

Shimpi, P. A. (1999). Risk mapping. In: P. A. Shimpi (Ed.), *Integrating corporate risk management*. New York: Swiss Re New Markets.

Snell, S. L. (1992). Control theory in strategic human resource management: The mediating effect of administrative information. *Academy of Management Journal, 35*(2), 292–337.

Tricker, R. I. (1994). *International corporate governance: Text, readings and cases*. New York: Prentice Hall.

Wang, J. M., & Kleiner, B. H. (2000). Effective employment screening practices. *Management Research News, Patrington, 23*(5/6), 73.

Westphal, J. D. (1998). Board games: How CEOs adapt to increases in structural board independence from management. *Administrative Science Quarterly, 43*, 511–537.

Zajac, E. J., & Westphal, J. D. (1996). Director reputation CEO-board power, and the dynamics of board interlocks. *Administrative Science Quarterly, 41*, 507–529.

APPENDIX. DEFINITION OF VARIABLES

1. HR involvement in strategic planning (HRIStrat): This variable was the average of involvement scores of mission statement, business strategy, HRM strategy, corporate values statement, and strategic planning process.

2. HR involvement in development of behavioral control mechanisms (HRICON): This variable was the average of involvement scores of performance management, performance measurements, code of ethics/ discipline for employees, and structured process of compliance with rules and regulations.

3. HR involvement in corporate governance structure at the board level (HRICGS): This variable was the average of involvement scores of board nomination committee, board audit committee, board compensation committee, report on corporate governance practices and achievements, charter on board's oversight responsibilities, and venue for communication between board and employees.
4. HR involvement in the development of risk management guidelines (IIHR1Q6).
5. HR involvement in the development of a formal corporate culture program (IIHR1Q19).
6. Implementation of the strategic planning process (PSTRAT): This variable was the average of practice scores of mission statement, business strategy, HRM strategy, corporate values statement, and strategic planning process.
7. Implementation of behavioral control mechanisms (PCON): This variable was the average of practice scores of performance management, performance measurements, and code of ethics/discipline for employees.
8. Implementation of corporate governance structure at the board level (PCGS): This variable was the average of practice scores of board nomination committee, board audit committee, board compensation committee, report on corporate governance practices and achievements, charter on board's oversight responsibilities, and venue for communication between board and employees.
9. Implementation of risk management guideline (IIPRQ6).
10. Implementation of a formal corporate culture program (IIPRQ19).
11. Link of acquisition functions with corporate governance objectives (GACQ): This was the average of scores of the link of such HR acquisition activities as defining required competencies, HR planning, job description, and selection with corporate governance objectives.
12. Link of development function with corporate governance objectives (GDEV): This was the average of scores of the link of such HR development activities as career management, counseling, development, documentation of individual competencies, succession planning, and training with corporate governance objectives.
13. Link of compensation function with corporate governance objectives (GCOMP): This was the average of scores of the link of such HR compensation activities as group or team-based compensation, individual incentive compensation, and profit or gain-sharing plan with corporate governance objectives.

14. Link of employee relations function with corporate governance objectives (GER): This was the average of scores of the link of such employee relation activities as discipline, employee access to business information, employee communication, compliance with company policies, and negotiation with corporate governance objectives.

15. Link of functions relating to managing the HR environment with corporate governance objectives (GMHRE): This was the average of scores of the link of such practices as health and safety, human resource information systems (HRIS), and total quality management with corporate governance objectives.

16. Link of acquisition functions with corporate risk management objectives (RMACQ): This was the average of scores of the link of such HR acquisition activities as defining required competencies, HR planning, job description, and selection with risk management objectives.

17. Link of development function with risk management objectives (RMDEV): This was the average of scores of the link of such HR development activities as career management, counseling, development, documentation of individual competencies, succession planning, and training with risk management objectives.

18. Link of compensation function with risk management objectives (RMCOMP): This was the average of scores of the link of such HR compensation activities as group or team-based compensation, individual incentive compensation, knowledge or skill-based pay, and profit or gain-sharing plan with risk management objectives.

19. Link of employee relations functions with risk management objectives (RMER): This was the average of scores of the link of such employee relation activities as discipline, employee access to business information, employee communication, compliance with company policies, and negotiation with risk management objectives.

20. Link of functions relating to managing the HR environment with risk management objectives (RMHRE): This was the average of scores of the link of such practices as health and safety, human resource information systems (HRIS), and total quality management with risk management objectives.

21. Perceived Organizational Performance: The initial factor analysis performed on the six Likert scale items (items one to six in part IV of the questionnaire) generated two factors. One factor constituted the outcome measures of performance (PPOUT) consisting of perceived performance in terms of sales growth rate, market share, and operating profits. The other measure of performance, the driver measures of

performance (PPINPUT), included perceived performance in terms of development of new product/service, human resource, and market.

22. Size: Organization size was measured in terms of the number of employees in 2002.
23. Organization Age (CoAge): This was measured as the difference of 2002 and the date of founding.
24. Industry: Industry as a dummy variable, where an organization was coded zero if it provided services; otherwise, it was coded 1.
25. Citizenship of Owners: This was measured as zero if the organization was a government-owned corporation, one if it was not for profit, two if it was predominantly held by Filipinos, and three if it was a multinational corporation.

AN EXAMINATION OF SHAREHOLDER–STAKEHOLDER GOVERNANCE TENSION: A CASE STUDY OF THE COLLAPSES OF ANSETT HOLDINGS AND AIR NEW ZEALAND

James C. Lockhart and Mike Taitoko

ABSTRACT

For decades the majority of contributions to governance practice have been compliance-focused while much governance research has been grounded in an agency view (Daily, Dalton & Rajagopalan, (2003), Academy of Management Journal, 46(2), 151–158). Much of that effort has failed to observe the key drivers of boardroom decision making. The objective of this research was to explore the shareholder–stakeholder tension within an organisation as it progressed through sequential forms of ownership. The results presented in this paper are primarily drawn from the immediate ex poste and ex ante events surrounding the collapse of Ansett Holdings Ltd and the latter government bailout of Air New Zealand. New Zealand's national airline provided a relevatory case (Yin, (1989), Case study research: Design and methods (Rev.ed.). Newbury

Corporate Governance: Does Any Size Fit?
Advances in Public Interest Accounting, Volume 11, 223–246
ISSN: 1041-7060/doi:10.1016/S1041-7060(05)11010-4

Park, CA: Sage), the opportunity to study a phenomenon previously inaccessible to research, because data hitherto unavailable 'entered' the public domain. However, when reinterpreted in light of direct input from key executives involved – benevolent informants – much of that data needs to be reconsidered to better understand why critical decisions were made. The Ansett collapse subsequently became the single largest corporate collapse in Australian history while the loss to Air New Zealand became New Zealand's largest-ever corporate loss. The decision by Brierley Investments Limited (BIL) to 'block' Singapore Airline's (SIA) entry into the Australian market, implemented through the high risk acquisition of the balance of Ansett, directly resulted in both 'collapses'. Decisions by the organisation's governance were found to have a direct impact on the performance of Air New Zealand through various phases of its ownership. While the 'collapses' are attributed to a failure of governance to act in the organisation's (stakeholders) interests. Growing tensions between shareholders and stakeholders were observed to be suppressed as the BIL dominated and led Board achieve complete control over decision making. There remains considerable opportunity to further governance research through the examination of business ethics, notably the view that appropriate ethics can be met by way of legislation (e.g. Diplock, (2003, April), Corporate governance issues. Securities Commission of New Zealand. Available from: http://www.sec-com.govt.nz/speeches/jds240403.shtml). However, the role of governance, particularly whom it is there to serve requires far greater attention on behalf of researchers. In the cases of Ansett and Air New Zealand the Board ceased to act in best interests of the organisation in favour of the major shareholder.

INTRODUCTION

In September 2001, Air New Zealand placed its wholly owned subsidiary, Ansett Holdings Ltd (Ansett), into voluntary administration. The subsequent failure to secure a rescue package or buyer for Ansett then accelerated its ultimate collapse. The Ansett collapse subsequently became the single largest corporate failure in Australian business history while the financial loss to Air New Zealand became New Zealand's largest-ever corporate loss. By financial year-end June 2001, Air New Zealand had accumulated a consolidated loss of NZ$1.4 b (billion). The airline's balance sheets showed that total liabilities had climbed from 53.3% of total assets in 1999, to 93.6% in

2001 with a corresponding fall in owner's equity from 48.4 to 6.4%. The New Zealand Government eventually provided Air New Zealand with $885 m of new capital, resulting in an 83% ownership stake, to keep it operating.

The objective of this research is to develop an understanding of the role of governance and strategy within Air New Zealand as it progressed through sequential forms of ownership. We use Johnson and Scholes (1999) model of determinants of purpose to explore shareholder–stakeholder tensions over the last two decades with particular attention being paid to the period of the collapse. The key results presented in this paper, therefore, focus on the immediate ex post and ex ante events surrounding the collapse of Ansett, and the latter Government bailout of Air New Zealand.

Guidance to case selection is typically provided by the theoretical issues to be developed and explored during the study: A process often mitigated by access and the availability of data. In contrast to much case research, Air New Zealand provided a relevatory case (Yin, 1989). A relevatory case exists when a researcher has the opportunity to study a phenomenon previously inaccessible to research. Therefore, research of such cases would only rarely involve more than a single case. The case presented here is also unusual in that data, especially that pertaining to boardroom events and the motivation for key decisions, was accessible for research.

LITERATURE REVIEW

A model of the key determinants of organisational purpose has been offered by Johnson and Scholes (1999) (see Fig. 1). Their model places corporate governance into the context of its relationship with the purpose of the organisation. The organisation's *purpose* is central to the model. By analysing the forces that acted upon Air New Zealand's purpose using this model, the key political and cultural aspects inherent within the organisation, manifest in shareholder–stakeholder tension, can be explored.

The introduction of ethics, cultural context and stakeholders into the determination of purpose appears to shift the obligations of governance well beyond the minimal compliance obligations those responsible have to shareholders (Johnson & Scholes, 1999). The process of governance, predominantly through the board of directors, is postulated as the only means through which these various forces may be best aligned.

The scope of the framework, notably the consideration of stakeholders, is a question that has been asked of corporate governance for decades (from

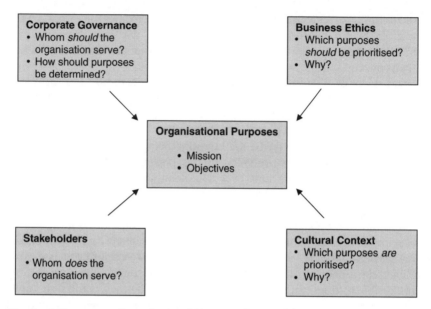

Fig. 1. Influences on Organisational Purpose. *Source*: Johnson and Scholes (1999).

Berle, 1931). At the heart of this debate lie the two seemingly disparate views regarding whom the organisation should serve and, therefore, how, corporate strategy should be determined, namely, Blake's (1999) *Shareholder School* and *Stakeholder School*.

Blake (1999, p. 28) observed that "the shareholder school focuses on shareholder value as the principal factor that the board should consider in its decision-taking".[1] This narrow view of profit maximisation (Shaw & Barry, 2001) is attributed to have gained support following the publication of Friedman's (1962) influential book, *Capitalism and Freedom*. According to Shaw and Barry (2001), Friedman's view is conducive to the laissez-faire operation of Adam Smith's "invisible hand" (p. 204). Support within New Zealand of Friedman's (1962) narrow view is evident in two reports (see Shaw & Barry, 2001; Henderson, 2001) published by the New Zealand Business Roundtable (NZBRT). In representing the NZBRT, Kerr (1996) believes that Friedman's narrow view is a way of making business "stick to its knitting". He also argued that the broad stakeholder view would see shareholders bear the cost of stakeholders' decisions. However, this view assumes that organisational performance is maximised when only shareholder's views are met and that stakeholders' views are, by some unstated necessity, at variance to organisational performance.

Kerr (1996) also alluded to the ineffectiveness of state ownership, a critical assumption in the sale of Air New Zealand. However, Charkham and Simpson (1999) observed that governance issues don't simply disappear as state-owned business passes into private ownership. They argue that the "the real problem is not who owns what, but what is done with the influence and power that ownership confers" (p. 17). A view that becomes apparent in the presentation of research results that follows.

While there remains much debate over the ethical stance of each school there is tacit agreement that the strong growth in the U.S. economy throughout the 1980s and early-1990s can be largely attributed to the widespread acceptability by boards and managers of the shareholder model (Finegold, 2001; Gates, 1998; Lazonick & O'Sullivan, 2002). There is also the view that much of the growth achieved through the shareholder model resulted from executives focussing on cost reduction in order to meet shareholders' expectations, while investment and growth opportunities were often missed or ignored (Hamel & Prahalad, 1994; Lazonick & O'Sullivan, 2002; Shaw & Barry, 2001). Therefore, while the practices of "denominator management" (Hamel & Prahalad, 1994, p. 9) and "downsize and distribute" (Lazonick & O'Sullivan, 2002, p. 15) created short-term shareholder value, in many cases it appears to have been at the expense of long term growth and business sustainability (Hamel & Prahalad, 1994; Gates, 1998; Conger, Lawler, & Finegold, 2001; Lazonick & O'Sullivan, 2002). The observation being made here is that while the shareholder model does not have to result in denominator management, its more common-place interpretation results in that end.

By contrast the stakeholder school ascribes that a wider range of interests be taken into account by the board, whether or not they add to shareholder value (Blake, 1999). Typical of this view, Charkham and Simpson (1999) argue that "companies have a broader purpose than to promote shareholder value... It is critical that shareholders recognise the complex social and economic relations that underpin wealth creation" (p. 13). A view upheld by the U.S. Supreme Court as long ago as The Depression (see Berle, 1932). This perspective is later observed to be well outside of the domain of the governance of Air New Zealand preceding the collapse of Ansett.

Although Kerr (1996) claimed that potential conflicts occur as a result of businesses meeting stakeholder expectations, Johnson and Scholes (1999) suggest that such conflict is quite normal within organisations. They claim that in most situations, "a compromise will need to be reached between expectations which cannot all be achieved simultaneously" (p. 211). The difficulty for the board and managers that follow the stakeholder model is the need for them to respond effectively to the various needs of individuals or stakeholder groups (Howe, 1997).

There is a view in New Zealand that catering broadly to all stakeholders, including society, not only destroys shareholder wealth but could also be illegal (Shaw & Barry, 2001; Kerr, 1996). In contrast, there is an emerging global view that businesses that *do* adhere to the broad view could better serve the needs of stakeholders while *creating* wealth for their shareholders. Von Tunzelmann and Cullwick (1996) claim that "outstanding companies worldwide... are consistently found to have built into their corporate strategies a strong social orientation which they have combined successfully with high returns to shareholders" (p. 45). Similarly, Collins and Porras (1997) found that the long term financial success of an organisation is more likely to occur by engaging all stakeholders in understanding and preserving the core values and purpose of the firm. While Hilmer (1998) admitted that, "even *if* [italics added] the managers of corporations are required to act only in the best interests of shareholders, they must inevitably take into account the interests of other stakeholders in order to maximise shareholder wealth" (p. 23). Johnson and Scholes (1999) model of the influences on purpose, therefore, provides a means through which the expectations of various stakeholders and shareholders are aligned with the purpose of the organisation – and vice versa – by deciding which strategies should be prioritised and why. This framework then provides the basis for determining why strategic decisions were made by Air New Zealand's Board of Directors.

In 1998 Dalton, Daily, Ellstrand and Johnson (1998) observed that agency theory had become the dominant framework for the study of corporate governance, a view reinforced in their more recent work for the Academy on governance through ownership. In that summary Daily et al. (2003) extend the observation of others that the results of much agency grounded research are inconsistent, a finding they then extend to ownership studies in general. Implications that the agency problem could well be overstated, or that the theory may be inappropriate for governance research remained unstated.

The authors did, however, observe the recent U.S. trend of attempting to align directors' interests with those of the firm. This trend marks a shift of the search for the agency problem among senior management, and particularly CEOs (see Dalton & Daily, 2001), to that among boards of directors (see Tosi, Werner, Katz, & Gomez-Mejia, 2000). Nevertheless, the research trend remains grounded in an agency view of the firm. From a practitioner perspective the agency view is manifest through increasing compliance being 'imposed' on boards through rules-based approaches such as the Sarbanes-Oxley Act or through more prescriptive approaches such as those of Higgs, and in New Zealand, recommendations from the New Zealand Stock exchange (2004) and the Securities Commission (2004) on appropriate board architecture and reporting standards.

The second phenomenon to evolve from the separation of the provision and control of wealth appears to be confusion between the *two* entities now supposedly responsible for organisational success – the board and management (whose collective activity contributes the management system). Attempts to assign distinct roles and responsibilities to the board began in 1966 with the publication of The Corporate Director by the American Management Association (Kristie, 1997) and have continued unabated to date (e.g. American Law Institute, 1992;[2] OECD, 1999, 2003). These broad functions are widely accepted, being endorsed by Hilmer (1998) and KPMG (2001) in the contexts of private business in Australia and New Zealand respectively.

No doubt the repeated publication of task-lists provoked Cassidy's (2000) remark that governance has degenerated into "a meaningless 'box ticking' exercise", a sad indictment on its understanding and practice. In direct contrast to these tasks Cochran and Warlick (1994) and Taylor, Chait and Holland (1996) have both argued that the board's contribution is strategic, the focus of governance being external whereas management's focus is internal. "Governance is strategy orientated whereas management is task orientated" (p. 10). Yet the typical lists of directors' duties are compliance related and largely ignore strategy, notable exceptions include those from both Pound (1995) and King (2002) who take a refreshingly holistic approach to the responsibility of governance.

Two features of these failures make them appropriate for case research. First, critical documentation remains in the public domain and second, the cause of the respective outcomes mark a significant departure from the heralded failures of Enron (Bryce, 2002), WorldCom, Tyco, Adelphia (Sonnenfeld, 2002), and Global Crossing (Zeff, 2003) whose Boards are not *directly* attributed for their failure.

CASE METHOD

The single most important condition for differentiating between data collection techniques is the type of research question being asked (Yin, 1989; Stablein, 1996). The case study (Dixon, Bouma, & Atkinson, 1987; Hakim, 1987) is the preferred strategy when examining contemporary events. Yin's

(1984, 1989, 1993) principles ensure that the researcher avoids the pitfalls associated with the *preferred technique method* identified by Ackerman (1965) and Gummesson (1991).

Research strategies may not, however, be mutually exclusive. A study may include an archival analysis or survey in a case study (Sieber, 1972). With respect to this study, given the complete lack of control over behaviour (Cook & Campbell, 1979) and the focus on contemporary events, suitable techniques for the data gathering process were restricted to the case study data collection and analysis supplemented by archival analysis. Substantive effort was applied to archival analysis through annual reports, histories and press statements from which focus was then applied to identify the decision making behind contemporary strategic events.

The combined approaches were considered necessary to avoid Christensen and Raynor's (2003) observation that "many academics and consultants...remain at this correlation-based stage of theory building in the mistaken belief that they can increase the predicative power of their 'theories' by crunching huge databases on powerful computers" (p. 70).[3] A view supported by Daily et al. (2003) observation of the lack of explanation produced by some two decades of governance research. The research design (Eisenhardt, 1989) also defines the degree to which results can be generalised (i.e. whether the obtained interpretations can be generalised to a larger population or to different situations). While the results, in this forum, relate solely to the case of Air New Zealand they contribute to a sector driven agenda for governance research in New Zealand.

Guidance to case selection is typically provided by the theoretical issues (Van de Ven, 1989) to be developed and explored during the study but inevitably mitigated by both access and the availability of data. The process of selection for this study was influenced first, by the successive organisational failures; second, the implicit role the Board of Directors appeared to take in contributing to that outcome and third, access to data of which critical points (documents) were in the public domain: a *relevatory case* (Yin, 1989). A relevatory case exists when a researcher has the opportunity to study a phenomenon previously inaccessible to research. The collapse of Ansett Holdings and subsequent government bailout of Air New Zealand provided that opportunity.

Christensen and Raynor (2003) remark that failure events may provide a better understanding of causality. However, the study of failure events has to be conducted, at best, opportunistically. Attempts to research organisational failure due to governance decision making are expected to be rare as the majority of evidence remains beyond the scrutiny of research.

While case selection was predominantly influenced through the nature of the case, access beyond the analysis of publicly available documents still had to be gained. Gummesson (1991) identified that access is the researcher's number one challenge. "Access refers to the opportunities available to find empirical data (real-world-data) and information" (p. 11). Case research typically requires cooperation from a person and/or company (Howard & MacMillan, 1991; Ladd, n.d.). Without key informants research was expected to be slow, and perhaps, unsubstantiated. Key informants within the organisation were gained either directly or through established industry contacts. Some key informants were often only prepared to confirm a hypothesis developed from material sourced from other third parties. Other contributors to the study included four senior managers and the airline's executives, industry commentators and researchers, and government ministers all of whom were interviewed using the exploratory, open-ended interview technique. With the exception of the Minister of Finance participants wish to remain anonymous.

Critical collaborators in both Ansett and Air New Zealand have requested anonymity, and further disclosure of the steps used to gain access to these select senior managers and executives would implicate them by way of the contributions made to this research. This stance is recognised as causing anxiety within the research community, given the requirement for repeatability. However, this is anticipated to become increasingly commonplace as the focus of governance research shifts from large data sets to boardroom decision making. The only way that research can occur, and the results be published, is to ensure the anonymity of contributors. In future, as board room decision making is explored in detail not only will contributors remain anonymous but the various organisations they represent are likely to demand the same respect. That outcome is still far from the case presented here.

THE CASE: RELEVANT HISTORY

Air New Zealand was established in 1965 through the name change of TEAL (Tasman Empire Airways Ltd), New Zealand's then international carrier (Rennie, 1990). TEAL had been a joint venture between Qantas (23%), BOAC (38%), the New Zealand Government (20%) and Union Airways (19%) – a wholly owned subsidiary of P&O Lines (UK) (Driscoll, 1979). Owing to the rapid development of international air travel in the late 1950s and early 1960s, and the growing importance of reciprocal landing rights, the New Zealand government eventually acquired 100% ownership in 1961 (Rennie, 1990).

The purpose (see Bart, 2004) of TEAL was to 'meet the needs of the people of New Zealand for air services between New Zealand and other territories, and to assist in the promotion of New Zealand's export trade and tourism' (Patterson & Wallace, 1997, p. 86). TEAL, however, remained a profit-oriented organisation having no obligation to maintain specific services in the absence of reasonable returns (Rendel, 1975; Holmes, 1982).

Air travel in the domestic market was provided by NAC (National Airways Corporation), also government owned. NAC was established in 1947 under the NAC Act of 1945 (Aimer, 2000). NAC's ownership remained with government up to and beyond its merger with Air New Zealand in 1978. Following the merger of NAC in 1978 Air New Zealand was immediately confronted with rising fuel costs, coupled with a devalued NZ dollar, deregulation of the U.S. airline industry, and the grounding of the company's DC 10 fleet (Aimer, 2000). The performance of Air New Zealand was also adversely affected by the Mt Erebus air disaster in 1979 when a DC 10 crashed in Antarctica. However, by 1984, and after further development of both domestic and international routes, the organisation was achieving annual profits of some NZ$80 m (million) p.a. (Patterson & Wallace, 1997). In 1986, and under the CER (Closer Economic Relations) agreement with Australia, the New Zealand government removed foreign ownership restrictions from the Air Licensing Act opening domestic routes to foreign competition, a position not reciprocated by the Australian government. Within two months Ansett Airlines owned by Ansett Australia (50%), Brierley Investments Ltd. (1999) (BIL, 27.5%) and the Newmans Group (22.5%) (Patterson & Wallace, 1997) was operating flights on the trunk route of Auckland, Wellington and Christchurch in competition with Air New Zealand. Seven months after establishment Ansett had purchased the outstanding 50% from BIL and Newmans. Air New Zealand reacted competitively reducing fares, enhancing onboard services, and investing in terminal facilities. Ansett's first year in New Zealand closed with a NZ$30 m loss, and BIL was reported losing some NZ$14 m on their investment (Patterson & Wallace, 1997), a phenomena that was to repeat itself at a much later stage.

In 1989 the government floated Air New Zealand for NZ$660 m to a consortium led by BIL (35%), the NZ public (30%), Qantas (19.99%), Japan Airlines (7.5%), and American Airlines (7.5%). The NZ government retained a 'Kiwi Share' enabling government to control changes in the capital structure, classes and transfers of shares, and board composition. The

Kiwi Share also appears to have ensured the continuation of non-profitable domestic routes in a manner not dissimilar to that of the earlier NAC Act.

In 1994 the Australian Government prepared to open their domestic market to New Zealand airlines through an 'open skies agreement' (Ballantyne, 1995; Goh, 2001) to create a single Australian–New Zealand aviation market. However, due to the perceived adverse impact this may have had on recently privatised Qantas they reneged only days before Air New Zealand was due to be granted access to the Australian market. Air New Zealand was then left with the only option of gaining access to the Australian market by purchasing 50% of Ansett Australia from TNT Holdings for A\$465 m, purchase approval was granted by the New Zealand Commerce Commission in June 1996. The acquisition created a 50/50 partnership between Air New Zealand and the remaining shareholder News Corporation Ltd. Air New Zealand also gained pre-emptive rights for the balance of the company.

Benefits from the acquisition appear to have been realised almost immediately. In successive years (Air New Zealand, 1997, 1998, 1999) both the Chairman and the CEO reported that sound progress was being made in integrating systems, reducing costs, market development and the integration of routes between the two airlines. At the same time Air New Zealand, with Ansett Australia, joined the Star Alliance alongside Singapore Airlines (SIA), United and Air Canada. An expansion strategy that was consistent with the stated policy of pursuing relatively low risk commercial opportunities. To fund the purchase the Board raised new equity through a 3:11 rights issue, drew down cash reserves of NZ\$350 m, and used NZ\$190 m of existing credit facilities. The net effect of prudent financing and sound management ensured that Air New Zealand's balance sheet remained sound and the airline continued to provide returns above the industry average.

THE CASE: FAILURE

In December 1998, BIL was reported as beginning to implement their business plan of increasing representation on the boards of strategic investments and taking a more active participation in their management (BIL announces business, 1999, April 23). Although the public announcement for this approach was withheld until late April 1999. The shift from passive investment to active involvement in governance and management appears to have been motivated by the continuing [poor] performance of many of the strategic investments held by BIL. Clearly, BIL considered they had the competencies required to extract greater returns from these investments by greater involvement (BIL policy, 1998). BIL increased their representation on Air New Zealand's Board from two of eight directors in May, 1999 to four of ten including that of Chairman in December. One respondent reported that at that time BIL began to realise that the return they expected from this investment (an international airline), 20% ROI, was not going to be forthcoming. The only exit strategy available to them, therefore, was via the sale of shares to a more benevolent owner. This they thought they had found in the form of SIA.

In March 1999, SIA conducted their third attempt to buy into the Australian market (Thomas, 2001), this time through the acquisition of News Corporation's 50% share of Ansett Australia (previous attempts were in 1991 with Ansett, and 1994 with Qantas). In order to 'block' SIA's entry, and force them to enter the Australian airline market via their own airline, the Air New Zealand Board now dominated and chaired by BIL's representatives, (BIL, 1999) exercised their pre-emptive rights and agreed to acquire the remaining 50% of Ansett. Air New Zealand purchased the remaining 50% (A$580 million) in June 2000 with debt capital, increasing their debt to asset from 51.5 to 82%, while their debt to equity increased from 106 to 465%.

Immediately after the acquisition the airline's long standing CEO, Jim McRea, resigned, Air New Zealand's chairman, and BIL appointee, then filled the position for some six months until a permanent CEO was appointed. At the time McRea stated publicly that with the final purchase he had achieved a lifetime's ambition. However, research respondents stated that management was not persuaded by the timing of the purchase, and the precarious financial state from which *they* then had to manage the airline. Further evidence of their concerns is evident in the behaviour of a group of senior managers, including the CEO, who immediately resigned (including the GM Operations International and GM International Affairs). Therefore, Air New Zealand was faced with the situation where the company had its lowest level of aviation experience at both senior management and board levels in its history. An outcome brought about by imprudent decision making on behalf of the Board.

In the 2001 Annual Report, acting chairman Jim Farmer discussed the difficulties that Air New Zealand faced after the purchase of the final 50% of Ansett Holdings Ltd. Farmer pointed to the high fuel costs and exchange rates as having a significant impact on the airline's profitability. However, he acknowledged that these influences had been foreshadowed in the 2000 Annual Report (Air New Zealand, 2001). The predicted increase in fuel prices was also mentioned in BIL's 2000 Annual Report. In that report it was claimed that the Ansett purchase and SIA's introduction would add considerable value to Air New Zealand, "despite the potentially damaging effects of higher fuel prices on near term earnings" (BIL, 2000). These reports imply that although increasing fuel prices significantly impacted on Air New Zealand's profitability, the impact was both predicted and expected. Recall that Air New Zealand had experienced these external shocks during the 1970s, however, the absence of an appropriate CEO during the period did little to ameliorate their impact on the airline.

Farmer also claimed that poor maintenance planning at Ansett had been identified after Air New Zealand had assumed management control from News Corporation. He stated "the consequence was unacceptable reliability and punctuality performance which in turn lowered customer satisfaction and manifested itself in declining market share" (Air New Zealand, 2001). However, marketing data showed that Ansett had been losing market share to Qantas from as early as 1994.

Immediately following the purchase of the first 50% of Ansett, Australia management established 23 joint project teams between the two airlines. The anticipated synergies between Ansett and Air New Zealand were quickly developed, yet the organisation's governance publicly blamed the imminent downfall on a lack of their knowledge or events well outside of their control. Those 23 project teams had been in place since the purchase of the first 50%, and research respondents reported that management knew fully well the extent of Ansett's capabilities in terms of its fleet, crew, engineering and ground staff.

One paragraph in Farmer's report that attempts to explain the reasons behind Ansett's collapse, possibly best sums up the predictability of the troubles that Ansett and Air New Zealand quickly encountered after the acquisition. Farmer claimed that:

> the deteriorating profitability of Ansett in a rapidly changing industry and [the] newly highly competitive domestic market in Australia, on top of poor financial performance of Air New Zealand's international operations, meant however that the short term demand for capital to fund Ansett's revival…was beyond the existing financial resources of Air New Zealand (Air New Zealand, 2001, p. 3).

The new CEO, Gary Toomey, found it impossible to trade his way out of the precarious position he inherited. By June 2001 Air New Zealand had accumulated a consolidated loss of $NZ1.4 billion. Total liabilities had climbed from 50% of assets in 1999 to 93.6%, and owners' equity had declined accordingly. In September Air New Zealand placed their wholly owned subsidiary Ansett Australia into receivership. The following month the New Zealand government provided the airline with NZ$855 million of new capital to keep it operating, effectively giving the government an 83% stake. The failures of Ansett Australia and Air New Zealand represent the largest corporate collapses on each side of the Tasman.

ANALYSIS

Air New Zealand's purpose was never stated explicitly. However, as in the case of NAC and TEAL, the government ensured that the airline remained a tool of national development that existed to meet the needs of the people of New Zealand. The airline's purpose for the period 1940–1989, as derived through Johnson and Scholes' (1999) model, is presented in Fig. 2.

Immediately post sale the new CEO, Jim Scott, employed a strategy of high growth through high expenditure. Scott's prediction of double-digit growth throughout the 1990s, and his desire to increase spending, possibly demonstrated his lack of understanding of the airline industry. The previous fifty years had proved that year-on-year double digit growth, as Scott had suggested, was unrealistic in the volatile airline industry. Increased competition as a result of deregulation made Scott's predictions even more unlikely.

Scott's retirement in 1991 saw the return of a CEO with vast industrial experience. Jim McCrea's thirty-year tenure with Air New Zealand returned the experience that was necessary at the head of the airline. McCrea's decision to immediately pull-back from the high-risk strategies that Scott had employed signalled his greater understanding of the inherent volatility within the industry. However, the Chairman, Bob Matthew (again representing BIL), commented that the financial returns in 1993 of 12.5%[4] fell short of those required to properly reward the shareholders, despite the difficult industry conditions during that period. McCrea's apparent satisfaction with the same results, imply that management considered such returns satisfactory under the prevalent conditions. The historical analysis of the airline demonstrates that the Board's expectations of higher than 12.5% under those conditions were unrealistic. These disparate views are indicative of a split in the expectations of the airline's performance between management and governance, yet during the next few years convergence was again achieved between the two parties.

Over time, the owners, in particular BIL, appeared to gain a better understanding of the difficult industry environment in which they had

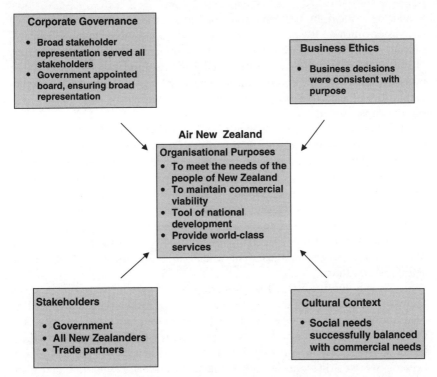

Fig. 2. Strategic Influences on the Purpose of Air New Zealand, 1940–1989. *Source*: Johnson and Scholes (1999).

invested capital. Matthew's annual reports demonstrate a shift in Board and owner expectations throughout the 1990s, as BIL's drive for unrealistic returns appeared to soften. The purchase of the first fifty percent of Ansett Holdings Limited was consistent with McCrea's strategy of growing an Australasian-based airline through prudent investment decisions. The subsequent rights issue meant that the investment did not significantly increase the financial risk, and the balance sheet remained strong.

Although purchasing the second 50% of Ansett was reported as always being a preferred long-term strategy by the management team, the purchase was expedited when SIA made an offer for the remaining Ansett shares held by News Corp. The purchase of the final 50% of Ansett placed Air New Zealand in an extraordinarily high-risk financial position. McCrea's long tenure with the company and success as CEO over the previous ten years would be critical in ensuring that the acquisition achieved the desired outcomes quickly. Respondents stated that the executive team set an implementation plan in place for the rapid and effective merging of businesses. However, McCrea's departure from Air New Zealand two weeks after the purchase of the final 50% of Ansett, impacted significantly on the implementation of effective merger strategies. Consequently, the merger was poorly implemented.

BIL Executive Chair, Sir Selwyn Cushing, stepped into the role of acting Chief Executive at the most critical period of the airline's history. However, with hindsight it became apparent to respondents that Sir Selwyn had actually realised the goals of the BIL business plan released fifteen months earlier, albeit at huge financial risk. BIL had increased its board representation in Air New Zealand, they had introduced SIA as a likely investment partner, and they had now taken an active management role in the airline. As a result they were now in a strong position to carry out their primary role of active investment management aimed at maximising and extracting shareholder value.

Sir Selwyn and the BIL/SIA dominated board now appeared to be more focussed on increasing the value of the A shares rather than implementing continuing merger strategies. Convincing the Government to increase the foreign ownership cap also became a priority: it would allow SIA to take a larger shareholding in Air New Zealand. BIL believed that the SIA shareholding would add considerable value to Air New Zealand, thereby increasing the value of their investment in the short term. However, the Board's attempt to gain an increase in the foreign ownership cap, failed to consider the reason Air New Zealand actually existed – a tool for New Zealand's economic development. Key influences on the organisation's purpose as at 1999, are presented in Fig. 3.

In support of these perspectives we observe that four months before the collapse of Ansett, Sir Selwyn Cushing stepped aside from his chairman positions on the Air New Zealand and BIL boards. Shortly afterwards he wrote to the Prime Minister. In the correspondence approved by the BIL board, and obtained for the purposes of this research, he stated that:

> BIL is an investment company. Its basic objective is to achieve an annual return of 20% on its shareholders' equity. The directors of BIL have a fiduciary duty to their shareholders, including 85,000 New Zealand residents, to seek to maximise the company's financial returns.

> Air New Zealand has consistently destroyed shareholder value in recent years by failing to achieve returns in excess of its weighted average cost of capital.

> (BIL, 2001)

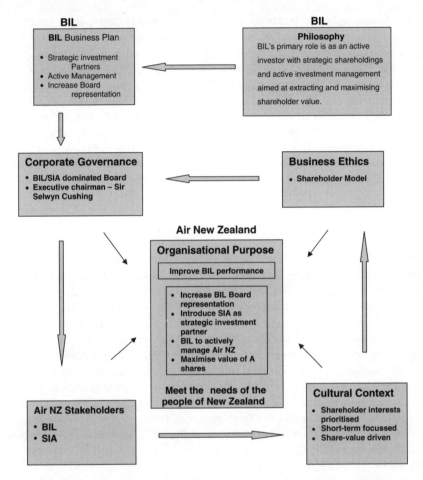

Fig. 3. Influences on the Purpose of Air New Zealand, 1999. Adapted from Johnson and Scholes (1999).

Despite Sir Selwyn's view of BIL's poorly performing investment, his comments go on to reflect the purpose of his company (BIL) and his faith in its investment strategies:

> BIL intends to exit its stake on Air New Zealand at some time…however, BIL believes the shares to be substantially undervalued at present and does not currently intend to sell its stake.

The Ansett collapse occurred exactly twelve weeks later, removing any chance BIL may have had of extracting the value they believed existed. The strategy adopted by the major shareholder, and systematically implemented through their domination of governance and senior management, was one of short-term profit maximisation. The growing shareholder–stakeholder tension, over the preceding decade, arguably dissolved in favour of the majority shareholder.[5] However, it was at odds with both Air NZ's ethical responsibility for the well-being of the nation, and gave little if any consideration to the wishes of minority shareholders. When BIL realised that their expectations of a 20% return on investment were not going to be met they sought an exit strategy through the sale of shares to SIA.

DISCUSSION

Despite the surprise expressed by its Chairman our research shows that Air New Zealand's management was aware of Ansett's declining profitability well before purchasing the remaining 50%. Note that this is at variance to publicly held and expressed opinions over the knowledge that Air New Zealand's board supposedly held and stated publicly about Ansett. The phenomena of rapid change was not new to the industry nor was it new to Air New Zealand. Management expected that Air New Zealand's financial performance would be poor as a result of the predicted increase in fuel price and the relative poor shape of Ansett's operations and performance. Air NZ knew this information and it was shared in the boardroom. The airline had anticipated raising capital for the purpose of reviving Ansett. More importantly, the purchase was prematurely undertaken even though Air New Zealand's immediate financial resources were never sufficient to fund the investment needed to revive Ansett.

The stakeholder model served Air New Zealand well throughout its first 60 years. At times there was conflict between various stakeholder groups such as those between the Government and the airline's management. Managers were constantly challenged to meet the needs of various stakeholder groups. The stakeholder model also provided a robust governance structure that allowed the airline to grow successfully over time – as a tool for national development. This outcome is entirely consistent with the relevant stakeholder theory discussed earlier (Collins & Porras, 1997; Finegold, 2001; Johnson & Scholes, 1999).

As BIL increased their power and influence over a period of two to three years, evident by their representation in the boardroom and domination over decision making, Air New Zealand's governance and strategy framework became more representative of the Shareholder Model. Strategies were formulated that better reflected the more short-term nature of the shareholder framework, which in this case translated to an exit strategy for the majority shareholder. As Hamel and Prahalad (1994) and Collins and Porras (1997) argue, the long-term sustainability of a business is undermined by boards and managers who pursue the narrow, short-term view to satisfy their shareholders only. We assert that Air New Zealand's poor performance after 2000 may have been reduced or even avoided if a broader stakeholder view had been maintained under private ownership. However, such a stance may not have resulted in the full ownership of Ansett, the remaining 50% being most likely owned by Singapore Airlines – one of Air New Zealand's Star Alliance partners. While this outcome was reported to have had merit to management it clearly was not in BIL's interests.

The Government and BIL both had high levels of interest in the strategic direction of the airline but for very different reasons. Consequently, both chose to exercise their power to influence the ownership structure of the business. Even though BIL owned large blocks of shares, it managed this investment for the benefit of majority shareholders (themselves), with little regard to minority interests. BIL's strategy was at odds with Air New Zealand's culture which reflected a deep understanding of the need to carefully nurture the airline through steady growth within a volatile industry. Historically, Air New Zealand had been led by people who understood aviation at both Board and senior management levels. They understood the industry, the need to balance wide-ranging and often opposing views of various stakeholder groups and individuals, and knew what their airline meant to New Zealand, socially and economically. Succession planning had ensured that the purpose of the airline was preserved.

Jensen (2000) argues that corporate governance mechanisms are necessary for controlling agency conflicts. However, this study has found that senior managers throughout Air New Zealand's history, with the exception of Scott and Sir Selwyn, were largely motivated by their desire to be involved in aviation. Jensen may rightly argue in this case that these managers were still motivated by self-interest. If so, then the agency view fails to recognise that a manager's self-interest may in fact be beneficial to the firm, its owners, and the broad stakeholder group. It follows that the requirement for monitoring may be reduced if such self-interest can be enhanced. Active investors who monitor managers and sometimes actively manage may also act out of self-interest (as in the case of BIL), and not in a manner that is strategically supportive or custodial for the organisation.

Both Cochran and Warlick's (1994) and Taylor et al. (1996) observation that the role of governance is primarily strategic is not supported by this study. In the case of Ansett and Air New Zealand the primary role of governance – some respondent's would state exclusive – was to maximise the wealth of the majority shareholder. Academic's assumption that governance acts in the organisation's benefit, while commendable, has in this instance been sorely challenged.

CONCLUSION

If strategy and governance have a material impact on organisational performance then it is likely that various ownership structures, which in turn influence both, will also influence organisational outcomes. Johnson and Scholes' (1999) framework of Influences on Organisational Purpose was used as the basis for identifying and examining the critical decisions that shaped and reshaped the purpose of the airline through its entire history. Governance and through it strategy – or the lack thereof – were found to have a direct impact on the performance of Air New Zealand through the last decade of intense study. While the deliberate attempt by the airline's major shareholder, Brierley Investments Limited (BIL), to 'block' Singapore Airline's (SIA) entry into the Australian market was the catalyst to both 'collapses'.

There has been much discussion surrounding the demise of Ansett and the financial losses incurred by Air New Zealand. However, this research demonstrates that the events that occurred after acquisition of the remaining 50% of Ansett were predictable – the airline had no financial capacity to absorb the ensuing adverse shocks. Air New Zealand had survived many challenges throughout its history, and its senior managers were aware of the risk of being involved in the increasingly competitive and volatile airline industry. However, as Ansett's performance declined and Air New Zealand's losses mounted, there appeared to be a level of either naivety or ignorance on the part of select components of the organisation's management system. Where risk had been reduced in the past through proactive strategy formulation and quick decision making, Air New Zealand's board was reportedly surprised by the rapidity of unfolding events.

Air New Zealand's chances of long-term survival were significantly eroded when the shareholder-structured governance and strategy model began to reflect a new purpose for the airline. The events that occurred after 2000 largely represented the 'industry noise' that had surrounded the airline throughout its history. This time, however, the airline's ability to avoid the familiar shocks had largely been dissolved in the pursuit of short-term profit maximisation on the part of the major shareholder, BIL. While the Board had the necessary power and control (Charkham & Simpson, 1999) to impose *its* desired strategy, this was at the expense of the organisation. In the absence of desirable competencies, the performance of the organisation rapidly deteriorated.

Corporate governance lacks a "unifying theory" (Tricker, 2000). The vast majority of contributions to governance practice are grounded in a compliance focused regime while much governance research is grounded in an agency view. There remains considerable opportunity to further research in this context from the perspective of business ethics, (Diplock, 2003) especially those related to the ongoing tension between shareholders and stakeholders.

NOTES

1. Note that Blake's classification of stakeholders encompasses shareholders. An alternate view, and not resolved here, is one where the concept of stakeholders excludes shareholders. Both stakeholders and shareholders remain recipients of the organisation's activity. Stakeholders are served through the organisation's purpose and processes, shareholders then receive the outcome (profit) from the pursuit of these activities.

2. Given that the Ansett collapse and the Air New Zealand bailout occurred prior to the world-wide surge in governance interest post-Enron indicative board functions adopted here are commensurate with the period in question.

3. Many contributions to research on governance appear to suffer from the same pitfalls, characterised by large data sets that provide the opportunity for precise quantitative analysis yet reveal little understanding of practice and often fail to contribute to theory.

4. Air New Zealand provided data to show that world airline cumulative profit margin for the period 1985–1999 was 0–2%.

5. BIL were the majority shareholder and are observed to have acted in their own interests, as opposed to those of the organisation. Little consideration was given to minority shareholders by the Board, and the independent directors remained surprisingly mute throughout the entire collapse of both airlines.

REFERENCES

Ackerman, J. S. (1965). On scientia. In: G. Holton (Ed.), *Science and culture* (pp. 14–23). Boston, MA: Beacon.

Aimer, P. (2000). *Wings of the nation: A history of the New Zealand National Airways Corporation 1947–78.* North Shore City: The Bush Press.

Air New Zealand. (1987–2001). *Air New Zealand annual reports.* Auckland: Author.

American Law Institute. (1992). *Principles of corporate governance: Analysis and recommendations.* Philadelphia, PA: Author.

Ballantyne, T. (1995, September). Big brother blues. *Airline Business*, pp. 88–91.

Bart, C. (2004). Boards involvement with mission statements. In: C. Bart, N. Bontis, & M. Head (Eds.), *Conference Proceedings of the 25th World Congress*, Hamilton, Ontario.

Berle, A. A., Jr. (1932). Corporate powers as powers in trust. *Harvard Law Review, 44*, 1049–1075.

BIL announces business plan (1999, April 23). *BIL Website.* Retrieved May 9, 2002 from www.bilgroup.com/6_news_article_69.html

BIL policy matters. (1998, December 4). *BIL Website.* Retrieved may 19, 2002 from the World Wide Web: http://www.bilgroup.com/6_news_article_69.html

BIL. (1990–2001). *BIL Annual Reports.* Wellington: Author.

Blake, A. (1999). *Dynamic directors: Aligning board structure for business success.* London: Macmillan Press.

Brierley Investments Limited. (1999). *Business plan.* [Downloaded from www.bilgroup.com/6_news_article_69.html]

Bryce, R. (2002). *Pipe dreams: Greed, ego, and the death of Enron.* New York, NY: Public Affairs.

Cassidy, D. P. (2000). Whither corporate governance in the 21st century? *Corporate Governance, 8*(4), 297–302.

Charkham, J., & Simpson, A. (1999). *Fair shares: The future of shareholder power and responsibility.* Oxford: Oxford University Press.

Christensen, C. M., & Raynor, M. E. (2003, September). Why hard-nosed executives should care about management theory. *Harvard Business Review, 81*(9), 66–74.

Cochran, P. L., & Warlick, S. L. (1994). Corporate governance a review of the literature. In: R. I. Tricker (Ed.), *International corporate governance: Text, readings and cases.* London: Prentice-Hall.

Collins, J. C., & Porras, J. I. (1997). *Built to last: Successful habits of visionary companies* (2nd ed.). New York, NY: HarperCollins Publishers.

Conger, J. A., Lawler, E. E., & Finegold, D. L. (2001). *Corporate boards: Strategies for adding value at the top* (3rd ed.). San Francisco: Jossey-Bass Inc.

Cook, T. D., & Campbell, D. T. (1979). *Quasi-experimentation: Design and analysis issues for field settings.* Chicago: Rand McNally.

Daily, C. M., Dalton, D. R., & Rajagopalan, N. (2003). Governance through ownership: Centuries of practice, decades of research. *Academy of Management Journal, 46*(2), 151–158.

Dalton, D. R., & Daily, C. M. (2001). Director stock compensation: An invitation to a conspicuous conflict of interest? *Business Ethics Quarterly, 11*, 89–108.

Dalton, D. R., Daily, C. M., Ellstrand, A. E., & Johnson, J. L. (1998). Meta-analytic reviews of board composition, leadership structure, and financial performance. *Strategic Management Journal, 19*, 269–290.

Diplock, J. (2003, April). *Corporate governance issues.* Securities Commission of New Zealand. Available from: http://www.sec-com.govt.nz/speeches/jds240403.shtml

Dixon, B. R., Bouma, G. D., & Atkinson, G. B. J. (1987). *A handbook of social science research.* Oxford: Oxford University Press.

Driscoll, I. H. (1979). *Airline: The making of a national flag carrier.* Auckland: Shortland Publications.

Eisenhardt, K. M. (1989). Building theories from case study research. *Academy of Management Review, 14*(4), 532–550.

Finegold, D. L. (2001). To whom are boards accountable? *Corporate Board, 22*(129), 17–23.

Friedman, M. (1962). *Capitalism and freedom.* Chicago: The University of Chicago Press.

Gates, J. R. (1998). *The ownership solution: Toward a shared capitalism for the twenty-first century.* New York, NY: The Penguin Press.

Goh, J. (2001). *The single aviation market of Australia and New Zealand.* London: Cavendish Publishing Limited.

Gummesson, E. (1991). *Qualitative methods in management research* (Rev. ed.). Newbury Park, CA: Sage.

Hakim, C. (1987). *Research design.* London: George Allen & Unwin.

Hamel, G., & Prahalad, C. K. (1994). *Competing for the future.* Boston: Harvard Business School Press.

Henderson, D. (2001). *Misguided virtue: False notions of corporate social responsibility.* New Zealand: Business Roundtable.

Hilmer, F. G. (1998). *Strictly boardroom* (2nd ed.). Melbourne: Information Australia.

Holmes, N. (1982). *To fly a desk: Sir Geoffrey Roberts, father of Air New Zealand.* Wellington: Reed.

Howard, W. H., & MacMillan, R. (1991). In search of excellence on the farm: An example of case research. *Agribusiness, 7*(1), 1–10.

Howe, F. (1997). *The board members guide to strategic planning: A practical approach to strengthening nonprofit organisations.* San Francisco, CA: Jossey-Bass Publishers.

Jensen, M. C. (2000). *A theory of the firm: Governance, residual claims, and organisational reforms.* Cambridge, MA: Harvard University Press.

Johnson, G., & Scholes, K. (1999). *Exploring corporate strategy* (5th ed.). London: Prentice-Hall, Inc.

Kerr, R. (1996). Does business have a social responsibility? *The Independent Business Weekly,* 13 December, p. 9.

King, M. (2002). *Executive summary of the King report 2002.* Institute of Directors South Africa.

KPMG. (2001). *Toolkit for the company director: The essential guide – New Zealand* (2nd ed.). Wellington: Author.

Kristie, J. (1997). Timeline: The evolution of 20th century corporate governance. *Directors and Boards, 22*(1), 37–46.

Ladd, D. R. (n.d.). *Notes on the use of the case method* (No. 9-373-894). Boston, MA: Intercollegiate Case Clearing House.

Lazonick, W., & O'Sullivan, M. (2002). Maximising shareholder value: A new ideology for corporate governance. In: W. Lazonick & M. O'Sullivan (Eds), *Corporate governance and sustainable prosperity* (pp. 11–36). New York, NY: Palgrave.

New Zealand Securities Commission. (2004). *Corporate governance in New Zealand.* Securities Commission New Zealand.

New Zealand Stock Exchange. (2004). *NZX listing rules.* Author.

OECD. (1999). *The OECD Principles of corporate governance.* [Downloaded from www.oecd.org/document/62/0,2340,en_2649_34813_1912830_1_1_1_1,00.html]

OECD. (2003). *OECD launches drive to strengthen corporate governance.* [Downloaded from www.oecd.org/document/41/0,2340,en_2649_37439_1841833_1_1_1_37439,00.html]

Patterson, D., & Wallace, J. (1997). *The Patterson files.* Otaki: New Zealand Wings.

Pound, J. (1995, July–August). The promise of the governed corporation. *Harvard Business Review, 73*(4), 89–98.

Rendel, D. (1975). *Civil aviation in New Zealand: An illustrated history.* Wellington: Reed.

Rennie, N. (1990). *Conquering isolation: The first 50 years of Air New Zealand.* Auckland: Heinemann Reed.

Shaw, W. H., & Barry, V. (2001). *Moral issues in business.* Belmont, CA: Wadsworth.

Sieber, S. D. (1972). The integration of fieldwork and survey methods. *American Journal of Sociology, 78*(6), 1335–1359.

Sonnenfeld, J. A. (2002, September). What makes great boards great. *Harvard Business Review, 80*(9), 106–113.

Stablein, R. E. (1996). Data in organization studies. In: S. R. Clegg, C. Hardy & W. R. Nord (Eds), *Handbook of organization studies* (pp. 509–525). Sage: London.

Taylor, B. E., Chait, R. P., & Holland, T. P. (1996). The new work of the nonprofit board. *Harvard Business Review, 74*(5), 36–46.

Thomas, G. (2001). Recipe for disaster. *Air Transport World, 38*(11), 50–55.

Tosi, H. L., Werner, S., Katz, J. P., & Gomez-Mejia, L. R. (2000). How much does performance matter? A meta-analysis of CEO pay studies. *Journal of Management, 26*, 301–339.

Tricker, R. I. (2000). Valedictory editorial: So-long, and thanks for all the fish. *Corporate Governance, 8*(4), 403–405.

Van de Ven, A. H. (1989). Nothing is quite so practical as a good theory. *Academy of Management Review, 14*(14), 486–489.

Von Tunzelmann, A., & Cullwick, D. (1996). *Social responsibility and the company:A new perspective on governance, strategy and the community.* Wellington: Victoria University.

Yin, R. K. (1984). *Case study research: Design and methods.* Newbury Park, CA: Sage.

Yin, R. K. (1989). *Case study research: Design and methods* (Rev. ed.). Newbury Park, CA: Sage.

Yin, R. K. (1993). *Applications of case study research.* Newbury Park, CA: Sage.

Zeff, S. A. (2003, April). *Post-Enron: The first uncertain steps, and the politics.* Seminar presented to the College of Business, Massey University, Palmerston North.

PART III:
THE NEXT STEP

AGENCY THEORY, ETHICS AND CORPORATE GOVERNANCE

John Roberts

ABSTRACT

This paper is an exploration of the potential place, if any, for ethics in corporate governance. It begins with the influential role that agency theory has played both in the conception and reform of corporate governance. Its grounding assumption of self-interested opportunism leaves little or no room for ethics beyond what pays. This conception is then contrasted with a Foucauldian view of governance in which ethics is explored in terms of how an 'ethic' of shareholder value has been promulgated in the last decade. The third section of the paper explores the contemporaneous explosion of interest in corporate ethics and social responsibility and suggests that there is a nascent disciplinary regime being assembled which may redefine the terms of shareholder value to include environmental and social performance. What is paradoxical about both an ethics of shareholder value and corporate responsibility is that they are effective only through creating a preoccupation with the self and how the self is seen, rather than the other. The final concluding part of the paper suggests that ethics, following Levinas, should be understood in terms of sentience and the 'responsibility for my neighbour' that this assigns. Such a view of ethics refutes the individualism that agency theory takes as the essence of human nature, and Foucauldian analysis suggests is the product of

Corporate Governance: Does Any Size Fit?
Advances in Public Interest Accounting, Volume 11, 249–269
Copyright © 2005 by Elsevier Ltd.
All rights of reproduction in any form reserved
ISSN: 1041-7060/doi:10.1016/S1041-7060(05)11011-6

249

*disciplinary processes. Its grounding in sentience and proximity however
offer it only a local role in corporate governance.*

INTRODUCTION

As academics we are perhaps not used to seeing a direct impact from our
abstract theorizing but in the case of agency theory one can point to the
profound impact that its assumptions have had in both characterising and
seeking to reform corporate governance practices. One of the reasons for the
success of this theory is that it has kept a similar distance from actual board
practices as those who are keen to understand and influence what goes on in
boards – investors and those regulatory authorities who act principally on
their behalf. Its negative assumptions about human nature have a natural
consonance with those who monitor boards remotely and who, as a result of
this distance, are fearful that their interests are being abused. We could
suggest that the value of the dismal assumption of self-interested opportunism is that one's confidence in others is seldom misplaced. Better to
assume the worst than to become disillusioned by having one's trust in
distanced others abused. But in the paper that follows, it is argued that such
fail-safe pessimism is much more productive than it imagines itself to be.
Rather than merely observe some truth about the opportunism of human
nature, as this belief has become embodied in boards in the attempt to
constrain and align self-interest towards investor interests, it has had the
effect of producing or at least promoting the very self-interested opportunism that it fears. Investors' distrust of remote directors has as its correlate a
certain attachment to self-interested opportunism – the self-interest of the
investor. To acknowledge both agency theory's deficiency and productive-
ness as a theory of the motives of the other would perhaps open the door to
a questioning of the other half of the equation – the assumed sovereignty of
the property rights of owners and those who represent these.

In order to explore corporate governance, not as a theory about how to
constrain and align a given 'self-interested' human nature, but rather as a
site for the production and reproduction of self-interested opportunism, the
paper shifts the focus of attention away from assumptions about human
nature to *practices and their effects* both objective and subjective. In this way
it attempts to offer an alternative account of the production and reproduction of self-interested opportunism both in directors and in investors. Performance measurement both within and beyond the corporation, and the

visibility it creates, is argued to have the effect of individualising the director. Such effects are most evident in the impact of both sackings and of share-options as a means to enforce what I will explore in terms of the ethic of shareholder value. But similar processes of measurement and the visibility it creates can also be seen to be driving the more recent enthusiasm for corporate social responsibility. From within an individualised subjectivity, ethics is at best 'the ethics of narcissus'; a concern to be seen and to represent the self-corporation as ethical. But ethics and the construction of ethical appearances are very different and the final part of the paper draws upon the work of Levinas to offer a counter view of the ethical capabilities of the person that is the complete antithesis of the assumed individualism of agency theory.

THE INFLUENCE OF AGENCY THEORY WITHIN CORPORATE GOVERNANCE

Agency theory has a number of manifestations. Jensen and Meckling's (1976) innovation was to insist that organisations should be seen as no more than a set of implicit and explicit contracts with associated rights. Alchian and Demsetz (1972) in contrast focused on the 'team production process' and the problem of free riding and monitoring within this. Fama (1980) looked to the potential of the managerial labour market to constrain and channel individual executive opportunism. These varied models of the nature of organisational relationships are constructed around a few simple assumptions that Donaldson (1990) characterises as a 'theory of interest, motivation and compliance'. As with neoclassical economics more generally, the basic unit of analysis is taken as the 'individual' who is preoccupied with maximising or at least satisfying their utility; conceived typically in terms of a trade-off between work and leisure. It is this combination of assumed autonomy and self-interested motivation that creates the problems within agency relationships; the relationship between a principal and those employed as 'agents' to serve their interests.

As applied to corporate governance it is the shareholder who is cast as the 'principal' and the problem, following the separation of ownership and control (Berle & Means, 1932), is how the principal can ensure that his 'agents' – company directors – serve the shareholders interests rather than their own. Either in the form of 'shirking', which in the governance context can be seen in terms of a lack of attention to maximising shareholder returns, or in terms of 'self-interested opportunism' – accruing wealth to themselves rather than shareholders – the principal is vulnerable to the self-interest of their agents. The remedies to this conception of the agency problem within corporate governance involves the acceptance of certain 'agency costs' involved either in creating incentives/sanctions that will align executive self-interest with the interests of shareholders, or incurred in monitoring executive conduct in order to constrain their opportunism.

As these assumptions have been read onto corporate governance, and informed its reform in recent decades, they have resulted in what are now an almost universal set of techniques and practices designed to control the conduct of executives both within the corporation and externally (Walsh & Seward, 1990). Inside the company, boards have essentially two means to exercise control over executives; they can fire them and they can give them incentives – share options, long-term incentive plans. For these levers to work, however, boards must be populated with 'independent' non-executives who are willing and able to monitor executive performance, particularly where there are potential conflicts of interest. The growth and development of both the number of non-executives on boards as well as the increased specification of their role and conditions of 'independence' has characterised board reform around the world. The separation of the role of chief executive from that of the non-executive chairman has been part of this; in the language of Cadbury committee (1992) it is intended that this ensures that no individual has 'unfettered' powers of decision. The creation of audit, remuneration, and nominations committees all staffed by independent non-executives, is also common and ideally ensures both the proper use of incentives and a high degree of monitoring of executive performance and decision-making. To these internal controls are added a range of external controls. Foremost here has been the focus on enhanced 'disclosure', and the 'transparency' that this allows, principally of financial performance but recently also of social and environmental performance (Zadek, 2001). The intention is that the share market is thereby better informed such that all relevant information is impacted into the share-price (Fama, 1980; Barker, 1998). There is also a market for corporate control (Cosh, Hughes, Lee & Singh, 1989) that ideally allows for weak management teams to be displaced by strong teams that will run companies to better effect for shareholders. In recent years at least at a policy level there has also been concern that shareholders – in the form of the large institutional investors – should take on their responsibilities as owners (Myners, 2001; ISC, 2002; Charkham & Simpson, 1998) through exercising proper scrutiny and influence both publicly and through their private contacts with investors (Roberts, Barker, Sanderson & Hendry, 2003).

The model described here of a combination of internal and external controls is what characterises Anglo-American corporations and by early 2001 there was a growing confidence that this model was the best means of ensuring effective governance, and that corporate governance practices in other jurisdictions should and indeed were beginning to converge upon this model (OECD, 1999). At this point the scandals of Enron, Worldcom and Tyco broke and these have at least temporarily shaken the confidence in and complacency about the Anglo-American model, and been the stimulus of yet further reform. In the United States, the Sarbannes-Oxley Act can be read almost as a perfect mirror of the collapse of Enron and perhaps suggests a loss of faith in the self-regulatory capacities of both boards and markets by increasing the criminal liabilities of directors. In the United Kingdom, the response has been more muted but has involved the further strengthening of the role of the non-executive within boards (Higgs, 2003) and of the monitoring responsibilities of investors in relation to voting and remuneration and activism (ISC, 2002). I would argue that in many respects these latest reforms merely repeat and reinforce the core assumptions of agency theory – that the problem lies in the self-interested opportunism of executives and can be remedied only through a mixture of increased independent monitoring, sharper sanctions and more appropriately targeted incentives that avoid 'reward for failure'. In what follows I want to question these assumptions and suggest that they are better seen not as the solution but rather as the source of the governance problem.

PRODUCING AND REPRODUCING SELF-INTERESTED OPPORTUNISM

The traditional path followed by critics of agency theory has been to offer a contrary set of assumptions about human nature. Perrow (1986) was one of the earliest organisational theorists to challenge the hegemony and adequacy of agency theory. He suggested that there was much that was good in seeing the potential for self-regarding behaviour but saw this primarily as a stimulus for investigating ways in which the cooperative potentials of agency might be reinforced. He noted a similarity between agency theory's negative conception of self-interest and a more routine feature of everyday life – our tendency, reinforced by distance, to attribute base motives to others. This is an important point for it begins to open up a question as to where the problem lies. As an attribution the problem is in the minds of investors rather than executives, and indeed Perrow argues that it might be important to enquire into the motives of the principals as well as the agents. In a similar vein Donaldson (1990), and later Donaldson and Dais (1991) have questioned the relevance of the negative assumptions of self-interested opportunism as these apply to directors; they offer the optimistic assumptions of McGregor's theory Y as the source of an alternative model of the director as 'steward'. A similar questioning of the relevance of economic theory for understanding organisational action has more recently been offered by Ghoshal and Moran (1996) in relation to Williamson's transaction cost theory.

Rather than seek to counter agency theory with an assertion of the contrary potentials for human goodness and responsibility, here I want to pursue a somewhat more complex line of argument by suggesting that human nature – both 'good' and 'bad' has itself to be understood as something that is produced and reproduced. From this perspective, we cannot know in advance about human nature, but must instead look to the practices through which it is shaped. Such is my intention here in relation to the production of self-interested opportunism amongst directors. The lesson that screams at us from the Enron and Worldcom scandals is that self-interested opportunism is alive and well within the boardroom. But if this is understood not simply as cause but also as an effect of corporate governance practices then this might allow a better, or in any case different, understanding of the 'problem' and its remedies, including the place, actual or potential, for ethics in corporate governance.

THE ETHICS OF SHAREHOLDER VALUE

Ethics are thus understood as the means by which individuals come to construe, decipher, act upon themselves in relation to the true and false, the permitted and forbidden, the desirable and the undesirable. (Rose, 1992, p. 144)

Superficially it seems outrageous to put ethics and shareholder value in the same sentence and yet, at least in the Foucauldian sense that will be pursued here, shareholder value has arguably become the ideal or ethic in terms of which executives have come to construe and judge their own conduct. Of course, in this sense, corporate governance has to be understood on a much broader scale than the focus that agency theory gives it – the relationship between directors and shareholders (Miller & O'Leary, 1993). As an ethic or ideal shareholder value now inhabits almost every level of the company as well as the minds of analysts, fund managers etc. Here, however, I want to focus on the subjectivity of the most senior managers and the paradoxical ways in which in the name of controlling self-interested opportunism agency theorists have contributed enormously to its elaboration.

Agency theory arguably embodies what Foucault would term a 'sovereign' view of power in which the problem for sovereign shareholders lies in getting self-interested directors to honour the rights of ownership, rather than their own interests. The dispersion of ownership made the exercise of shareholder power difficult, and only the reconcentration of power in the hands of large institutional investors has allowed the possibility of a reassertion of the rights of ownership (Monks, 2001). Power in this conception lies, or should lie, with the shareholder/owner and must be used to induce compliance on the part of the agent/director. In other words, the problem of governance lies with executive autonomy and the ways in which this can be used to serve their own interests. The remedy is to constrain the exercise of this autonomy through close monitoring by non-executives and others. As with media interest in issues of corporate governance, the focus here is on the exception – the corporate failure, the sackings and board conflicts, the signs of obvious executive excess or greed. My focus here on the ethic of shareholder value follows Foucault (1979) in insisting on the dispersed and relational nature of power, and on the way in which power should be understood in its operation not as something which constrains and restricts, as if from the outside, but as something that is productive of reality and in particular of subjectivity. Power in this sense works not against but through shaping the exercise of executive autonomy. It is evidenced not so much in the failure of governance as in the gradual inculcation of norms through which individuals come to govern themselves and each other. Power in this productive sense is part of what allows us to understand how Enron can happen at the end of a decade of governance reform; Enron speaks not of the failure but rather the success of corporate governance (Deakin & Konzelmann, 2003).

Governance for Foucault involves 'the conduct of conduct: a form of activity aiming to shape, guide or affect the conduct of some person or persons' (1979, p. 2). Within such a view the operation of relations of power is inseparable from the development of particular ways of knowing. Here, rather than attempt to trace the myriad practices, techniques and programmes through which the transitory hegemony of shareholder value was installed in the last decade, I have the more modest objective of redescribing some of the key elements of what agency theory sees as mechanisms for monitoring and control in terms of their normalising and individualising effects on those who are subject to them.

Elsewhere, in drawing upon Foucault's work to explore the operation of systems of accountability within organisations (Roberts, 1991, 1996), I have suggested a key role for management accounting information in creating the most authoritative 'field of visibility' for the 'results' of action. Its representations of activity in terms of budgets, cost and profit centres, organises the content and process of routine accountability by comparing individual to individual, department with department, one accounting period with earlier periods. Although the person is rarely constituted as such within accounting representations of activity in terms of cost, profit, margins etc, amongst their most important effects are those they have upon people who are subject to the visibility they create and the surveillance that they make possible. Foucault (1979) suggests that in the knowledge of such visibility we make power play 'spontaneously upon the self' and internalise the power relation in which we 'simultaneously play both roles'. So the routines of accountability advertise the standards of utility in terms of which the future security of the self is seen to depend, but in the process become the lens through which we come to monitor, judge, understand and seek to govern our own conduct and its consequences, and the conduct of our peers.

Such processes 'individualise' by creating a permanent narcissistic preoccupation with how the self is seen and judged; in the mirror of accounting one discovers oneself as an 'individual'. Our preoccupation with self can be purely defensive such that, in order to avoid the shame and humiliation of being singled out as a failure, I seek to prejudge and correct my conduct in the light of expectations. Or the individualised self can take the more assertive form of a positive identification of the self with the 'results' achieved. Here success can act as a sort of 'lure' in which the hierarchy is taken as an index of personal value, and progress towards its apex becomes a measure of one's success in making something of myself (Grey, 1994). Part of the lure is the promise of an ever more complete autonomy that progress up the hierarchy seems to offer. But, in practice, such success depends upon one being able to continuously demonstrate one's own utility both through doing better than one's peers and through securing the conformity of subordinates. Whilst it is perhaps easy to see how such disciplinary processes serve to hold the self and others in place at lower and middle ranges of the hierarchy, the effects of disciplinary mechanisms on those who reach the top of the hierarchy have some unusual aspects.

Foucault suggests that the 'individual' is not just the 'fictitious atom' of an ideological representation – for example within law or economics – but is also a reality 'fabricated' by the technology of power that he calls discipline. By definition those who reach the 'top' of organisations have in the process learnt how to manage themselves successfully within the disciplinary processes of the firm. Within its self-defining processes of comparison, differentiation and ranking, they have marked themselves out as 'successful' and 'powerful'. Achievement of the top jobs contains within it the fantasy of becoming the one who governs rather than is governed. Those who reach those pinnacles are therefore particularly prone to believing that they have, as it were, passed through the mirror in which they were held to account by others and have realised a complete autonomy.

Numerous studies of the effects of power upon the executive mind suggest the sorts of dangers that can be associated with accession to high office. At the very least having succeeded within the terms of the hierarchy there is both surprise and resentment at finding that the imagined autonomy of the top job in practice opens their conduct to new and indeed more intense forms of scrutiny and accountability both within board processes and externally (Useem, 1993). At worst, however, 'success' and the very considerable powers associated with high office can reanimate infantile fantasies of omnipotence and omniscience. A person can thereby become convinced of their own perfection, scornful of the abilities of others and punishing of any expression of difference or dissent. They can lose sight of any sense of institutional obligations and come to see the organisation as if it were a personal fiefdom. They can develop a sense of personal moral superiority such that they come to think of themselves as somehow set apart; a law unto themselves (Kets de Vries, 1989; O'Neil, 1993; Zaleznick & Kets de Vries, 1985). In the context of a board they can continue to struggle for imagined autonomy through seeking to dominate decision-making and establish the sovereignty of their will. In this way the self-interested opportunism that agency theory takes as its founding assumption, can be seen as a reality that is fabricated by the operation of disciplinary processes within the firm rather than as something that is essential within human nature. Paradoxically, the very means through which agency theory proposes to constrain such opportunism can be seen only to reinforce and reproduce it.

By all accounts the last decade has seen a massive intensification of the scrutiny of companies and those who run them. On the investor side this can be traced to the reconcentration of ownership in the hands of large institutions that now have both the means and the need to more closely scrutinise corporate conduct. The global scope of these investors, as well as the intensification of competition between them, has motivated a much more intense scrutiny of company performance, as well as the emergence of shareholder activism. A whole host of proprietary valuation techniques have been developed during the decade to support and enable this – EVA, EBITA, Holt – through which different funds can scrutinise the sources of value within companies, seek to compare different companies and sectors, as well as differentiate their our investment style from others (Froud, Haslam, Sukdev & Williams, 2000). At a more micro level one can point to the emergence of quarterly league tables ranking the investment performance of different funds as well as the highly incentivised nature of fund manager' and analyst' remuneration. Within this increasingly intense and complete 'market for information' sell-side analysts play a key role both as sources of information and commentary; their incorporation within larger investment houses ensuring that such 'information' is motivated by the desire to generate turnover (Barker, 1998).

On the corporate side, repeated 'governance' failures have led to a huge increase in both the quantity and scope of corporate disclosure, as well as much tighter regulation of the methods of such disclosure. Investor relations is now typically the responsibility of a dedicated department with its own permanent staff (Rao & Sivakumar, 1999; Marston, 1999). Top executives, in particular the CEO and finance director, now spend up to a quarter of their time on managing the relations with investors (Pye, 2001). This includes both public presentations around the time of results announcements to analysts, and as many as 50 or so individual meetings with large existing or potential investors and their analysts (Roberts, 2003). Whilst the traditional focus of academic research has been on the efficiency of these information flows, and the degree which accurate information is impacted into the share price (Fama, 1980), this is again to ignore what is arguably amongst the most important 'truth effects' of such intense scrutiny – the way in which, in the knowledge of such scrutiny, the ideal of shareholder value is thereby installed in the minds of senior executives.

This remote scrutiny has been reinforced by the internal governance changes described earlier; the separation of roles of chairman and chief executive, the increase in the proportion of independent non-executives, and the development of their sub-committee roles in relation to risk and audit, nomination and remuneration. Here, I want to look by way of an example at the use of executive dismissal and remuneration as means to align executive self-interest with the interests of shareholders, and the paradoxical consequences that have flowed from these.

One consequence of increased investor scrutiny has been a growing awareness of the short-term nature of senior executive tenure. The average life span of a FTSE 100 chief executive is now just over four years (Higgs, 2003). This repeated severance of individuals and institutions – typically when they come to be seen as obstacles or impediments to value creation – in a sense makes a reality of Jensen and Meckling's account of organisation as no more that a nexus of implicit and explicit contracts. Subjectively it arguably works against any identification with the institution, and instead encourages executives to get the best lawyers to work over the details of their contracts (Ghoshal & Moran, 1996). It establishes what in the life span of an institution is a very short time horizon for achievement that possibly precludes a deep understanding of products, and markets and instead emphasizes the importance of largely financial means for realising immediate visible improvements in returns to shareholders. So if occasional executive sackings advertise to all the likely transience of tenure in the top job this is then matched through the positive incentives associated with executive remuneration. From an agency perspective, levels of executive remuneration at any moment in time offer clear evidence of the agency problem – executives are seeking to enrich themselves. But in the strange world of motivational essences upon which the theory is constructed, the solution to such problems of executive greed can only be thought about in the same terms as the problem itself. The only remedy is to develop incentives – share-options – as a mechanism through which the self-interest of executives can be aligned with the interests of shareholders (or at least their agents).

Although there seems to be no evidence of a link between pay and performance but only pay and company size (Conyon & Peck, 1998) the remedy, at least in the UK, to the growing levels of absolute pay has again been thought about in conventional governance terms – control through closer monitoring and transparency. In practice, the process that has been thereby elaborated has had the perverse effect of bidding up executive pay. Companies, typically with the help of compensation consultants who can legitimate their decisions, establish a process through which the pay of their own executives is compared with that of executives in comparable companies and industries. The rationale that is pursued in such comparisons frequently suggests that to attract and retain the best executives a company should pay in the top quartile. The inevitable result is the gradual ratcheting-up of relative levels of executive pay (Ezzamel & Watson, 1997). Transparency here has the perverse effect of heightening awareness of comparability which, when combined with assumptions about the managerial labour market, has served not to constrain but inflate levels of executive pay.

Managers gradual embrace of the ethic of 'shareholder value' can be seen to have been made much easier through the way in which their own personal rewards were so generously and pointedly tied to share-price performance. Alan Kennedy writing before the collapse of Enron offered the following characterisation of executive action in pursuit of shareholder value.

> Suddenly managers everywhere were making decisions solely on the basis of whether the outcome would spur their stock prices even higher. If core costs cuts were called for so be it, whatever the long-term consequences. If internal costs were slow to come out, turn to your suppliers and demand dramatic reduction in their costs as a price of continuing to do business with you. If cutbacks in research and development were necessary to make the numbers, then cut back R&D. If those steps failed to produce the desired outcome in the stock market, take the money that might have been invested in building the business for the future and use it to buy back stock on the market. And if all that still did not drive up the stock price, cook up another blockbuster deal to get Wall Street's attention.
>
> (Kennedy, 2000)

Despite these sorts of warnings, it was only with the collapse of Enron that the perverse effects of such crude incentivisation began to become visible. What is odd, however, is that the systemic nature of these effects is still difficult to grasp and instead there is a search for some sort of scapegoat – the accounting profession, the criminal executive, the compromised non-executive – as an explanation (O'Connell, 2004). The explanation that is repeatedly refused is that it was the ethic of shareholder value that had all too successfully been implanted in the executive mind as a guide to 'good' conduct (Bratton, 2002).

ETHICS AND CORPORATE GOVERNANCE

In the above I have sought to juxtapose two contemporary accounts of the causal relationships that shape corporate governance. On the one hand is agency theory's account of the relationships between investor (principal) and the director (agent). Here it is the assumption of self-interested opportunism that is the driving causal assumption and from this flow a whole range of prescriptions for monitoring and control, both internally and externally. The second account of governance that I have sketched gives a causal role, not to some assumed human essence, but rather to the myriad techniques, programmes and practices through which executive conduct comes to be made visible, and the ways in which this visibility shapes the 'individualised' subjectivity (self interest) of executives. What I want to explore in what follows are the awkward implications of both these accounts for anything like an ethic that might inform corporate governance.

It is hard to find a place for ethics within agency theory assumptions (Shearer, 2002). Moral hazard is ensured by the prevalence of self-interested opportunism and at best can only be constrained. At most ethics has the form of a trade, that must be justified in terms of some threat or benefit that accrues from ethical conduct. Superficially it seems perverse to talk, as I have, of an ethic of shareholder value, but what is particularly awkward here is the way in which this is possibly a more accurate account of how shareholder value comes to function as a guiding ideal for conduct. Thus whilst for agency theorists, at least in terms of securing legitimate property rights, ethics can only be ensured through external monitoring and controls, in the disciplinary account, shareholder value is indeed an ethic; an ideal in terms of which the self is judged, worked upon, improved. It is not amoral self-interest but rather a morality of self-interest. If ethics are always only a matter of the ideals that shape conduct, then shareholder value has indeed become an ethic, and Enron executives can perhaps only be accused of excessive zeal.

One of the dangerous sources of blindness in agency theory concerns its rather mechanical sense of causality. Because executives are greedy, *therefore* investors, regulators, etc. have no choice but to treat them with suspicion. Responsibility is thereby projected elsewhere and there is a strange inability to see the self-fulfilling potentials of investor assumptions and the ways in which their own conduct contributes to producing the problems that they locate elsewhere in others. At least the disciplinary account suggests that the 'individualised' mentality of executives (and investors) is socially produced and reproduced. In what follows, I want to argue that this individualised self can be understood as both our best hope for ethics in corporate governance, and as an absolute obstacle to ethics.

One of the paradoxes of the last decade is that, along with an intensification of the demand for shareholder value, we also witnessed a huge explosion of interest both academic and practitioner in business ethics, corporate social responsibility and corporate citizenship. How can we account for this proliferation of ethical concern? As with the emergence of shareholder value it can be seen to be to involve multiple sources of influence. It was in the 1970's that Milton Friedman (1988) famously argued that 'the only responsibility of business was to make a profit'. Such a clarity of moral purpose arguably took place against the backdrop of an assumed division of responsibility within the confines of the nation state, such that business should be free to pursue purely economic objectives, since the State and other institutions could be trusted to have regard to wider ethical concerns, including the legal framework within which businesses operated. Arguably globalisation has fractured this comfortable ethical division of labour. The retreat of the State from its welfare role under the combined pressures of fiscal crisis and the threats, real or imagined, of globalisation, means that we can no longer count on this source of protection (Beck, 2000). Part of the growth of interest in business ethics can perhaps be traced then to these institutional shifts, and the concomitant recognition of the power and relative autonomy of the large trans-national corporation (Korten, 1996). One can also point in this respect to the rise of the single issue focused NGO as a channel for political concerns that the State is no longer willing or able to champion. Their particular skill, learnt over the decade, lies in targeting individual companies and making them the object of adverse publicity. Only certain companies are vulnerable to such targeting – retail and extractive transnationals were the early objects of attention – but over the decade more and more companies have discovered that they are vulnerable to what has come to be internalised and managed within companies as 'reputational risk'.

The corporate response to these new forms of risk and scrutiny has been varied. It has now become almost compulsory, at least for larger corporations to have a written code of ethics or business principles; even Enron had one. These can be used both internally and with suppliers to advertise standards of acceptable practice. Those who have discovered themselves to be at risk from reputational damage have also begun to publish environmental and social reports, alongside their financial reports. For perhaps far too many companies such codes and brochures seem to represent the full extent of their embrace of the ethical. But in others social and ethical standards have been integrated into performance appraisal, and at least a nascent form of 'triple-bottom line' accounting had begun to be developed (Elkington, 1997).

Beyond the corporation the large accounting firms have begun to get involved in acting as auditors for such reports and there is a growing business in the provision of social and environmental audits. New international standards for such reporting are being developed. At the same time the large institutional investors have begun to develop an interest in socially responsible investment. In the UK, for example, in part through the recognition of the growth potential of 'ethical' investment products, the Association of British Insurers have recently published their own code of conduct, new indexes such as FTSE for Good have been established, and within individual fund management companies typically someone now monitors not just corporate governance but also SRI. Such private sector initiatives are then encouraged by national ministers for social responsibility, and by EEC green papers, global reporting initiatives, World Bank programmes and the United Nations 'global compact'.

What can perhaps be observed in the above, at least in embryonic form, is the emergence of a whole new disciplinary apparatus, modelled along the lines of management and financial accounting, concerned with comparing, ranking, and differentiating firms in terms of their social and environmental performance. CSR in this respect has provided a unifying point of focus for the development of multiple new forms of knowledge, new methods and objects of measurement and calculation, and new representations of corporate conduct. If the analogy with financial reporting is appropriate then as a correlate of the development of this new field of visibility we might hope to see the emergence of a new from of executive subjectivity that adds social and environmental responsibility to the ideal of shareholder value. For some these new forms of ethical accountability are the best hope that we have for something like ethics in business (Zadek, 2001). My own appraisal of these innovations is sadly more ambivalent, for such changes seem only to add new terms of reference and judgement to the 'individualised' mentality that they continue to promote.

What I have developed elsewhere and will merely reprise here is the suggestion that all that is invoked here is 'the ethics of narcissus' where the problem of ethics is cast merely in terms of the desire to be seen to be ethical (Roberts, 2001a, 2003). In one early and very famous corporate social report titled 'Profits and Principles. Does there have to be a choice?' the first line of which reads 'we care what you think of us'. What is put at stake through these new forms of ethical visibility is the corporate reputation along with the reputation of individuals who are closely identified with the corporation. At its worst, the proliferation of ethics codes and environmental and social reports can be viewed as a knowing and cynical attempt to counter criticism through the repair of the corporate imago (Power, 2003). There is often something peculiarly post-modern about the labour involved in the representation of the corporation as ethical and responsible. The work often takes place on the surface of the corporate body in public or community affairs departments, and involves no more than the commitment of considerable corporate resources to the preparation of codes, and the publication of reports that often do no more than seek to represent more publicly the work that is already being done.

If ethics is to be judged in terms of its effects then the prime beneficiary of such presentations of corporate goodness are corporations themselves. Since

reputation damage arises from negative representations of corporate conduct by NGO's and the press, it is quite easy to use codes and reports as the
means to offer counter, positive representations. Subsequent criticisms of
the corporation can then be countered by reference to the codes and reports,
and failure thereby localised in the figure of the deviant employee rather
than the corporation that becomes in a sense irreproachable in its stated
ideals. Such positive external effects are complemented by important internal consequences, for the embrace of ethical or sustainable values can be
seen as a vital way in which staff's positive identification with the corporation is protected or enhanced (Willmott, 1998). Far from constituting a
change in the governing values that inform and shape corporate conduct,
this manufacture of ethical appearances can be seen more properly to actually serve the conduct of 'business as usual'. It furnishes the corporate self
with a new narrative of responsibility without requiring anything new or
different beyond the work of a few individuals at head office.

Less cynical and arguably more consequential than this purely external representation of the corporation as ethical or sustainable is where external
reports and codes begin to be complemented by new forms of internal
measurement and reward. Through mechanisms such as triple bottom line
accounting or the balanced scorecard, the new corporate values arguably
begin to reshape governance through adding new points of focus, creating
pressure for new kinds of action and innovation and rewarding (and sanc-
tioning) different kinds of behaviours. At least compared with the more
cynical forms of external representation, the development of new forms of
internal visibility have the potential to change the terms of the calculus that
defines success for people at every level of the hierarchy. But there are some
severe limitations to these new technologies.

One can only measure what one thinks to look for and since many impacts are external to the corporation there is often simply a lack of awareness of what should be being represented. Measurement can also only
capture what is amenable to quantification. Whilst some environmental
impacts are perhaps relatively easy to observe, quantify and thereby internalise, it has proved much more difficult to generate a generic and yet
meaningful way to represent social impacts. Finally, there are all sorts of
benefits to be gained from what is a peculiarly arbitrary dislocation of the
'economic' from the 'social' from 'the environmental' (Bauman, 1993). It is
easy for responsibility for different elements to be distributed within an
organisation in such a way that the complex interrelationships between say
local employment, the physical environment and community impacts are
neither understood nor managed. Disaggregation also has the benefit of

allowing the easy coexistence of corporate ideals – profits and principles – while displacing the dilemmas, choices and responsibilities that these might involve to those lower down the hierarchy who must now finds ways to demonstrate to their bosses that they are both profitable and principled. Incentivising performance around such disaggregated measurements also offers the peculiar prospect of competing with one's peers to demonstrate one's ethical or sustainable credentials; as with all measurement there is always the potential for an awkward disjunction between conduct and its remote representation.

CONCLUSIONS: ETHICS AS RESPONSIBILITY FOR MYSELF OR AS RESPONSIBILITY FOR MY NEIGHBOUR

The question raised by the above analysis concerns whether, for all the self-preoccupation that it produces, such disciplinary processes applied in the service of profits with principles is all that we might hope for, or reasonably expect to realise by way of business ethics. The answer here depends critically upon how ethics is understood; on how we come to understand and conceive of our ethical capabilities. Kohlberg (1986) in his seminal account of the different stages and levels of moral development pessimistically concludes that most morality is simply a matter of convention; it is to conform with the norms of one's group or society and such conformity is motivated by the desire for approval and belonging rather than any concern for or with the other. The disciplinary account I have offered above of the ethic of shareholder value, possibly augmented with some ideals of social responsibility, plays upon a similarly normalised preoccupation with how the self is seen and judged both by others and by myself. The obvious paradox here is that ethics increasingly has the form of an ever more complete self-absorption, rather than something that has much to do with others (Shearer, 2002).

The counter view of ethics or ethical capabilities that I want to offer here is drawn from the work of Levinas (1991) and, in particular, his last book 'Otherwise than Being or Beyond Essence'. This is an almost impossibly difficult read but for my purposes here it is helpful in revealing the limits of the individualised view of the self that agency theory takes as the essence of human nature and Foucault suggests is the effect of the operation of disciplinary technologies. Whereas we might typically think of ethics as a branch of philosophy, or as an application of moral reasoning to our conduct, Levinas as a phenomenologist was seeking to find the ground of ethics in experience. Ethics for him is not about philosophy or a choice freely made, but rather is to be discovered in human sentience and what he calls the 'assignation of responsibility for my neighbour' that comes through this sentience. He is suspicious of sight which he talks about as the 'sensible conceptualised' and looks to the others senses in an attempt to point to the ways in which 'the other affects us despite ourselves'.

For me the value of this approach to ethics is that it offers a way to escape the individualism that characterises both our own 'disciplined' consciousness and much theory (Roberts, 2001a). Whereas we might baulk at the idea that the self should be characterised as essentially opportunist it is nevertheless difficult not to conceive of the self in atomistic terms – of the self as some sort of entity. Levinas here draws a distinction between the 'ego', which is the field of self-consciousness that discipline plays with, and the 'psyche' which he describes as 'the soul of the other in me'. This distinction is then read onto two very different senses of identity. On the one hand there is our reflexively constituted sense of self which he insists is no more that an 'ideality' – a synthesis of 'aspects and images, silhouettes and phases'. Here disciplinary techniques provide the ideal in terms of which reflection is turned back upon itself. But at the level of the psyche Levinas insists that identity comes to us from outside in the assignation of responsibility; identity in this sense can only be realized as 'non-indifference' to my neighbour. What he seems to be seeking to describe is an openness to the other at the level of the psyche/sentience that is always already there and through which I find myself already caught up (assigned) responsibility for my neighbour. The language he uses to describe following this assignation is quite violent – he talks of being penetrated, denuded, cored out. Responsibility he insists 'goes one way' – my responsibility for my neighbour. It is without limit – 'there is always one more response to give'. It cannot be passed on – it is uniquely mine. It is 'despite the self' and yet offers no promise of success. Rather than a self that draws comfort and apparent solidity and value from the story I tell myself of who I am, and seek recognition of from others – successful, responsible etc – the identity that emerges through responsibility is defined only in relation to the other.

> The word I means 'here I am', answering for everything and everyone. The self is on the hither side of rest; is the impossibility to come back from all things and concern oneself with oneself. Responsibility in obsession is a responsibility for what the ego had not wished, that is, for the others (1991, p. 114).

Following Levinas the image of the individual that informs agency theory can be seen to be a mirror image; it is the image of the self as seen from outside which then, as a concept, comes to haunt the perception of self and others. Levinas argues that the reflexivity of the ego – the constant repair of the self-image – has the effect of encrusting, thickening, doubling the self. Within such processes ethics becomes the story I tell myself of my own goodness (often supported by stories of others' relative badness or the reverse). But this is only a story and its reflexive maintenance – our preoccupation with self – is precisely what forecloses the assignation of responsibility for the other who is right next to me. The problem of ethics in corporate governance from this point of view is not about how to get ethics back into business but rather of exploring how our ethical sensibility is routinely blunted. Here the account I have given of how accounting as a system of visibility has the effect of installing distant interests in the minds of all those who are subject to it, can be seen to effect a sort of ethical reversal in which the defence of the self is privileged over our felt responsibility to others. It teaches us to be thick-skinned, it looks to others to reflect the value of the self and thereby sees only itself. It would be wrong to suggest that thereby there is no place for ethics in business. Governance, as Miller and O'Leary (1993) insist is always 'congenitally failing' and one can find ready examples, in both the boardroom and shop floor where people routinely go out of their way for others in the routines of their work. But as Bauman (1993) has observed, given that Levinas' account of ethics depends upon sentience and proximity, it is difficult to see how we can give more than local reach to our moral concerns without inevitably being forced back on disciplinary technologies – measurement, comparison, calculation, visibility – and their contrary individualising effects if we want to give more than local reach to our moral concerns.

REFERENCES

Alchian, A., & Demsetz, H. (1972). Production, information costs and economic organization. *The American Economic Review, 62*, 777–795.

Barker, R. (1998). The market for information – Evidence from finance directors, analysts and fund managers. *Accounting and Business Research, 29*(1), 3–20.

Bauman, Z. (1993). *Postmodern ethics*. Oxford: Blackwell.

Beck, U. (2000). *What is globalization?*. Cambridge: Polity.

Berle, A., & Means, C. (1932). *The modern corporation and private property*. New York: Macmillan.

Bratton, W. (May 2002). Enron and the dark side of shareholder value. *Tulane Law Review*, *76*(5 & 6), 1275–1362.

Cadbury, A. (1992). *Report of the committee on the financial aspects of corporate governance.* London: Gee & Co.

Charkham, J., & Simpson, A. (1998). *Fair shares: the future of shareholder power.* Oxford: Oxford University Press.

Conyon, M., & Peck, S. (1998). Board control, remuneration committees and top management compensation. *Academy of Management Journal*, *41*(2), 146–157.

Cosh, A., Hughes, A., Lee, K., & Singh, A. (1989). Institutional investment, mergers and the market for corporate control. *International Journal of Industrial Organization*, *7*(1), 73–100.

Deakin, S., & Konzelmann, S. (2003). After Enron: an age of enlightenment? *Organization*, *10*(3), 583–587.

Donaldson, L. (1990). The Ethereal hand; organisational economics and management theory. *Academy of Management Review*, *15*(3), 369–381.

Donaldson, L., & Dais, J. (1991). Stewardship theory or agency theory: CEO governance and shareholder returns. *Australian Journal of Management*, *16*, 49–64.

Elkington, J. (1997). *Cannibals with Forks; the triple bottom line of 21st century business.* Oxford: Capstone.

Ezzamel, M., & Watson, R. (1997). Wearing two hats: the conflicting control and management roles of non-executive directors. In: K. Keaset, S. Thompson & M. Wright (Eds), *Corporate governance: economic and financial issues.* Chichester: Oxford University Press.

Fama, E. (1980). Agency problems and the theory of the firm. *Journal of Political Economy*, *88*, 288–307.

Foucault, M. (1979). *Discipline and punish.* Harmondsworth: Penguin Books.

Friedman, M. (1988). The social responsibility of business is to increase its profits. In: T. Donaldson & P. Werhane (Eds), *Ethical issues in business: A philosophical approach.* Englewood Cliffs, NJ: Prentice-Hall.

Froud, J., Haslam, C., Sukdev, J., & Williams, K. (2000). Shareholder value and financialisation; consultancy promises, management moves. *Economy and Society*, *29*(1), 80–110.

Ghoshal, S., & Moran, P. (1996). Bad for practice: a critique of transaction cost theory. *Academy of Management Review*, *21*(1), 13–47.

Grey, C. (1994). Career as a Project of the Self and Labour Process Discipline. *Sociology*, *28*, 479–507.

Higgs, D. (2003). *Review of the role and effectiveness of the non-executive director.* London: DTI.

Institutional Shareholders Committee (2002). *The Responsibilities of Institutional Shareholders and Agents – Statement of Principles.* London.

Jensen, M., & Meckling, W. (1976). Theory of the Firm: Managerial behaviour, agency costs and ownership structure. *The Journal of financial Economics*, *3*, 305–360.

Kennedy, A. (2000). *The end of shareholder value: the real effects of the shareholder value phenomenon and the crisis it is bringing to business.* London: Orion.

Kets de Vries, M. (1989). *Prisoners of leadership.* New York: Wiley.

Levinas, E. (1991). *Otherwise than being or beyond essence.* Dordrecht: Kluwer Academic Publishers.

Kohlberg, L. (1996). *Child psychology and childhood education.* London: Longman.

Korten, D. (1996). *When corporations rule the world.* West Hartford Conn: Kumarian Press.

Marston, C. (1999). *Investor relations meetings: Views of companies, institutional investors and analysts.* Edinburgh: The Institute of Chartered Accountants of Scotland.

Miller, P., & O'Leary, T. (1993). Accounting expertise and the politics of the product; economic citizenship and modes of corporate governance. *Accounting Organizations and Society, 18*(2–3), 187–206.

Monks, R. (2001). *The new global investors.* Oxford: Capstone.

Myners, P. (2001). *Institutional investment in the United Kingdom: A review.* London: HM Treasury.

O'Connell, B. (2004). Enron.Con: "He that filches from me my good name … makes me poor indeed". *Critical Perspectives on Accounting, 15*, 733–749.

OECD. (1999). OECD principles of corporate governance. OECD Publication Service.

O'Neil, J. (1993). *The paradox of success.* Maidenhead: McGraw-Hill.

Perrow, C. (1986). *Complex organizations: A critical essay* (3rd ed.). New York: McGraw-Hill.

Power, M. (2003). Auditing and the production of legitimacy. *Accounting, Organizations and Society, 28*, 379–394.

Pye, A. (2001). Corporate boards, Investors and their relationships: accounts of accountability and corporate governing in action. *Corporate Governance: An International Review, 9*(3), 186–195.

Rao, H., & Sivakumar, K. (1999). Institutional sources of boundary spanning structures; the establishment of investor relations departments in the Fortune 500 Industrials. *Organization Science, 10*(1), 27–42.

Roberts, J. (1991). The possibilities of accountability. *Accounting, Organizations and Society, 16*(4), 355–368.

Roberts, J. (1996). From Discipline to Dialogue: individualising and socialising forms of accountability. In: R. Munro & J. Mouritsen (Eds), *Accountability: power, ethos and the technologies of managing.* London: International Thompson Business Press.

Roberts, J. (2001). Corporate governance and the Ethics of Narcissus. *Business Ethics Quarterly, 11*(1), 109–127.

Roberts, J. (2001). Trust and control in Anglo-American systems of corporate governance; the individualizing and socializing effects of processes of accountability. *Human Relations, 54*(12), 1547–1572.

Roberts, J. (2003). The manufacture of corporate social responsibility: constructing corporate sensibility. *Organization, 10*(2), 249–265.

Roberts, J., Barker, R., Sanderson, P., & Hendry, J. (2003). In the Mirror of the Market; the disciplinary effects of company shareholder meetings. IPA Conference Paper, Madrid.

Rose, N. (1992). Governing the enterprising self. In: P. Heelas & P. Morris (Eds), *The values of the enterprise culture: the moral debate.* London: Routledge.

Shearer, T. (2002). Ethics and accountability: from the for-itself to the for-the-other. *Accounting, Organizations and Society, 27*, 541–573.

Useem, M. (1993). *Executive defence: shareholder power and corporate reorganisation.* Cambridge, MA: Harvard University Press.

Walsh, J., & Seward, J. (1990). On the efficiency of internal and external corporate control mechanisms. *Academy of Management Review, 15*(3), 421–458.

Willmott, H. (1998). Towards a new ethics? The contributions for post-structuralism and post-humanism. In: M. Parker (Ed.), *Ethics and organizations.* London: Sage.

Zadek, S. (2001). *The civil corporation: The new economy of corporate citizenship.* London: Earthscan Publications.

Zaleznick, A., & Kets de Vries, M. (1985). *Power and the corporate mind.* Chicago, IL: Bonus Books.

BEYOND LAW AND REGULATION: A CORPORATE GOVERNANCE MODEL OF ETHICAL DECISION-MAKING

Jack Flanagan, John Little and Ted Watts

ABSTRACT

Large companies are the dominant forms of wealth creation in society today. As well as providing jobs and export income, they are key influences on social cohesion. We ignore how companies are run at a peril to us all. However, today investors are increasingly concerned about the ethical behaviour of those who run companies. Regular disclosures that directors and executives have behaved unethically reflect badly on the corporate sector as a vehicle for investor funds. By comparison, Australian company directors are increasingly stating that there is already too much concentration on the mechanisms of corporate governance, indicating that they will happily tick the boxes, but do little more.

In the latter part of the 20th century, companies discovered mission. The key elements of any mission must include the major corporate participants – investors, suppliers, customers, employees and society. The role of management is to develop a structure that can operationalise the mission. Such an approach puts ethics – how we treat other people – at the core of a company's activities. Trust is a critical element in how

Corporate Governance: Does Any Size Fit?
Advances in Public Interest Accounting, Volume 11, 271–302
Copyright © 2005 by Elsevier Ltd.
All rights of reproduction in any form reserved
ISSN: 1041-7060/doi:10.1016/S1041-7060(05)11012-8

the interests of these stakeholders are taken up in decision-making and embedded in strategy, plans and action on the ground.

In the aftermath of significant corporate collapses in the 1980s and then again at the start of this century, companies also discovered corporate governance. According to the much referenced Cadbury Committee in the U.K., corporate governance is the system by which companies are directed and controlled, i.e., a the system of checks and balances for effective resolution of conflicts and control over the exercise of managerial power.

This paper suggests that an alternative "professional" approach to governance is likely to be more effective. Today, the role of management is to "add value" and contribute to the "good" of society. This good is the collective set of stakeholder interests entrusted to the governing board to look after. A governance model that integrates the human good with the operations of 'mind' in terms of learning and leadership highlights eight distinctive "products," the eighth being valued products and by-products delivered to each stakeholder. The model is structured around the person's capacity to ask four categories of questions, including those that provide orientation and direction.

The model is used to examine a contemporary governance issue experienced by the board of directors at the National Australia Bank Limited.

INTRODUCTION

The Latin etymology of "governance" can be found in the term "guberna-tor," which refers to the direction giving for a ship. An alternative etymology is from old French word "governance" meaning to control, or in a state of being governed (Farrar, 2001, p. 3). Governance can also refer to a "system of management" (Macquarie Dictionary, 1987) or "the controlling, directing, and regulating of influence, and a mode of living or behaviour" (Oxford English Dictionary, 1933).

We can thus immediately see two distinct arms of the word governance. Firstly, it refers to what drives the *behaviour* of directors and executives in directing and controlling a company. This gives rise to questions about the motivations, skills and ethics of the people charged with this duty – namely the board of directors. Secondly, it refers to the *systems* by which the activities of the company are controlled by those given that responsibility, and focus is placed on identifying the elements of a corporate governance system, and testing the effectiveness of the system against changes in the internal and external environment.

Directors, stock exchanges, governments and the majority of researchers in Anglo-Celtic countries appear to have adopted the latter definition of governance, with a major emphasis being placed on finding the set of rules that will effectively control the behaviour of directors. According to the much referenced Cadbury Committee in the U.K., corporate governance is the *"system* by which companies are directed and controlled" (emphasis added) (Cadbury, 1992). According to the Cadbury Committee, managers needed to "be *free* to drive their companies forward, but exercise that freedom within a framework of effective *accountability"* (emphasis added). According to the committee, companies needed to implement a system of checks and balances for effective resolution of conflicts and control over the exercise of managerial power (Charkham, 1995, pp. 2–5).

The argument promoted was that competitive pressures made it imperative that company management remain free to do as they wish, but provide some form of reassurance to shareholders and other stakeholders that they were seen to be accountable. A definition of governance based on a "system of accountability" was firstly more understandable to directors and their advisors, as they were familiar with systems of accountability imposed by corporations legislation as reflected in disclosed financial statements. Secondly, a system definition was simpler to implement, as the "remedy" appeared more concrete – a new series of rules – as opposed to trying to grapple with a definition based on directors' motivations, skills and ethics.

In this paper, we argue that a regulation of corporate governance via systems of rules is unlikely to be effective – in the sense that we will continue to suffer from unexpected corporate crashes where boards of directors appear not to have acted in the interests of shareholders or other groups – and a more fundamental approach is necessary. To develop effective corporate governance measures that can provide guidance, we assert that directors need to understand what governance should mean to them. They need to be able to name its core attributes and establish a link to ethical conduct. They need to understand also that practical outcomes emerge for improving the quality and effectiveness of their own governance.

Although a "person" ultimately exercises governing powers, governance is complicated by the notion of juridic persons. Corporations are legal constructs designed to represent collectives of individual persons and interests. Thus, corporate governance needs to embrace shared personal values and collective values if boards are to operate effectively.

What is obvious, at this stage in the establishment of governance principles, is that there is no definitive definition of governance *that suits all
parties*. The issue is not, of course, "governance" per se. The real issue is
who controls the activities of the company, for whose benefit is control
exercised, and how are demands for accountability met? Control is difficult
to observe because of a lack of transparency in board decision-making,
leading to a perceived lack of accountability of boards and executives for
their actions. If directors are to meet calls for greater governance, they need
to understand the relationship between personal character, decision-making,
leadership and the public outcomes of governance; and what mind and
matter have to do with governance and the organisation.

These are some of the orienting issues that give rise to the ideas we put
forward in this paper. They are focused primarily on the governance responsibilities of boards of directors that characterize many organisations in
society.

GOVERNANCE AND THE DUTIES OF DIRECTORS

Figure 1 provides one way of mapping the way in which researchers have
tried to observe governance as practised in companies. We can observe the

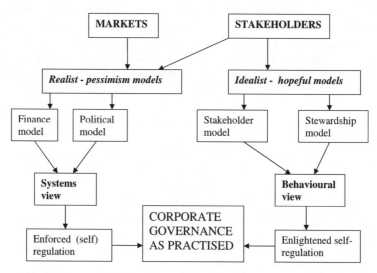

Fig. 1.   Research Pathways to Observing Governance as Practised.

impact of corporate governance practices on markets, and vice versa, via share price movements. We can also observe the impact of stakeholders – significant shareholders, institutional shareholders, regulators, chief executive officers (CEOs), directors and others – on corporate governance practices. Hawley and Williams identified four models of corporate governance: the finance model, the political model, the stakeholder model and the stewardship model (1996). We dichotomise Hawley and Williams models into two meta-models of governance practices. Firstly, the realist–pessimist models, incorporating the finance and political models that together give a systems perspective of governance. Secondly, the ideal – hopeful models, incorporating the stakeholder and stewardship models that together give a behavioural perspective of governance.

The realist–pessimism models are so called as governance is imposed on, or grudgingly accepted by, management as a price for stakeholder involvement. The finance model relies on the functioning of highly liquid capital markets to discipline managerial behaviour through the selling and buying of shares. Applying this model, directors and managers will adopt governance attributes that keep investors investing in their shares (Hawley & Williams, 1996). The political model focuses on the power distribution between managers and investors. It encompasses situations where shareholders, or their representatives (fund managers, directors) seek to influence company policy by negotiating voting support rather than by buying and selling their shareholdings (Pound, 1993, p. 83).

The two models form a systems view of corporate governance as they focus on the control attributes of the corporate governance system in place, and test the elements of the system as indicators of director behaviour. The control attributes can be external (monitoring by shareholders and creditors, regulatory and legal system, the market for corporate managers) or internal (management compensation plans, monitoring by directors, the internal management market) (Farinha, 2003, p. 4; Bushman & Smith, 2001, p. 238; Garvey & Swan, 1994). These models are consistent with the establishment and effective workings of societal systems of justice (Rawls, 1971). The systems view of the workings of organisations is so widely accepted, that most research undertaken assumes that this is a reasonable explanation of the relationship between managers and stakeholders.

The ideal – hopeful models regard altruism and ethical behaviour as alternative valid determinants of management behaviour. The stakeholder model sees the management maximising the wealth of shareholders while meeting the conflicting needs of all stakeholders. Secondly, the stewardship model views directors and managers as responsible stewards who should be relied upon to run the firm unfettered in the interests of all stakeholders (Hawley & Williams, 1996). The ideal–hopeful models comprise a behavioural view of corporate governance that sees "care for others" as a significant determinant of action (Gilligan, 1982). Testing these two models requires observation of the behaviours of directors in companies as they attempt to control the activities of managers and employees – a difficult exercise to carry out.

While all four models can be used to explain the behaviour of managers and directors, the finance and political models have received most attention. Corporate governance is seen as an additional control mechanism put in place to provide evidence that management is acting generally in the interests of shareholders and not expropriating shareholder wealth for their personal consumption. The agency theory, on which these observations are based, assumes that all parties – including directors and executives – act out of self-interest. A major assumption behind the finance model of corporate governance is that the elements of the "governance system" are used by outsiders as signals for buying and selling shares. Thus, part of the role of a governance system is to keep the market well informed, increasing market efficiency and liquidity.

Researchers adopting the political model have focussed on the conflict between managers and owners in companies and made the assumption that the distribution of power between them is not solely a result of the market for corporate control. The political model looks at non-market forms of influencing corporate governance. The political model still adheres to the assumption of self-interest and agency conflict but views agency problems as subjects for the political system to deliberate on. Agency costs are viewed as entitlements to be allocated by the political system rather than costs to be controlled (Hawley & Williams, 1996, p. 8).

The groups with the potential power to influence corporate governance are dominant shareholders, institutional investors (through fund managers) and boards of directors. Dominant shareholders may inhibit governance activity as they can monitor their interests directly (Black & Coffee, 1994). Institutional investors hold a portfolio of shares that represents major market indices. The absolute dollar amounts invested in shares has grown rapidly, giving institutional investors an incentive to incur costs to become informed and monitor their investments rather than to inform their buy or sell decisions (Pound, 1993). Until recently institutions seem to have been loath to exercise their voting power (Carlton, Nelson, & Wiesbach, 1998). Directors have always possessed the authority to execute almost any reform that critics of current corporate governance practices might want, but outsiders cannot easily observe whether they exercise that authority (Hawley & Williams, 1996, p. 9), and little is known about how directors actually make decisions (Bushman & Smith, 2001, p. 289).

A major assumption that is not tested by the realist–pessimism models is the self-interest assumption that lies behind the theory of agency conflicts. Self-interest may be valid as an average or dominant motivation, but is unlikely to reflect the motivation of all players in the corporate game at all times. Altruism and ethical behaviour are also likely to influence director behaviour. It is hard to believe that no directors have ethical principles and that self-interest is the only motivating force. Directors are likely to reflect the ethical views of the community and it is unthinkable that they leave their personal values and ethical approaches out of decision-making with regard to boardroom decisions. It is likely that most directors are conflicted by the struggle between the self-interest urge, their ethical principles, concern for others and their sense of justice. The purely self-interest view of director decision-making and the purely ethical view of decision-making are unlikely in themselves to explain all director behaviour. We know that directors can exercise significant power to benefit themselves at the expense of company shareholders apparently without being monitored by shareholders or other outside groups (Turnbull, 2000), so it is important to understand how directors cope with this struggle.

From our review of the literature, we sensed a gap in the understanding of the social dynamics of board functioning. Despite the increase in corporate governance research adopting a systems view, one statement is repeated often by the researchers, "we actually know very little about the internal operations of boards" (Bushman & Smith, 2001, p. 289). Sonnenfeld (2002, p. 2) has pointed out that many failed companies carried all the external hallmarks of good governance, with independent directors with large personal stakes in the shares of the company, demonstrating a range of skills, with audit and compensation committees, and codes of ethics. The remedies prescribed for improving corporate governance have all been *structural*, whereas the key to governance is *social*. Boards of directors have to develop a "virtuous cycle of respect for each other, trust and candour." (Sonnenfeld, 2002).

A constant claim is the need to get more sunlight onto, and more fresh air into, corporate governance issues because we do not know how directors make decisions, what factors they take into account, the pressures on them, and the values and ethical principles that guide their deliberations. Commentators talk of a need to change the culture in the boardroom (Knight, 2004). However, before you can change culture you need to establish that the ethos of the organisation is consistent with the culture change envisaged.

Directors need to ask themselves whether any proposed change fits with their personal ethos and any explicit or implicit corporate ethos? Any cultural change needs to be consistent with the ethos of those who control the organisation, and that ethos in turn will inform the organisation's culture and stated mission. Unless these factors are addressed early, it is likely that a strategy adopted that is not consistent with the organisation's ethos culture and mission will fail.

A change in corporate governance practices requires an investigation and evaluation of the personal ethos of the directors and executives, an analysis of the culture in place, and an evaluation of how the ethos and culture affect decision-making to see if there are deficiencies in governance practices. Such an evaluation by company boards is likely to be spurred on by more effective monitoring of governance practices from outside companies (taking a systems view) and a greater understanding of their decision-making behaviour by the directors themselves (taking a behavioural view).

A PERSONAL GOVERNANCE SYSTEM: THE MISSING LINK?

The behavioural view of governance brings into focus the personal powers and authorities of directors. In most cases, the initiating and orienting powers and authorities are bestowed on directors, in trust, by others, as a medium of control, accountability and communication about the direction, purpose and good for which the company is established. The directors in turn delegate and entrust to others.

In relation to their mandate, directors guide the organisation for which they are responsible and held accountable. Their role is dependent upon but separate from their person, evident when one leaves a board and another takes their place. Their work is to communicate, seek advice, make decisions, and in so doing draw on personal attributes of experience, intelligence, judgment and capacity for decision.

Officers of a company are expected to act ethically, that is, to take full cognisance of the interests that the firm's stakeholders directly or implicitly entrust to them when making their decisions. The set of these interests, we call *the good*. Another way of describing the good is to think in positivist notions with regard to the evolution of successively higher complex systems that are *better* than those that went before. One of the better things to evolve is our ability as humans to reflect ethically on the choices confronting us

(Dunne, 2004, p. 1). In their ethical decision-making role, directors face numerous conflicts of interest, such as that between their desire to further their own interests and the fiduciary obligations that are imposed on them by corporations legislation.

With increasing calls for accountability, directors need to rebut claims about any abuse of their powers, by being seen to be accountable to shareholders and others. By focusing on a system definition of governance, directors, stock exchanges and many researchers have adopted the view that there are explicit, objective principles of governance available that, if implemented, will ensure that boards will not only be seen to be fully accountable for their actions, but will actually act in a fully accountable manner. The definition of governance adopted in practice, the system definition, provides a two-dimensional model of governance, as it assumes that the system reflects the actions of directors and the values that drive those actions, whereas we do not know this just from the existence of an apparently working system.

What we assert is that directors today need to arm themselves against even the perception that they are benefiting themselves at the expense of other stakeholders, and need well-developed ethical governance guidelines for doing so. There appears to be a growing awareness that directors need to be better prepared for the sorts of issues that will confront them. Most directors see this as an education in the process of the company's business, such as reading financial statements and understanding key performance indicators, so that directors will be "alert and worried about finance, strategy, and the CEO," (Buffini, 2003, p. 4).

While such skills are important, we believe a director's education needs to go much further than a mere understanding of the external factors relating to company operations. It should include an education about factors internal to the directors themselves – about how they think and feel about the situations that face them – in effect to develop an internal system of corporate governance that will guide their own actions.

Understanding a company's situation, by itself, is not sufficient to provoke directors into "right" action. Did the directors fully grasp the significance of those external realities that were pressing upon them? Was their grasp compromised by fear and distrust? Were true judgment and decision at work? Were courage and charisma needed to give effect to decisions? Were the decisions taken appropriate for the situations they were facing? A solution that provides a course in rational decision-making and business ethics is simplistic. Decision-making is more complex than most models suggest, and business ethics is not an optional add-on.

One place to look for a solution – which tends to be overlooked – is the linkage between thinking and doing, between the models of the world and the models of the mind. If strategy is derived from ideas, what is the basis of generating good ideas? How do directors know whether an idea is a good one? Who is right? And how do they deal with strong emotions that can often influence their thinking and acting? How do they protect themselves from the failures of their colleagues to use their minds well?

We have sought to find a place for these kinds of questions in a dynamic model of personal and corporate governance. The starting point for our basic model of governance is to ask questions about what nourishes the growth of organisations and what prevents it. At the heart of a company stands the person, individually and as a group or board. Each person brings with them their past history and present circumstances. To make sense of the world we live in, each of us needs to understand as much as possible about what is going on. The phrase "knowledge is power" is not an empty statement. The basis of all understanding is the desire to know, which manifests itself in a conscious drive to engage with the task of understanding, which itself requires an openness to all possibilities. This is represented by the vertical line in Fig. 2. However, how are we to be sure that we understand the world correctly? Understanding poorly or misunderstanding can have dire consequences for our decisions.

In his seminal work *Insight* (1957), the Canadian philosopher, Bernard Lonergan provided an answer to this question with the explication of a generalised empirical method of decision-making that focussed on four operation norms: be attentive, be intelligent, be reasonable and be responsible when assessing issues to arrive at a decision. At the level of responsibility, we need to assess any likely action against the good we intend by that action. This will result in decisions that the decision-maker knows are ethical.

On a corporate board, the good held in trust is what is desired by the shareholders, the customers, the suppliers of materials, services and finance, the employees, the government and the community, as well as the executive management and the board of directors, that is the various stakeholders. To understand this good, held in trust for all the stakeholders, is at the heart of the organisation. To operate out of it is the core task of the board of directors, through sharing the company's ethos, values and mission, and shaping the company's strategy and policies.

At the level of the board, each director has three essential aspects of his or her job to manage. Firstly, to understand the task itself, and to find their particular role and voice in that task – engineer, lawyer, accountant, strategist, generalist – and how best to contribute to it. Secondly, to co-operate

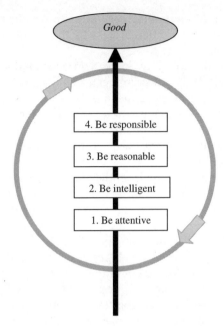

Fig. 2. The Basic Model of Personal Governance.

with others on the board, learn to work constructively with others and to have one's voice heard. Lastly, learn how to manage oneself. This is perhaps the hardest and most critical aspect of being a director. Directors should know and be themselves. They need to open themselves to the demands of what has been entrusted to them. They should have the courage to put contrary views and to judge when to do so. To do this effectively requires a model of knowing oneself, of personal governance, that most people never stop to think about. It is a model based simply on the power of questioning. Yet in company failure after company failure, we are informed that directors did not ask the right questions. We need to understand what stops, and more importantly what would help them to ask the right questions.

Our model is constructed on the generally unexamined or unnoticed attribute of human living, namely one's powers of enquiry and capacity to ask questions. The questioning system of enquiry is one we are all familiar with from the operation of courts with cross-examination, the holding of public enquiries and royal commissions, senate estimates committees, and the media questioning of people in powerful positions. A culture that allows people to ask all sorts of questions provides a good indicator of authenticity in the culture, as such questioning generally exposes the truth surrounding events often portrayed in a different light by those with much to lose from the truth coming out.

People naturally do not want to be held accountable if some of their decisions are suspect. If their decisions can be hidden behind a veil of silence or obfuscation, decisions can be made on the basis of values close to the hearts of those making them, but that other stakeholders find unacceptable. However, if there is a culture of openness, and questions asked are answered honestly, then a culture of trust will be built, based purely on the way questions are addressed.

When we monitor a company from the outside, it is impossible to observe the character of the directors and their integrity in making decisions. Directors have many ways of erecting smokescreens to hide what they are doing and how they are doing it. A key question for outsiders should be who controls the questioning in the company? Our thesis is that the control of questioning in the organisation should reside at the board level, and provide the locus of control in the organisation. Questioning by and of board members is the source of openness and accountability by corporate management. Our guide to effective questioning comes from Lonergan's hierarchy of operational norms: be attentive, be intelligent, be reasonable and be responsible. Lonergan (1971, pp. 8–9) analysed how we can do this systematically.

THE POWER OF THE QUESTION: A DYNAMIC STRUCTURE THAT INITIATES AND DRIVE CHANGE

Questions by their nature seek answers, which generally lead to further questions. Answers are often so satisfying that we overlook the power (of inquiry) that gave rise to them in the first place. Answers, nevertheless, provides a novel way to classify questions and open a fresh approach to the cybernetic topics of control and communication, which some regard as the essence of governance. Fig. 3 provides the basic model exploded to reveal the questions associated with each operating norm classified by the answers they seek. The model shows the internal dynamic system of questioning, brought to consciousness, with the operating norms being the inputs, the question being the process and the answers sought being the output.

The model describes a set of mental powers that we all, often unknowingly, or inadvertently, use in daily life. The thinking operations, though

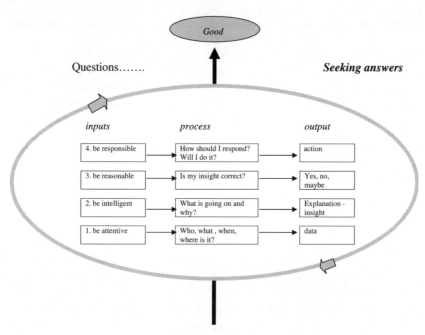

Fig. 3. The Internal Dynamic System of Questioning.

invisible to others, are accessible to the person thinking. Thus, in carefully observing one's own mental activity, anyone can discover and identify the set of thinking operations or powers within oneself, and describe them as constituting the four levels, each level building on the level below. To Lonergan (1957), the key to the development of understanding was insight. An insight unlocks the mysteries of a puzzle and leads to understanding.

The good detective novel sustains our interest until the last page where the clues assembled confirm a most unlikely hypothesis based on insights that only the master detective has, but which he or she eventually reveals to the reader as the only explanation, and red herrings are seen for what they are. Within organisations where ideas and information are freely exchanged and in which there is open inquiry, new insights will more easily develop. Equally, where information is not exchanged and where inquiry is suppressed, insights will not arise, get crushed or are lost.

There are four steps in the basic questioning model (see Fig. 3). At the first level, there is a need to be attentive to the data – from all sources, external and internal. Questions such as who, what, when and where give access to the basic data on which we can work. At the second level, we need to explore that data applying our intelligence to it to find out what is going on and why. This level seeks explanations and we expect those explanations to yield insights that link the various explanations of the data. At the third level we need to apply reason, and ask whether our insights are true or correct. Answers we derive can be yes, no or maybe, and require the exercise of judgment. Our judgments may direct our attention back to gathering more data seeking more explanations, because we do not really understand the situation, or propel us forward to the fourth level. At the fourth level we need to take responsibility for our actions and ask, with the choices confronting us, how should we respond, and will we do anything?

The key to this process is understanding, and the key to understanding is insight. Insight can take a long time to come, or can occur in an instant. We can assist its delivery by being persistent with our questions. Recall trying to solve a puzzle, and you will probably recall the whole gamut of human emotion. Were you tempted to abandon the venture: did you feel stupid (rightly so, for level 2 is the measure of intelligence and, not being there, you can *feel* stupid), did you get angry at yourself and at others, and so on?

As Lonergan points out, insight is the prime source of personal power. It energises and enlightens. You can relish and delight in the insight and celebrate that you, at least, understand. You have enriched the data with an insight, grasped the unity in the data, and enriched yourself with the new understanding you now have.

Yet insights are not enough. They can be wrong. Processes and methods are needed to ensure, not only, that insights occur but are thoroughly tested and evaluated, for they have the potential not only to lead to enlightened decision and action but also to mislead. Insights, by their nature, are open for revision. Hard work is often needed to validate and confirm what our insight, hunch, or intuition has suggested.

In moving from insight to judgement, we test our understanding and seek to be free of illusion or error. Here the driving precept is to "be rational." We test our insight by relevant questions against the data of experience, to arrive at a confident "yes." If an insight stands invulnerable against all questions, our insight becomes a judgment. With a correct judgment we can say a definitive "yes" or "no" and, in this, exercise publicly our powers of assent.

THE POWER OF THE QUESTION: A SOURCE OF BOARD CONTROL AND ACCOUNTABILITY

Directors need to be aware of the relationship between their personal dynamic structure of questioning that is invisible to others and the public manifestation of that questioning that can be depicted now as a structure of control. It represents control over one's own thinking, the self-management of one's being. It also represents control through cooperation with fellow board members, taking a leadership role when necessary and intervening in debate that you think is getting away from the main issues.

At the lowest level, being attentive requires the directors to be in touch with the real world, collecting and processing the data from all senses and memory to enable them to perceive what is and what is not possible. At the next level, applying their intelligence to derive insight and understanding, they will develop ideas and concepts that need to communicated to others either verbally, in written form or via diagrams, so that they can be tested by further questioning. At the third level they apply reason and judge whether their understanding is real, true, or highly probable. This is a judgment that needs to be shared with others so that again it can be questioned and tested. At the fourth level they need to act responsibly, taking into account the good entrusted to them. At this level the directors will engage in a dialectic as they test their competing ideas and concepts and the truth of their insights against each other. The outcome should be an insight that they can all hold to be probably true that will guide change in the organisation and give them evidence that they collectively have a structure that controls the decision process for the benefit of all stakeholders. For the organisation to change and develop for the betterment of all stakeholders, application of this structure of control by the board as individuals and as a group needs to be more explicit.

Our first observation is that this dynamic structure of questioning and control within a board of directors should generate a set of products that add value to organisation decision-making (see Fig. 4). At the lowest level, being attentive should lead to questions indicating that a director is cooperating, engaging in research, or requesting research, to collect evidence about the topic under discussion. This research output needs to be made explicit and available to all concerned.

At the second level, being intelligent requires some interpretation of the data, and one of more insights to what has occurred. The insights give rise to possible explanations of the situation and opportunities for action that

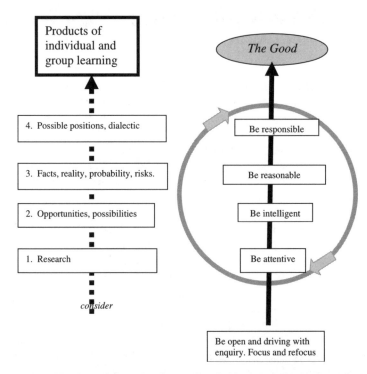

Fig. 4.   The Boardroom Products of Individual and Group Learning.

could be taken to resolve an issue. Also these possibilities and opportunities need to be make explicit and available to all concerned in the decision.

At the third level, applying those insights, directors can identify which of the possibilities best represents the reality of the situation, which of the possible explanations indicates the truth as they believe it. It may be possible only to specify a probability that any single explanation represents the truth of the situation, and any attendant risks should be made known. Finally at the fourth level, directors can engage in a dialectic that brings to light the different understanding and conceptions of truth that each director has arrived at and spell out the possible positions that the company can take, with the object of making a choice that achieves change in the corporation's strategy or policies, but in a manner that reflects all points of view, and is consistent with the good that the organisation is striving to achieve.

The products identified in Fig. 4 are the manifestation of individual and group learning by board members. Each subsequent product is a function of the products developed lower down. Errors at lower levels, such as poor research, faulty explanations of the data and quick acceptance of one explanation above others, lead to errors at higher level and poor choices to solve problems.

A second observation to be made is that we are dealing with inquiry as a structure turning on itself. The image of a wheel is appropriate here. A wheel has a core, a rim, an inside and an outside. It also can change directions. The set of questions selected sets direction. Another set of questions provide drive for the wheel to turn. Another set of questions can open out and expand the rim. Directors need to focus intently on the issues at hand, and refocus to ensure that they are doing enough research, making interpretations that provide correct insights, ascertaining the reality they are faced by and acting responsibly to make choices that satisfy the interests of all stakeholders. These are onerous and never-ending responsibilities. Like footballers, directors cannot afford to take their eyes off the ball.

A final observation is that there are two attributes or competencies integral to inquiry. Firstly, that personal drive and energy prevail and give focus until all relevant questions are satisfactorily answered. Secondly, there needs to be a personal disposition towards openness, for there is no limit to the number of questions that we can ask and the answers we can find. Unless these attributes are found in and collectively accepted by directors, there will be no drive, energy, or openness within the board. The measure of competence and skill which each director possesses in each of the attributes of 'good mind management' translate directly into what the Board possesses. This is the strength of our model.

Of course, directors need always to be aware of sources of bias on the 'ground' in which they operate (institutional oversight, embedded bad practices, poor policy, etc.) and in themselves (a narrow view, prejudice, closed mind, etc.). The overcoming of bias is a personal project and challenge requiring directors to be open, share information about themselves, seek expert opinion when necessary, test their views openly and constantly ask questions. This is a tough task, requiring positive-thinking application to arrive at a genuine understanding of each situation.

On a board of directors, there is a risk to the relationships on the board in asking questions as a perceived, but often unintended, judgment on the questioner's competence. If the questioner is insecure, then defensiveness, distrust and evasion may occur. The asking of questions that might disturb the smooth running of the meeting is the Achilles heel of corporate governance. The factors that stop questioning relate mainly to the perceptions of individual directors about themselves and how they are perceived by powerful others on the board. Factors that stop questioning on a board include:

• Fear
• Lack of knowledge
• Lack of interest
• Lack of engagement
• Not wishing to disturb group harmony
• Not wishing to be seen to be different
• Topic seen as being of specialist interest
• Being put down in past questioning
• Intimidation by powerful others
• Pressure to come to a consensus
• Defensiveness of others

These factors would all be familiar to directors at some time or other. Some are the personal responsibility of directors and some are owned by the board itself. Directors need to realise that they can help themselves to be better questioners, and the board as a group needs to help individual directors to be better questioners, by encouraging such factors as:

• Openness
• Encouragement
• Courage
• Reading board papers well in advance
• Being prepared prior to meetings
• Having time to reflect
• Board protocols to encourage questioning
• Acknowledging that all questions are valid and acceptable
• Valuing all members' contributions

APPLICATION OF THE DYNAMIC MODEL OF CORPORATE GOVERNANCE

The positive approach that informs much research into governance assumes a fact-value dichotomy with value-laden statements not being susceptible to empirical testing because they lack objectivity (Simon, 1976). Positivists steer away from ethical issues as being unsuitable for rational analysis. As Stewart points out, an alternative approach, the "good reasons" approach, says that ethical positions and decision choices can be rationally evaluated by observing the arguments used to support them (Stewart, 1988). Lonergan takes this a step further by demonstrating that the four stage structure of control comprises the structure of objective decision-making. The decision-maker experiences, understands, and then judges the truth or existence of alternative courses of action. In making a choice between alternatives, the decision-maker additionally judges the value of each alternative. For Lonergan (1957, pp. 399–409), objectivity is overcoming bias and prejudice when making judgements and decisions, driven by our unique desire to know and understand. A true judgement is one that can satisfactorily answer all the questions posed at any one time. It is exemplified by the precepts, "be attentive, be intelligent, be reasonable, be responsible."

It is rare to have certain judgment on management issues. Mostly there is a high degree of uncertainty and risk. Certain relevant questions may not easily be answered, or the data is incomplete and costly to obtain; or experience may be lacking. Our judgments are hedged and so are our actions. One can seriously err, however, by prematurely reaching judgment and stopping all further questions. It is a common mistake to make judgements on the basis of incomplete or faulty data. It is also a common mistake to jump from data to judgement, bypassing explanation and insight. Here, great challenges and dangers await company boards. The solution to overcome these risks is for constant, frank, vigorous open questioning and discussion between board members on all critical decisions, and development of the dynamic questioning structure of control we have outlined, to provide each director with sufficient "mindfulness."

Given the personal focus of our model, based on individual powers of inquiry, we now wish to locate the model's general features within a practical map of governance. First, in terms of orientation, the wheel will turn in the direction set by the primary task and purpose of the organisation, which establishes the 'good' it sets out to achieve. This 'good' is the set of valued products that each stakeholder implicitly or explicitly entrusts to the directors to take care of, which represents the heart of the organisation. We use a threefold notion of good: particular good, good of order and the personal human good (Fig. 5).

Particular good, in relation to a firm, can be seen through the eyes of its stakeholders as immediate goods or benefits: the return on investment, positive cash flow, profit margins accruing to owners; a just wage for workers, a safe workplace; quality products accruing to customers; and fair dealings with suppliers and customers.

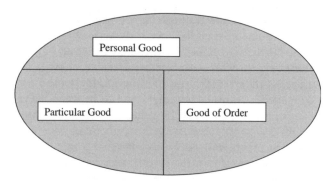

Fig. 5. The Threefold Notion of Good.

The good of order refers to those things which ensure that particular goods keep coming. It includes organisational sustainability and growth, work opportunities for employees and suppliers, and the reputation of the organisation. Personal good, in our use of the term, refers to the set of ultimate reasons why we act. Finnis (1980, pp. 86–89) proposed a set of seven basic human goods found after self-examination as to why we act. He defined them as: life itself, knowledge, achievement, aesthetic experience, harmony with oneself, harmony with others and harmony with higher sources of meaning (spiritual harmony).

The term "good" is used here in the sense that Finnis uses it, to describe a value that is desired for its own sake. The value on which he places most attention is knowledge, and he is at pains to indicate that a basic value, like knowledge, is not a moral value, but rather an intrinsic value (1980, pp. 59–65).

Within the corporate context, we can apply the products of individual and group learning by deliberating on the good, to produce a set of necessary value-adding products that will operationalise good for the stakeholders and when implemented lead to organisational effectiveness (see Fig. 6). These will be products of individual and group leadership, in the sense that authentic leadership requires personal and collective esponsibility and a free commitment to the decisions made.

The products of directors' individual and group learning, applying our dynamic structure of questioning, will be firstly, as they demonstrate their responsibility to the stakeholders, an explication of the values, mission and vision that drive the company.[1] It is not sufficient for the CEO or board to understand this. All employees, customers and suppliers must understand

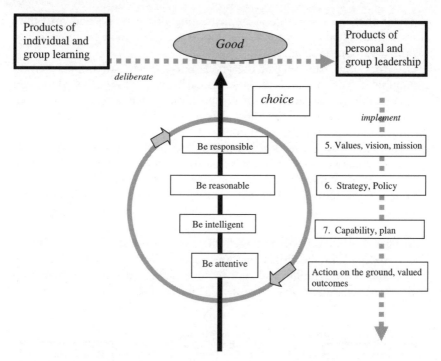

Fig. 6. The Boardroom Products of Personal and Group Leadership.

it too. Secondly, the values and mission must devolve into strategies and policies that are explicitly consistent with the values and mission of the organisation and are judged by the board to represent what the company should be doing. Thirdly, those strategies and policies must devolve into a plan of action that is consistent with the values and mission and within the capabilities of the staff to deliver. The plan must make sense to those who have to implement it as well as the board and executive who developed it. Lastly, the plan must result in action on the ground, in the real world, that is consistent with the good entrusted to the board, and with solving the real issues facing the organisation. When this occurs the result will be outcomes valued by all stakeholders, and genuine development will have occurred.

We can now assemble the dynamic structure of control based on the power of questioning with the four value-adding products that are the result of directors' individual and group learning and the four value-adding products that are the result of implementing this learning and providing effective individual and group leadership to provide a model of governance for the organisation (Fig. 7).

Directors' understanding of the good shapes organisational choice and commitment. This is what is at stake, primarily, in what is entrusted to them by stakeholders. The deeper their grasp of, and commitment to, the good, the more consistent will be their decision-making with the stakeholder groups. The deeper their understanding of the dynamic structure of control, the more ethical will their decision-making be, in the sense that it complies with their personal values and the values that they have collectively agreed will guide their deliberations. Secondly, they will commit resources through a strategy consistent with the good. Thirdly, they mediate the good through their delegation to management, to plan and build organisational capability and to deliver it by action on the ground. Directors need to ensure that the trust placed in them by their stakeholders is reinforced by their decisions, and is reflected in the firm's ongoing reputation. Loss of this trust can contribute to catastrophic and sudden collapse. The media and regulatory bodies are increasingly alert to violations of this trust.

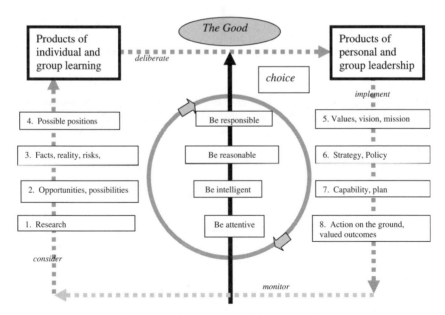

Fig. 7.   The Dynamic Structure of Corporate Governance.

Our four levels of inquiry are represented within the wheel in Fig. 7. These indicate the personal and collective performance of directors and the board, and those to whom the board delegates or entrusts its requirement. The path that the wheel will take, carved out by "leadership." The set of eight "products" around the wheel represent progress, going clockwise around the wheel. Progress is determined by monitoring the outcomes of action against the insight that lead to action and the good that the board is seeking to serve. The process is endless if a sustainable organisation is to be developed and maintained.

We have sought to find a pivotal place for questions in a dynamic model of personal and corporate governance. Our model reveals, in its full unfolding, a complex fabric of trust, power, authority and personal competence. If our model is to be useful, it should reveal all key components of governance in relation to each other – such as values, operational roles and other stakeholder interests. It should also reflect the dynamic nature and structure of governance – the need to consider data, its interpretation, an assessment of the reality of the situation, the need to deliberate and evaluate possible positions against the good of all stakeholders, the need to implement decisions in a way consistent with good entrusted to directors, and lastly the need to monitor the action taken and the outcomes derived against the insights developed and the good entrusted to directors.

The wheel thus turns a complete circle, and the next round takes up fresh data from the "ground" – to be further interpreted and tested, again creating a new round of dialectic. The wheel's hub remains the centre of power and energy for this model. This is the centre of the person, or the measure of personal integration, drive and openness, capacity for insight, judgment and decision, achieved by those involved in the circle of cooperation.

Apart from the eight "products" of the circle, a critical component of our model is the structure of the "good." To what extent do directors need to bear all these "goods" in mind, or is only one to be considered, namely, profit? Our notion of the "good" is that it is "integral." Boards cannot aim exclusively for one good without considering the impact on other goods. If great financial wealth was generated by a company but the country was laid to waste and all the citizens became sick, it would not be possible to say that a company had produced any good, as the costs (human and environmental) would be obvious to all and would outweigh any financial benefits attributed to the relatively small group of owners. In reality, of course, the costs and benefits are more difficult to ascertain. Directors need some guidance then to weigh the economic benefits against the economic, social and environmental costs of their actions. Directors need to sensitise and educate themselves to be competent to identify the good affected by their decisions, use a model of decision-making that is consistent with their personal and organisational values, and have a means of implementing decisions that is consistent with their values and the good they want to create. This is our basic structure of governance.

NATIONAL AUSTRALIA BANK AND ITS FOREIGN EXCHANGE LOSSES: EVIDENCE OF POOR USE OF THE PERSONAL CORPORATE GOVERNANCE MODEL?

Even a cursory glance at the National Australia Bank (NAB) 2003 annual report indicates that the bank had probably one of the most comprehensive corporate governance systems in place within any company in Australia. The report set out the responsibilities and functions of the board, including the review and monitoring processes for compliance with prudential regulations and standards. The board had audit, risk, nomination and remuneration committees, all of which had a majority of independent, non-executive directors.

The corporate governance charter of the board covered continuing education of directors by allowing for management to give presentations to assist non-executive directors to gain a broader understanding and knowledge of the group. The charter stated that the company's values included a requirement that the business was to be run ethically and with integrity in observance of the company's code of conduct. Lastly, the governance charter covered whistleblower protection stating that the company did not tolerate fraud, corrupt conduct or regulatory non-compliance, and would not take reprisals against those coming forward to disclose such conduct (Annual Report, 2003, pp. 62–69).

The company displayed all the manifestations of a company that provides for education of and monitoring by the board, that had a code of conduct that should have allowed for contrary views to be addressed in a fair and open manner, and that should have provided an environment for personal and organisational growth. Yet a relatively minor issue tore this façade apart.

The issue that provoked a crisis for the board of the NAB was the disclosure in January 2004 of an unspecified loss generated by unauthorised trading in foreign currency options by four dealers in late-2003. The traders had bet that the Australian dollar would fall against the U.S. dollar, whereas it had strengthened. If the bet had come off, NAB would have made a profit and the subsequent turmoil would not have occurred – at least not at that time.

Nobody outside the board of NAB knows what was the actual sequence of events that led to the announcement of the unauthorised currency trades, nor what actually happened in the board meetings. As with all public knowledge of undisclosed issues we can only speculate as to the possibilities.

The point at issue was not the loss itself, but the unauthorised trading that was used to hide it, and what this said about the risk management controls employed by the bank. According to a guidance note issued in 2002 by the regulator of the Australian finance industry, the Australian Prudential Regulation Authority (APRA), the board of directors should have been actively involved in risk control as it was "an essential aspect of the business to which significant resources need(ed) to be devoted" (APRA, guidance note 113.1, 2000).

The initial issue was the failure of the bank's risk management system, but the subsequent, more damaging issues were firstly, the board's initial attempt to place blame for the risk management failure on "rogue traders," and to dismiss market speculation of a large loss as "fanciful." The CEO, Frank Cicutto, announced that an internal enquiry would be carried out by PricewaterhouseCoopers (PwC) to value its currency options portfolio. When this strategy failed to sooth adverse media comment, blame was placed by the board on the only female director, Catherine Walter.

The dominant issue was identified immediately by the media, but not by the board of directors, as a governance issue, with a daily barrage of questions from the media speculating about what must have occurred and what the appropriate remedies should be, filling the void left by the board's reluctance to communicate openly with the media (Durrie, 2004). A statement by one of dealers involved, that the derivatives trading was undertaken with full management knowledge, cast doubt on the boards explanation of the losses incurred, and indicated that aggressive trading might have been part of the bank's operating culture (Oldfield, 2004).

The bank's chairman, Charles Allen, reluctantly revealed that the bank was having difficulties valuing all 22,000 currency options in its portfolio, and that fictitious, profitable trades between its London and Melbourne offices had been undertaken by the traders to hide their losses, indicating both a problem with risk management policies and the audit of such activities (Oldfield, 2004a).

Allen stated that the board would take whatever action was necessary to restore investor confidence in the bank, but the market and media perception was that a remedy concocted behind closed doors would not suffice. The public pressure proved too much for CEO Frank Cicutto and chairman, Charles Allen, both of whom resigned their positions before the PwC report was published, being replaced by John Stewart and Graham Kraehe, respectively.

The PwC report published in March 2004 put the total foreign exchange loss at $360 million, highlighted a complacency among board members, and an unwillingness by the board to question the actions of management, especially after APRA had written to the chairman of the board questioning currency control breakdowns at NAB nearly a year before, in January 2003. APRA's query did not get to the audit committee until May 2003, where it was attached to a summary prepared by management stating that the problems were minor and being addressed. PwC found that financial control and risk management systems were deficient. For example, when traders made $41 million profit in one day against a budget of $37 million for the year, nobody on the board questioned such an unusual gain. Also the daily volume of the bank's own capital being traded on the markets, called value at risk (VaR), according to its 2003 annual report was $22 million, three times that of the other three major banks combined (Kohler, 2004). The PwC report found 800 breaches of trading limits, and a consistent pattern of misreported profits going back several years, with critical trades being placed in September when trader bonuses were calculated.

The PwC report was critical of the audit committee which during 2003 was responsible for risk management and financial control. A risk committee was established in August 2003, but did not meet during that year (Annual Report, 2003, p. 65). The PwC report suggested that the audit committee was too quick to accept management explanations rather than making its own inquiries. At the time, the audit committee members included Graham Kraehe, Peter Duncan, and was chaired by Catherine Walter. When a risk committee was established in late-2003, Kraehe moved from the audit committee and Duncan became a member of both the committees. These moves indicate that Kraehe and Duncan regarded themselves as the key directors who could supervise risk management, yet subsequent blame for the risk management failure was instead placed on Walter, who was stood down as audit committee chair (Cornell, 2004; Frith, 2004).

APRA then published its own report that confirmed the findings of the PwC report, and strongly condemned the bank management for inadequate oversight of its currency desk, and criticised the audit committee for becoming too focussed on the process of financial reporting and audit, without questioning substantive issues and warnings that were surfacing at the time. APRA also criticised the bank for an excessive focus on profit, risk taking and winning (Baker, 2004). To demonstrate the seriousness with which it viewed the NAB situation, APRA required NAB to lift its minimum regulatory capital from 9 to 10%, close its currency options trading room, and stop using an internal model for calculating market-risk capital. These moves would have a serious dampening effect on profits, affect dividend payments, lead to a downgrading of then bank's credit rating and put downward pressure on its share price (Oldfield & Boyd, 2004).

Applying our model of governance with the centrality of enquiry and seeking answers to questions, we would ask whether the board individually or collectively addressed the relevant issues. Our starting point is to ask enough questions. There is specific evidence here of the board ignoring key flags being waved before them. The PwC report indicated that several early warnings were given to the board, but they were all ignored (Boyd, 2004). Directors were not attentive to the data (APRA's query, the huge one-off profits on trading, the daily volume of VaR being traded) and carried out no research of their own. They apparently did not understand the significance of the data being presented to them. They got no insights into what was really occurring in the bank, being soothed by management claims that all was well.

The board reaction to the PwC report was to place the blame squarely on the chair of the audit committee, Walter. She refused to go quietly, stating that the PwC report lacked "independence" because PwC performed significant work for the bank, and had a partner on the board. Walter claimed that the PwC report had been influenced by NAB's risk committee members before it release. The problem escalated into a public brawl when the chairman Graeme Kraehe called an extraordinary general meeting (EGM) to have Walter dismissed.

In retrospect, both Kraehe and Walter can be seen to have been protecting themselves but at the expense of the bank's reputation and their own. Kraehe tried to garner support from major investor groups, but they in turn called for the removal of several or all directors and the timely removal of Kraehe himself (Oldfield, 2004b). Having realised that he could not save himself, Kraehe cancelled the EGM, after the board and Walter agreed that she and two other directors would resign immediately and Kraehe would resign by mid-2005 (Bartholomeusz, 2004).

Where was the evidence of spirited debate in the boardroom focussing on these issues so that directors could decide what the situation was in reality and could judge effectively how to deal with it? The company's governance charter covered director education, ethical conduct and whistleblowing, yet only Walter had a reputation for regularly asking probing questions of the company's executives (Cornell & Oldfield, 2004). The call by the seven other independent directors for Walter to resign from the board because of her criticism of the PwC reporting process smacks of payback for being seen to be different with her constant questioning, as well as being an attempt to scapegoat Walter for problems that were obviously collective in nature. No director emerged from the incident with an enhanced reputation.

Directors acting individually, as a board, or in committee appear to have failed to put relevant questions to management (Knight, 2004). Had the board ignored these early warnings or had their questions been deflected too easily by management? When the information received is dissonant with one's expectations, the response can be twofold. Firstly, it can be treated as a temporary aberration (poor risk management) that can be fixed (being provided with a sequence of remedies that are being implemented by management). Secondly, directors can instigate research to confirm or deny the early warnings. Executives of NAB appeared to respond defensively to information critical of their actions, delaying communication and attempting to water down its impact.

The directors were put on notice, when these early warnings surfaced, to gather the necessary data so that they could better understand what the problem was. As knowledge of options trading is generally poor, yet in NAB it contributed a significant percentage of profit, it was incumbent on directors to understand how the bank's profits were being generated. Directors' understanding of the situation was incomplete and the judgements they would arrive at were likely to be flawed. One director even admitted that directors had not been active enough in questioning management.

As a consequence, the solutions arrived at were also flawed. Board members acted defensively to protect their own positions rather than promote practical reasoning (most appears to have been flawed and poorly conceived), the performance of the board appeared amateurish rather than skilled and the action proposed (sacking Walter, calling an extraordinary general meeting) exacerbated problems rather than solved them.

The decision to sack Walter and her refusal to go quietly focused attention on her motivations. Was she being obstructionist and disloyal as it was implied by comments in the press, or was she applying a personal set of values to the situation? Some insight to her motivation can be gleaned by comments made by her at a Melbourne Law School graduation where she said, "You should actively manage your personal and economic balance sheet. That way you can judge whether you are appropriately allocating your time and energy between revenue-enhancing activities and soul-enhancing activities. Testing the sum total of these activities against your personal values will help you recognise whether you are living the values you espouse" (Gottliebsen, 2004).

Walter appears to have effectively utilised her own corporate governance system, but seems to have been at odds with the board's collective governance system – and the two must work together. Did she fail to convince fellow directors that they collectively should get more information, or did she fail to ask the questions herself? All directors appeared ill-informed about the nature of the problem with the currency trades and its potential to cause harm unless effectively resolved.

Other board members appear to have used the collective board governance system to hide deficiencies in their personal governance systems by seeking to paint Walter as the cause of the problem, when in reality her culpability was no greater than other members of the board.

NAB does not appear to have had a specific mission or values statement, despite claims in its 2003 annual report that such a document existed to guide action. This could have been a fundamental problem for decision-making in the bank. Where does an employee, manager, or director look for guiding principles against which to evaluate actions being proposed? The strategy certainly did not provide any. Without such guidance, which flows down into policy and plans, decisions were made against the value promoted most often – namely the "high performance" culture outlined in the bank's strategy (Annual Report, 2003).

CONCLUSION

If the only good that drives an organisation's leadership is economic value, it is likely to get into trouble eventually, as goods such as knowledge, skilled performance, cooperation and practical reasoning are likely to be sacrificed for economic gain. Such a sacrifice will always have a limited lifespan. It could be a long one, but it is always limited, as those involved will eventually believe that someone else is getting a better share than they are, or want to protect their share at all costs, costs which they want to be borne by others.

Governance systems are being rapidly constructed in a forlorn attempt to give the impression to outsiders that decisions will be taken with ethical considerations uppermost in the minds of directors and managers. However, to avoid falling into the economic trap, directors and other executives need to better develop their personal governance systems, both individually and in concert with each other, to overlay the corporate governance structure of their companies.

The role of boards is changing in our major companies. A regime of accountability is replacing a regime of "trust us" to do the right thing. Corporate governance systems have been seen by boards and executives as a way of deflecting criticism of what they actually do, but it has had the opposite effect of focusing greater scrutiny on board activities. A board is now no different to a production department or marketing department in that it is required to add value to the organisation, and a growing number of fund managers are starting to ask directors just how they do this.

Our model of governance attempts to provide directors and executives with a model to guide their activities as they demonstrate how they add value. It is not a simple model in outline, but considers all the relevant attributes to be considered by directors. Directors would do well to heed the call to understand their own values, decision-making attributes and the factors that guide them, both for their own sake and for the sake of their company's ongoing sustainability. Directors can monitor their personal integrity, and the board's collective integrity by being attentive, intelligent, reasonable and responsible in managing and sharing their experience, insight, judgement and decisions. This requires an interaction between questioning, knowing your own knowing and attending to the good before promulgating mission statements, strategies plans and action.

NOTES

1. For example, Westpac Banking Corporation Limited in Australia refers to its mission, vision and values as its DNA, as an indication of how fundamental they are to its ongoing existence (Westpac, 2004).

REFERENCES

Australian Prudential Regulation Authority (APRA) (2000). *Trading book and trading book policy statement*. Canberra.

Baker, P. (2004). Profit is king at all our banks. *Australian Financial Review*, March 25.

Bartholomeusz, S. (2004). Zero tolerance a lose–lose trend. *Australian Financial Review*, 8 May.

Black, & Coffee (1994). Hail Britannia? Institutional investor behavior under limited regulation. *Michigan Law Review*, *92*, 1997–2087.

Boyd, T. (2004). Ineffective board failed to query actions. *Australian Financial Review*, March 13.

Buffini, F. (2003). Skill development crucial for directors. *Australian Financial Review*, 11 April.

Bushman, R., & Smith, A. (2001). Financial accounting information and corporate governance. *Journal of Accounting and Economics, 31*, 237–333.

Cadbury, A. (1992). *The financial aspects of corporate governance.* London: HMSO.

Carlton, W., Nelson, J., & Wiesbach, M. (1998). The influence of institutions on corporate governance through private negotiations. *Journal of Finance, 53*, 1335–1362.

Charkham, J. (1995). *Keeping good company.* Oxford: Oxford University Press.

Cornell, A. (2004). Sacked scapegoats say system at fault. *Australian Financial Review*, March 13.

Cornell, A., & Oldfield, S. (2004). NAB's long nightmare. *Australian Financial Review*, March 27.

Dunne, T. (2004). The next evolution of ethics. *Writings of Tad Dunne.* Toronto. http://www.wideopenwest.com/~tdunne5273/NxtEvEth.htm

Durrie, J. (2004). Damning insight into NAB. *Australian Financial Review*, January 20.

Farinha, J. (2003). Corporate governance: A survey of the literature. *Working Paper*, CETE, Universidade do Porto, Portugal.

Farrar, J. H. (2001). *Corporate governance in Australia and New Zealand.* Melbourne: Oxford University Press.

Finnis, J. (1980). *Natural law and natural rights.* Oxford: Clarendon Press.

Frith, B. (2004). Walter a risky domino play for NAB. *The Australian*, March 23.

Garvey, G., & Swan, P. (1994). The economics of corporate governance: Beyond the Marshallian firm. *Journal of Corporate Finance, 1*, 139–174.

Gilligan, C. (1982). *In a different voice.* Cambridge: Harvard University Press.

Gottliebsen, R. (2004). A long time coming but it's now Cathy go home. *The Australian*, March 28.

Hawley, J. P., & Williams, A. T. (1996). Corporate governance in the United States: The rise of fiduciary capitalism. A review of the Literature. *OECD background paper*.

Knight, E. (2004). Full of arrogance just like the old BHP. *Sydney Morning Herald*, March 25.

Kohler, A. (2004a). Bank was playing a whale of a game. *Australian Financial Review*, January 28.

Lonergan, B. J. F. (1957). *Insight: A study of human understanding.* London: Longmans, Green & Co. (reprinted by University of Toronto Press, 1992).

Lonergan, B. J. F. (1971). *Method in theology.* London: Darton, Longman & Todd.

Macquarie Dictionary (1987). *The Macquarie Library* (3rd ed.). Sydney: Macquarie University.

National Australia Bank (2003). *Annual Report.* Melbourne.

Oldfield, S. (2004a). NAB crisis deepens as losses mount. *Australian Financial Review*, 20 January.

Oldfield, S. (2004b). Kraehe puts old NAB hands on notice. *Australian Financial Review*, 1–2 May.

Oldfield, S., & Boyd, T. (2004). Regulator punishes NAB. *Australian Financial Review*, March 25.

Pound, J. (1993). The rise of the political model of corporate governance and corporate control. *New York University Law Review, 68*, 5.

Rawls, J. (1971). *A theory of justice.* Cambridge: Harvard University Press.

Simon, H. A. (1976). *Administrative behaviour* (3rd ed.). New York: Free Press.

Sonnenfeld, J. A. (2002). What makes great boards great. *Harvard Business Review*, September.

Stewart, D. (1988). The decision premise: A basic tool for analysing the ethical content of
    organisational behaviour. *Public Administration Quarterly*, Fall.
The Oxford English Dictionary (1933). London: Oxford University Press.
Turnbull, S. (2000). Corporate governance: Theories, challenges and paradigms. *Working
    paper*. http://papers.ssrn.com/paper.taf?abstract_id = 220954
Westpac Banking Corporation Limited (2004). *Social Impact Report*, Sydney, at http://
    www.westpac.com.au/internet/publish.nsf/Content/WI + Social + Impact + Report

EFFECTIVE CORPORATE GOVERNANCE REFORM AND ORGANISATIONAL PLURALISM: REFRAMING CULTURE, LEADERSHIP AND FOLLOWERSHIP

David A. Holloway and Dianne van Rhyn

ABSTRACT

Spectacular corporate failures including One Tel, Ansett, HIH, Enron and Worldcom and the recent fiasco with National Australia Bank are evidence of a legitimacy crisis in current corporate governance practices. This paper analyses the organisational impact of recent "best practice" guidelines and the recommendations for reform. We conclude that substantive concerns still exist and it is likely that companies will utilise a "tick the box" approach emphasising form over substance governance changes. We argue for a two-fold approach to embed effective ongoing reform. The first involves cultural change(s) at the boardroom level to develop a "real" team approach. This would embrace the use of constructive conflict in the decision-making process and also incorporate elements of trust and openness. Constructive conflict, we argue, leads to real and effective boardroom behavioural changes.

Corporate Governance: Does Any Size Fit?
Advances in Public Interest Accounting, Volume 11, 303–328
Copyright © 2005 by Elsevier Ltd.
ISSN: 1041-7060/doi:10.1016/S1041-7060(05)11013-X

The second strand of reform proposes that such changes should be extended into the internal decision-making (enterprise governance) arena. Such a move towards organisational pluralism devolves decision-making and allows greater employee involvement in the "running" of organisations. It also entails a significant re-framing of organisational values, culture and followership. The leadership role becomes one of facilitation and support not the current dominant "command and control" mindset.

1. INTRODUCTION

Spectacular corporate accounting scandals and failures including Parmalat, One Tel, Ansett, HIH, Enron and Worldcom are evidence of a worldwide crisis in current corporate governance practices, and symptomatic of a deep malaise in corporate culture and values. This paper briefly reviews the recent developments calling for reform in Australia (and overseas) as typified by the 2003 Australian stock exchange (ASX) Corporate Governance Council findings and recommendations. It also explores recent ethical developments (Malpas, 2003; Ciulla, 1998) as they relate to management and leadership functions, including developments in the literature on participative decision-making. We argue for a more effective group approach to decision procedures in the boardroom and an enhanced collective involvement by internal stakeholders (employees) in the organisational decision-making process.

Corporate governance and what makes good governance has been contentious locally and internationally since the global stock market meltdown of the late-1980s (Goodjik, 2003; Sonnenfeld, 2002; Baker & Owsen, 2002; Vinten, 1998; Firstenberg & Malkiel, 1994; Leighton & Thain, 1990). High-level corporate failures during the late-1980s and early 1990s such as Bond Corporation and Quintex Corporation in Australia and Polly Peck and BCCI in the United Kingdom (U.K.) had initiated moves towards reform. Recommendations for change accelerated in the late-1990s and in early 2000s with further major corporate failures in the U.K. and Europe; high profile examples such as Enron, Worldcom and Tyco in the United States; Harris Scarfe, OneTel, Ansett and HIH in Australia; and most recently Parmalat in Italy.

This has resulted in a perceived legitimacy problem and what could be classified as a "...general crisis in corporate governance"[1] (Bargh, Scott, & Smith, 1996, p. 170). A series of reports (government and non-government) in several nations have resulted in supposed enhanced "best-practice" corporate governance guidelines and suggestions for changes culminating in legislation enacted in the United States – the Sarbannes-Oxley Act in July 2002 (The Economist, 2002), aimed at curtailing (misbehaving) senior managers of corporate entities.

The paper is primarily an analytical and normative one, constructed in two parts. It moves from the macro and a focus on corporate governance to the micro and the need for change to flow from boardrooms and cascade down through the workplace. The first part of the paper is a focus on the corporate governance reform "best practice" recommendations internationally as well as in Australia and the legislative impact of the Corporate Law Economic Reform Program (now the Audit Reform and Corporate Disclosure Act) – CLERP 9. The analysis shows that concerns still exist and it is possible that companies can continue to utilise a "tick the box" approach emphasising form over substance when implementing governance changes. We argue for a two-fold approach to embed effective ongoing reform. The first involves cultural change(s) at the boardroom level to develop a "real" team approach. This would embrace the use of constructive conflict in the decision-making process and also incorporate the twin elements of trust and openness. Constructive conflict, we argue, leads to real and effective boardroom behavioural changes.

The second part of the paper calls for the extension of the notion of robust, effective social systems and teamwork beyond the corporate boardroom walls. It calls for organisational pluralism in that lower-level (as well as higher-level) organisational actors have direct involvement in the decision-making process. We argue for more active involvement by employees through participative decision-making and enhanced levels of direct staff ownership in the organisation. This entails "quantum" changes in organisational values, culture, followership and the prevailing senior executive top-down approach to decision-making. The leadership role, we advocate, then becomes one of facilitation and support, not the current dominant "command and control" mindset.

2. CORPORATE GOVERNANCE REFORM PRESSURES

In the international arena, there has been a series of inquiries and reports since the beginning of the 1990s with the aim of identifying necessary changes to corporate governance practices. These are covered in greater detail in Holloway and van Rhyn (2003) and hence we will not focus on these elements here. Suffice to say that virtually all had the aim of constructing guidelines and principles for the composition, roles and disclosure concepts that "should" be used by the board of directors in companies around the world. Very few of these have been subsequently enshrined within a legislative framework other than the introduction of the Sarbannes-Oxley Act in America. The Act applies to all 14,000 firms listed in the U.S.A. including those based overseas and requires CEOs and CFOs to certify in writing that the company's annual financial reports are true and fair (The Economist, 2002, p. 49).

The main result of these developments is a general international convergence on "best-practice" recommendations particularly with respect to the expanding role of chairs and independent directors. In the next section, we will clarify how these outcomes have influenced the regulators and in particular the Australian federal government.

3. AUSTRALIAN CONTEXT

Australia is not isolated from international events, a governance crisis has also occurred here. There have been recent major, and very public, corporate failures ranging from the retail sector (Harris Scarfe), telecommunications (OneTel), aviation (Ansett) and insurance (HIH). This is in addition to well known past failures such as Alan Bond's Bond Corporation and Christopher Skase's Qintex Corporation. Although not suggesting similar demise is facing National Australia Bank, the behaviour of the board in March 2004 is indicative of the lack of governance. These outcomes did not generate the same response as occurred in the U.K. and other international jurisdictions. The ASX has recently produced its own set of listing requirements in this area. This has been followed by the Federal Government's implementation of the Corporation Law CLERP 9 reform proposals on 1 July 2004.

3.1. ASX Corporate Governance Council (CGC)

The ASX has taken a proactive stance and formed a plenary council of a number of stakeholder groups (21 in all) including business, the accounting profession, investor groups, company secretaries, company directors and the Law Council. The result is a 75-page document detailing ten principles and comprehensive guidelines about operationalising "best practice" corporate governance. This is given effective regulatory weight in the same way as the U.K. "comply or explain" approach. ASX listing rule 4.10 requires companies from 1 January 2003 to disclose in their annual reports the extent to which they have followed or elected not to follow these best practice recommendations (2003, p. 5).

None of the principles effectively addresses the concerns Justice Owen (HIH Royal Commission) raised of a "paper exercise" and the ability of senior management to merely look like they are doing "the right thing" (Owen, 2003, vol 1, p. 133). Most if not all of the CGC guidelines can be met without necessarily changing the level of business risk or the degree of corporate misbehaviour or even outright failure.

The ten principles are: lay solid foundations for management and oversight; structure the board to add value; promote ethical and responsible decision-making; safeguard integrity in financial reporting; make timely and balanced disclosure; respect the rights of shareholders; recognise and manage risk; encourage enhanced performance; remunerate fairly and responsibly; and recognise the legitimate interests of stakeholders.

In practice, perceived problems with the principles are already emerging. A 2004 study by KPMG has identified that companies in Australia are struggling to implement the two key principles 4 and 7 (Walters & Andrews, 2004). Principle 4 is similar to the requirements of the Sarbannes-Oxley Act in that CEOs and CFOs are required to submit in writing to their boards that the corporation's financial reports present a true and fair view of the operational results and financial conditions. Only 20 of 68 companies in the study disclosed a CEO and CFO sign-off or stated that they had complied with this principle. The KPMG report stated "there is a debate about whether this principle adds value, and concern that CEOs and CFOs need clarification" (p. 71). The analysis revealed that there was even less compliance with principle 7, which covers statements about the integrity of risk management and internal control, and requires confirmation if risk management and control compliance are both efficient and effective.

3.2. CLERP 9 Requirements

Australian federal government intervention has resulted in the Corporate Law Economic Reform Program (Audit Reform & Corporate Disclosure, CLERP 9) Bill being released for comment on 8 October 2003. It has subsequently passed through Parliament (late in June 2004) and has a commencement date of 1 July 2004. The primary objectives of the Act involve promoting transparency, accountability and enhancing shareholders rights. According to the Department of Treasury it will augment auditor independence, achieve better disclosure outcomes and improve enforcement arrangements for corporate misbehaviour (Treasury, 2003). CLERP 9 does, however, propose to extend the reform processes beyond the narrow boundaries of the corporate governance recommendations and principles produced internationally and in this country.

The business media and popular press attention and reaction have focussed primarily on the proposed provisions, which enhance directors' responsibilities and the additional shareholders rights in relation to executive remuneration packages. In future shareholders will be able to comment on, and take a non-binding vote on the mandated remuneration disclosures for executives and directors (Dawes, 2003). To date, comments at industry forums and from the accounting profession have been generally positive about the contents of the Bill with concerns focussing primarily on the issue of continuous disclosure and associated penalties for companies that do not comply with this requirement (Brown, 2003; Anonymous, 2002).

One of the most important provisions, we would argue, relates to the need for the annual directors' report to include a more detailed operating and financial review of the company's performance. This is to be sufficiently detailed to enable shareholders and others to make an informed assessment of the company's current position and future strategies. In addition, the legislative requirement for CEOs and CFOs to make a formal written declaration to the board of directors that the annual financial statements are "true and fair" takes Australia down the U.S.A. path of the Sarbannes-Oxley Act. It would certainly have a sobering and salutary effect on company senior executives if, in future corporate failures, some senior management personnel are taken away in manacles in the back of police vehicles if this provision is breached.

It is highly unlikely, however, that any current or proposed corporate governance models or systems could effectively prevent senior management misbehaviour or even corporate failure. This raises a serious conundrum. Does a "best practice" corporate governance model result in improved corporate performance and prevent poor or fraudulent management decision-making?

4. BEST PRACTICE CORPORATE GOVERNANCE (ONE SIZE FITS ALL?)

We can distill the world's best practice model from the above developments and pronouncements made across the different nation state jurisdictions.

Such a construct would supposedly deliver better governance and one would expect better corporate performance.

The elements that would be the part of such a best practice model would start with the most critical role identified by all the reports and recommendations. That role is the chair of the board, which would be a non-executive position with enhanced responsibilities in relation to decision-making, management oversight and information gathering: this would also have expanded legal responsibility beyond that expected of other independent directors. The structure of the rest of the board would comprise of executive and independent directors with the majority of the membership being non-executive. One of these would also be a designated senior independent director separate from the chair. The independent members would also chair and fill exclusively the membership of the key sub-committees (audit, remuneration and nomination). Again, this would be expected to enhance the management oversight role as well as better comply with the fiduciary duty expected of independent directors.

The other essentials would include a publicly available code that would explicate the governance/ethics protocols to be used by the board; a relatively small sized board (the average is 11 directors); professionally designed and conducted induction training for new directors as well as ongoing professional development; independent directors to have at least 2–3 years term to retain appropriate corporate knowledge; a tighter definition of independence for prospective directors to avoid conflicts of interest; and, an appropriate range of board directors ages and skill sets including financial, industry knowledge, strategic skills and representation of immediate community and general society interests.

It is highly questionable as to whether this "one size fits all" approach will be effective. Smaller sized public companies may well not benefit from such tight prescriptive requirements that will clearly add to their governance structures and costs (Brayshaw, 2003). Indeed, Australia may not have sufficient number of suitably qualified potential independent board members. One cannot legislate and require governance reforms that in the end are dependent on "real" behavioural changes at the board level and need more than a form over substance approach. In addition, it is still problematic whether good governance structures necessarily correlate with good corporate performance.

4.1. Does Good Governance = Good Corporate Performance?

An increasing body of research is concluding that there is no or only weak connections between corporate performance and best practice elements of good corporate governance. This is particularly so in relation to elements such as size of boards, percentage of independent directors and duality of chair and CEO. Edwards (2003a) argues that "...there is a U-shaped relationship between size and performance: the addition of members adds to the skill mix...it is not numbers per se which are important but the effective integration of the skills and knowledge base of the board with the company's needs at any given time" (p. 29).

Empirical tests of board attributes have been carried out in a number of countries.[2] In the U.K., a study of the impact of companies applying the Cadbury committee recommendations analysed 115 companies between 1992 and 1995 and found little evidence of corporate improvement (Laing & Weir, 1999). In the U.S.A., a study by Bhagat and Black (2002) concluded that there was no correlation between long term firm performance and board composition specifically in relation to the board majority being independent directors (p. 232). A survey of Canadian companies, Allaire and Firsirotu (2003), found that the 25 Canadian companies with the best governance scores performed more poorly than the 25 companies with the worst governance scores. Sonnenfeld (2002) points out that both good and bad companies have adopted the "right" corporate governance practices and many good companies have not. Following good-governance practices does not automatically produce good boards or good corporate performance.

A comparative study of the U.S.A., U.K. and the Netherlands listed companies also found weak correlations but did point out that there is an over-focus in the extant literature on measuring the financial dimensions of company performance (Maassen, 1999). Finally, in Australia Kiel (2002) studied the top 348 companies listed on the ASX and found few connections between board size, and composition and company performance. Rather, he identified human capital factors especially board members' mix of skills and knowledge as being important for firm success.

This growing body of evidence suggests that although sound board structures and process are important, they are not by or of themselves sufficient to ensure enhanced corporate performance. This is complicated further when one considers the organisational and individual "cultural" mindset in relation to decision-making that is prevalent amongst the majority of senior executive echelons in both the private and public sectors.

4.2. Managerial Decision-Making Prerogative: Likelihood of Real Reform?

The concept of managerial prerogative has developed over time such that senior managers of organisations believe they are solely responsible for all the key decisions merely because of the organisational position they occupy. This is closely connected to the additional desire of senior management to maintain *control* over strategies, decisions, the future, customers, employees, markets etc. (Mintzberg, 1994, pp. 201–202). This enables senior management to feel more comfortable and in charge of what is "going on" in the organisation.

The development of this notion can be traced back to the evolution of professional management. Ownership of the firm's equity was separated from control of the firm's assets by the senior executive through their exercise of the management function. Berle & Means in their seminal treatise (1932) clearly explicated this classical view of the public corporation by tracing historical events in the business domain from the Civil War to the Great Depression in America. Thus management, specifically the chairman of the board, the CEO and other senior executive effectively assumed control over corporate affairs. In practice, it enabled senior executives to have the ultimate say in selecting board members and in defining the role and responsibilities of the board of directors (Leighton & Thain, 1990).

Jensen and Meckling (1976) explained this view through their (positivist) construct of agency theory which asserts that managers of public corporations, although agents of the shareholders, will act in their own self-interest possibly to the detriment of the shareholders. Agency theory therefore focuses on constructing contractual mechanisms to limit and/or control this self-interested managerial behaviour. Central to this concept is that board directors who carry out this monitoring function should be independent of management who are in essence being monitored by them (Cohen, Krishnamoorthy & Wright, 2000).

More recent arguments by Jensen have focussed on the failure of internal control (via the board) over management (Jensen, 1993) and management's willingness to sacrifice profitability for growth and size (Jensen, 1988), which are additional exemplars of this notion of self-interested behaviour to the detriment of the long-term interest of the firm. This could be explained by the existence of management compensation packages that incorporate performance bonuses and share options that are linked to profit and size criteria as reflected in share prices. Jensen, despite this condemnatory analysis, does not support external limits being placed on the prerogatives of top management because in his view that would damage economic efficiency, promote greater degree of micro management by the State and interfere with the operation of free capital markets (Jensen, 2001).

Another perspective, on corporate governance focuses on managerial hegemony where senior management acts as if corporate governance is an unavoidable annoyance with board structures, processes and mechanisms that are mainly ineffectual and primarily symbolic (Wolfson, 1984; Galbraith, 1967). The board of directors is in reality dependent on management for information and is therefore limited to ratifying management decisions and satisfying regulatory requirements for the existence of such governing bodies. The board in effect becomes a passive body filled with friends and colleagues of the senior executive that helps (only?) to initially set and then increase senior management's monetary compensation (Core, Holthausen, & Larcker, 1999).

A different viewpoint, emerging from the strategic management literature, is the resource dependency perspective which is a more benign view of the function of the board of directors. As distinct from the agency theory approach, the board of directors works closely with management in a collaborative approach at the broader strategic direction level (Williamson, 1999; Boyd, 1990). The directors, particularly the independent members, bring with them expertise and skills plus the additional bonus of providing contact and access to external resources that would benefit the firm in the medium to longer term.

It is important to note that none of these approaches involves stakeholder groups in the process of corporate governance. They focus exclusively on the relationship (positive or negative) between the senior management and the board of directors. The theories espoused do not even include the shareholders as a primary stakeholder group in the governance arena. This is a serious deficiency. In the later section, this paper argues strongly for the involvement of a wider set of stakeholders in the governing process.

5. EFFECTIVE "REAL" REFORM – BOARD CULTURE, BEHAVIOUR AND PERFORMANCE

It should be acknowledged here that there is, however, a less individualistic and managerial approach to decision-making in companies in parts of Europe. Instead, there is a greater willingness to use a more participatory approach and allow enhanced stakeholder involvement, particularly employees and shareholders, in both the governance and internal management of companies.[3] The discussion that follows relates to Anglo-American organisations, but is not necessarily representative of the European cultures.

Real ongoing reform requires substantive changes to actual behaviour in the boardroom. Sonnenfeld (2002) constructs a particularly positive response to the conundrum of managerial prerogative and the adoption of a "form over substance" approach to governance of organisations. He argues that it is not the rules and regulations of the governing process that count but the way people work together that is vital. Therefore, what distinguishes exemplary (effective) boards is that they are robust, effective social systems (2002, p. 108). In other words they exhibit a healthy boardroom culture. We argue this is the most critical of the additional elements needed to ensure that good governance practice is translated into "better" organisational performance. Justice Owen supports wholeheartedly such a response. Jack Welch, a former CEO of General Electric, also advocates this approach as opposed to a tighter set of governance rules "The characteristics you want are integrity, common sense and willingness to speak out" (Gottliebsen, 2003, p. 21). Edwards (2003b, p. 13) adds in addition other less tangible factors such as "...behavioural integrity, skills, relationships, leadership...".

Vital elements in constructing such a culture would be to create a climate of trust and candour with full access to relevant information; effective governing body teamwork which avoids groupthink and social loafing;[4] encouragement of open dissent and debate; members/directors changing roles regularly; individual accountability of members/directors for their roles to the rest of the board; and, regular reflection and evaluation of the board's own performance (Sonnenfeld, 2002, pp. 109–112). In particular, the need for active debate and open questioning of management is seen as central to this "healthy" process.

The key to this "healthy culture" is open debate and discussion. This means that directors must have the capacity and willingness to challenge each other's assumptions and beliefs and rely on integrity, personal fortitude and external trust to allow for opposing viewpoints and challenging questions. Sonnenfeld's analysis shows that "...the highest performing companies have extremely contentious boards that regard dissent as an obligation and that treat no subject as undiscussable" (2002, p. 111). In this way they avoid the problem of groupthink where conformity and consensus are seen as virtues. We argue that this would be better interpreted as "constructive" conflict, rather than just mere dissent, where the aim is to deliver more robust and effective decision outcomes. One needs to build, at the corporate governance level, robust and effective teams. In this scenario, the roles of the chair and the independent directors are central to guaranteeing that this robustness occurs by ensuring that both individual and collective voices/ opinions are heard and valued.

Given that there is little correlation between good corporate governance and good corporate performance, there is need for "real" reform to be extended in such a way as to enhance organisational performance. This can be achieved, we argue, by continuing the cultural reform process within other parts of the organisation and thereby extending the notion of robust, effective social systems and teamwork beyond the boardroom walls. Extension into the general workplace would occur through the use of effective workforce empowerment and participative decision-making processes which then cascades through all layers of an organisation. The next section of this paper focuses on the key elements required to deliver such a level of "quantum" organisational change.

6. EFFECTIVE "REAL" REFORM – INTERNAL GOVERNANCE AND ORGANISATIONAL PLURALISM

The extant management and accounting literature with its prescriptive edge limiting organisational power, authority and decision-making to the hands of senior management requires alteration and a shift in focus if effective participative governance is to be adopted. The new approach is to involve employees from the commencement of the organisational decision-making cycle, by permitting and encouraging active involvement, full participation in and psychological ownership of the process. The result is a form of organisational pluralism in which internal organisational actors at all levels (high and low) across the firm are involved intimately in the decision-making process(es). This would be further enhanced if employees also have an ownership stake in the business. This acts as an effective counterfoil to the shortcomings of management "...failing to communicate a vision, planning problems, not matching vision with processes, not being committed..., failing to lead by example, demonstrating inconsistencies of attitudes..." (Waldersee & Griffiths, 1997, p. 10).

6.1. Participative Decision-making

A change in the internal management approach towards a more participative and facilitative style would be a positive step. Within the European context, Goodjik (2003) posits a stakeholder model of collaboration with management that extends throughout the organisation and is not limited to governance and strategic planning issues. He argues, "The stakeholder model assumes a partnership between management and stakeholders, a partnership seen as a real dynamic and changing process of dialogue" (2003, p. 225). The main stakeholder group in this instance, however, would be limited to employees. This would enhance internal governance procedures and act as a precondition for good corporate governance allowing for more effective value creation for the firm.

Holloway (2004) argues for an approach in which employees/staff can be involved closely in the strategic planning process and the operational decision-making areas in both the public sector and the private sector. In his study of University strategic planning he calls for a move that would ensure that "…decision-making powers are cascaded down through the layers of the organisation" (2004, p. 13). The result is an inclusive, not exclusive, decision-making methodology that taps into the adaptability and self-organising capability of the workforce and helps to unleash the full potential of the organisation.

Does this proposed participative approach work? What are the benefits? There are two strands of literature that argue positively in favour of just such an intellectual turn. The first is grounded in industrial relations research. The notion is that employees should have control of the organisation as a whole and to discover new, and presumably better, ways for organising work – a form of workplace evolution. The argument is that the idea of participation is central to notions of democracy, which apply to most social institutions, including politics, community, family and school. It therefore should naturally apply to the workplace (Ciulla, 1998, p. 74). Benefits for organisations identified in this literature are presumed to be self-evident.

The second strand is grounded in organisational development literature in the management discipline. Most of that literature has focussed on quality of worklife, job enrichment and employee motivation – primarily normative concepts. A seminal paper by Black and Gregersen (1997) analysed and brought together the major findings in the academic and practitioner literature. They took a multidimensional view that examined the degree of integration of participation and decision-making processes and their relationship with job satisfaction and performance. The results clearly identified that the greater the degree (or depth) of employee involvement in five key decision-making processes – identifying problems, generating alternatives, selecting solutions, planning implementation, and, evaluating results – the greater the level of job satisfaction and job performance. It should be noted that this refers to individual not collective outcomes for worker participation. This and other similar studies (Ashmos, Duchon, McDaniel & Huonker, 2002; Witt, Andrews & Kacmar, 2000; Tremblay, Sire & Dalkin,

2000; Latham, Winters & Locke, 1994; Pearson, 1991) have empirically validated the organisational benefits of participation in decision-making.

The elements for corporate success are: the extensive use of work teams from senior executive teams downwards; emphasis on flexibility, adaptability and learning; strong support for innovation and creativity; performance rewards being team-based; information shared openly; managers acting in a facilitative role and the atmosphere being the equivalent of working in a small business (Garratt, 2000, pp. 133–138). The end result is a more collectively oriented approach to decision-making and performance evaluation that becomes organisationally pervasive.

One element that needs cognizance is the importance of having more than psychological ownership of corporate processes and outcomes. The latest studies on the relationship between actual ownership and corporate performance bring into question the modern notion of the need for externally recruited professional management teams that would supposedly deliver "better" corporate performance. The notion of ownership involvement by not only families but also other senior executives and the members of the organisational workforce (employees) would certainly be one way to ensure effective involvement and commitment to ensuring good corporate performance.

6.2. Ownership and Corporate Performance

A recent study by Anderson and Reeb (2003a) of the American S&P 500 index[5] found that one third of the top 500 non-financial companies had substantial family ownership averaging around 18% of equity in the business. Their initial hypothesis (consistent with existing literature) was that minority shareholders would be adversely affected by family ownership. Their main finding, however, was that these firms with a substantial family ownership component had a better corporate performance than non-family firms. In addition, when family members take on the CEO role, firm performance is better than with outside CEOs. McCrann (2003, p. 40) explains this under the general rubric of having "...skin in the game". In other words, having ownership exposure to the results of the business acts as a powerful incentive to ensure long-term commitment to success.

Earlier studies had similar results. Morck, Shiefer and Vishny (1988) studied the relationship between management (founding family) ownership and the market valuation of 371 publicly listed firm and concluded that this was positive and increased as ownership levels rose. Controlling for size, industry and managerial ownership, studies have revealed that firms controlled by founding families have greater value, operate more efficiently and have lower levels of debts. They have also shown that a subset of descendent-controlled companies performs even more efficiently than the usual type of founder-controlled firms (Anderson & Reeb, 2003b; McConaughy, Matthews & Fialko, 2001; McConaughy, Walker, Hendersen & Chandra, 1998).

These findings prompted BusinessWeek magazine to carry out an additional study in which they quantified these findings. They tracked family companies over the past decade and identified average shareholder return of 15.6% for family companies when compared to 11.2% for non-family companies in the S&P 500. In addition, the analysis showed that return on assets averaged 5.4 versus 4.1%; annual revenue growth was 23.8 versus 10.8%; and, profit growth of 21.1 versus 12.6% (Business Week, 2003, p. 1). The speculative explanations offered for this difference ranged across a number of factors including greater passion for the enterprise; being born to lead (a strange notion); quicker decision-making; significantly enhanced staff loyalty; investing (and reinvesting) in longer term growth strategies; and, having no absentee landlords at the board governance level. These explanatory assertions are yet to be tested empirically.

So how can these benefits be harnessed and the effects transferred to other corporate entities? We argue that these positive results could be transferred if both large and small organisations allowed and even encouraged increased ownership by employees in the business. The notion has intuitive appeal. This would be another version of having "skin in the game" and would certainly act as an incentive for increased participation in the decision-making process. Despite some difficulties and failures in 100% owned employee ventures, there are many other stories of success with employee ownership and involvement in what could be classified as examples of "small c" capitalism (Macleod, 2003; Taylor, 2000; Goyder, 1979). When combined with the literature on participative decision-making and self-managed, devolved organisations this makes a compelling "story" for contemporary organisations to explore (Hope & Fraser, 2003; Garratt, 2000; Pasternack & Viscio, 1998; Purser & Cabana, 1998).

6.3. Reframing Organisational Culture and Values

The key question is how to achieve a significant shift in organisational culture, when the intransigent nature of managerial prerogative and the current imbalance in power relations, management self-interest and ego is readily apparent. First there would need to be a major change in the pre-vailing senior executive mindset. Such a depth of change requires key senior personnel, in addition to the CEO, acting as "champions" and advocates of a "quantum" change process.

The organisational values need to be re-framed. The key drivers of pure economic-rationalistic notions of corporate performance such as enhancing shareholder value and high returns on equity need to be changed and wid-ened. These need to be the outcomes of sound organisational performance not the primary drivers in the first instance. This calls for a shared and participative process to determine as an organisational community what these values and personal virtues "ought" to be and to what extent they should be legitimately informing and influencing the operations and finan-cial outcomes of the business.

Sonnenfeld (2002, p. 110) argued that the construction of a climate of trust and candour along with the encouragement of open dissent were vital to the building of an effective and robust social system at the board level. We would extend this notion further and argue that trust should not exist solely in the boardroom and is, in fact, absolutely critical to effective functioning throughout the organisation and "...forms a kind of social glue, keeping humans together..." (Gustaffson, 2003, p. 1). When something goes wrong at the individual level, then one needs to examine more closely the moral structure of the organisation as a whole. The need then in collectively re-framing organisational values is to put trust at the centre and to have all other values and virtues espoused as flowing from that core. The arguments for the acceptance of other virtues such as honesty, integrity, authenticity, sincerity and loyalty would then be as subsets of trust. Gustaffson puts this as

> Trust then, forms the whole within which social credibility can function. The general level of trust in a society or culture, thus, forms the precious chalice containing all goodness, all virtue. This means that not only virtues like loyalty, friendship and trust-worthiness depend on trust; all virtues do...
>
> In this way, virtues can be seen as semi-stable personality traits – as "character". They are, however, not exclusively individual personality traits. To the same degree they are networks of expectations, of trust. For a virtue to exist, there must be a possibility of somebody trusting in it, a willingness or predisposition within the social network (2003, p. 3).

The objective of this reframing is to develop and accept the concept of shared governance (Lu, 2003). The resulting revised organisational rela-tionships can lead to a justifiable claim that they are the features of an ethically expert organisation (Malpas, 2003). Further, it takes the institution down the path of what Hegelsen (1995) calls the "web of inclusion". The web structure is a pattern of relationships and connections instead of iso-lations and divisions characterised by permeability within and beyond the organisation. This permeability allows attention to be focussed on "...what needs to be done rather than who has the authority to do it" (p. 21). It makes the organisation more egalitarian and participatory because a per-son's position and value is defined according to what s/he contributes not merely the role or authority s/he possesses.

A hint of caution is necessary at this juncture. In the Miller, Greenwood and Hinings seminal paper on change management, they identify that or-ganisational change of the required magnitude should best be described as "quantum". There are significant barriers to such change not least being that such "...upheavals threaten the rewards, reputations, and power of elite executives" (1997, p. 73). This in itself becomes problematic.[6]

6.4. Contemporary Leadership

The role of leaders in these newly reframed organisations – having evolved from the changes that emanate from such a move into a more collectively oriented decision-making approach – will also change significantly. The hero-style chief executive who makes all the big/key decisions that defines an organisation and sets the future course should now be an endangered spe-cies. The academic, practitioner and business education literature are con-verging in that the notion of complex decision scenarios and environmental complexity and uncertainty necessitate team approaches and a redefinition of the role of leaders to one of coaching, support, facilitation and coun-selling (James, 2004; Lazlo & Nash, 2003; Raelin, 2003; Switzer, 2003; Bisoux, 2002; Parry, 2002; Bolman & Deal, 2001; Wheatley, 1999; Thomas & Willcoxson, 1998; Ciulla, 1998).

There is also a growing wave of literature that surfaces concepts of ethical and even moral principles and forefronts for organisations, both private and public, the idea of principle-based forms of practice and decision-making (Malpas, 2003; Gustaffson, 2003; Lu, 2003; Marshall, 2000; Dalla Costa, 1998; Badaracco & Ellsworth, 1989 – to name but a few). Malpas argues that in the organisational context, ethics is integral and "...essentially con-cerns the establishment and maintenance of relationships and as such is fundamental to organisational success" (2003, p. 1). These notions are being extended into the area of leadership despite a prevailing notion that a lead-er's sole responsibility is to find effective, and pragmatic solutions to or-ganisational problems in which ethics plays no part (Ciulla, 1998). Not only is the role of leadership being reassessed in light of ethical and moral insights but also the vital role of followers. The role of business educators in this process is vital and they are certainly aware of and actively promoting a "sea change" in moving from an industrial to a post-industrial leadership paradigm (Bisoux, 2002).

The "turn" is reflected in (some) Australian organisations as well as overseas. Michael Chaney, the retiring CEO of Wesfarmers, is an exemplar of this process of leading more by example than by authority. He used Trevor Eastwood, the previous CEO, as his mentor in developing an approach in which he states, "...a team of good people can contribute a lot more than an individual" (Switzer, 2003, p. 43). He realised that it is more effective to use a collaborative approach embedded in an informal, collegial office atmosphere and minimising the negative aspects of a traditional leader's "...huge ego" (2003, p. 43).[7]

Again, a note of caution needs to be cast on this wave of reform fervour. Despite the growing movement to a more enlightened approach to the management and leadership of contemporary organisations, it is still evident that by far the majority of organisations do not subscribe to this reframed worldview. It raises the puzzling conundrum as to why there are still so many traditionally focussed organisations in both private and public sectors. The speculative answers provided in Boyett and Boyett range from resistance to an organisational cultural change from an emphasis on individuality to one of a collective nature; the team approach being perceived as too time consuming, risky and inefficient; managers feeling threatened by a loss of control, status and responsibility; and, even that the transition from a traditional to high performing organisation is simply too hard to accomplish and sustain (1998, pp. 140–141).

More important, we argue, is the need to ensure that the key negative elements are countered effectively. These are the current imbalance in organisational power relations; executive self-interest often embedded in executive compensation and performance bonus schemes; and, (large) managerial egos. In addition, the Miller et al., findings about any proposed "quantum" organisational change that such "...upheavals threaten the rewards, reputations, and power of elite executives" (1997, p. 73) needs to be taken into account. It is critical, therefore, that there are champions for just such a change throughout an organisation from the top to the bottom.

Leadership in this scenario will need to be exercised at all organisational levels to ensure a successful transition to what Ciulla (1998) argues is "true" empowerment in a process of moral commitment to sincerity and authenticity.[8] Wheatley views this as a natural move to autonomy and self-determination but uses a scientific underpinning of chaos theory and quantum mechanics to explain the need to do so (1998). We would argue in favour of this move from a pragmatic as well as an intellectual base. Organisations that have taken this path have out-performed their competitors.[9]

Strategically agile and the newly successful organisations will be essentially self-organizing systems that progress and succeed through initiative and self-control with little or no need for intervention from senior management. The role of the leader(s) becomes reconceptualized as one of facilitation and championing the new decision-making paradigm (Hope & Fraser, 2003; Garratt, 2000; Pasternack & Viscio, 1998; Purser & Cabana, 1998).

Effective leadership is still vital to current and future organisations but is now redefined from the more traditional "command and control" approach to a "coach, consult and guide" role that maximises the human potential of the whole workforce not just an elite coterie at the top of an organisational pyramid.

6.5. Reconceptualised Followership

The current "reading" and construction of the notion of followership also needs to be significantly reframed in this revised organisational context. Followers cannot remain passive and powerless receptors of leadership inspired wisdom. The role of followers is no longer to be negatively cast as "passive sheep" following unquestioningly a strong leader who makes all the key decisions. Instead, their role changes to one that is an "active" followership at times interchanging the leadership – followership role and mantle of responsibility and interactivity.

In organisations even leaders play followership roles depending on their position within the organisational hierarchy. Organisations need, however, at whatever level organisational "actors" can be construed to be followers, those who can be labelled as either dynamic, courageous or our preferred term "active". The idea is to avoid an organisational outcome aptly described in the de Jouvenal quote "...a nation of sheep begets a government of wolves" (Kelley, 1992, p. 34).

There is a small but growing body of literature that advocates a recasting of the traditional role of followers (Chaleff, 2003; Raelin, 2003; Dixon & Westbrook, 2003; Kelley, 1992; Hollander, 1992; Vanderslice, 1988; Litzinger & Schaefer, 1982). The call is to reconstruct the "traditional" notion of "follower", which tends to be a negative stereotype: typical followers supposedly display a passive and uncritical approach to work as well as lacking initiative and a sense of responsibility for outcomes. Such followers merely perform assigned tasks given to them, and then stop awaiting for the next task. Active followers on the other hand are able to think for themselves, either individually or collectively as required; they exhibit characteristics more often associated with risk takers (and leaders); they are usually self-starters and problem solvers; they are rated highly by their peers and their nominal organisational superiors. We argue that these types of "actors" have discarded the pejorative "follower" label; instead they are equal and active participants in the decision-making process(es).

The result of such a transformation naturally impacts on the senior management role in addition to the proposed changes to the leadership role espoused in this paper. Senior managers, that are retained in this reframed organisation structure, take on more of a "mentor" or "boundary rider" role. They would act normally only as advisors or may be called upon when there is a decision-making impasse or inter-personal disputes that remain unresolved. The resulting organisational structure has few(er) hierarchical layers and should be applicable across all organisational sizes and types. A large organisation is in the end only an aggregation of smaller strategic business units. The end result of this series of advocated changes (cultural and behavioural) is to not only enhance corporate governance but also to maximise the opportunity to construct better corporate performance outcomes.

7. CONCLUSION

The critical analysis in this paper shows that concerns about the shape and future of corporate governance changes still exist and it is highly likely that companies will utilise a "tick the box" approach emphasising form over substance changes. In this scenario, it will take further major corporate scandals and failures of the magnitude of the recent Paramalat affair and the recent NAB fiasco for the realisation that reform has been no more real than the fable of the emperor's new clothes. Real reform requires cultural and behavioural changes at the boardroom level, thereby creating effective social systems that utilise an effective teamwork approach to decision-making.

It is clear that one cannot mandate corporate governance changes either by way of merely recommending and gently prompting or by legislating for "good" governance in corporate entities. This move is not achievable by fiat. We instead argue that the move should be from the micro to the macro. Change of behaviour and approaches to decision-making internally within organisations will filter up to the macro system-wide boardroom level and result in enhanced governance practices. Anything else (or less) will invite what will inevitably be mere lip service paid by organisations, both private and public, to the reform process.

The construction, however, of what this paper has proposed as robust and effective social systems throughout an organisation will yield positive outcomes for those institutions with the fortitude to take such divergent paths from the mainstream. This will result in real and sustained internal as well as corporate governance reform(s) emanating from the significant cultural, leadership and followership reframing process. Active participation by all – who wish to be involved – means that the changes will percolate through the organisation. These organisations realise that they are filled with living, breathing, and feeling human beings who need more than a pay cheque, more than a performance review and more than a promotion to be effective and committed enterprise-based citizens. The organisational future waits to be written.

NOTES

1. Corporate governance has no universally accepted definition but is generally accepted as the practice of companies having boards of directors whose role is primarily one of setting broad policy and strategic direction plus oversight and control over senior management and corporate financial performance (ASX, 2003).

2. Attributes include composition – size of boards and mix of directors; characteristics – directors backgrounds and skill sets; structure – board organisation and information flow; and, process – decision-making activities and the conduct of board meetings (Korac-Kakabadse, Kakabadse & Kouzmin, 2001, p. 25).

3. This is best illustrated by the practice in the Netherlands and Germany of having two company boards. The Supervisory Board is composed entirely of independent directors representing shareholders and employees. This board (termed the Raad van Commissaren in the Netherlands) monitors and supervises the corporate strategy, while the board of directors constructs the corporate strategy and carries the ultimate and fiduciary responsibility for the results of the company (Goodjik, 2003, p. 232).

4. Social loafing is where group members do not participate effectively in groups and rely on other members to do the work and groupthink refers to group mediocrity in decision-making by chasing consensus (falsely) at all costs (Baker, Barrett & Roberts, 2002, pp. 328–331).

5. This index consists of the 500 largest corporations (by market capitalization) on the U.S. stock exchange.

6. The literature on change management is replete with examples of unsuccessful change management projects particularly when internal resistance is encountered (Kotter & Cohen, 2002; Graetz, Rimmer, Lawrence & Smith, 2002; Hay & Hartel,

2000; Maurer, 1996). The normative practitioner literature on the other hand proclaims that "...change is a very normal, *universally* (italics in the original) necessary, and urgent aspect of organisational life" (Miller et al., 1997, p. 72). Its necessity is supposedly self-evident. Thus, to achieve successfully the magnitude of change being advocated here will require the overall goodwill, commitment, acceptance and active involvement of all participants in the change process from the top to the bottom of the organisation.

7. A number of selected quotes captures this shift in the contemporary role of leadership:

> Leadership today is about values, working with people, building consensus. It's about thinking about a greater good than yourself. It's not about the guy on the white horse anymore (Ciulla – Chair of Leadership and Ethics – Jepson School at the University of Richmond, cited in Bisoux, 2002, p. 29).

> Leadership, among other things, is about empowering people to manage themselves. And it's about using one's personal power to win the hearts and minds of people to achieve a common purpose (Gill – Director, MBA in Leadership Studies – University of Strathclyde, cited in Bisoux, 2002, p. 29).

> There has been a huge shift in our thinking. Our tendency has always been to look to an individual for leadership. But now there's an understanding that leadership is not always correlated with positions of power and authority. It is something that can come from anywhere in an organization or community. It can manifest itself in many different ways (Alexander – President, Center for Creative Leadership, Greensboro, cited in Bisoux, 2002, p. 28)

8. Ciulla is concerned that in many cases empowerment programs are not genuine. "Authentic empowerment requires leaders to know what they are giving away and how they are changing the relationship between themselves and their followers... Power is a defining aspect of this relationship... Bogus empowerment attempts to give employees or followers power without changing the moral relationship between leaders and followers...Without honesty, sincerity and authenticity, empowerment is bogus..." (1998, p. 84).

9. Examples of successes include: AT&T Credit Corporation, Federal Express, Weyerhauser, Motorola, Kodak, Hewlett-Packard, GE Appliances, Eli Lilly and Knight-Ridder (Boyett & Boyett, 2000, 138–139). Similar experiences exist in other parts of the world particularly in Europe and would include Svenska Handelsbanken, Borealis, Asea Brown Boveri, Syncrude Chemicals and Sequoia Oil paradigm (Hope & Fraser, 2003; Garratt, 2000; Pasternack & Viscio, 1998; Purser & Cabana, 1998).

REFERENCES

Allaire, Y., & Firsirotu, M. (2003). Corporate governance and performance: The elusive link. *Journal of Armand Bombardier Chair Working Paper*. Montreal: University of Quebec.

Anonymous. (2002). Changing the future of corporate reporting. *Australian CPA, 7*(10), 12–14.

Anderson, R. C., & Reeb, D. M. (2003a). Founding-family ownership and firm performance: evidence from the S&P 500. *The Journal of Finance, 58*(3), 1301–1328.

Anderson, R. C., & Reeb, D. M. (2003b). Founding-family ownership, corporate diversification and firm leverage. *Journal of Law and Economics, 46*(2), 653–684.

Ashmos, D. P., Duchon, D., McDaniel, R. R., Jr., & Huonker, J. W. (2002). What a mess! participation as a simple managerial rule to "complexify" organizations: Employee participation in decision-making. *Journal of Management Studies, 39*(2), 189–206.

ASX Corporate Governance Council. Principles of good corporate governance and best practice recommendations. Sydney: Australian Stock Exchange; March 2003.

Badaracco, J., Jr., & Ellsworth, R. R. (1989). *Leadership and the quest for integrity*. Boston, MA: Harvard Business School Press.

Baker, E., Barrett, M., & Roberts, L. (2002). *Working Communication*. Queensland: Wiley.

Baker, C. R., & Owsen, D. M. (2002). Increasing the role of auditing in corporate governance. *Critical Perspectives on Accounting, 13*, 783–795.

Bargh, C., Scott, P., & Smith, D. (1996). *Governing Universities. Society for Research in Higher Education*. Buckingham: Open University Press.

Berle, A. A., & Means, G. C. (1932). *The modern corporation and private property*. New Brunswick, New Jersey: Transaction Publishers reprinted in 1991.

Bhagat, S., & Black, B. (2002). The non-correlation between board independence and long-term firm performance. *The Journal of Corporation Law, 27*(2), 231–274.

Bisoux, T. (2002). The mind of a leader. BizEd September/October, 26–31.

Black, J. S., & Gregersen, H. B. (1997). Participative decision-making: An integration of multiple dimensions. *Human Relations, 50*(7), 859–878.

Bolman, L. G., & Deal, T. E. (2001). *Leading with soul: An uncommon journey of spirit*. San Francisco: Jossey-Bass.

Boyd, B. (1990). Corporate linkages and organizational environment: A test of the resource dependence model. *Strategic Management Journal, 11*, 419–430.

Boyett, J. H., & Boyett, J. T. (1998). *The guru guide: The best ideas of the top management thinkers*. New York: Wiley and Sons.

Brayshaw, G. (2003). Optimising board performance and good corporate governance through an effective review and evaluation process. *Corporate Governance Symposium CPA Australia*, Perth, Australia, pp. 1–10.

Brown, K. (2003). CLERP 9 bill on the table. *CA Charter, 74*(10), 21.

BusinessWeek. Family, inc. BusinessWeek Online November 10 2003, Available (http://www.businessweek.com:/print/magazine/content/03_45/b3857002.htm?mz)

Chaleff, I. (2003). *The courageous follower: Standing up to and for our leaders*. San Francisco: Berret-Koehler.

Cohen, J. R., Krishnamoorthy, G., & Wright, G. (2000). *Corporate governance and the audit process*. Working Paper, Boston College.

Core, J. E., Holthausen, R., & Larcker, D. F. (1999). Corporate governance, chief executive officer compensation and firm performance. *Journal of Financial Economics, 51*, 371–406.

Ciulla, J. B. (Ed.) (1998). *Ethics: The heart of leadership*. Westport: Praeger Publishers.

Dalla Costa, J. (1998). *The ethical imperative: why moral leadership is good business*. Reading, Massachusetts: Addison-Wesley.

Dawes, J. (2003). What's new. *CA Charter, 74*(11), 60–62.

Dixon, I., & Westbrook, J. (2003). Followers revealed. *Engineering Management Journal, 15*(1), 19–25.

Edwards, M. (2003a). Academic take on corporate experience: The lessons of good governance have their place in universities. In: The Australian, Higher Education Supplement. p. 29.

Edwards, M. (2003b). Review of New Zealand tertiary education institution governance. New Zealand Government Ministry of Education.

Firstenberg, P. B., & Malkiel, B. G. (1994). The twenty-first century boardroom: Who will be in charge? *Sloan Management Review*, *36*(1), 27–35.

Galbraith, K. (1967). *The New industrial state*. New York: New American Library.

Garratt, B. (2000). *The twelve organizational capabilities: Valuing people at work*. London: HarperCollins.

Goodjik, R. (2003). Partnership at corporate level: The meaning of the stakeholder model. *Journal of Change Management*, *3*(3), 225–241.

Gottliebsen, R. (2003). World's greatest boss says it's no time for wallflowers. In: *The Australian, Business Supplement*, 18 June, Melbourne, pp. 21 and 24.

Goyder, M. (1979). The mondragon experiment. *Personnel Management*, *11*(3), 24.

Graetz, F., Rimmer, M., Lawrence, A., & Smith, A. (2002). *Managing organisational change*. Queensland: Wiley.

Gustaffson, C. (2003). What kind of morality is trust *Electronic Journal of Business Ethics and Organization Studies*, *8*(1). Available at http://ejbo.jyu.fi/index.cgi?page = articles/0301_4

Hay, P., Hartel, C. (2000). Managing change and resistance to change: A theoretical guide for practitioners and researchers. Working Paper Series 88/00: Monash University Department of Management, Victoria; 1–16.

Hegelsen, S. (1995). *The web of inclusions*. New York: Doubleday.

Hollander, E. P. (1992). Leadership followership, self and others. *Leadership Quarterly*, *3*(1), 43–54.

Holloway, D. A. (2004). Strategic planning and Habermasian informed discourse: Reality or rhetoric. *Critical Perspectives on Accounting*, *4/5*(15), 469–483.

Holloway, D. A., & van Rhyn, D. J. (2003). Corporate governance reforms: The emperor's new clothes. *Proceedings of the 4th Multinational Alliance for the Advancement of Organisational Excellence*, Melbourne 1–6.

Hope, J., & Fraser, R. (2003). *Beyond budgeting: How managers can break away from the annual performance trap*. Boston: Harvard Business School Press.

James, D. (2004). A game with no rules. *Business Review Weekly*, *11–17 March*, 64–65.

Jensen, M. C. (2001). Value maximization, stakeholder theory, and the corporate objective function. *European Financial Management*, *7*(3), 297–317.

Jensen, M. C. (1993). The modern industrial revolution, exit, and the failure of the internal control systems. *The Journal of Finance*, *3*, 831–880.

Jensen, M. C. (1988). Takeovers: Their causes and consequences. *Journal of Economic Perspectives*, *2*, 21–48.

Jensen, M. C., & Meckling, W. H. (1976). The theory of the firm: Managerial behaviour agency costs, and ownership structure. *Journal of Financial Economics*, *3*, 305–360.

Kelley, R. E. (1992). *The power of followership: How to create leaders people want*. New York: Bantam Doubleday.

Kiel, G. C. (2002). Board composition and corporate performance: How the Australian experience informs contrasting theories of corporate governance. *5th International Conference on Corporate Governance and Direction*. Henley.

Korac-Kakabadse, N., Kakabadse, A. K., & Kouzmin, A. (2001). Board governance and company performance: Any correlations? *Corporate Governance*, *1*, 24–30.

Kotter, J. P., & Cohen, D. S. (2002). *The heart of change: Real-life stories of how people change their organizations.* Boston: Harvard Business School Press.

Laing, D., & Weir, C. M. (1999). Governance structures, size and corporate performance in UK firms. *Management Decision, 37*(5), 457–464.

Latham, G. P., Winters, D. C., & Locke, E. A. (1994). Cognitive and motivational effects of participation: A mediator study. *Journal of Organizational Behavior, 15*(1), 49–63.

Lazlo, C. & Nash, J. (2003) Six facets of ethical leadership: An executive's guide to the new ethics in business *Electronic Journal of Business Ethics and Organization Studies, 8*(1). Available (http://ejbo.jyu.fi/index.cgi?page = articles/0601_1)

Leighton, D. S. R., & Thain, D. H. (1990). The role of the corporate director. *Business Quarterly Autumn*, 20–24.

Litzinger, W., & Schaefer, T. (1982). Leadership through followership. *Business Horizons*, 78–81.

Lu, X. (2003) Shared governance: The ethical and practical method for corporate success *Electronic Journal of Business Ethics and Organization Studies, 8*(1). 1 Available (http://ejbo.jyu.fi/index.cgi?page = articles/0801_4)

Maassen, G. F. (1999). *An international comparison of corporate governance models.* Amsterdam: SpencerStuart.

Macleod, G. (2003). *From Mondragon to America: Experiments in community economic development.* Canada: UCCB Press.

Malpas, J. (2003). Making ethics work. Corporate Governance Symposium, CPA Australia, 27 August, Perth, Australia, 1–4.

Marshall, E. M. (2000). *Building trust at the speed of change: The power of the relationship-based corporation.* New York: American Management Association.

Maurer, R. (1996). Using resistance to build support for change. *Journal for Quality and Participation*, 56–63.

McConaughy, D. L., Matthews, C. H., & Fialko, A. S. (2001). Founding family controlled firms: Performance, risk, and value. *Journal of Small Business Management, 39*(1), 31–49.

McConaughy, D. L., Walker, M. C., Hendersen, G. V., Jr., & Chandra, S. M. (1998). Founding family controlled firms: Efficiency and value. *Review of Financial Economics, 76*(1), 1–19.

McCrann, T. (2003). Putting some family values into corporate governance. In: The Weekend Australian, Money & Investing, 40.

Miller, D., Greenwood, R., & Hinings, B. (1997). Creative chaos versus munificent momentum: The schism between normative and academic views of organizational change. *Journal of Management Inquiry, 6*(1), 71–78.

Mintzberg, H. (1994). *The rise and fall of strategic planning.* London: Prentice Hall.

Morck, R., Shiefer, A., & Vishny, R. W. (1988). Management ownership and market valuation: An empirical analysis. *Journal of Financial Economics, 20*(1/2), 215–293.

Owen, N. (2003). The failure of HIH Insurance. *HIH Royal Commission*, 1–3.

Parry, K. W. (2002). An exploration of social processes of leadership in organisations in New Zealand. *Proceedings of the Australian and New Zealand Academy of Management Conference.* Victoria, 1–8.

Pasternack, B. A., & Viscio, A. J. (1998). *The centerless corporation: A new model for transforming your organization for growth and prosperity.* New York: Simon and Schuster.

Pearson, C. A. L. (1991). An assessment of extrinsic feedback on participation, role perceptions, motivation, and job satisfaction in a self-managed system for monitoring group achievement. *Human Relations, 44*(5), 517–537.

Purser, R. E. P., & Cabana, S. (1998). *The self-managing organization: How leading companies are transforming the work of teams for real impact.* New York: Simon and Schuster.

Raelin, J. A. (2003). The myth of charismatic leaders. *TD March, 57*(3), 47–54.

Sonnenfeld, J. A. (2002). What makes great boards great. *Harvard Business Review September,* 106–112.

Switzer, P. (2003). Leading by example. *CA Charter December, 74*(11), 42–43.

Taylor, R. (2000). A paean to job ownership: A pioneer of worker co-operatives appeals for wider staff stock options. In: Financial Times London, 14.

The Economist "I swear..." The Economist, 17 August 2002;11 and 49.

Thomas, J., & Willcoxson, L. (1998). Developing teaching and changing organisational culture through grass-roots leadership. *Higher Education, 36,* 471–485.

Treasury CLERP Paper No. 9: CLERP (Audit Reform and Corporate Disclosure) Bill 2003. The Department of Treasury, 8 October 2003, Available (http://www.treasury.gov.au/contentitem.asp?pageId=&ContentID=700).

Tremblay, M., Sire, B., & Dalkin, D. B. (2000). The role of organizational justice in pay and employee benefit satisfaction, and its effects on work attitudes. *Group and Organization Management, 25,* 269–290.

Vanderslice, V. J. (1988). Separating leadership from leaders: An assessment of the effect of leader and follower roles in organizations. *Human Relations, 41*(9), 677–696.

Vinten, G. (1998). Corporate governance: An international state of the art. *Managerial Auditing Journal, 13*(7), 419–431.

Waldersee, R., & Griffiths, A. (1997). The changing face of organisational change. CCC Paper No. 65, Australian Graduate School of Management, University of New South Wales, Sydney.

Walters, K., & Andrews, B. (2004). Snapshots: Matters of principle. *Business Review Weekly,* 71.

Wheatley, M. J. (1999). Leadership and the new science. San Francisco: Berret-Koehler.

Williamson, O. E. (1999). Strategy research: Governance and competence perspectives. *Strategic Management Journal, 20,* 1087–1108.

Witt, L. A., Andrews, M. C., & Kacmar, K. M. (2000). The role of participation in decision-making in the organizational politics-job satisfaction relationship. *Human Relations, 53*(3), 341–358.

Wolfson, N. (1984). *The modern corporation: Free market versus regulation.* New York: McGraw-Hill.